A Tale of Two Sisters

A Tale of Two Sisters

Life in Early British Colonial Madras

The Letters of Elizabeth Gwillim and Her Sister
Mary Symonds from Madras 1801–1807

Patrick Wheeler

Peter Lang
Oxford · Bern · Berlin · Bruxelles · New York · Wien

Bibliographic information published by Die Deutsche Nationalbibliothek
Die Deutsche Nationalbibliothek lists this publication in the Deutsche Nationalbibliografie; detailed bibliographic data is available on the Internet at http://dnb.d-nb.de.

A catalogue record for this book is available from the British Library.

Library of Congress Cataloging-in-Publication Data
Names: Wheeler, Patrick, author. | Gwillim, Elizabeth, 1763-1807, writer of letters. | Symonds, Mary, 1772- writer of letters
Title: A tale of two sisters : life in early British colonial Madras: the letters of Elizabeth Gwillim and her sister Mary Symonds from Madras 1801-1807 / Patrick Wheeler.
Description: Oxford ; New York : Peter Lang, [2021] | Includes bibliographical references and index. |
Identifiers: LCCN 2021016297 (print) | LCCN 2021016298 (ebook) | ISBN 9781800791671 (hardback) | ISBN 9781800791688 (ebook) | ISBN 9781800791695 (epub) | ISBN 9781800791701 (mobi)
Subjects: LCSH: Gwillim, Elizabeth, 1763-1807--Correspondence. | Symonds, Mary, 1772---Correspondence. | Women--India--Chennai--Correspondence. | British--India--Chennai--Correspondence. | Chennai (India)--Social life and customs. | Gwillim, Henry, Sir, 1760?-1837.
Classification: LCC DS486.M2 W49 2021 (print) | LCC DS486.M2 (ebook) | DDC 305.40954/82--dc23
LC record available at https://lccn.loc.gov/2021016297
LC ebook record available at https://lccn.loc.gov/2021016298

Cover design by Brian Melville for Peter Lang

Cover image: A drawing, and some of the text, from one of Elizabeth Gwillim's letters, showing herself at her writing desk, facing the portraits of her mother, family and friends. This is surrounded by examples of her bird paintings. Author's collection.

ISBN 978-1-80079-167-1 (print) • ISBN 978-1-80079-168-8 (ePDF)
ISBN 978-1-80079-169-5 (ePub) • ISBN 978-1-80079-170-1 (mobi)

Published by Peter Lang Ltd, International Academic Publishers,
52 St Giles, Oxford, OX1 3LU, United Kingdom
oxford@peterlang.com, www.peterlang.com

This publication has been peer reviewed.

Contents

Illustrations

Acknowledgements

Considerable thanks are firstly due to Michael Wigan and Ray Cocks. I must also express my gratitude to Victoria Dickenson, Anna Winterbottom and the staff of the McGill University Library and Collections, Montreal, to the staff of the British Library, London, particularly in the Asia, Pacific and Africa Collection, to Ben Cartwright of the South Asia Collection Museum, Norwich and to the staff of the Manuscripts and Special Collections Library, University of Nottingham. I would also wish to thank Rosemary Raza, Arthur Macgregor and, hitherto, the late S. Muhtu of Madras for general support.

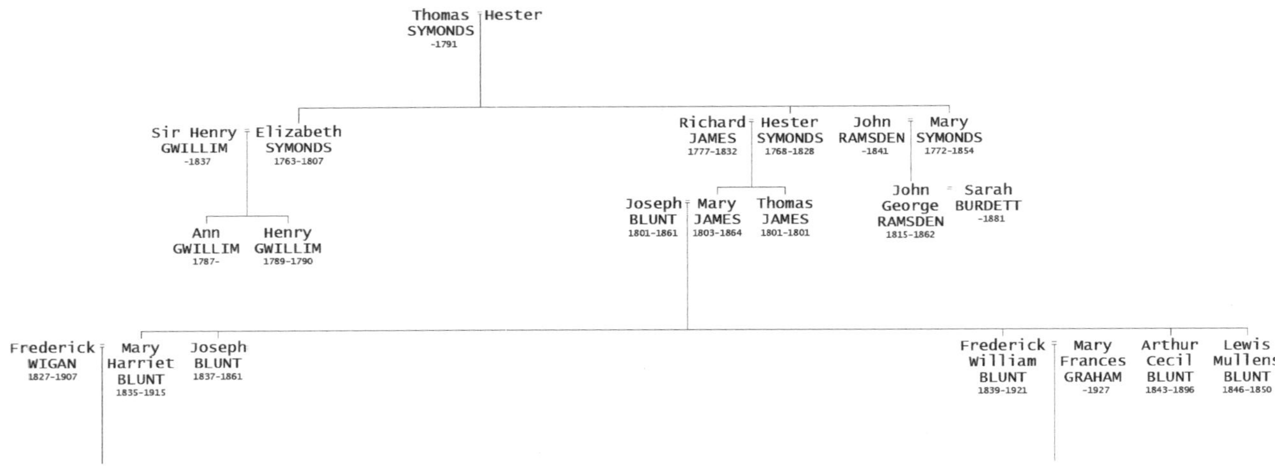

Symonds family tree – earlier years

Introduction

A squally and turbulent night had finally ebbed into a pearl-soft dawn rising calmly on the ship's starboard side. The two ladies dressed in their respective cabins in the roundhouse of the ship, the Honourable Company's East Indiaman, the Hindostan, and made their way up the steps of the quarter gallery to the poop deck. They had some inkling land was nearby, after months at sea, lately passing through miles of empty Indian Ocean. In the distance, to the left, they and the crew could just discern a grey line on the horizon and, before long, other ships riding at anchor in the roads outside what can only have been Madras. Late morning a 15-gun salute was made to the flagship, and was responded to with three cheers and, by midday, the anchor was dropped and a further, lesser, salute was made to Fort St George on the shoreline.[1] After four months at sea they had at last arrived, in July 1801, although they still had to make the perilous journey ashore, crashing through the surf in an undecked masulah boat. Although made deliberately flexible, the two women quaked as it corkscrewed from wavetop to wavetop in the hands of ten spray-soaked straining oarsmen to the haven of the shingle, and to the rhythm of their chanting.

The two ladies were Elizabeth Gwillim, who had travelled with her recently knighted husband Sir Henry Gwillim, and her younger unmarried sister Mary Symonds. Sir Henry had been appointed Puisne Judge to the Supreme Court of Judicature at Madras, assisting the new, and first, Chief Justice, Sir Thomas Strange and another puisne judge, Sir Benjamin Sullivan. Also in their company were two young men, Mr Henry Temple and Mr Richard Clarke, both appointed as clerks to the court. During their seven years in Madras these two women wrote numerous letters home, sometimes lengthily, in which they described in detail their lives,

1 Logbook of Honourable East India Company's Ship Hindostan, India Office Records, British Library, London.

occupations, interests and prejudices. Only these letters survive.[2] There are none received by them from family or friends, but they remain a remarkable resource for an insight into day-to-day life in British Indian Madras, and by inference much of India, at the dawn of the nineteenth century. They were written at much the same time that Jane Austen was writing her novels in England, and although they can never compare for style, clarity and wit, they are fact, not fiction; they are history. The reality of being women meant that there was little description of political, economic or military events, and they are therefore a window into the social life of an otherwise male world, far removed from the certainties and reassurances of their English homeland. In a way this enhances their value, as they give us such a sharp perspective on life at that time, uncluttered by masculine concerns; a social anthropology of early British India. Letters are somehow a more revealing source than journals, giving a more personal and intimate glimpse of society; a hint of illicit disclosure in a relaxed and fluid style. Journals are often written with a suspicion of eventual exposure to public gaze, and may therefore be intrinsically more restrained.

Despite the limitations of commentary imposed by their sex, the two women's letters, and lives, were also coloured by the experiences of Sir Henry Gwillim's life in Madras. During the course of his Madras career he found himself increasingly at odds with the Governor and Council of this Presidency town, and also his senior colleague, the Chief Justice. As this progressed, so the two sisters became more distant from, and critical of, both the men and women of the British community, partly self-imposed and partly a polite ostracization. Until the middle of 1803 the governor of Madras was Lord Edward Clive who was son of the much better known Robert Clive of Plassey fame, but was himself rather less distinguished, preferring gardening to deliberating upon matters of state, which he left largely to his council. He was succeeded by Sir William Bentinck as Governor in 1803. The chief justice was Sir Thomas Strange, who presided throughout Sir Henry's time there, and altogether for some fifteen years, apart from a period of absence in England in 1805 and 1806. The third judge, a puisne

2 Elizabeth Gwillim Letters, and those of Mary Symonds her sister. 1801–08 MSS Eur C240. India Office Records, British Library, London.

judge, like Sir Henry Gwillim, was Sir Benjamin Sullivan, and there were senior naval and military personnel and powerful members of council such as William Petrie. The rest of Madras's working British population consisted of civil servants, traders, soldiers, young East India company writers, hopeful adventurers and a little human detritus that had washed up from unknown sources. It is difficult to ascertain the total numbers of British in Madras at the beginning of the 1800s, but it must have been a few thousand, many of them ordinary soldiers and sailors and not listed in the directories of the time, as neither was any woman. What is known, however, is that in the years 1801 to 1807, whilst the sisters were in Madras, the total number of British buried there was 3362, suggesting the overall population was not inconsiderable.[3]

Throughout the years that the sisters were in Madras there was increasing politico-legal tension. This is covered in more detail elsewhere. In summary, however, there was growing antipathy against the crown-appointed court by Governor Bentinck, who believed the charter of justice exercised by the Supreme Court might protect subversive Indians from prosecution and control, making insurrection easier. Doubtless it also curtailed some of the less respectable tendencies of the colonists. He would in fact have preferred to abolish the crown court and, after a while, even gained the support of the Chief Justice, Sir Thomas Strange. This antipathy to the crown appointed judiciary was a feature of life within the other Presidency towns in India. Sir Henry Gwillim opposed these attitudes, and supported the rights given to the Indian people as much as to the British, which led to an increasing gulf between him and the Madras establishment. This was not helped by a serious personality clash between him and both Bentinck and Strange, reinforced by Gwillim's irascible and prickly temperament. In the end, charges were laid at his door, and his career in India was cut short by his recall in 1808, alone, his wife Elizabeth having died in 1807.[4, 5]

3 Madras Ecclesiastical Returns, Asia, Pacific and Africa Collection (APAC), British Library, London.

4 See final chapter.

5 Cocks, Raymond, *Social Roles and Legal Rights: Three Women in Early Nineteenth-Century India*. The Journal of Legal History. 2002 Vol. 23, No. 2. pp.77–106.

These events are of considerable relevance to the lives of his wife, Lady Elizabeth Gwillim, and her sister, Mary Symonds. Both arrived in Madras, full of excitement and anticipation, and plunged themselves into the social whirl and visual delights of a strange and fascinating culture. Elizabeth became deeply involved in numerous interests, and immersed herself in the country and its people, whereas Mary concentrated on the European life. She was after all single, and her best future lay in finding a suitable husband, for the lives of women in those days were completely dependent on the patronage of men. As Elizabeth wrote, 'I shall leave the White people to Polly and tell you a little about the Black people.' Polly is of course Mary, and at first sight her letters seem superficial, even flighty, but closer inspection reveals a serious and intelligent analysis of the people and events of the time, which sometimes verged on tart opprobrium aimed at her peers, as the family becomes more detached from the social hub with the gradual fall from grace of Sir Henry. Elizabeth, on the other hand, had no real reason to plunge herself into the life of British society, other than unavoidable dinner engagements and balls, because she was married, with a household to run, and a fiercely intelligent interest in the Indian world around her. She wanted to know as much as she could about Indian culture, religion and daily life, and learnt the local language to this end. Despite this, both women became more defensive as life became more politically strained for Sir Henry, and they felt themselves to be slightly ostracized by the society in which they had by right of seniority and precedence found themselves. As relationships became subtly more tense, one can detect an increasing asperity within the two sisters' letters; a waspish inclination to disparage the behaviour, origins, attitudes and abilities of their peers. Eventually they were found to be upholding Sir Henry's politico-legal contentions. The two women had a close and friendly relationship with Thomas Strange and his wife in the initial years, but this became more distant and strained as events followed their course. There was particular irritation at Strange's sudden and unexplained return to England in 1805, which was believed to be self-serving, and this eventually proved correct. It had placed a great burden of work on Henry Gwillim's shoulders, in that he was effectively covering all the court work alone for nearly two years.

It is interesting that the East India Register and Directory for 1803 and 1804 shows Lady Gwillim to be a directress of the Female Asylum (Orphanage), along with Lady Clive, the then Governor's wife, which was very much to be expected for women of their standing within that community. Lord Clive was governor of the institution. By 1805 Lady Clive's place had been taken by Lady Bentinck, whose husband had become governor, but Lady Gwillim's name was no longer present, although by right it should have still been.[6] It was possible that she was nudged out of her role because of the differences between the two husbands, or that she resigned graciously in support of her husband.

Elizabeth was interested in horticulture, which developed into a desire to learn botany, in which she received instruction from at least two notable local botanists, Dr Johan Rottler, a French missionary-botanist,[7] and Dr James Anderson, Physician-General in Madras,[8] to the extent that she had at least one specimen named after her: Gwillimia Indica Rottler. In addition, and most important of all, she and Mary were consummate artists. Some of Elizabeth's extraordinary watercolours are held in the Blacker-Wood Library at McGill University, Canada, having been found in London in the 1920s. These are mostly ornithological, some large, measuring three by

6 The East India Register and Directory for 1803, and 1804, Asia, Pacific and Africa Collection (APAC), British Library, London.

7 Botanical Journal of the Linnaean Society Vol 113, Issue 4, 1993 p.351 – 388. Dr Johan Rottler was a French botanist and missionary from Strasbourg who collected more than two thousand plant specimens from southern India which he sent to Europe. Many ended up in the Royal Botanic Gardens, Kew. His initial appointment in India was at the Danish Lutheran Mission in Tranquebar, and he later transferred to an English mission in Madras.

8 Anderson, James. Oxford Dictionary of National Biography. ref:odnb/476. James Anderson was a surgeon and horticulturalist of Scottish origin who rose through the ranks of shipboard medicine eventually becoming surgeon-General in Madras and, after the formation of the Madras Medical Board in 1786, he was appointed Physician-General. As a noted botanist and horticulturalist, he planted mulberry trees in an attempt to establish a local silk industry, and also encouraged the growth of American cotton, sugar cane and coffee. In addition, he planted a notable botanical garden which did not survive. There is a memorial statue of him in St George's Cathedral, Madras and he is remembered as a man of great compassion and generosity to the poor of Madras.

two feet, and therefore clearly life-size or more, and exquisitely executed, with well-preserved colour and line.[9] The most interesting thing is that they precede the work of John James Audubon by more than twenty years. Somehow they seem a little more natural, and perhaps this has something to do with Audubon's technique, which was to shoot the birds first and hold them in place with a metal framework. Elizabeth, however, usually painted from life and had to work quickly because the birds would not eat or drink whilst captive. She had a very skilled, but somewhat self-willed, elderly assistant who was able to keep the birds peaceful, and relatively still, while she painted. They were then released. Inevitably she had to paint shot specimens from time to time, but she still had to work quickly as they quite quickly became unlovely companions in that heat. She also painted botanical specimens and some other animals, but most of these seem to have been lost. Mary was not supposedly such an accomplished artist, but she painted very finely, and particularly concentrated on Indian life and landscape. Much of her work is held at the South Asian Collections Museum in Norwich. Both their letters often make reference to George Samuel, and it is clear that they wrote to him about their drawing and painting and so must have known him well, and had very probably received instruction from him in England. George Samuel (1770–1823) was a well-known landscape painter of the time, who exhibited regularly at the Royal Academy.[10]

The interest in Indian matters was profound, and Elizabeth's observations on the character of the Hindu people were perceptive and valid. In October 1801 she wrote, 'They are the mildest people in the world. They go on praying to their god, sowing rice, weaving cloth, and eating curry just in the same way as they have done these three thousand years.' Little has changed, in a rural context at least, in the two hundred years since. In the early years they were both fascinated by the customs, dress, foods, flora and even the climate, apart from the dreaded 'land winds'. Despite the pleasure in the food available, they were often asking for special requests from home, such as hams, ketchup, confectionery and unavailable herbs and, besides

9 ElizabethGwillimpaintings. <https://archive.org/search.php?query=subject%3A%22Gwillim%2C+Elizabeth%2C+--+1763-1807.%22andpage=2> or more easily 'archive.org' and search for Gwillim, Elizabeth

10 Samuel, George. Oxford Dictionary of National Biography. ref:odnb/24604

edible goods, they would request English seeds, clothing, hats, china, jewellery, even fire irons and especially drawing paper and watercolours. The time from request to delivery cannot have been much less than a year. At the same time they were sending plants, seeds, presents of shawls, fabrics and various trinkets to their family and friends. Elizabeth was much intrigued by Indian history and tried to describe some of the particularities of Hinduism to her mother. She also described, in some detail, the various Hindu festivals that she attended; the intricacies of dress and dance, the ritual, fireworks, illuminations and finely detailed carving of the carriages, all fascinated her. In describing Indian religious dance she wrote, 'Their dancing is very little like ours; they never step upon the toes but keep the knees bent, and tread on the outside of their feet and move in a very small space .... they dance for an hour within the space of a sheet of paper, the feet all the while in constant motion.' It would be hard to improve on this for accuracy of observation. In order that she could more deeply study the history and religion of the Indian people, she learnt competent Telugu, the language of the region, and she could also write it adequately *(see note 11 of 1801, page 29)*.

Much of the correspondence is studded with chatter about family and friends, and occasional less than flattering comments about other Madras residents, especially from Mary, and especially after the initial honeymoon period had waned. Names are scattered through the letters, and most are family or close friends. Others are young men travelling home, or officers on East India Company ships, who acted as couriers for letters and packages. Some of these young men, and others recently arrived in India, such as William Biss, would stay in the Gwillim household, often for long stretches. They would be company for the male members of the household, such as Sir Henry Gwillim himself, and his young protégés Richard Clark and Henry Temple. Elizabeth and Mary also much enjoyed hosting these young men. Mary, because she was nearer their age group, and considering marriage, albeit rather languourously, and Elizabeth because she was childless, her husband was overworking, and was often absent, and her maternal disposition encouraged her protective instincts. Young men were often bored, isolated and lonely and unsurprisingly susceptible to the charms of Indian women and, more so the Anglo-Indian, who were frequently very beautiful and, if born of a man of means, reasonably well educated. In Calcutta at that time, three-quarters of young bachelors kept at least one bibi, or mistress. Half of the children baptised there in the Anglican churches were illegitimate, and of mixed parentage.[11] One-third or more of all British wills left all a man's possessions to one or more bibis, or their offspring.[12] It is unlikely Madras was much different. Elizabeth, and many such contemporaries, tried to protect young men from these temptations. They and their contemporaries were only a small factor in the gradual suppression of the bibi and of the Anglo-Indians. Much more important was the intolerance demonstrated by the growing body of church ministers and missionaries, and the gradually increasing exclusion of the Anglo-Indian from government employment.[13]

If women were concerned about young men, the age of girls about to be married was another consideration, although one they could do less about. The age of consent for a girl was much lower at that time and, although they often thought a girl too young, they railed against the thought of decrepit men aged 50 to 60 years marrying girls of 15 or 16, which was common practice at that time.[14] Although appalled by the prospect, they blamed the girls as well, 'their own sordid dispositions have made them prefer age and riches when they might have married men suitable to themselves in years and with fair prospects, but without much ready money'.

The unabridged letters contain 155,000 words, which is a great deal of quill and ink for two women. On one occasion Elizabeth wrote a letter that was almost 10,000 words in length; more a dissertation than a chatty note. The need to write was paramount, partly out of a desire to share their experiences but also tacitly, or sometimes not, to invite a reply. News from home was desperately sought, and all the time there was that lurking anxiety that the next letter might reveal an awful event. Doubtless the feeling

11 Robb, Peter, *Sex and Sensibility, Richard Blechynden's Calcutta Diaries 1791–1822* (Oxford 2011).

12 Dalrymple, William, *White Mughals. Love and Betrayal in Eighteenth Century India* (London, 2002).

13 Wheeler, Patrick, *Ribbons among the Rajahs. A History of British Women in India before the Raj* (Pen and Sword History, 2017).

14 Ibid.

was the same amongst their English family, and always there was the ever present, but unspoken, fear that one might never see loved ones again. So the scratching of quills was a frequent sound, but most especially when word passed around that a ship was due to sail, and letters were hastily gathered to be put into the packet for that ship. 'I have three people standing by me and hurrying me to conclude.' This often led to hasty scrawling and dubious punctuation. Awaiting a reply could entail months of agonized silence while the adverse monsoon winds, or one of the other hazards of the sea, prevented ships reaching the Coromandel Coast. A gap of at least four months without correspondence was the norm in the winter months, and then letters that were several months old could arrive in bundles of six or more from one correspondent. Although the sisters claimed that even a few words were welcome they, in fact, preferred much more in the way of news. There is in the letters a continuous underlying current of homesickness. 'A ridiculous little shabby note from James, for which he may expect a good trimming when I have more time to write. This letter to come 15,000 miles consists of six lines of business, and two more of apologies for not making it shorter!'

Another major occupation, and point of comment, was the management of staff. Everyone had servants, and it was commonplace, even usual, to have 'half a hundred' as in the Gwillim household. The roles were legion, from that of the Khansaman, who was Muslim, who purchased provisions and superintended the table, down to the Chaprasi who acted as a footman and runner, carrying messages. In between these they employed dishwashers, clothes washers, horse carers, grass cutters, water carriers, coolies, palanquin carriers and so on. Language difficulties were usual, which is one of the reasons why the women learnt a local tongue. An important initiator of a requirement for so many servants were the arcane religious and caste differences between Hindu and Muslim, which caused great difficulties in food handling for obvious reasons. Higher caste Hindus would not even touch a clean plate in case it had been defiled, for fear of loss of caste. The pariahs,[15] or lower caste individuals, were of course available

15 The word Pariah is mentioned throughout the text and was the word, incorrectly used by the British, to describe the lowest caste in India, or outcaste. They once formed some 20% of Indian society in Madras and were proud of their ancient, possibly Dravidian origin. As their population increased they were obliged to take

for any unpleasant job that needed doing. The two sisters' feelings about their staff were cautious but amicable. Like everyone else they depended on them hugely; they wondered at their practices and lifestyle; they didn't entirely trust them not to pilfer, but they greatly admired their consideration and kindness.[16]

Within the letters two circumstances appear that are not a feature of the normal social landscape. The first is their ability, as women, to visit a zenana.[17] Mary's description is therefore highly unusual, as it was forbidden for any man other than husband or brother to enter a zenana, and there are therefore few first-hand accounts even by women. Mary's comments, although given with her usual offhand and slightly disdainful manner, thus become very revealing. The other situation was unique, and that was the Vellore mutiny, a little discussed event from 1806 which preceded the Great Uprising of 1857 by half a century. This bloody and violent sepoy rebellion, only 85 miles away, is described from contemporary accounts by both sisters whilst, like the other British residents of Madras, fearing increasingly for their own lives. The underlying causes are reported, and many of the details, and there is a reassuring demonstration of sympathy with the point of view of the Indian sepoys for reasons which seem today very reasonable, but obviously didn't to some supervisory authorities at that time. Their reaction may have been partly enhanced by the deteriorating relationship with Lord Bentinck, knowing that he was held partly

---

up 'unclean' tasks such as the burial of corpses, which probably led to the suggestion they were outcaste. The word pariah derives from the Tamil paraiyen, meaning drum beater, and today they are listed as a Scheduled Caste in Tamil Nadu. See also Yule, Henry. Hobson Jobson: *A Glossary of Colloquial Anglo-Indian Words and Phrases, Etymological, Historical, Geographical and Discursive.* (London 1903; Oxford 2013)

16 For more on servants in early British India see: Wheeler, Patrick. *Ribbons among the Rajahs. A History of British Women in India before the Raj.* (Pen and Sword History 2017): Parkes, Fanny *Wanderings of a Pilgrim in Search of the Picturesque* (London 1850): Roberts, Emma. *Scenes and Characteristics of Hindostan with Sketches of Anglo-Indian Society. Volume 1* (London 1835; 2005).

17 See also: Parkes, Fanny *Wanderings of a Pilgrim in Search of the Picturesque* (London, 1850).

responsible for the mutiny's occurrence, and as a consequence recalled by the Company's Board of Control.

When they arrived in India, Elizabeth was aged 38, having been born in Hereford in 1763. She married Sir Henry Gwillim in London in 1784 and it would appear that she had two children, Ann Gwillim born 1787 and Henry in 1789. There is no mention of any children with these names in the correspondence, only the children of her sister Hetty at home, and those of friends. It is likely that they both died in infancy, and this is confirmed for Henry. When Elizabeth arrived in India she had been married for 17 years and it wasn't to be for much longer. In December 1807 she died somewhat unexpectedly, with no clear cause being recorded. Her letters reveal a relapsing febrile illness which she treated with cinchona bark; effectively quinine. It seems possible, therefore, that her death could be attributed to a malaria-related illness, such a common scourge at that time, although typhoid, dysentery or some other infectious illness could have been the culprit. She was buried under a rather austere flat headstone, inscribed in Latin, just inside the entrance to St Mary's Church within Fort St George. Every visitor walks across her bones without realising the remarkable talent and intelligence of the person over whom they are passing. Ten months later, in October 1808, Sir Henry, his still unmarried sister-in-law Mary, and good friend Richard Clarke, took passage home in the east Indiaman Phoenix which, after a perilously stormy voyage, reached Capetown in January 1809. Romance flowered amongst the cut-away masts, rent topsails and sea-swept quarterdeck and later that same year Mary married Captain John Ramsden, the commanding officer of her ship home. Five years later she had a son. Sir Henry Gwillim did not languish too long in the isolation of widowhood and married Elizabeth Chilman in 1812. One must suppose she did not live up to her name as he lived until 1837, reaching an age of almost 80 years. Interestingly Richard Clarke, then a civil servant in the East India Company, seems to have retained a lifelong friendship with Mary and her new husband. He was to become a significant legatee, along with Mary and one other relative, in John Ramsden's will of 1841. He had also married a family friend, Mary Thoburn, in 1809.

Inevitably, where letters were often written in haste because of pressure to prepare them for a ship's packet, the punctuation is sparse or confusing.

Also, where two sisters have written about the same subject, there is some repetition. An editing process was therefore necessary, but this was confined to adjusting some punctuation, minor restructuring of unclear sentences, and avoidance of duplication. Furthermore, some paragraphs consisted of arcane gossip about obscure friends in England which make no contribution to the value of the letters as a social history document. Altogether therefore, editing has resulted in a shrinkage in size of about ten percent. The letters retain their immediacy and freshness as a record of life in India far away from Jane Austen's England but still reflecting the same social codes of that era.

Letters of 1801 and Commentary

Commentary

The volume of correspondence in the two sisters' letters home is inevitably short for the first year. After all, they only arrived in Madras in July, the 26th precisely, having set sail from home waters at the end of March the same year. What is more, they seem not to have put pen to paper until October, although there may have been other letters which are lost. One must presume that writing home to their mother and sister would have had a high priority.

The first letter is actually from Portsmouth, just prior to departure, and describes the rush and bother of leaving; Elizabeth *(often called Betsy by her sister, who is herself sometimes referred to as Polly)* hinting at the misfortune of parting from the glamour of London, having revelled in her presentation at Court. There is an interesting reference to the possibility that adverse winds might delay departure for a month, emphasizing the all-powerful influence of the weather in the days of sail. Thereafter it is all about India, with a wealth of description and chatter. There is little mention of the voyage, other than Sir Henry Gwillim's constant sea sickness, which must have been a disheartening and disabling experience, especially over four months, for any traveller with negligible experience of the sea and ships. This inevitably would have included the majority.

From then on the descriptive flow resonates with excitement (14.10.1801); the trees, the fruit, the gardens and the copious use of flowers for any occasion. Then follows the description of the equally copious number of servants, and their highly specific purposes, the pleasure of numerous balls and dinners, and particularly one given by a Mrs Chinnery who was almost certainly the sister-in-law of the renowned portrait artist of that period. Their immediate social circle consisted particularly of the other two judges; Sir Thomas Strange, the Chief Justice, and Sir Benjamin

Sullivan. Both came round regularly, especially, it seems, whilst the Gwillims were serving a dressed gammon at table that they had brought from home.

Mary, the younger sister, begins to describe her own venture into painting (14.10.1801). Her interest is very much that of the lives and appearance of the ordinary Indian, the manner of the different castes and the general native way of life. She also describes their living arrangements and their dress, especially their abundant gold jewellery. Elizabeth writes in a more serious vein, already feeling the weight of household responsibility with so many servants to organise. The contents of the table are a preoccupation, and she throws herself into a familiarity with local horticulture. Her growing interest in Indian cultural behaviour is manifested by her description of religious ceremonies (7.10.1801), especially that for employees working with tools. This requires that they have time off work, and money to purchase the unfortunate beast who is about to be sacrificed. Each of the Gwillim family appears to be asked to contribute in turn, which only adds to the size of the eventual feast after the sacrificial ceremony. This Elizabeth describes fully, and goes on to give a general introduction to the manner of Indian houses and places of worship, and to offer insight into the intrinsically peaceful and resilient nature of the people. In the main she viewed them as having lived through history implacably watching successive invasions wash over them, and yet having ultimately survived little changed. It is as if she saw this almost infinite view of these people, pursuing their unchanging agricultural practices, somehow conferring an advantage against all-comers. Some might view this as patronising, but the intention is complimentary. It is clear already that she prefers the Hindu to the Moslem. So their first six months pass by, the impression being steadily gained of their enchantment with India and its culture, and their respect for its mild, patient and philosophical people.

Letters

From Elizabeth Gwillim to her mother. Portsmouth 1801.

You will be surprised, perhaps, to receive a letter dated from this place, where we may possibly stay a long time. We received a summons from the Purser on Wednesday, which was not regarded, but the wind proving fair, and the convoy lying ready, with orders to sail instantly, we were informed on Thursday we had not a moment to lose. Mr Clarke, Rich and Temple set off at 12 o'clock at night and we three followed with four horses at eight the next morning, after having sat up all night. When we arrived here, very much fatigued, we were informed that the wind, having suddenly changed, every ship had been obliged to put back for the Downs, so we are now waiting for the wind, and they tell us it is likely we may not go off for three weeks or a month. I do not know whether you will be sorry that this hurry has prevented Mr Gwillim from being knighted. He received directions to attend the levy for that purpose on Wednesday last, but the King's illness prevented him from having the levy, and many were obliged to return home dressed *(in court dress)*. On Friday, he was to have attended a private one for that purpose, but for that we could not wait. For my part I have no regrets about it, as it adds nothing to the respect of his situation, but he was desired to accept, and it had been done long ago but for the confusions in the change of Ministry, by which everything has been delayed. We think ourselves very fortunate to have had all material things settled. Had it not, God knows when it might, for the seal of the court was sent down to us in this place only a few hours ago. We expected to have sailed without it. It would not have prevented Mr Gwillim from receiving a salary but he could not have done an atom of business till it had arrived. For my part I have got all my preparations in excellent order, but I have laboured and travelled so much to do it that I have not had one moment to myself. I like my black man and maid very much. I do not know whether you read that I had been at court, because in several papers it was put down as Mrs Gwillim by Mr Yorke, instead of Mrs Gwillim by Mrs Yorke. She and Mrs Carew offered to take me. I was much pleased to go with her. Mrs Carew sent her chair and chairmen for me, and Mrs Toussaint made all my clothes and I was dressed there. I assure you I have not looked so well in a great many years, as I did in my hoop and blond lace. I have had it all packed up for a ball dress. I was not at all frightened, and Mrs Yorke was full of encomiums, Mr Gwillim tells me, on my management of my hoop, and greatly admired my dress which was excessively pretty, all white crepe, satins and blond lace. I should have gone again next Thursday if I had stayed in London, as it is expected you should take leave if you have time. It was a remarkably pale drawing-room, and everybody very fine, being the first show after the mourning. The Bishop of Ely was with me, and extremely good-natured in going about the room to enquire who everybody was that I wanted to know about, and upon the whole therefore I was extremely entertained. Mr John Yorke, the Bishop's brother, whom you have seen, has made me a present of a most magnificent centrepiece for my plateau, of cut glass and silver. He had it packed at the silversmiths. I have the pleasure to tell you that we are all well and in good spirits, but we were very low all yesterday. Mr Gwillim was much affected at leaving London so suddenly. I never saw him lower, but he has quite recovered today. To add to our lowness, yesterday we were in the greatest fright all the way we came. General Stewart, the Commander-in-chief, was ahead of us, and indeed every person. The horses were much tried on the road. One of the horses had been twice already on the last 10 mile stage, and on the same day. With us was the third time, and the poor thing wanted to lie down all the way, though it was a very fine horse, but you may suppose it did not help our fright to find ourselves so late, and that our surprise was great to hear that whilst we had been labouring to get here, the ships were moving back again.

The Ethiops mineral[1] I began to take when Ned was in town did me great good, and I have been as well since as ever I was. I sent this in a parcel to town, to Hetty, and shall write again soon to you. I beg to hear from you; you may write without fear as we cannot go for some time.

1 Ethiops mineral: Mercuric sulphide, HgS, prepared as a black solid by the reaction of mercury and sulphur, and formerly used medicinally as an anthelmintic and tonic. Undoubtedly toxic, like all mercury compounds.

From Mary Symonds to her mother. 14th October 1801.

I hope you have from time to time received several letters through Hetty, which I have written during the passage out and since our arrival here. Betsy and I had written a large packet which we intended to go by a ship, which should have left this place some weeks ago, but is still here under repair. In my last letter, I could give you very little more satisfaction than by saying we were all arrived safe and well, as we had not then seen anything of the country. I have now the pleasure to say that we like it very much, and I think it will agree very well with us upon the whole. Betsy has, since she embarked at Portsmouth, had better health than I have known her to have for years before, and I was never better in my life. Mr Gwillim has indeed been a good deal frayed, but has no serious illness. He suffered a good deal from seasickness on his passage and, since he came here, he has had the prickly heat which is a very violent eruption, and itches violently, but all people here congratulate him and say it is considered a most favourable symptom, and that persons who have it at the outset generally enjoy very good health here. Besides this, he had an accident which was very troublesome to him.[2] His servant set a jug of boiling water on the ground behind him when he was dressing. He stepped back suddenly and it fell over his leg, and scalded him very badly, but Betsy immediately applied a great quantity of oil to it, and when the surgeon came to see it he thought it looked so cool and well that he chose to continue the same application, and it healed very fast, but he was obliged to keep himself on a couch for a fortnight. He is now quite well, and has no other complaint but the bites of the gnats, ants and other little insects which abound this month, but we are now every day expecting the rains to set in, which destroy all these little plagues, and we are told that we shall then have four months of fine cool weather, just like fine spring weather in England. I think this a most beautiful country. Here there are a variety of fine trees, and a delightful verdancy. We drive out every morning from

2 It is interesting to note that Mary refers to this as an accident, rather than the clumsy error of a servant, which might have been the response of many. It much reflects the character of the family.

five to seven o'clock at which time it is quite fresh and cool. There is the greatest variety of roads that can be made in a flat country and, whichever one takes, one is sure of a fine avenue, or a beautiful lane, shaded by the tall bamboo intermixed with the gum arabic tree which abounds here, and is the most elegant tree that I ever saw. The largest trees that resemble English foliage are the tulip tree, the banyan and the mango. These are common in the public roads, but we have a great number of very fine trees in the gardens. About half past four o'clock in the evening one can walk or ride out again for an hour and a half, very pleasantly. We have a great many native vegetables which are very good, but altogether unlike anything in England. The fruits also I think very good. The melons are not equal to those you have, but the pineapples are excellent and the mango, plantain and the Malacca I like very much. The last of these makes a taste very much like gooseberries, having an agreeable tartness in it. There is a good deal of visiting in this place, which is very pleasant when one is quite at leisure, but I assure you it is difficult to do anything as the houses are all open, so that people come in unawares unless one shuts oneself up in one's bedchamber. Dinners and balls are very frequent, and dancing is much pleasanter here than you would think it could be in so warm a climate, as the rooms are quite open and the evenings are very cool and pleasant. In most of the dining rooms they have two men who stand in the opposite corners of the room with very long fans made in the form of flags. They are much ornamented with painting and brass, and they are made of a sort of grass which, when dampened, gives out a very agreeable perfume. These cool the room very much. Most ladies have servants who fan them during dinner, and stand behind their chairs for that purpose. So you see, great pains are taken to prevent our feeling any inconvenience from the heat. The kitchens, and other offices, are built at a little distance from the house. These people are very excellent cooks, but they have a very odd way of cooking. All their utensils are very simple, but elegant in their form. The kitchen is a long room with large arches in the wall, formed like the mouth of an oven about 2 feet deep. In this place they light a fire of sticks for roasting, and the spits are turned by boys who are apprentices to the cook. The boiling is generally done over charcoal fires which are lighted in earthen pots and stand out in the garden on any convenient place. They boil and stew everything in earthen vessels which they have in all sizes, and various pretty shapes. The cooks are also very good confectioners, and make all sorts of mixtures of eggs milk and sugar, as good as possible, and custards trifles etc. The milk is remarkably rich here, and eggs are very plentiful. The price of fowls is about 10 pence a couple, for such chickens as you would generally boil at home, but they have here two other sorts of fowl. The capons are as large as a very fat hen turkey, and the other sort of full-grown fowl is about the size of the Dorking fowl which you have in London.[3] The larger size turkeys here are the most monstrous things you can conceive, and look like a mountain on the table. Provisions are in general very cheap, and so are the servants' wages, but the quantity of food you are obliged to put on your table, and the number of servants you are obliged to keep, make housekeeping quite dear enough. The servant who dresses your hair would on no account empty the washstand basin herself. You must keep one for every purpose, yet it is in this respect much worse in Bengal and other parts of India than it is here. We have a butler to order the dinner and someone else to go to the market to buy it. He, in turn, has two servants to carry it home, and the Butler has a second butler under him, a man to write out his accounts, and a servant to clear the plates. Each horse you keep has two servants who do nothing but attend to him, and if you keep poultry there must be one for each sort, as the same woman who takes care of ducks never interferes with the chickens etc.

The gardens here are very handsome, as we have a great variety of beautiful shrubs which grow very high and bloom very profusely. Many of the finest roses have extremely handsome blossoms and their thick foliage conceals the long bare stalks of the palm trees which spread only their graceful tops. They form a fine contrast in the groves, and are constantly waving their long branches in the most stately manner. The great abundance of sweet scented flowers gives rise to many pretty customs amongst the natives here. Whenever they mean to compliment you they present

3 The Dorking chicken is one of the oldest British breeds, dating possibly back to Roman times. It was particularly prevalent in the southern English town of that name from whence it was sent to the London markets.

flowers to you, not plucked with leaves and stems as you gather them, but pressed out as you may do cowslips or Jasmine. They use sometimes white and sometimes pink flowers for this purpose. When they have pressed them they take the fibres of a plant which are as strong as a fourpenny thread, and they string them upon these as close as possible, passing the thread through the bottom part of the flower head so that it forms a rope of about an inch in diameter. This they present in wreaths of a yard, or 2 yards, long. At the time the nabob was enthroned, these wreaths were presented to all the company, and the nabob himself placed them round the neck of the principal persons, and also presented them with a small parcel of the Betel nut which the natives have done up in leaves, gilded over. They strew flowers on the graves of all their friends occasionally, and when any person of consequence dies they weave a cloth to wrap round the body. They then take wreaths of flowers, as I have described, and plait them into each other exactly as a weaver does his threads, fixing them into a frame, or loom, for that purpose. The tombs of great persons are very handsome buildings, and I am told that the inside of some of them is kept constantly hung round with flowers, and six or eight men are employed in any one of them, to renew them daily.

We were, last night, at a grand ball given by Mrs Chinnery, at which there were about hundred and fifty persons.[4] They danced in the house, which was finely lighted and dressed with flowers. The supper was in the garden where a table was laid near 300 feet long upon carpets. Over the table was an awning of green cloth bordered and supported on each side by columns of large bamboo, round each of which an immense quantity of the branches of trees, and flowers, were bound, so that it had the appearance of a beautiful long bower. It was lighted by more than a hundred wax lights, all burning in cut glass shades. Altogether it had a very brilliant appearance. Balls of this sort occur every week, but the suppers are generally in the house.

4 This is very probably the wife of John Chinnery, a civil servant of the East India Company, and entrepreneur. It is unlikely his brother George Chinnery was there, a celebrated portrait artist, as he did not arrive until the following year, having left his wife in Ireland. See Chinnery, George: Oxford Dictionary of National Biography: ref:odnb/5311

I am endeavouring to make a set of drawings of the different castes, and descriptions, of the natives of this country, to give you all an exact idea of their dresses, but I fear I shall not have more than one or two to send with this, as the ships, I am told, will sail sooner than expected, and it is difficult for them to suit their time to mine to draw them, but as another ship is expected here daily, which will leave this place in a short time for England, I hope to make a packet by her. I have written my letters on India paper for two reasons. First, it is much cheaper than Europe paper and, secondly, that I think you will like to see what they make here. It is poor stuff.

If you can get some mushrooms at any time, a little ketchup or a few preserved apricots, we shall be much obliged to you for them. The two gammons of bacon Ned was so good as to give us have turned out very fine. One, and the half of the other, have been dressed for different companies here. They were much admired and eaten at luncheon clean to the bone. Sir Thomas Strange[5] and Mr Sullivan *(the other puisne judge)* came every day whilst the first lasted. I hope your dear boys are all going on well. By the time you receive this you will have another stout lad, I suppose, ready to run amongst the party. I hope you will have this letter pretty soon as Admiral Rainier[6] goes home in this fleet, and therefore it is expected they will not be delayed anywhere on their passage. If I had time, I could lengthen it out to a quire of paper but, as it is, I fear you will be tired and I must close it this moment as the ship sails tomorrow. All sorts of English pickles are greatly valued in this country, not only by the Europeans, but also by the natives, who steal them from you if they can get at them in any way, and eat them privately. Their laws forbid them to eat or drink anything which has been touched by an inferior, so that their cooking is always done by one of their own caste. This they strictly adhere to with all things that they are indifferent about, but their passion for these pickles is so great that they condescend to eat them though made by us, whom they

5 Sir Thomas Strange (1756–1841): First Chief Justice of the Supreme Court in Madras, 1800–1816. Oxford Dictionary of National Biography: ref:odnb/26640

6 Admiral Peter Rainier (1741–1808) was Commander in Chief of the East India station from 1794 to 1805. See Oxford Dictionary of National Biography: ref:odnb/23028

account the lowest of all, and class with the outcastes. One cannot trust a jar of pickle even with the Butler, but I am obliged to give out a little at a time in a saucer and to observe that it is brought to table, for they cannot resist it. They have no vinegar in this country, but what is brought from England, and for that we pay about six shillings a quart, so they could not afford to make them if they knew how.

The three little figures *(drawings)* I have sent are an Ayah, or lady's Portuguese maid, a little Moor boy who is the sort of servant generally kept to wait on single ladies at dinner, and a woman lackey whose business it is to put water in the bedrooms, and to sweep their floors. This sweeping she performs with a little rod or broom in her hand, and in the other hand she has a dust shovel which they call a fan. It is made of chip or cane, of which materials they make a great number of useful and elegant utensils, footstools, dinner things, baskets in the form of boxes to hold millinery or clothes of any sort. They look very ornamental in the rooms, as they colour them and plait them in very pretty figures. They also make mats for the floors with cane, which are very durable. Most of the houses are entirely covered with them, as the floors are of chunam, which is a sort of stucco. They colour this to represent marble of different kinds. In squares, this has an elegant appearance, but the colour comes off on one's clothes very much, when it is not matted. They also make blinds of the cane, which are painted green to prevent the glare of light from coming in too strong. The fronts of the houses are quite open. A house generally consists of five rooms, or halls, of an equal size in the centre. The first (to which you ascend by a very wide flight of steps) is called a veranda. The rooms are divided only by columns, or in arches, so that the whole of the sitting rooms lie open before you when you enter. Besides this you have two wings of three rooms each; and these make chambers and library. If you have gentlemen visitors, they sleep in bungalows which are small, very pretty, houses built in different parts of the garden. Mr R. Clarke has one of these, which is very comfortable and pretty. It consists of a sitting room with verandas on three sides of it, a room over that, and on the top of all a little slight room with a thatched or matted top, and the sides are all round of Venetian blinds. In this he sleeps at present, and thinks it very cool and pleasant, but when the rains set in the lower room will no doubt be better. None of the windows in this country are glazed. They are very large and have fixed Venetian blinds, very strong, which fasten like shutters. You shall have some sketches to give you an idea of the houses very soon, I hope, and of many other things, as I shall not suffer myself to be idle where there is so much matter of curiosity, which I know my friends will be glad to have related, and drawn, even in the slightest manner. I beg you to give my compliments to all who do me the favour to enquire after me, and most affectionate remembrance to Ned, Nancy and the dear boys

From Mary Symonds to her sister Hetty. 14th October 1801.

I have sent a long letter for mother directed to you, and left it open that you may read it before you forward it. I send three little figures, which I fear my mother will be disappointed to find of such a small size that they will require her best spectacles to discover their ornaments. The necklace, bracelets and earrings of the lowest servants are of the finest gold. Some of the better order of women are quite loaded with gold and jewels but in these ornaments consist their whole wealth; they call them joys. Some wear large rings in the nose and have their toes and fingers covered with rings. They have no furniture in their houses but an earthen vessel to boil their rice and curry in, and some 'chip' baskets. Their whole dress consists of a long piece of cloth or muslin, which they wrap about themselves in an elegant manner. If I had drawn their figures of a larger size you would perhaps have had some difficulty and expense in getting them through the India house, or else I must have troubled some person to get them on-shore and so have used that interest which would convey a better thing. If you choose to keep the whole collection as I send them you must copy them for my mother or else desire her to return them to you. I could wish you to show them to G. Samuel and tell him that he shall have some *(pictures of)* houses and choultries and pagodas[7] very soon, that is to say we

7 A **Choultry** is a resting place, an inn or caravanserai for travellers, pilgrims or visitors, and were open to all to provide shelter from adverse weather, or wild animals, especially overnight. A **Pagoda** was the term incorrectly (as Elizabeth Gwillim

propose setting about them after the rains are over, when for two or three months we shall be able to sit out of doors several hours in the day as the weather will be cool and clear. I hope, now we are settled, that I shall be able to send something for the curious by every opportunity. If you are in the habit of making the preserves as we did formerly, it will not be taken amiss that you add a few measures of fine high flavoured strawberries into your stew pan for us as they turned out, I think, finer than any other of our preserves, but they are all very good, and greatly treasured here. They were only boiled into jam the same as raspberries, with a good deal of sugar.

PS. We did not forget the third of this month and we had a goose on Michaelmas day.

From Mary Symonds to her sister Hetty. Undated

I had almost a mind to be lazy and not to write to you by this opportunity, but I now think the enclosed company *(in picture format)* may be able to afford you some entertainment and, as I have had my share of amusement in making them, it is but fair you should now have yours. However I fear I shall have some difficulty in explaining them to you. I intended to make a great many more, and to fix them in a box to represent a street *(something like a pop-up book)*, but I fear if I do so you will have some trouble in getting them passed at the India house. They are done very slight, but I promise you some good drawings by the next ships. This method I invented to give you some idea of the population of this country. I intended to place the rows of people very near to each other in a box, and they would then be about as thick as the people are here in the streets. To a stranger it appears quite dangerous to drive through them,

emphasizes in her letter of the 7th March 1804) used by the British in India to describe a Hindu temple, with its classical design, as opposed to today's common usage for structures of this kind in China or Japan. Confusingly, a *pagoda was also a unit of currency*, being a gold coin minted by the East India Company in Madras, and worth 3.5 Rupees. According to the letters one pagoda was worth eight shillings and sixpence or, in modern UK currency, 42.5 New Pence. Therefore a Rupee then was worth just over 12 New Pence.

but the horse keepers, who march by the side of the carriage, make a horse noise calling them to go out of the way, and they contrive to divide off while you pass, and I have never heard of an accident. I have written the names on the backs of these things. I shall send you a great many figures done in the same way, as there are an immense number of employments which I can describe better in that way than any other. Toddy is a liquor which is drawn from the coconut tree.[8] It is thought very wholesome if drunk early in the morning, before the sun rises, and as soon as it is drawn from the tree but, if it is kept till the sun is up, it becomes fermented and has an intoxicating quality for which the natives drink it. I have drawn a toddy man, who is distinguished according to the custom by a cocoa palm leaf. The carriages of the natives are extremely elegant, particularly the hackery, which is drawn by milk white bullocks. I intend sending you an accurate drawing of one very soon. In the meantime there is one in one of these rows, which may give you some little idea. You will also see a curious method of carrying children. Two women carry a long bamboo stick, with a piece of cloth tied to it in which the child is put. One of the rows consists entirely of women with chattys *(pottery)* and brass pots; I intended to bend it round and make a little well in the middle to show the manner of drawing water. It is never done by men, and the man would be much despised who should go near enough to hear the women's conversation there. The high caste women never carry the pots on their heads, but on the shoulder, and the Brahminy women never touch any earthen pot. They only use the brass ones. They are also distinguished by wearing cloth like trousers, as the men do, the other women wear theirs straight round, like petticoats. I have written to Nancy Green and, if I had time, I could write a great deal more to you but, as the ship sails this evening, I dare not stay any longer. I hope to write again very soon. Pray tell James and George Samuel[9] that they are impudent fellows for not writing to us and,

8 A specific coconut palm is used – Borassus Flabellifer – called palmyra, or a date palm. The relevant tree is often just called a toddy palm. The sweet sap is collected in jars at the head of the tree, and very rapidly ferments. If distilled, arrack is produced. Today sugar cane is often used.

9 Noted landscape painter of the day; d.1823. A presumed friend and former tutor. See note 10 to Introduction, *page 6*.

if they don't set about writing soon, I shall begin a new plan with them and write them such long tedious stories as shall tire their sleepy heads too much to read. What a set of correspondents have we left behind us; I declare you are the only one that deserves to be called a friend, or that seems to be sensible of our absence. Your letter, and my mother's, gave us the greatest pleasure, but we were very sorry to hear that the children were not well. I hope you will not miss any opportunity of writing, if it is but a few lines at a time.

From Elizabeth Gwillim to her mother. 7th October 1801.

Since we came here Polly and I have changed sincerely. She has become the writer as I have had much domestic business. You must not therefore be surprised to see so little of my hand. Besides I have had a good deal to write to Lizzie Thoburn, which no one else could do, about seeds and plants. I have sent many sorts, but like enough nothing new. I think you would like this country very much. There is nothing to complain of but that it is a little too hot. Here it is perpetual summer. The trees and grass have almost constantly the fresh verdance – (*sic – verdant state*) of May. A few weeks of dry weather dries up the grass which is always short but it does not make it very brown and one night of rain, with this heat, turns up a fresh crop, and every place is like green velvet. Upon the trees this drought has no effect as it has with yours. Philosophers have a way of accounting for this, but I do not well understand it myself. Their freshness is not preserved by dews or fogs, for we have neither. The trees are large and tall and the whole place is like our parks and gardens, with every beauty that there can be in a flat country. Neither plants nor trees have their leaves eaten by insects, nor curled up by them, as yours are, with what we call blights. They are perfectly clean and fresh and most of them bloom all the year.

I never write two lines without an interruption. All our rooms are open here and have great folding doors thrown open. It is like living in public. The houses may properly be called Garden houses. They are like handsome summer houses in English pleasure gardens, but with more apartments. Everyone walks in and presents himself before you, unless you have particularly directed to be private. As a part of a history of the manners of the place I will tell you what I was interrupted about since I sat down.

The gardener or Maistry as they call him, the headman with three under him, and two boys in regular order, the youngest first and the gardener last, walked up to the front of the house and into the hall where I am sitting and, after making a Salaam, that is putting their hands to their foreheads and bowing to the ground, they stand upright before me. They cannot speak a word of English, nor I of Malabar, which is their language *(In fact Tamil. See note 22, Chapter 1802, page 90)*. Therefore, their entrance being obtained by the servants who are lying about, one comes forward as an interpreter, he being greater than they, like other folks in office, talks to them in a loud voice, lowering it to me in a most farcical manner. He explains to me that this is a feast day for praying to God for all those employed with tools, and that they are desirous of two days' holiday to go to see the God, and request me to give them a rupee and half, that is about three shillings and sixpence or 3/9, to buy a sheep to kill in front of the tools and spades, which are for that purpose carried to the back part of the garden, where the sheep is to be slaughtered, cooked and eaten. After this they generally spend the night in a sort of revelry, going to the pagodas and making music more horrible than any noise was ever heard, seeing dancers and jugglers, and so forth. These kind of feasts seem frequent, as are all their days of recreation, and of religious ceremony - indeed religion and amusement seems to be always united with these people. When I had granted their request, the servant desires to know if I will say any more to them, and finding I am done he says most authoritatively, Salaam, that is he bows and goes. This they call making a Salaam for a sheep. The Carpenters, I understand, made their Salaam to Mr Gwillim[10] this morning, and are also to kill their sheep. When Mr Gwillim's new palanquin came home we were obliged to have two sheep killed before it could be used. There are 13 palanquin men, 12 bearers and one cook who performs his business in a shed, where they sleep at the back of the garden. They modestly requested only a rupee apiece for the two sheep but, when they came, they looked so long-legged and lean that Mr Gwillim gave them another rupee for pity, and desired them to change them for fatter ones. They make stews of it, so lean meat does as well as fat. They call their stews curry, from

10 Sir Henry Gwillim is often referred to as Mr Gwillim, or even Mr G.

the name of a leaf they put in them. They eat boiled rice for bread and the vegetables they stew with the meat. They drink no strong liquor; water is their beverage. It may therefore be allowed them to pepper their stews very high. They eat little animal food, and the spice is necessary to warm their stomachs. Medical people begin to find that Europeans do not require to have their dishes seasoned so highly, as they are used to having them, the spice being to the natives what our wine is to us. It is not necessary to take both. It is curious to go through their markets as the provisions are almost all vegetables. They have indeed a good deal of fish but in a street a mile long where every house is a shop, and has a standing before it with chiefly vegetables. There will not be above one or two butchers, with a kid or two being cut up, or a sheep. The different sorts of people here were not easily explained to me before I saw them, but they are easily distinguished when one sees them; not indeed the minute divisions of castes, for they do not know them all themselves, but the different nations. The population of this place, with its towns and villages in a square of about 7 miles each way, is not I should think much less than in London. The people seem to swarm in the roads, and what makes it appear strange is that there is no appearance of dwelling places for them. Our Garden houses stand in the middle of the gardens, and are seen from the road. The pagodas *(temples)* rise among the trees and are shaded till you come near them. The choultries are low buildings *(wayside shelters)*; mere porticoes with only sometimes an apartment at the back. They are of stone, and richly ornamented with carved work, but the exuberance of foliage conceals all but the front. This gives them an air of solemnity that is a beautiful contrast to the general gaiety of the country, and the fresh verdure, the constant show of blossom, the groups of people with their light graceful dresses, and over all the bright clearness of the sky, gives the whole place an air of cheerfulness that I have never seen equalled. Neither the mosques, nor these, rise high however. Their dwelling houses in the town are seldom more than one storey high, with just a ground floor. There are rows of trees generally before the houses, on each side of the street, and besides this there are gardens at the back, so that these are not seen till you go through. The villages are still more concealed, and they are for the most part in the groves of cocoa palms in the neighbourhood of some choultrey or pagoda, both of which are very numerous. They consist of a set of houses made of palm leaves, little larger than beehives, and plaited and thatched with the same, or with Palmyra leaves, another kind of palm. These villages are in their thousands. The pagodas are places of worship of the Gentoo[11] people and the choultries are for the reception of travellers, and built by them. The mosques are, as you know, the moormen's places of worship. We have Portuguese, Armenian and English churches in the towns. I generally, as I have heard most people do, call the Indians Gentoo, but the Gentoo, Hindu, Malabar[12] and Brahmins are all one set, these names being distinguished amongst themselves only to imply their employment, or at least the set of employments that may be used by that caste of people. Thus Brahmins are the priests, but they have also other trades they may perform, but none can be done by anyone other than such as belong to that caste. He may make different things, and all may be servants to us or to one another, may be poor or rich, but a worker in iron must breed his son to it, and so must a worker of leather etc. These people are the original inhabitants of this country and though they have been invaded and governed by most warlike people, they are still ten to one, at least, of all the other nations who, enticed by their beautiful country, have been endeavouring to destroy them for these thousand years past. Their extraordinary laws, and their numbers, have done much towards preserving them that their courage would not have led them to attempt, and they go on praying to their god, sowing rice,

11 The word Gentoo is possibly from the Portuguese gentio, meaning gentiles, or heathen. It has in the past been applied to all Hindus, but by the turn of the 18th century it particularly meant the people of the south, centring on Madras, and specifically its 'black town'. In the minds of the British it frequently referred to both the people, and their language, which in this region was often Telugu, being the main spoken language along the eastern coast of the Indian peninsula. It is this language that was incorrectly called Gentoo. See letter of 7.3.1804 and Yule, Henry. *Hobson-Jobson: A Glossary of Colloquial Anglo-Indian Words and Phrases, Etymological, Historical, Geographical and Discursive*. (London 1903; Oxford 2013) Elizabeth Gwillim makes it reasonably clear in her letters that she could both read and write Telugu. See letters of 3.8.1802 and Oct/Nov 1803. She translated a legendary tale of St. Thomé (7.3.1804) and sent it home but this was lost with the ship Prince of Wales in June 1804.

12 Tamil-speaking. See note 22, 1802, *page 90*.

weaving cloth, and eating curry just in the same way as they have done these three thousand years. They are the mildest people in the world. They are not like the moor men, a ferocious people enervated by luxury, by turns voluptuaries or slaves, but a mild, patient, people possessed of every useful art but that of defending themselves from their enemies. They seem to have no pleasure in or thought of revenge, otherwise one might say they might have had the satisfaction of seeing their invaders either sink into idleness and luxury, or destroyed by each other, whilst they had lost nothing they value. The Earth produces so abundantly, and with so little labour, what they require, and much more, that they do not feel much wrath when others partake of that with them which might only otherwise be wasted. Foreign delicacies they never require. It may seem an absurd distinction to say that they are not effeminate, but feminine in their manner, not depraved but gentle. They have the virtues and the vices of us women; patient, mild and attentive. They are pusillanimous; they are cowardly and deceitful; their frauds are like those of children and they have neither shame nor fear when they are detected. They seem to know no power to resist temptation, and therefore to have no shame of doing ill and, as to fear, they never appear themselves to have any resentment of good or ill, and if punishment has taught them to fear, it only gives rise to new frauds without preventing them from doing amiss. They are a small people with soft voices, not squeaking, of a fine brown colour and not sooty black. Their features are delicate and their hair waving and not curled. Their teeth are white and their mouths red with chewing betel. Their noses are small and neatly made, but rather low-bridged, except in some castes. The Brahmins have higher noses. I fancy that I know them at first sight. It may be mere fancy in me, but they know one another's caste by the features, which is not wonderful as they never marry out of their caste. Their dress is always white, with borders, and sometimes a red turban. The moor men are a handsomer people; taller; higher noses, and a grander air about them. Their dress is richer and their pale trousers or petticoat, is of striped sapphire or mixed with gold, and their turbans are more showy. Their government may now be said to be done away with. They are in our power, but the people are numerous, particularly here on the coasts. They retain little of the ferocity of their character in the expressions of their faces, but enough to give them an air that distinguishes them from the Gentoo's mild looks [11]. I could not mistake them. The moor women are particularly showy. They and the Gentoo are covered with gold ornaments, and all indeed have a carriage that would be admired in our best stage figures. The people calling themselves Portuguese are, as well as the moors, as dark as the Gentoos. These are a sad set. They pretend to have descended from the Portuguese but it is not so in many instances. They are the refuse of all sorts, and sort of Christian, but yet who partake in all the superstitions of the natives, and know nothing but profligacy. They are not so numerous as the Moors. The women wear a petticoat, and some of the men affect to wear European clothes. The next people are the English, whom I soon discovered not to be more than one in a thousand of the others, but I am told we are not near so many. Is it not a strange thing to see ourselves thus masters of a place? You never meet an English person but in a carriage or in a palanquin. The sepoys, that is the black soldiers, have all the manners of ours. Even now when I see the regiments of them, whether horse or foot, I cannot help being surprised when I pass by and look back at the black faces drilled by our people. They have so much the same air, and they think so much of themselves that there is no danger of their befriending their own countrymen. In my morning rides, I used to pass the camp we had here for some time, and I was much diverted to see the corporals drilling the awkward squads, and young beginners, so completely. The corporals have exactly the same cares and affectations as those in the Park *(i.e. a park in London).*

I sit to write exactly opposite your picture, with Hetty's, the two Thoburn's, and Nancy Green.[13] I seem to be talking to you. Having seen no land since I left England, I cannot persuade myself I am so far off. I sent a letter off in a hurry to Lizzie Thoburn, when I first landed, and have just had it back, so I have sent it with these things. Polly has also sent letters. The worst business of all is the writing. The ship we sent those by had an accident, and did not leave. I long to hear from you. I begin now to get settled and feel at home, and the weather is becoming cooler than it was. It is

13 Close friends in England.

like a fine warm summer in England, and I do not think it is too hot. When we came the land winds prevailed, which are very hot and unpleasant. This climate affords many pleasures and, if there were not some drawbacks, we should all be coming here. The moonlight nights are charming, and I long sometimes to have you with me to see one when the fine warmth of the night, and the sea breeze cooling the air, invites us to sit out on the terrace before the house. The moon so bright, shining on the trees, the grasshoppers chirping, and the sepoy tinkling his little wild tune on a sort of guitar on the one side of the garden. The sea roaring at a distance, which I hear as I lie down in bed. Tuberoses and sweet flowers smelling pleasantly, and all these without the least fear of catching a cough or cold. When I am telling you something, I find other things necessary for the story, and that makes me make sad digressions. You do not perhaps know, as no servants sleep in the house, that everybody has three or four sepoys to keep watch in the garden. They keep guard by turns night and day, go home to their meals, and sleep under the trees or on the steps of the doorway. It is a kind of terrace, the length of the house, of eight or 10 steps up, and balustrades on the side on which we put china pots with flowers, and lean over to listen to the surf of the sea. It rolls in here prodigiously, like it does at Borth sands which Hetty will know, and I hope she will read this before it comes to you, for I mean it for both of you. I hope that some conveyance will soon give me an opportunity of sending it, for I have been much hurried this time. We expect the Georgina packet daily, and that will be in England before the Lord Thurlow, which this letter is intended to go by.[14] I am very much obliged to Ned and Nancy for the bacon and we have half a Gammon now. I

14 The Georgina and the Lord Thurlow were both ships. A packet is the bundle of post brought or taken by a ship. The packet remained open until the ship was about to sail when some warning was given that the packet would close and there was a general rush to complete letters in time. There could be considerable unpredictability as to when ships would sail, and thus packets close, and so the sisters and their contemporaries often left their letters 'open', by which they meant available for adding new pieces of news as the days passed before the packet shut. There was no obligation for them to be 'open' for examination or censorship, as the latter did not exist for personal correspondence.

have desired Polly to say how useful it has been. Only old bacon will carry, and this came to us as nice as when it set out.

Since I wrote this I have been invited by the servants to see the ceremony they hold for their sheep killing. We have a great many outhouses here called godowns. In a small room within a small square or courtyard, where the carpenter keeps his wood and does his work, the ceremony was held. In that room they made up a small kind of temple, like a scene in a play, with little pillars having flowers twisted round and shaped into it; others crossed it at the front, on the top. Long leaves of palm were set which, bending forward, formed an airy kind of pediment. At every point of each leaf bowed over some oleander flowers. The pillars were dressed with all kinds of flowers, and the ground spread over with leaves and all around spades, hoes and iron tools of every description; rollers etc, bound round with flowers suitable to their forms, and all arranged very prettily. On the floor of this little stage, as one may call it, was a pyramid of fruit and palm leaves, with the flowers of the palm forming a long spike which, when bent over, looked like a fountain. Here they placed a quantity of flowers, fruits and sweetmeats, of every colour, with lamps and two candles, and a fire burning on a plantain leaf in front, on which they strewed Bergamia continually.[15] The head carpenter and gardener, without their turbans, and a Brahmin also bare headed, were doing the ceremony. The Brahmin, sitting on his hams, was chanting for a long time and occasionally sniffing up the smell of the Bergamia. The others were tending it, and all the fruits were roasting a little with the fire. All the rest of the people were standing outside the place by now, and then devoutly bowed and held their hands together, as we do when we pray. At last the fire goes nearly out, and with the Brahmin in a sort of ecstasy the people are desired to enter the place, one at a time. They fall down flat on the floor and, holding their noses over the expiring fire, sniff it up eagerly, arise and go out. This done, the Brahmin puts the leaf of fire not yet extinguished into the carpenter's hands. The motion restores the flame a little, and he then brings it outside where all crowd round him and hold their hands over the flame, and sniff it. Then

15 Citrus Bergamia, or Bergamot Orange, is a fragrant citrus plant, not unlike lime, which is often used to scent food or perfumes.

he puts it out by crumbling it, after which each person makes a salaam and receives a portion of the ashes, which he spreads on his hands with great devotion, smells it, and rubs it on his forehead making that white, and what remains goes on his breast. Fireworks were then lighted and let off, and the ceremony was ended by their picking out a plate of things, which they presented to us when we departed. I should have told you that the poor sheep were all this while tied up to a post in front of this altar, for such I consider it. The festoons of flowers that ornamented it were excessively pretty. The sheep are not to die till tomorrow morning, and so the altar therefore remains in place.

I have a thousand things to say to you of love to the children, but you know of our love for them and are, I daresay, desirous to hear how we like this strange country. So I keep on telling you what we see, rather than in guessing what you are at, which I hope anyway soon to hear. May God bless and preserve you and believe me your dutiful daughter.

From Elizabeth Gwillim to her sister Hetty. 17th October 1801.

Some awkwardness may arise which you must excuse, as I can manage no better at present, not being as yet acquainted with any person belonging to ships. The gentleman who brings this brings also two trees, and a basket and packet of seeds for Mr Whitley.[16] His name is Livingstone, if he should call. He is a surgeon, and I was introduced to him to do me this service and am in hopes he will come out again. He thinks he can take onshore two shawls for me, but this cannot always be done. If he finds any difficulty, they must go to the India House and he will tell you how to get them out, or will employ a person to pay the duty. If this is done, Mr James *(Hetty's husband)* will please to enquire the expense, pay it and

16 Reginald Whitley, 1754–1835, was a frequent English correspondent on botanical and horticultural subjects. He was often the recipient of samples sent home. He was the business partner of Frank Thoburn, whose family, particularly daughters Lizzie and Mary, were close friends of Elizabeth Gwillim and Mary Symonds. Frank Thoburn had founded a nursery in Cromwell Road, Brompton, Kensington, in 1784 and had a particular interest in exotic plants. After Thoburn's death Reginald Whitley became step-father to the two Thoburn girls.

charge it to Mr Gwillim. I would have sent over more shawls, but for this difficulty. If they are thus paid for, let me know what, as if not heavy it is worthwhile sending them. They are both orange coloured; one will make you a square and James a waistcoat, and the other will do the same for Mrs Gwillim, and I would beg you to send it to her for that purpose. This is a bad time of year for getting them, as they come from Bengal and no ships have lately come. There is no square shawl to be had so you will take what you can. Tell Mr Whitley my seeds would not grow as English seeds seldom succeed. The seeds from the Cape are hung up in bags in a basket, and hung up in cabins as they do here. Swindon's seeds from England grow, and begin to be in great repute and are done up in varnished pasteboard. I have sent him some in both ways, and I hope they will grow.

I wish I had brought a hundred more out of Mr J's shop of Scotch muslins and cambric muslins. Give my best love to James.

Letters of 1802 and Commentary

Commentary

The first letter of year two is dated February, in which Elizabeth tells her mother that she has just received six letters from her sister Hetty dated May, and therefore written nine months beforehand while they were at sea. The realisation of the inconvenience of the monsoon system in the receiving and sending of correspondence had become apparent. During the winter months the north-easterly monsoon winds prevented sailing ships from heading in that direction, and onwards up the east coast of India, and the offshore surf at Madras became so great that it was not possible to land small boats. There was therefore a dearth of mail, although it is interesting that newspapers could arrive overland, although taking four months in times of war. Outward correspondence had to await the lessening of the winds when ships could both arrive but also sail away with the wind at their backs, and before the stronger headwinds of the south-westerly monsoon arrived in the mid-summer months. The dates of letters from India therefore followed the movements of ships, and there were two main peaks of epistolary industry from February to May and from August to October, although other matters necessarily dictated the movements of ships, not least the activity of French privateers.

After a brief discourse on these matters, in this first very long letter to her mother, Elizabeth's characteristically enquiring mind moves on to the weather and, just as lightly, skips on to entomological matters with the interesting, but questionable, pleasure to be had from eating white ants, or termites. Already we see the focus and passion that she has for subjects that catch her imagination, and which develop in so many interesting ways in the coming months and years. In true British fashion the weather is a regular topic for discussion, and it is interesting to note the susceptibility of the Indian British to the temperature changes of monsoon time with references to gout, rheumatics, coughs and colds and the great value placed on flannel as a wearing apparel, even by the Indian people. From the weather it is of course a logical jump to horticulture, and she launches into a detailed description of the vegetables available to them and the differences and similarities to what they were used to in England, weaving this into a general topographical outline of the Madras district. Throughout her descriptions one is aware of a depth of knowledge already in existence, and a charm of simile that must have been a pleasure to read in distant England: 'the fine cut mimosa as light and thin as a piece of lace', and the beauty she finds in the flowering bindweeds hanging in 'fantastic festoons'.

In this same February letter she then launches into an elegant description of the 'garden' houses in which she and the other Indian British lived, which were clearly as elegant as her description, and of a neoclassical, Italianesque, design of which a precious few still survive. With an almost unrecognised descriptive contrast she then describes, with no less interest or detail, the houses of the native Indians. Finally the letter must end, which she does with a graphic flourish describing a man's reaction to finding the queen termite ant in a nest: 'He pops it into his mouth, her Majesty being esteemed a particular delicacy.'

It is at this point that the sisters refer to their house by the sea in an area of Madras called St Thomé, where then and now was to be found a large Catholic church. The house had been extended by the landlord and during these preparation they stayed for some months in a house loaned to them on St Thomas' Mount *(not to be confused with St Thomé. The Mount was some eight miles to the southwest, and inland)*. They appreciated the coolness and airiness of the elevated situation there. The family seem to have retained possession of the St Thomé house throughout their time in India and enjoyed the proximity of the beach and the sea, and the refreshing sea air. Even when they were living elsewhere, Sir Henry regularly rode there in the mornings for work purposes. Interestingly there is a map of Madras from 1854 on which one can discern a building, not far from St Thomé, called Gwilliamhouse – written as one word. *(See illustration)* It is hard to escape the conclusion that this might be the original Gwillim house, although it is impossible to be certain. It lies behind the coast road, not far from the sea, and its position would do well for what is described by the sisters. There is still the relic of an old garden house in that area which is now a school for the deaf, but it seems unlikely that it is the same building. Furthermore it doesn't accord with Mary Symond's depiction of their house in some of her paintings.

The next letter was written in the same month, but to her sister Hetty. Here one can detect the first hint of home sickness as she describes how she sits at her desk to write, surrounded by paintings and miniatures of family and friends, and also the apprehensive excitement in receiving letters after a long period of silence. Inevitably there was a growing concern after so long that such correspondence might bring bad news, those times being ever ones of uncertainty arising from the fragility of health and life. She also describes the beach and coastline which remind her of familiar parts of coastal Wales, and she spends some time being taken about by her palanquin boys watching the surf – 'just like Barmouth' *(a coastal town in Wales)* – and buying fish of all sorts. Soon, however, she writes about sending presents home, especially the wondrous Kashmir shawls then available, and very different from today's massed-produced objects. If there was no friendly person to carry such objects home, they had to be taken to the India House in London, where they could only be collected by paying a prohibitive duty. Somehow the East India Company felt it reasonable to charge their employees for returning presents home. Goods were frequently smuggled ashore on arrival in Britain, and there is a reference to this in Elizabeth's letters of September 1803 and March 1804. In subsequent letters, and years, it is clear that the Symonds sisters cultivated several young friends, officers and ships' surgeons to carry goods for them in both directions. Unexpected names such as Prosser, Livingstone, Templar and others, stand out in this context within the pages of the letters. Almost immediately the two sisters are entranced by the textiles to be found in India; not just the variety, but the intensely beautiful detail with which they have been decorated; much of it hand painted. Such exquisite fabrics are now only to be seen in the Victoria and Albert Museum, London. Equally extraordinary is their ability to withstand the rigorous washing practices, which destroy English made fabrics, and take out the colour promptly. There is already a hint appearing of later restrictions to exporting Indian fabrics to

Europe, the British policy being subsequently one of encouraging its own cotton trade by exporting in the reverse direction.

At this stage both women are indicating their drawing and painting interest, but perhaps feeling somewhat diffident about their abilities in this new and strange context. Mary confesses that she has taken up painting miniatures of women. She can source some of the materials from India, or even China, but others she needs from home. She would like George Samuel, friend and landscape painter, to write with instructions; a rather distant and slow correspondence course. Her letter of that February already betrays another major interest, that of the social life around her, with extensive gossipy news about this person and that, and she invites the same from her sister in England: 'A chit chat letter, which seems to place us amongst you all, is what we most desire to receive.' Her own chatter extends to detailed descriptions of her contemporaries in Madras, with a particular delight in pointing out how several grand and exalted ladies have very humble origins. Here one has the first intimation that Mary was inclined towards snobbishness. There is also the first suggestion of her realisation of the age disparity between husband and wife, so often present in British India, when she refers to a girl of 20 marrying a man in his mid-40s. It was far from uncommon at that time to hear of girls of 15 marrying men of 50 odd. At the same time Mary recognised, and relates, the fact that a high proportion of British civil employees in India then had Indian, or more commonly Anglo-Indian, wives or partners, and she makes the perhaps surprising statement that half the women in the Madras community at that time were of mixed race. 'Most of the civilians have these blackey families.' The children of better-off men were often sent for education to England, to give them a better chance in India. The main effect of this was to make the young women more marriageable, thus perpetuating the interracial mingling. The young Anglo-Indian men, however, had struggled to get employment ever since Cornwallis denied them this chance some twenty years earlier. As referred to in the introduction, three-quarters of young men in Calcutta up to 1810 kept at least one bibi *(concubine)*, and half the children baptized at St John's Church in the 1780s were of mixed parentage, and illegitimate.[1] There is little reason to believe things were much different in Madras, and it is clear that even men of consequence and station in that city had 'natural' sons or daughters, in other words of acknowledged illegitimacy, and of mixed race. Mary refers further to this in a later letter, dated 10 Oct 1804, where she emphasises the existence of the large number of mixed race children of soldiers and poorer officers, many of whom were accommodated in government schools *(then called asylums)* but for whom employment later proved difficult. As prejudice increased against Anglo-Indians, and even Indians, so these schools gradually disappeared in subsequent years. Mary seems herself to have been almost as much attracted to the Indian men of her acquaintance as many young European men were to the women, especially when a rich and exotically robed Nabob entertained her. Dalrymple refers to a number of women at that time who cohabited with, or even married, Indian men of consequence.[2]

In that first year are found the initial comments about two important subjects, food and fashion. The latter regularly appears throughout the letters, with regular requests for new items to be sent out from England. Food is a perpetual interest but Mary, being a little more impetuous, additionally encourages her sister in England to chide their friends for not writing, and also encourages her to go shopping with her husband's money in order to buy things to send to India. She then even confesses, with the imprudent egocentricity of unmarried youth that, for her, going to a ball takes precedence over writing a letter.

Elizabeth is, not unexpectedly, just as excited by the prospect of gifts from home, but there is a noticeable difference in that she is also just as concerned that she should find worthwhile things to send back home as presents, and that they should suit the recipient. She also reveals an early interest in what was to become a major preoccupation during her time in India, namely horticulture, in particular at that time the growing of vegetables and the availability of other produce for the table, including game, meat, fish and shellfish. Mary, whose personality is rather more complex,

1 See notes 11 and 12 of Introduction.

2 Dalrymple, William, *White Mughals. Love and Betrayal in Eighteenth Century India* (London, 2002)

reveals a tendency to incongruity in that she complains about her inability to communicate with the native Indians in 'black English' and yet, in the same letter, she expresses no interest in learning a local language despite the fact that the whole of the rest of that household are learning Telugu, Malabar *(Tamil)* or Persian, particularly Elizabeth. As she stoically perceives, this reflects their relative interests; 'I shall leave the White people to Polly and tell you a little about the Black people.' Elizabeth's motive for language learning was inevitably related to her profound interest in Indian history, culture and religion. In an extraordinary letter to her mother of July that year, she starts with the above memorable sentence, which so clearly defines the difference between the two women. She then hurls herself into a lengthily descriptive outline of the Hindu religion, and paints entrancing and detailed pictures in words of the various religious ceremonies that she has attended. This must have taken some time as this letter, by no means her longest, is 5,500 words long; no mean effort with a quill pen. One has the impression she might have written for longer because, as she says in October; 'I am always curious to enquire about their customs, and here there are so many different peoples that it takes a long time to distinguish one set from another.' It is fair to say however that her portrayal of Indian history is inevitably from a colonial standpoint, however much she sought out and narrated details from Brahmins, and other reliable sources. Although she attempts, furthermore, to classify the castes in Indian society, it is likely that purist Indian sources would take issue with the accuracy of her categorization. It is also fair to say, however, that what is truly compelling here is not so much the detail that she delivers, but the fact she is interested at all, which would have been uncommon among her peers.

Early reactions to servants are contained in that first full year. Mary, perhaps characteristically, is inclined to emphasize any laziness and lightfingeredness. Elizabeth, with typical goodwill, emphasized their gentleness, kindliness and cleanliness, and also the abilities held by those of higher caste. She also intimates that cruelty and impatience is to be found amongst employers.

The correspondence for the latter part of the year; mainly October; is mostly about the weather, the desire for a top up of their confectionary stocks, and their appreciation of Lord Clive, Governor of the settlement and son of Clive of India.[3] He appears to have been a most agreeable person, although not such an effective administrator, but his wife was much appreciated by both sisters. Mary's footnote to the year was a succession of names and social prattle, but entertaining enough, although rather typical of her. There is much family news, and an amusing, but uncharacteristically earthy, passage where Elizabeth reveals a puckish side to her personality in relating the misunderstanding caused by the diction of the Indian servants, such that they make an English -ch sound like -sh or, specifically, 'shit' for 'chit'.

As a finale to the year, Mary describes the delightful efforts of the staff in decorating the house in lavishly green fashion to celebrate Christmas, a religious holiday unrecognized in their own faith, and yet into which they enter with gusto, even giving small presents to their masters. She is even more impressed by the local Nabob's contributions and by the Muslim street entertainment in the days afterwards.

So their first full year closes, and they face an incommunicative winter. The overriding impression is of excitement and pleasure in their Indian way of life, and all they have seen and learnt of local culture.

Letters

Letter from Elizabeth Gwillim to her mother. 5th February 1802.

I received six letters from Hetty written in May, which is the only account I have had from England since we left. Those letters were written in great haste, but were a very pleasant relief to me, as it appeared you were

3 Clive, Edward; First Earl of Powis. Oxford Dictionary of National Biography. ref:odnb/5696. Edward Clive was a reasonable administrator, but not the forceful negotiator that his father was. Early in his career in Madras he was involved with the planning for the attack on Tipu Sultan at Sriringapattanam, and later the administration of the newly acquired territories of Tanjore and Arcot. It seems that affairs of state were often inclined to give way to a deep interest in horticulture: Dalrymple, William, *The Anarchy: The Relentless Rise of the East India Company* (London, 2019).

recovered from the illness you had when I went away. It was the greatest surprise to us to learn that she had not by then lain in *(been delivered of her baby)*. I trust in God she had a good time, but it is very long to wait to hear of an event which was so near. It is now eight months since those letters were written. I wish we were as well off for private intelligence as we are for public. The newspapers come here overland, and we have had them constantly at four months after their date which, considering the distance, and that when the world is at peace we may have them still quicker, is a great matter. The timing of our arrival in this place was unfavourable to us in respect of hearing from, or writing to, our friends and, I daresay, long before this comes to your hand you will have thought it strange not to have heard. But besides that, this season has not permitted us to write for some time. Some accidents, which have prevented ships from calling here on their voyage to England, have been a problem. One was detained, on some occasion or another, which was to have taken up passengers here in November, and for which many made up packets *(of letters)* to send, but was obliged to go on another course after all, for fear of some privateers. These privateers were soon afterwards taken. I wrote, as we all did, by the Thurlow to you and, from that time to this, we have been constantly told to prepare letters, but so many disappointments have followed all the promises, that nobody is inclined to begin, and I think it likely enough that the first ship that calls will find nobody prepared. I am, however, so desirous that you should know everything of our goings on that, in spite of the small hopes I have, I am determined to begin. The months of November, December and January are what is called here the monsoon, that is the rainy season. The surf of the sea is very great on this coast, and therefore during this period it is thought unsafe for any vessels to lie near the coast. In this season, at the commencement of the monsoon, the flag is struck, and not put up again till it is over, to indicate that no ships are to remain in the harbour or roads, nor to come into them.[4] As great numbers of vessels of different sorts are constantly lying here at other times, this circumstance of itself gives the natives and settlers a

4 Flown from the flagstaff in Fort St George, on the coast, from which signals would usually be made to ships offshore.

melancholy idea. Indeed, it produces a great change in the appearance of the beach, which generally presents a most lively and busy scene. The country ships, that is the coasting vessels, have begun to come in and, with a few ships of war, we have near a hundred but these make little show. When we came here, the roads were crowded with ships of a large size, and we expect every day to see them again in the same state, and for nine months in the year frequent opportunities will occur of writing. There are so many things you will likely wish to know of this place, that I believe it matters not which I begin with. As we have now been here six months, you will expect to hear something of the climate. When we first landed on the 26th of July we had land winds, with sea breezes in an evening, but it was thought late for the land winds to continue. The natives count the season of the land winds a healthy time, and I believe it may be so to all people who are careful and patient. They prevail April, May, June and July. This wind is a strong breeze and, in the degree we had it, very pleasant to me at first, but we soon found the effects it is said to produce, sometimes the one and sometimes the other. It can give a dryness of the skin as if sand had blown on it, and I found it impossible to keep my hair from curling to a perfect frizz. At other times, as it blows over you, it draws out so great a profusion of perspiration that you get your clothes quite wet, but what is remarkable is that this wind, which is in itself so hot, makes everything else cold. Of course this sweat is as cold as ice, and the consequence of being in cold water may be easily guessed. It gives cramps in the legs, and spasms in the back and neck, and young men who go to sleep in liquor in the open air, which from impatience and foolhardiness they frequently will, occasionally get such cramps and spasms as are never cured. This effect of producing sweat is most common in sleep, and therefore all prudent people shut up the windows on the side whence this wind blows, and in daytime close the Venetians to keep out the light, which is the best way of keeping out the heat. The sea breeze generally sets in of an evening, and is delightfully refreshing. We none of us found any bad effects. In September and October, the heat of the climate is considerably abated, but they told us we should suffer much from the flies which would swarm into everything, but I found the accounts much beyond the truth. The trees, plants and the air are all extremely free from insects, but they come to the candles in an evening. They are chiefly the common small black fly, but these I never saw more numerous here than at Brompton *(a more rural home outside the City)*. There are no Blue Bottles or wasps, nor any stingers. There are small moths of various kinds, from an almost invisible size to the bigness of a sixpence, a few small things of the lady-fly kind, and of different colours, but very rarely does any large beetle come into the house. The grasshoppers are the most impertinent, and they are of all sizes and colours but, though very pretty, their noise is extremely troublesome and sometimes, when they hop upon one's arms or face, one is not quite sure that it is not a more offensive insect, but a fright is soon over however, for they are too busy a race to remain long in a place, and I believe few people are afraid of, or have much dislike for, them. The other tribe we have, that come occasionally to the candles, are very curious. They are the white ant which, in their first state, burrow in the ground to the quantity of bushels. In this state, when found, and they are watched for always, they are dug up and sold in the bazaar, much as we might sell elvers or shrimps. They are esteemed a great delicacy, and all the people of the country are only fond of them for stews. A nest of them, as you may suppose, frequently gets to a state of perfection and come out unobserved, and they then fly about as other insects do. They are said to have their wings only one day, but what truth may be in this I cannot say, but this I have observed, that though they fly into the rooms in hundreds, they all leave their wings behind them and walk off without them as perfectly, and as well, as ever. They generally alight, and run about the table not using their wings other than to obtain a place to walk in. In walking they shed their wings, just as the petals would be shaken off a bunch of May flowers. I could get a paper full of these wings, which are thin and brown. I enclose a sketch of the insect. I have now given you a list of our annoyances in the insect way, and I suppose I shall have no occasion to add to it as September and October are the months in which they come. In November they all disappear and even the grasshoppers are much quieter. In these months the air is generally cooler, but with not so fine a sea breeze. At night though, we have occasional heavy showers of rain which gives a freshness to everything, and makes the day very pleasant. We have had only one thunderstorm since I came here, which was at that time. I do not think it was more violent than I have seen in England, but it lasted a great part of the night. No accident happened that we heard of. Lightning seldom does harm in these hot countries. Before the monsoon, it lighted every night as soon as the sun set. The clouds have the most fantastic forms and the lightning shoots from different parts of the sky in the most beautiful manner. It is perfectly harmless, and therefore even I look at it with the greatest pleasure. Indeed, we are so much used to it in going about from house to house of an evening, that I look upon the sight of it as a great part of our pleasure and, if the lightning has not been bright, I feel as much disappointed as I do in England if the sun has not finally set. One evening at a ball at Lord Clive's *(Governor of Madras at that time, and son of Robert, Lord Clive)*, where there are very large glass lustres, the lightning shooting through the windows upon the cut glass lighted it up onto the dancers under them, and produced one of the finest effects I ever saw. In November the monsoon begins and everybody rejoiced that the weather would, after the rain, become cool; but though it disagreed with few Europeans I was much disappointed. The rain is heavier than yours in the same season and, with it, little abatement of heat, at least not enough to induce one to shut oneself up, or to put on additional clothing, other than ought to be done for the rains. The heat makes the damp so penetrating that every place is full of it. It is exactly the effect of a very sudden hot thaw, and gave me the same feelings, and the same complaints, I have in England when a great frost breaks up violently. I got a crick in my neck, and rheumatic stitches in my breast, exactly the same as yours, and I was plagued with them at every turn till I found myself obliged to take to all my English clothes again. My flannel petticoat and jacket, a shawl to go out in, and a good blanket on the bed, and if I had done this earlier I should have saved myself much pain. Flannel is most valuable here. The natives beg, buy and steal it. Even Mr Gwillim sleeps in a flannel waistcoat. The seasons in this place are exactly like England, with the difference being the degree of heat. November brings here exactly the same effects as in England. People who are gouty are laid up here at the end of October, and beginning of November, just as they are in England, and it continues in the same way. All the servants and exposed people get coughs also, and for two months our servants have been coughing quite as much as ever I heard a family in my life. I do not believe there were at one time two in 10 that did not have a cold or cough. What we have had they call a very mild monsoon, and I think it must have been. We had heavy rains, sometimes for two days and nights without ceasing, but no wind of enough consequence to call a storm, nor any thunder, and the ships might have stayed here all the monsoon with great safety, but this is not to be relied on and accidents have happened. Between the rains there are generally four or five of the sweetest days that can be imagined, and then again two or three days of rain. This is the great gardening time, and as the rains of the spring and the return of the sun warms your climate in England to the sweet temperament of May and June, so here by means of the rain and the retiring of the sun we are cooled to the same state, and the latter half of December, and this month, are like one of the finest seasons of May and June. Whatever plants we have, which cultivated in England either flower, or are fit for food in June, are ready at this time here. Christmas Day is kept exactly like May Day and every house, and every person, is draped with garlands of flowers. Boughs are fixed to the entrances of the houses, and people entertain their friends with green peas. French beans are here all the year, and are very good when of our kind, but their hedges are all full of a wild sort, or indeed sorts, for there are several, a little inferior to ours, but more abundant and to be had all the year. They climb up every tree and bower over their hedges, which are covered with the profusion of their flowers, sometimes white, but more frequently pink or lilac, and very beautiful. Some of these beans are shelled and boiled as broad beans and are not bad. Others are used as we use ours, but they are as broad as two fingers. They cut them small, however, and they are so much alike that I ate them several times without knowing, nor should I have known if I had not been told, although I thought them rather more mealy. We have potatoes only half the year, and the new potatoes are just come in. They do not grow here but are brought from the northward. I have eaten asparagus several times but they are miserable small straws. They are very sweet and would no doubt, as a few do, grow occasionally to a good size. They have been but lately introduced. Turnips and carrots are always to be had, but they are small. The cabbages are chiefly what we call cutters, or cabbage plants, and people who attend to their own gardens have cabbage, but no broccoli or cauliflower. The endive is large, and as white as snow; beetroot small; lettuces small; mustard, cress, radishes, mint in great abundance, onions, cucumbers and spinach. Sage is also good, and parsley grows very well, but the seed ought to be fresh from England at every opportunity, for the seed will not do a second time. It is excellent the first time, but the second it becomes like Chervil and, after two or three times, as rank as fennel. The seed I brought out would not grow. It got damp by some means, but a gentleman who came in the same fleet brought some, and I have had parsley from him, and he has given me a bed full of roots which do well. As the parsley becomes fennel, so the fennel gets as strong as aniseed. Thyme and marjoram I have not seen, and lost what I brought out that was dried. Here in this country are an infinite number of vegetables, some of which I am fond of; yams, a large coarse kind of potato, and a very small sweet potato, like frostbitten ones. Greens and sorrels of several sorts, but what the natives chiefly use are the seed vessels of plants. Almost all the plants and trees of the country are of the pea or bean shaped flower, and produce pods of various forms, and these they use in their stews, either shelled or young. The tamarind is a large tree of this kind, and is as agreeable to them as any other bean, for they generally put lime juice into them, or the acid of tamarinds. They have several things of the cucumber and gourd kind, which are excellent stewed, and also some other seed vessels. As the hedges and trees yield so many things, you may suppose they do not much labour in their gardens, but they keep the beds neat enough to give them some edible greens. Their gardens look more like shrubberies, with flowering trees that bloom like laburnum, and the bladder, or Senna. Some are very handsome, which you will not have seen, and all bloom profusely and have the lightest foliage, waving in the air. This country is now truly beautiful. There is no spot uncultivated, but is either used for coconut groves, mango groves (or orchards, as you would call them), pleasure grounds, gardens or rice fields. The rice looks exactly like thick crops of wheat, and I should not have known it without plucking it. It is at present green. Some crops of millet are cut and brought in, and some other small grains.

The sea is a fine object on one side, and on the other there are low ranges of hills. The first begins 7 miles from the sea; the houses are on the plane of this space, and the rice fields and towns are intermixed. The roads are cut into so many directions, winding towards the innumerable houses and villages, that I have as yet not the least notion of the plan of it, and the servants tell me "if my mistress every day go out for one year she will every day see some new road". Therefore, when I go out in the carriage, I tell them to take us anywhere for a pretty ride, and we see sweet scenes as there can only be in a flat country. The houses are all beautiful palaces of white marble embosomed in lofty trees. The enclosures of the rice and corn fields are very irregular, some small, and others like common fields in England, with groves and plantations of tall trees and flowering shrubs of every form, more various than you can guess. There is the great leaf of the cocoa palm, each one of which is a load for a strong man, and which he binds up and carries on his head or shoulder like a deal plank, and the fine cut mimosa, many of which are as light and thin as a piece of lace (the gum arabic is the finest of all). These groves and corners, and the full hedges, give a remarkable richness to the look of the cornfields. Never were seen such beautiful hedgerows as are on each side the roads, and dividing every field and garden, and the plants for hedging are as various and as beautiful. One plant is exactly like hawthorn, and grows in the hedge or runs up into a tree and, without plucking it, you could not know the difference, and therefore the English are fond of it for their fences. However it has no thorn, and the flowers are more like mignonette in appearance, and small.[5] The hedges have trees of various kinds growing in them. Another favourite hedge plant has nothing but leaves. It is extremely verdant, thick, bushy, tall and like lacework. Bamboo, also, is plaited into a rich-looking hedge and, throwing itself upwards, rises in plumes like light feathers 60 or 80

5 This could be Reseda, also known as the mignonette, which is a genus of fragrant herbaceous plant native to Europe, southwest Asia, North Africa and northwest India. It could equally be Lawsonia Inermis which is known as the henna tree or the mignonette tree. Decorative henna is derived from it, and it appears to be more like a hedging plant, which is what Elizabeth is describing. The preceding, and subsequent, sentences in this letter clearly indicate her already keen interest in horticulture.

feet high. Some people like the American aloes, which have not that stiff look you might imagine. The various kinds of bindweeds that everywhere abound, hang down, and cling about the branches of the trees, where they find support and form the most fantastic festoons. Also convolvuluses of various sorts, and beans with many wild gourds. These binding plants, profuse of flowers, clinging about the Indian plants of large size, are to me the most beautiful, as well as the most novel, kind. There is a plant, a kind of breadfruit, yielding a large fruit as big as a pineapple, and with leaves not unlike a pineapple but soft and pliant, and bending down. This has a wildness and grandeur in the look of it, particularly where it shoots up into trees, that is most delightful to a stranger. Wild sugarcane, and the prickly pear, or Indian fig, are also used for hedging. I think Edward James would not be sorry for a shipload of this hedging stuff, if he could make it grow. With these plants, a hedge may be formed in a short time that a tiger could not pass, for the closeness and strength of the thorns.

We have four rivers in this place, none of them navigable within some miles of here, and then only for boats. They are very shallow streams, but broad, when there has been rain, and banks rich in wood in many parts.[6] They wind about the plain in a most irregular manner, and there are a great many bridges over them, besides innumerable fords which, being causeways well-made in the dry seasons, are quite safe, and we seldom go out to dinner without passing one two or three of these. These rivers run into the sea at this place, and some of them come down the country 40 or 50 miles, and they enliven the country exceedingly. The great beauty of this place is that if you quit the seaside you have always a river on one hand or the other, or else a tank, by which you are to understand a lake, partly natural, but aided by all the dams being carefully kept up. Some of these tanks are many miles long and are very fine pieces of water. Many of the houses are built on the banks of them, with flights of steps to the water. Agriculture is carried on here in a manner just the reverse of yours, and so is gardening, for as you raise beds for the vegetables and leave a sunken path to walk round them, here they sink the bed about a hand breadth and

6 There are now three rivers: Adyar, Cooum and Kosathalaiyar.

the path around is raised. This is in order to retain the water, which is of course much exhausted in the day.

As you are a great architect[7] I think you will like to hear something of the buildings here, which are much talked of. But I hardly know how to begin a subject so various. The houses of all Europeans are nearly equal as to goodness and size, in whatsoever situation the dwellers are, for building is cheap and young people generally build them, and they are let out afterwards and sold. They are all like pictures of Italian palaces, with flat roofs or balustrades. I hardly know what to compare them to that you know of, for they look like marble and are all built with columns, but it is a lighter kind of building than fine churches in London, and much more beautiful architecture than the inferior ones. Lord Tilney's house is like a great many of them, with a double flight of steps outside, but many are only pavilions with nothing above the ground floor, which is the case of the house we live in. They are the prettiest houses, but the upstairs houses, as they call them, have more air. These houses are built of brick and cased over with chunam. This is a finer lime than the plaster of Paris, and it is made of the small white shells which the rough surf occasions the sea to throw up in great quantities. To prevent their being carried back with the tide, there are fishers who with a peculiar kind of net drag them out of the surf. They are then carefully cleaned and burned. The stucco made of this lime, and called chunam, bears a polish almost equal to white marble but, as is generally said, is I think more like the polish or glaze of very smooth white china. The walls, columns and balustrades are all polished. The walls of rooms are sometimes painted, as stucco rooms in England, of pale green-blue. Some people colour the chunam, for the outside of the house, of a light grey in

7 Elizabeth's mother was married to Thomas Symonds, who was an architect and monumental mason and, from 1753, a freeman of the city of Hereford. He was responsible for a number of fine monuments and he was for many years surveyor to the dean and chapter of Hereford and endeavoured without success to get them to take effective steps to prevent the collapse of the west end of the Cathedral, which finally occurred on Easter Monday, 1786. He was not dismissed from his post as ineffectual after the collapse of the tower, as has been suggested, he retired from his post instead. Following his death in 1791 his wife continued the business. See Gunnis, Rupert. A Dictionary of British Sculptors, 1660–1851.

imitation of the grey granite of the country, leaving the columns, pilasters etc white. The floors are also of this chunam, coloured according to the fancy of the owner, and here it so exactly resembles marble pavements that I should not have known. Our house has black and white squares for the sitting rooms, and in the other rooms a light tint much used. Some have dove and black squares, or all dove, which is neat. They mark it in squares so deep that it would deceive anybody.[8] We have folding doors in all the rooms, which are half way green-painted Venetians. The windows are all Venetians, and no glass, but we can thus exclude the light, and yet have air from room to room through the whole house. They are generally all open, and there are always as many doors as windows: never any plain wall or side of a room, but only piers between. These have girandoles, or glass shades, but the rooms will not admit of much furniture. There are verandas at the back and front of the house, and in these the dinner etc is generally laid. The other rooms are called halls, and are used as drawing rooms or sitting rooms. The dinners look very pretty laid out in these verandas, open to the garden and well lighted up. There is a balustrade between the columns on which they set flowers. The first dinner I saw I thought it wonderfully striking, particularly from the number of servants waiting with such extremes stillness, and so delicately dressed all in white muslins and white or figured turbans, and large gold earrings. Besides one's own servants, everybody who dines with one brings one or two with him so that if we sit down to dinner twenty, or three or four and twenty, there are at least thirty servants waiting at table. The greater part of these people will come in palanquins and each palanquin has from nine to 19 men and two lanthorn men. These set the palanquins under the trees before the doors, and lie down to sleep, or talk till they are called. If it be all night, the carriages wait in the same way, and they together form very pretty groups under the trees. I think nothing of the kind can exceed the beauty of an evening ride to see all the houses lighted up, and people dining or dancing in the verandas with the attendants lying about the garden, particularly at a ball when if there are 150 people or 200, which is generally the number, there

8 For details see Balfour, Edward: The Cyclopaedia of India and of Eastern and Southern Asia, Commercial, Industrial and Scientific (India, 1885).

will be 400 to 500 or more of these people in their muslin dress scattered under the trees before the house. The fort is very handsome from the fortifications. It has several handsome squares in it and the buildings are all in the same style as the garden houses; higher but with flat roofs. The church, and some public buildings, rise above them. In a view, it looks like prints one has seen of views of Grecian cities, all temples and no middling houses. The Black town is the most curious in view. It presents such a variety of objects: streets full of palaces such as I have described - English, Portuguese and Armenian Christian churches, Hindu pagodas and Moorish mosques and tombs, and when you go through the streets the various businesses carried on, and the lower buildings which form the extent of the town, are equally curious. It is very large, and the streets have at the corners names written up in Malabar *(Tamil)* and English, and the houses are numbered.

The houses of the natives make no show, but look neat enough where the streets are regular, which is pretty much the usual case. The streets are not paved but broad; the people walk on the middle way. The sides are raised 1, 2 or 3 feet with steps up at every house but the space before every house is appropriated to it, and not intruded on by passers-by. The roof of the house overhangs about three feet, in the way of our pent houses, and overshadows a solid raised part like a platform on which people sit by day, and where they frequently sleep at night. The door is small and low, with a carving in wood over it, and the wall of the house has no window onto the street, but is painted according to the fancy of the owner with a tiger hunt, or dancing girls, and flowers in borders or plain stripes. These paintings are in watercolours, painted on the white wash just in the same style, and with about as much skill, as paintings are done on the walls of rooms in our farm houses to imitate wallpaper. When you go in at the door, there is a short dark passage with a seat on each side, and of the same plaster as the wall, on which they sit or sleep at night. This brings you into a little square of about 10 feet each way which, if it be a small house, is shaded by a vine frame covered with some kind of gourd, which gives shade. In this place all the cooking is done on pans, and at night they sleep on the seats, and in the open parts or verandas, unless it rains, when they use the closed dark rooms, for to exclude the heat they also keep out the light. If the house belongs to a proper person, they have a small staircase which leads up to the same kind of place above. In that case, these verandas above have carpets on them, and here they sit to do their work, or to keep their accounts, and use these upper dark rooms for sleeping, and the under parts for the servants for cooking etc. In such a house therefore the square would be paved, and no tree over it, but the cooking and slop water are thrown over it, which is drained off but serves to keep it cool. Beyond this square there is another, which is a kind of yard where the cows are kept, and sometimes a garden beyond, but their gardens are more frequently a mile or two from the towns, in places appropriate to that use. These kind of houses are much cooler than our large houses. They have a very thick wall, and the light coming down in the middle does not heat it as ours are heated, which are exposed all round. They never sit in a draught of air, although they indeed lie down in the open air when staying in choultries, but when in a house, or near buildings which bring currents of air, they always get a wall at their backs, generally on three sides of them. Europeans think the more air the better, and build their houses like lanterns so that one can never get out of a draught of air, and the rooms are too hot and too cold at the same time. They are certainly beautiful buildings but many regret that they have not the coolness of the native houses. I have drawn a plan of a native house on the back of this, and have made rounds where the pillars are, which are always used within to support it, but not always on the outside. The workmanship is always neat. The walls are of brickwork, stuccoed over with chunam, and the roof pantiles, both without and within, do not have ceilings but are of a fine wood the colour of oak, varnished and carved. The pillars are of the same wood, very slender, and with such a capital as you sometimes see supporting an oak gallery in a church, and indeed their verandas or galleries are very much like those in a church.

Of their utensils I shall tell you elsewhere, but this is grown too long a letter and, as many ships are departing, I shall send some letters by each and this shall be one of them, as it is. I shall direct my letters to Hetty, whether they are to you or to her, and leave them open for, as there are so many things to tell you about, I shall not like to say the same thing twice. I daresay you have thought me a very negligent correspondent, but when I was on board ship I did a good deal of drawing of such things as we caught, and left Polly to write. When I came here I had to go about looking at houses, and arranging it when I got one. Lastly, I did not like to send my letters at the same time as hers, as a ship was then about to sail which, being overladen, sunk in the harbour, but no person was hurt. It was full of rice intended for your use in England. My letters were only brought back to me many weeks afterwards. Some I have sent by the Thurlow, which I hope you will have in March, and some I have kept, hoping to send better editions by other ships expected to leave later. How I have been disappointed, I have related in the first part of this tedious letter.

In order to finish this, so far as it goes, I may as well fill the paper by telling you what I had omitted, that the white ants have in each nest one as large as the end of a finger, which is called the queen ant. As soon as a man find this he pops it into his mouth, her Majesty being esteemed a particular delicacy. She is said to taste like a lump of thick cream or marrow. In fact these ants have little to do with the common ant, and seem more like bees, but without either their virtues, or their mischievous stings. We have two kinds of ants which might infest houses, a large black kind and a very small red sort. These are only kept out by constant sweeping, for if we do not sweep the house they will do so, and if you leave many crumbs on the floor they are soon carried off. The red ones bite one a sharp bite, and eat everything of the sweet kind, to prevent which we put the beds to stand on little square stones grooved and filled with water over which they cannot pass. Tables that contain anything sweet have the feet set in four china basins made strong and shallow for the purpose.[9]

From Elizabeth Gwillim to her sister Hetty. 11th February 1802.

To you who are our best, and almost only, correspondent we owe a thousand thanks. Your letters, and those you have enclosed to us, are all we have seen since we left England. The two Mrs Clarke enclosed for you, and which came to us in November by the Apollo, were a most acceptable pleasure, though being dated so early as April the 18th, and not bringing us news of your delivery, we were still in a state of anxiety. Before you have this, you will no doubt think us negligent about writing. How it has

9 These protective cups are still to be seen in the more isolated parts of India.

happened I have dilated upon fully to my mother. Her picture, and the miniatures, hang over my dressing table where I write, so I have all my friends before me. See, here we are, pray look at us *(a sketch is inserted in her letter)*. I have made my poor mother a shocking face, but it is a hasty piece and she must excuse it. Nothing I brought out has been admired equal to my mother's picture. Mr James' return of his rheumatic complaint gives us much concern. I hope it will not become a frequent visitor to him. I entreat you will not waste a line in making excuses for him in not writing. I know him much too well to be at all surprised, and can form a complete notion of him after the labour of the day, sitting down to write a letter and the pen dropping out of his hand, as the book used to do. I had written a long letter to my mother on which I shall write No. 1. before the fleet arrives. We heard of it as it passed Ceylon and the Coast, some days before they anchored, and you may judge we suffered great agitation. Mr G. desired me to agree with him, if the letters came late, not to open them till next morning. They came on an evening, and were brought to him, but he could not rest. Fortunately they contained no ill news, except that I should have been glad to have heard a better account of my mother. She bears the winters very ill. I wrote a letter for my mother and you jointly; a letter to Lizzie Thoburn, and sent some that had been returned to me from a ship that sunk in harbour, together with seeds for Mr Whitley by Mr Livingston, Surgeon of the ship Lord Thurlow. I hope you will receive them safe in March. He undertook to carry two shawls for me, directed to you. He told me he thought he could get them on shore for me but, if he found he could not, rather than they should be confiscated he would put them in the India House, from whence they could be had by paying the duty which I requested him to ask Mr James to pay him, having no other mode of paying it. If there should be a necessity, I shall beg the favour of Mr James to charge it to me. I shall be glad to know what is paid, that I may guess whether it is worthwhile to send such things or not. The cry here is that it is by no means worthwhile to send shawls, or anything else, to England if you are obliged to pay the duty, and as yet I know nobody to carry things for me who will care for them. Everybody that goes home likes to take all he can for himself, duty free. However, ships will be going now very frequently and, by sending one now and then, I shall soon be able to send you some to keep you warm. I am much vexed that, in my hurry, I forgot to give Mr Livingston a letter to introduce him to your attention and, as a selfish reason, because he expects to return here immediately, and would take care of anything sent back to me. Also, he is a very respectable young man, and was introduced to me by a friend of ours with whom we were very intimate on board ship; a surgeon who came out to settle here. It is of particular importance to entrust seeds to some person's care, but of all that I shall write to Lizzy. Mr James said something, once or twice, about sending shawls over and therefore, on a separate bit of paper, I shall set down the particulars relative to the purchase of them here, and also of the muslins of this country, for Bengal muslins are as dear here as in England, indeed dearer, unless you get some friend to chase them for you in Bengal, where you always have to buy more than you want. The one shawl I sent was for Mrs Gwillim *(Sir Henry Gwillim's mother)*, and the other for you. I have bought some more for friends and shall send these, and one for you, when I can get them carried home one at a time. The regulations with respect to sending the manufactured goods of this country are really absurd, or are at least carried to an absurd length, and I find the strictness here is much beyond that in England. I could, for very little money, send you things that would delight you if they would let them pass, but they will not allow even made up things to be sent. I wish I could send you the counterpane of my bed, which cost me about 40 shillings and is 4 yards each way. You never saw anything as rich as the painting on it. The town of St Thomé, about 3 miles from here along the sea beach, is full of manufactures of chintzes and counterpanes, with painted clothes for women of the richest patterns. I call them painted, for so they literally are; one person draws all the outline, and others put in the colours sitting on the ground, and they will come to your house and paint you any pattern you like on a sheet, or what cloth you choose to give them. I need not tell you how permanent the colours are. They indeed get brighter the more they are washed, though they lay all clothes on the sand here to dry, which takes out all English colours. Coventry blue thread for marking does not last above four or five washings. The borders of printed handkerchiefs disappear. Port wine goes clean out the first washing, and brown cotton stockings are no longer brown after one washing. I think you would envy me if you saw a washing of clothes come home. It looks all as if it was quite new, and the stockings are treated the same and I should buy them in any shop for real, but for seeing the marks. How they are ironed, and how they are folded, I cannot guess, but you might sit upon a dozen gowns that have come folded up, without disturbing a fold and yet, when you open them there is not a tuck nor hem that is not picked out as if it had just been made. Whatever shapes the gowns are, it is the same; despite ruffling and gimp, and fancy sleeves gathered up in places, they iron amongst it all, or press it in some way or other that it seems as if just made, and as white as snow. The clothes I had washed, when we first landed, covered half a room over, and quite astonished me when I saw it brought home, for the old brown kitchen dusters and calico towels, which I could never have washed in London to look decent, and which were besides mouldy by lying in the ship, were brought us white as any piece of new muslin. The heat of the sun bleaches everything out at once, but I think it also rots other things, but particularly linens. The English muslins and calicos wear admirably well, better I think than the Indian ones, but the linen cloth is worn out sooner than you could think. They beat it on the pieces of rock, in the rivers where they wash, and the linens cut directly. As to hems, whether of calico or linen, about four or five washings beat them entirely out and they must be done again. They say here that the washermen beat the linen, and whatever else they know to be European articles, and that they sing all the time that they beat, Europa, Europa, Europa. The Moor people have very pretty manufactures. The Gentoo people are most fond of white, with coloured borders woven in, but the Moorish people delight in having all the richest colours that they can put together. Their trousers, which are as full as petticoats and much the same thing, only divided, are made of satins of the most elegant stripes and patterns, whether for men or women. Over these the men wear shawls, or satin short pelisses, shawls around the waist, or over their shoulders and on their heads. The women wear coloured muslin over their drawers, or gauze robes, with broad gold borders, and a piece of the same gauze also bordered, with gold wove in, of the size of a long shawl which they hang at the back of their heads and spread over their shoulders in any fanciful way. It covers them, but does not conceal any part of their dress. Their cholis, or little bodices, are also of the most showy colours and patterns. I speak now of the common Moor women one sees about, or the girls of the town as we should call them, or dancing girls, or the wives of common people, for the wives of great men are finer, but of these I shall tell you in another place. The Moorish shopkeepers, who sell these things, spread them on mats before their doors, as earthenware is spread in England. They sleep or eat in the middle of the day, but about four o'clock in the evening an assortment of goods is spread out and the night market begins. The streets are crowded with people buying, and all are fully dressed at that time of day; I would give anything to send you some of their dyed muslins or gold gauzes, but they will not let a bit pass. Several people have tried to get some sent, but I have heard of no one who has succeeded. When spread out, their manufactures look most splendid.

Our house is near two miles from the Fort, and the Fort is built close to the sea. The walls are very handsome, with barracks under them, and at low water you can walk under them. The beach is like Borth Sands, or Barmouth, but the horses here have not strength enough to draw a carriage along the sand; you must either get out and walk, or go in a palanquin. The ground on which the Fort is built stands out a little to the sea, and the shore hollows in in a slight curve, from the Fort to St Thome; a large town; and you see the one place from the other, as Aberystwyth appears from the rock. It is three miles from the one place to the other and, as I am fond of the sea, I take the palanquin and the men always walk in the first breaker, for they wear no shoes nor stockings, and they feel no inconvenience in doing so. I fancy myself in a boat or a bathing machine. There is no land to be seen, the breeze comes fresh, and the sea is so much alike in all places that I can hardly persuade myself I am so far from you when everything looks so exactly like the place we have been in together. The sea appears to me to come in exactly as it did at Barmouth, rolling in with a monstrous surf, which extends farther out here, however. There is the same fine sand dimpled over with the same kind of shells, but I never saw any seaweed, nor any of that jelly-like substance which we used to find in Wales, and which I suppose is produced on the rocks as seaweed is, and we have no rocks here near the sea. The shipping does not anchor in front of this part but, passing this and the Fort, they anchor between the Fort and the Black Town and on that side the land retires back very much. There all ship business is carried on. On this side we have nothing but fishing, which is most amusing to me. I daresay you have often heard of the cattimarans used by these people. Catty means a bundle, and muram means wood, and therefore cattimarans, as we call them, are bundles of wood. By the way, Mrs Edward James is very fond of calling old maids old cattimarans, and you may tell her that when she has a mind to be affronting she need not use a foreign language but say at once, you old faggot. The surf is so strong that no ordinary boat can stand it, therefore all the fishing is done on these cattimarans. They are made by tying the trunks of three or four trees, each about as thick as a man, together with ropes made of the bark of the cocoa palm. They are seldom above ten feet long and only tied in a few places so the water comes through of course.[10] In general each of these has a man and a boy, or two men, but sometimes only one. One person only rows at any time; he has only one stick for this purpose but, sitting as a tailor does, he dips in one end on one side, and the other end on the other side, as quick as lightning. What he uses is only a straight lath: the nets are laid on the place before their feet and they are themselves naked except a small piece of linen. They meet the surf with the greatest indifference, though every wave buries them for a second or two; they appear in another place stretching their nets, or drawing them in, without seeming to have been interrupted. I have watched them for an hour together, thus appearing and disappearing by turns. There are hundreds of them, always out as far as your eye can search, and sometimes the surf appears to extend as far. One sees only white waves and these spots, as they look to be, popping up and down. I frequently make the men set down the palanquin, which they like well enough to do for they are all fond of the sea. If a cattimaran comes to shore, which they generally do, we buy fish from them and by this means I have seen a great variety of fish that I should never otherwise have seen, for they never bring home from the markets

10 These craft are still to be found along the coast of southern and south-eastern India. They look exactly as they used to, except they are now powered by a home-made outboard motor rather than human effort. The name derives from the Tamil word for logs bound together – kattumaram.

any but a few particular kinds. All the rest go by the name of palanquin boys' fish, which is indeed all the name I can get for any of them. Many of them are very nice, and more to my taste than the other kinds, but they are smaller sorts of fish, much like little trout and lasprings *(old term for smolt)*, and there is a small kind the same as whitebait, about a penny a plateful. These they dress very nicely: they stick them on bents *(a firm stalk of grass)* through the head, and then fry them quite stiff and they look excessively pretty, and eat the same as whitebait. There is another kind much more like an anchovy than our sprats are, and indeed I think they are anchovies. Besides these, there are many curious fish, such as the Ink fish which I should not like to eat, but I buy for about 8 pence, or 10 pence, as many as I like for myself, and a day's provision for the nine palanquin boys who are ready enough to run with me along the beach to St Thome and back for such a treat. Mr Gwillim has not failed to eat fish above one day in twenty since he came here. We have no lobsters here, but we have prawns as large as the tail of a middling lobster, and exactly the same, but there is no inside to them so we mix some crab with it and it makes a very fine lobster-like sauce. We have shrimps of all sizes, and another thing very unlike any creature I ever saw. The first I saw these at a table I thought they had been made from sweetmeats, and then varnished. They are very nice, but so little to eat and take so long a time to get at, that as little as they are, they are not worth much. However, they are sweeter than any of the other kinds; they are neither crabs, prawns nor lobsters. They have no tail, nor claws large enough to eat, only a body, and so it is like the inside of a lobster; they boil to a pale pink. The children catch these, and small crabs, along the shore as they run about the sand, whilst their fathers are fishing. These things look very pretty in a dish, and make fine soup or curry. Mr G. enjoys it all exceedingly when we get any new fish or vegetable which, by going about, I bring home.

We talk a great deal to the servants, some of whom are very good and intelligent, indeed they are the only people to enquire of, for few of the white people care of anything but having it all as like home as possible, and have no pleasure in enquiring into the customs of the people, or the productions of the place, unless they are likely to turn to account. The men like money and the women like visiting.[11] The greater part of them would not turn up their eyes to look at an object for which they would make up a party, and go 20 miles, to see in England. Mr G. asks the servants why they did not bring us any fish got by chance. They always say "Gentlemen cannot eat that fish"- then he asks them if they themselves can eat it, "yes" they say, "black people very much like that, but gentlemen can't eat, no custom" *(not accustomed to it)*. But they are extremely pleased to see you eat any of their kind of things and, since they discover our wish to try it all, they are constantly bringing some new kind of vegetable, many of which are very excellent. Of fruit for tarts, they have a great variety, quite as good as gooseberries or apples. There is certainly one very pleasing thing in the servants; they all enter into your pursuits. They are constantly bringing me flowers and insects, and are pointing out things to me as we go along. They also have some extraordinary notions of grandeur. Hares are very plentiful here, but rabbits are dear. A hare costs but little, but a rabbit eight shillings, for there are none other than those some gentlemen keep, and so few that I find they must be carefully checked before you buy them. By means of some directions to the servants, we got the hares dressed much in our own way. I wished once to have one for our company, and desired among the rest of the servants it might appear cooked in the same style. However, it was not brought in and, as I had observed the butler was disturbed when I asked him to get it, I enquired why it had not been done, upon which he said he was very sorry, but the cook and he had both agreed that all the company would laugh if a country hare was brought to so handsome a dinner. He promised me he would not fail to get a rabbit next time. They always call them country hares contemptuously, and I believe are perfectly convinced that it is from stinginess that I order them, and I have never so far prevailed as to have one for our company. They have a great pride in setting out the dinner, because everybody brings his own servant with him, and it is a matter of conversation. They spare no pains in dressing the table with flowers, and my plateau and figures *(table decorations)* are just to

11 In other words many of the other British in the settlement were unlike the two sisters, particularly Elizabeth, and were more concerned to lead an English style of life.

their taste. I am glad I brought out a china desert set, for there is so much glass here that they do not value it, though it costs so much. And there is no china here except mine, and a few things Sir Thomas Strange has. Both that, and my Wedgwood, have been admired beyond everything. Except at Lord Clive's, I do not see any Wedgwood but what looks as if it had been bought in Covent Garden, as much as for pattern as shape.

Well, I will put no more in this letter, as I do not know how they are to leave. I am just preparing for opportunities. I have drawn a few birds, and the cochineal insect, and plants, but I have not managed to do any other drawings yet. I hope I shall, but the views here are quite beyond my sketching. Visiting, and being unwell in the monsoon, and the fact that every time I go out, I come home just as tired as if I had been at an exhibition of pictures.

From Mary Symonds to her sister Hetty. 11th February 1802.

I have written several letters to you since my arrival in this country, or rather have scrawled over several sheets of paper and I fear I shall go on in the same slovenly manner for I cannot persuade myself to begin to write till the ships are almost ready to sail, and when I do begin, I find I have so much to say to you that I have no patience to write well. It was a great satisfaction to us to receive a letter from you by the Apollo, though the information we gained by it was not as satisfactory as we hoped it might have been by the time it was dated, for how you could have kept up till so late in the day I cannot conceive. We had great pleasure in hearing of Miss James and Miss Turnson spending the spring with you, as James must have had fine walks and plenty of amusement in showing them the lions about London. I have seen them both, but it is a long time since I saw Miss James; it was when she was at school at Miss Williams's. She was then a very handsome girl, and I daresay she is much improved since that time. Your new drawing room will be an additional inducement to me to endeavour at improving myself in drawing. I am at present incapable of giving you any satisfactory representations of this country, or of the people, and consequently cannot send you anything that will be worthy of a place on this wall; but my anxiety to give you an accurate idea of these people makes me send you some little daubs from time to time, by way of illustration to our letters. Now we are pretty well settled, I hope to get a good deal of time for drawing and, now we have peace with France, I suppose our opportunities for sending and receiving letters will be much more frequent. This letter will be sent by the Sir Stephen Lushington; she was one of the fleet we came out with. I sent a letter to you on our arrival here by a Mr Williams when he went home. He was a shipmate of ours when I entrusted my packet to him. I believed him to be unfortunate in being obliged to return so soon, but I afterwards learned that he is a most abominable fellow. I hope he did not contrive to scrape any acquaintance with you.

Captain Marsh arrived here yesterday, February the 15th, and I have this morning had the pleasure of reading two letters from you (the last of which is dated August 29), one from my mother, one from Mrs Morgan and some from Mrs Chambers, and I thank God heartily for the comfortable news you tell me of your own, and the dear little boys', health. Indeed, your letters are much more pleasing to us than all the public news in the world, so do not waste time and paper in apologies on that account. A packet of newspapers, whenever you have an opportunity of sending them, will afford us a great deal of amusement, and give us all the particular circumstances. Most of the great events which take place in Europe are sent here overland to the government, and to several great merchants' houses who have regular correspondence. A chit chat letter, which seems to place us amongst you all, is what we most desire to receive. I entreat you to continue your present plan of telling us all that occurs for, if it were not for your letters, we should feel ourselves quite friendless and forgot; not a word have we had from the Brompton family, nor have Sir Henry's family troubled him with any heavy packets. A little of Mr John's humour would be very acceptable, and enliven us much. I am very happy to hear he is about to be married. If it is true, I suppose you will see the lady, and pray give us some account of her for I dare say he will not give himself the trouble to gratify our curiosity with any particulars, and I have reason to think he will not even give me an opportunity of congratulating him. You will now be able to judge of his true character. He used to appear very differently at home and abroad. If he receives his friends in the same cold manner in his own house, as he used to do in his father's, I suppose it will no longer be attributed to the restraint he is under from those he lives with. Notwithstanding all his uncertainty, I have however a great regard for him and wish him all the happiness in the world and, should I ever be fortunate enough to have a house in England, he will be a very welcome guest.

I intend writing to G. Samuel by this ship, because I think he will be glad to hear from me, though he has not asked me to write. His time is very precious and therefore I shall not expect to hear much from him. You have not mentioned Mrs Burnside's death in any of your letters, nor does Mrs Shepheard say anything of it in hers. This I am much surprised at, as I saw it in a newspaper of the latter end of April 1801 which was, you know, soon after we left England. I often wish to give you some idea of our acquaintances here, but sometimes it appears a very difficult undertaking and, at others, a very useless one, yet it may be pleasant to you to know who they are, and you may occasionally meet with some of their connections. One name I know I have heard James mention as well known in the Muslim world; a Mr and Mrs Brown. He is a son of Brown, of the firm of Brown and Rogers; we are not very intimate with the lady as she was near lying-in when we arrived, and has not been out much since she recovered. He is a fine young man, rather dashing, and we are told he was very much so before he married, and was also a good deal in debt. She was a Miss Sewell; a relation of one of the first merchants here. Another of our acquaintances is a Mrs Chinnery,[12] who may be a relation of your friend of that name for aught I know. I am told she is the daughter of an innkeeper on the road near Stamford Bridge. She is, however, one of the finest ladies in this place. They give splendid balls, and it is observed of the lady that she wears the most expensive dresses of anybody, and seldom appears twice in the same. But the grand lady of all is a Mrs Dick; her husband is the highest member of Council who is married, in consequence of which she takes place over everybody in the settlement, just as the Lady Mayoress does in the City. I believe he is very rich. She is rather pretty and at least 20 years younger than he is; her father is a tailor at Charing Cross; his name is Douglas. She has a brother here who is a writer. Living with Mr Dick is

12 See note 4, 1801, page 20.

a Miss Boyd; a niece of the Alderman's. She is about 50 years old and she came out here about a year or two ago with Mr D. She dances away at the balls, and attends all the public amusements of the place; some people say she is a good sort of woman, and only came here at the particular request of Mr D., with whom she had been very intimate for some time, but others are of the opinion that she intends to captivate. The most intimate acquaintances I have are the three daughters of a Mr Wescott. His wife died about a year ago. The eldest of the young ladies is about 20; the second is 18 and the youngest 13 years old, and they have with them a governess, a Miss Williams. She is rather a handsome girl, and clever enough, but has a good deal of the Godwinian school, and the modern dash.[13] Two of the young ladies were married on the last day of the year; the eldest to a Mr Maitland, a merchant in a considerable house here. He is about 43-years old. We think Mrs M. very much like Lizzie Thoburn in her person, but it is only in her person, for her manners are exactly opposite. For as Liz is too anxious a temper to let herself be comfortable, so this good lady is so very easy and indifferent that she takes no pains at all to make her friends comfortable. Besides this she is very vain, and not very wise. The second, who is married to a Mr Rowley a rich Company's servant, is remarkably plain in her person. She has not however her sister's faults; she is attentive enough, and her husband is remarkably so, and a very good-natured man. He has settled £10,000 upon her, which sum was paid into the hands of trustees before the wedding. He is a young man, about midway between 40 and 50, or rather nearer to the latter number of years. I have not chosen this family for intimates on account of their merit, for I do not much delight in these, but their father was particularly attentive and kind to us when we first arrived here, and continues to be so. He has been intensely desirous that his daughters should be very much with us, and Mr Rowley is the same. Mr Westcott is a very proud old man; he ranks very high in the civil service of the Company, and was very rich at one time but he lost all his property by some speculation. I fear I shall tire you with descriptions

13 After William Godwin 1756–1836, a philosopher, and prolific writer, who became well-known for his politically radical, even anarchic, views., He was married to Mary Wollstonecraft, and father of Mary Shelley. See Oxford Dictionary of National Biography: ref:odnb/10898

of people you know nothing about, but you may read them at your leisure, or let it alone altogether if you like. We have a great many more whey faced ladies, for the society here is very large, but at least half the women are half caste, that is they are the children of English men by black women. These girls are sent home to England to be educated, as it is called, that is to learn to dance, to squawk and to strum. I have not met with one tolerable voice in the place amongst the women. Sir Benjamin Sullivan's *(co-judge at the supreme court)* family are very numerous and very curious. Two daughters and a son arrived here since we did. He has a son and a daughter, one of the girls lately arrived, who are half caste. This other girl is just 15, and she and her brother, a man of about 20, are children by a French woman who he met with in Germany. She had been a kept mistress of the Emperor Joseph. He brought her here as his wife, and she was received as such, however she grew tired of her spouse and went off to England with another gentleman, who now keeps her in London. Soon after this affair took place Mr Sullivan married a lady here, stating that he was divorced by the Archbishop of Paris. By his wife he has had 10 children, six of them are living with her in England where she is gone to superintend their education. Most of the civilians have these blackey families; the Misses are sent home to learn to give themselves a few airs, and then return here to be provided for by marrying military men up the country. When his work is completed a man of about 60 is at liberty to return to England with a pretty young wife and a family of small children!!! You will wonder why I say the civilians have half caste children to provide for more particularly than the military men. The reason is that the latter are always moving from one station to another and the children are forgot, or perhaps never known to them at all, besides which the military young men have not as good incomes, and therefore cannot afford to educate and provide for them.[14]

14 Many mixed-race offspring, probably the majority, were natural children, meaning that they were born illegitimately but that their existence had been acknowledged by their fathers. This situation was clearly common in India at that time and it had no relationship to class, or the lack of it. Leading figures in Madras, who are identifiable from these letters as being in this category, are Sir Benjamin Sullivan, Puisne Judge in the Supreme Court and colleague of Sir Henry's, Mr Strange (presumed to

We have had a great deal of amusement going forward; most of it I have been to, but the evenings and mornings are so cold that Betsy has not been able to bear them. At first all the medical people advised her to rise early and drive out before breakfast, but she caught cold every time she tried so Mr Ord, who attends her, observing this, has advised her not to rise till the sun has been up sometime, and always to take a cup of coffee first. I must tell you that Mr Ord has a brother in Cheapside. I recollect the name on a sign, John Ord and Company, but I do not remember what trade it is, but I believe a considerable one. But to return to the pleasures of the place, I must tell you that I have a great many good friends who are always ready in offering to carry me with them to any balls, or shows, that are going forward. I have chosen one lady, my near neighbour, with whom I generally go; Mrs Trent, the wife of General Trent. She is a very quiet, pleasant woman, and rather pretty. They have been in England, and returned to this country about two years ago, and they intend to return home in another year. The officers of the Scotch Brigade gave a ball on St Andrew's Day, with a very grand supper under tents in the garden. The Nabob and all his attendants were there. They were all dressed very finely in shawl dresses with embroidered silver sashes and turbans. The Nabob wore a muslin dress, richly ornamented with silver, a sash all of silver and a turban the same; besides a great quantity of jewels, and the plume which was presented to him by the governor at his coronation. I believe I have not written to you any account of the Nabob. He did Sir Henry the honour to write him a friendly note requesting him to fix a time when he might pay us a visit. The next morning being fixed, he came to breakfast with his son, and about 60 attendants, about six of whom were of high rank and sat down to the table with him. He is a very fat, tall young man, of a rather lively countenance; he talks a great deal and eats voraciously. Betsy expressed a wish to see some of the largest elephants and he very politely sent nine the next morning, all richly caparisoned, and their faces beautifully painted in scrolls winding in the course of the muscles. I mounted one; the elephant kneels down and a stepladder is placed against his side

---

be Sir Thomas Strange's brother), and Dr James Anderson, Physician-General and botanist.

for one to mount. The rider, or driver, sits on the neck; behind him is a seat divided into two square apartments: these are lined with rich silk or velvet (the one I was in was green velvet) with cushions of the same to support the back and arms. Each of the apartments holds two persons very commodiously, but you must squat like a tailor. Over the seat is a dome supported by four small pillars at the corners. The dome is lined with velvet, richly ornamented with gold stars. It is also fringed with a deep gold fringe, and a great many large gold tassels about it. When you are seated, and the steps replaced on the animal's side under a rich cloth which covers him all over, he rises up with a motion just like the rocking of a ship, and you are forced to hold fast whilst he rises or you would be thrown out. When he is up he trots tolerably fast, and the motion is easy and pleasant enough. I think it must be an agreeable way of travelling as they are very surefooted, and one should see the country all round.

The freemasons gave a grand ball and supper on St John's day. All the gentlemen of the Lodge appeared in their jewels, and all their insignia. The wives were distinguished by blue and silver sashes, and blue ribands embroidered with different devices in silver, relating to the rank of their husbands in the Lodge. The rooms were decorated with festoons of blue silk and painted transparencies. Lord Clive gave a ball on the Queen's Birthday, in the same style as the others, and the supper was in the garden under tents.

I have lately been three mornings to the races and you will be surprised when I tell you I have been almost starved with cold, though I had on a cloak and a double shawl. I set out from home at five in the morning as we have six miles to drive to the race stand. The sun rises at a little past six o'clock, but there is so much dew at this time of the year that it has very little power till eight or nine. I am no judge of the racing sport, but I believe the two first days it was very good; the third however was the most amusing to me as there were several absurd pony races and, what was very curious and quite laughable, a camel race and an elephant race. The elephants, besides their riders, had each a man pulling them by the tail and belabouring their sides with a large stick, but no one attempted to get the start of the other. They all made as much haste as they could, and came in in the same order they were out. The veranda, which is built for the accommodation of the company, is in a most beautiful situation commanding a very fine view. If I had Mrs Ratcliffe's pen I would draw it, but as you see mine is a very sorry one. I cannot undertake such a task.[15]

I assure you my finery wears out apace, and one wants a great variety for meeting the same people every day. Pray call on Mr Wilby and get a small stock of ornaments from him when you send, for those I had from him have been very useful. I should like a few things from the jewellers, but not very expensive ones. At Hyde and Scribes, and such places, you will meet with fancy beads which are much esteemed here. My brown beads are much admired, which I bought there; I think they called them Egyptian. Be sure to send me some necklaces and bracelets of the patent pearls. I should like the necklace to be about the size of a pea, each bead, and the bracelets smaller; about three rows each if the small clasps are worn. If not, you will buy them of one row, or 10 rows, according to the fashion. Also a pair or two of the patent pearl drops for earrings. Do not buy any of the pearl beads smaller than this O, *(circa 4 mm)* for the very small real pearls in this country are not dear but, if of a large size, they are immense. Betsy has some of the patent ones, which she brought out with her, and she is the only person who has them here. Even the pearl merchants take them for real. One told Betsy that her plain drop earrings were worth 900 pagodas, and he would not believe they were false till he weighed them. All our clothes have been very much admired, and borrowed by 20 people for patterns. Now, you know, we did go about a good deal for them, and got all the varieties we could, but the people who send out things to their friends here do not, in general, choose well. They buy the dearest things they can get, and by that means all get the same things. I am very glad I did not afford a patent lace gown. Here there are several, and one of English muslin, smartly made and trimmed, is thought quite as much of. A variety of taste in the make and trimming is everything. Be sure to send flowers and fancy feathers, and some shoes and gloves occasionally, and don't forget the magazine of the fashions, that we may see how to put them on. I should like something made at Mrs Lancaster's now and then. The people

15 It is possible, but uncertain, that Mary is referring to Mary Ann Radcliffe 1746–1818, a feminist, and author of a number of popular gothic novels at the beginning of the 19th century. If so, she is less well known for her art.

all have Miss Brace's things here, and Miss Trench's *(various London dress-makers)*; I like to have mine different if I can. I shall send a drawing with this, of which Betsy has written a description, and therefore I need not say anything on the subject except that it is a sad representation. I shall also send one of the old tailor who works in the house. Betsy says he put her in mind of some of the people described in the Arabian nights' entertainments. I have painted a table and some other things about the house, and I have drawn some butterflies and other insects but, somehow or other, I do not find much time to draw. Going out in the morning for exercise, and in the evening for pleasure, along with preparations for the latter, take up a great deal of time; and I have a good many notes to answer every day. I do the housekeeping business too, which is a good deal of work, for I am obliged to keep everything locked up in a storeroom and to give out every day to the different servants a proper quantity for the day's use. I cannot trust them with more; they are such pilferers. I must tell you how they contrived to cheat me of the candles. I gave them out a proper number and they cut a piece off each before they set them up. This I should not have found out soon had a lady not told me to observe that, and I found they really had done so. This is a good instance of the kind of thefts committed by the natives in general. They are not handy enough to break open any place, or to steal any large thing, but they are always at their petty thefts.

I don't think I ever told you anything about the fruit of this country. I must own I was disappointed in them at first. The flavours are so different from anything I had been used to and, in general, so very powerful. I am now quite reconciled to them and I like them nearly as well as the English. We have two or three sorts of oranges: the sort most esteemed is very high flavoured, but not very juicy. Another, which I prefer, is sweet and very full of juice but not much flavour. A third sort (the worst of all) seems to be something between a China and a Seville orange. The pines and melons are exactly the same is in England. One of the best fruits is the pumplemoos *(sic – clearly a grapefruit)* which is the same as the shaddock of the West Indies. They grow about the size of a large melon and are in fact a great overgrown orange of a very fine sort. The mango is very much admired, and is a very fine fruit. Also, it is very high flavoured, and I think very agreeably, but those who dislike them say they are like turpentine, tow and treacle tied up in a rag and sucked. The guava is shaped like a codling: its texture is exactly a mellow pear, and it has something of the flavour of strawberries. The plantains grow in large clusters; sometimes above 20 in a bunch. Each plantain is about 6 inches long, and an inch and a half in diameter. Horn is the most common sort, which is white, but there are a great many varieties. They differ in size and colour; some are green and some red, but they all grow alike in clusters. It is unlike anything in England in its taste, and I am very fond of it. I want to tell you also of a curious fruit which I forgot before. It is called a rose apple by the Europeans. It is the size and colour of an apricot, but it has an eye like a medlar. It is a delicate green, and the texture is exactly an apricot, and when you break it open it is loose from the kernel as an apricot is when over ripe. The taste is exactly roses and sugar, elegantly mixed and not too sweet. The kernel is green (with a very thin brown shell) and tastes the same as the green part of a rosebud: it has just that astringency, and the crispness of it.

I desire you will tell the Bromptonians[16] that I don't think they deserve to be remembered at all and I don't know that I shall write to Liz. It is so shabby of her not to send us a line, when we had left them above half a year before the last fleet sailed. I have sent a great many scoldings in this letter and I am very angry with everybody that they don't write to me. Be sure to send us all the pretty things you see which you think will be useful to us, whatever their nature may be. I may venture this commission to you as I know you have no immoderate idea of expense. Don't be lazy: going out shopping will do you good and teach you to spend your husband's money: he has not time. I fear I have told you some of this before, so I believe I must make memorandums of what I write lest I give you the same dish twice, and I am sure you will think once quite enough. This writing is really too bad and I am ashamed of it, but my pen is quite worn out and pens are very dear, so I am obliged to be saving them, and wearing them down to stumps. Besides, I am going to a ball and cannot give time to write well, for the packet closes tomorrow and I have two more letters which I want to write. I desire you will give my love and a hundred kisses

16 Those who live in Brompton. The reference to Liz suggests that it is their close friends the Thoburns.

to dear James and my little nephew Tom. Pray take care of him, that I may see him a stout fellow 6 years hence, (the term of my transportation will then be expired). If I were to adopt your plan of making spots for all the kisses I want to send, I must take a sheet of paper and spot it all over. Pray give some to Liz and Mary and Mama, and if James has no objection you may give one to Regi, but they are too precious to bestow even though he has been a sufferer with his poor ear.

From Elizabeth Gwillim to her sister Hetty 12th February 1802.

I entrust this to a private hand who assures me he will put it in the office at the first port of call, and that means you will have it a fortnight before the letters by the packets of which we have written several. The ships which have been at Bengal called here a few days ago, and sail on Sunday. I purchased several things to send, but have got no conveyance for them. A Mr Chalmers, who is taking his wife home, and family, has undertaken to carry one shawl, or a bit of shawl for a waistcoat, which I was very anxious to send to Mrs Holland. The waistcoat is for Mr Williams. I bought a shawl for you, and hoped to have been able to send it, and a waistcoat for James, and one or two other waistcoats of the same pattern which I wished to have distributed, besides a bit of muslin to make Lizzy and Mary a gown each, but I fear I shall not be able to send them unless Captain Marsh will take them when he goes but, though I have sent to every place, I cannot yet find him out. I conclude therefore he lives on board. I have wished you joy of the little baby, who I hope will live and do well, in a long letter to you: 14 sheets to my mother, and to you. I think you will not have patience to read it all. We owe you a thousand thanks for your letters. I hope you will be able to continue the same kindness, for we should have felt ourselves most forlorn creatures but for you. I wish I could do something for you here the while, or perhaps you would like one of my black maids to help you. This present one I have lies asleep under a tree all day, in all her rings and pins, and has a large star in the one side of her nose, made of rubies set in gold, which disfigures her not a little. Our clothes are in great request, or at least have been. I do not know whether this fleet has brought anything newer but, by your account, not much except that you tell me it is the fashion to be dressed in buff, and I assure you I thought the ladies completely so here, when I first saw them. They astonished me not a little. I have not been able to imitate them, on the contrary I am now, and have been three months, in all my English clothes.

Mr Gwillim has had a bilious illness. During his sickness on board ship he brought up a great deal of bile. He has been remarkably well and was getting fatter, but the truth is he would not let well alone for, being so well, he thought nothing would hurt him, and being very fond of malt liquor he drank a bottle of ale every day for six weeks or two months, which everybody says is very bad in this country and it is not one in a hundred who can bear it. To amend all, he drank milk three mornings and I assure you he eats very hearty. At last he got very uneasy and took some rhubarb, but that only stirred up the bile. He was ill six days, and was obliged to take some specific, but thank God I do not think he looks the worse for it. He has now a great charge neither to drink beer nor milk. The custom here is to rise at 5, or in winter at 6 in the morning, to have tiffin at one and to dine at 7 o'clock, and go to bed at 10. Mr G. has a great aversion, as you know, to eating before dinner. He used to take nothing but a cake, and I took half my dinner at tiffin time and half at seven o'clock.[17] This mode agrees with nobody: everyone cries out against it, but nobody alters it. Lady Clive and a few others tried much, but she could only get leave to eat her own dinner at three o'clock. It disagreed with both of us and therefore we have begun upon a new plan. I believe there may be half a dozen families who do the same: we have no Tiffin, and dine regularly at three o'clock. We have our coffee between five and six, and if we have company or dine out, we consider it as supper for, though it is called seven o'clock, it is near eight before we sit down and 10 when we rise from the table, at which time everybody runs home, or out to balls. This mode of life is quite comfortable to me. When I sup out I fancy myself at your friends in Oxford Street, for we have turkeys that you could not see over, a round of beef, boiled roast beef, stewed beef, loin of veal for a side dish and roast

17 Tiffin is a small meal at different times of day in different parts of India. It may be a mid-morning snack, lunch or tea, but perhaps most commonly lunch. It isn't an Indian word, deriving from an English colloquial term meaning to take a little drink.

pig; capons as large as hen turkeys and, in short, a scandalous waste of provisions, or rather of our money, for there are enough ready to eat the food: very few things are dear.[18]

Richard Clarke *(Sir Henry Gwillim's clerk)* has a place which is worth 500 pounds per annum which, as he has no expenses, is a great thing to so young a man. He lives with us, and there are no dreams of spending money in this place, at least none such as he would ever enter into. All balls are given, or subscribed to, for other families at least more than anybody could attend. Dinners are always given at home. There is no going to the tavern except to play billiards. Some men gamble very high and play hazard. There has been but one play since I came, and I did not see it; it was just the day after we came. We have had one concert.

From Elizabeth Gwillim to her sister Hetty 18th March 1802

We all wrote to you, and sent you various packets and letters by the ships which left this place on the 18th of February. I thought to have written further to you by the last ships but they sailed very suddenly. I had hardly time to send a few seeds on board for Mr Whitley. In the bag of seeds I put a small bag with some seeds strung for beads, and wrote on that bag from Mrs James. I had no time to explain about them. They are not a seed of this part, but are sold for ornament, and some ladies wear them. I thought it likely they would pass with the seeds, otherwise they would be taken. They are cheap enough, rough as those were, and I think handsomer than when polished, but some people like them better when polished, but then they are dearest. I shall therefore get some done to send you, and some to Nancy Green, as you may like to give them away to a friend. They look very well with a small gold bead between each. They are here called fakirs' beads. The fakirs are a sort of religion who travel about and beg with their families, and they wear these beads. Here there are also a set of beggars belonging to the Hindus, called pandarams, who wear them. These people

18 Gargantuan meals were the norm in Georgian British-India, with sometimes four times as much food placed on the tables in India as there would be for a similar occasion in England. See Wheeler, Patrick, *Ribbons among the Rajahs. A History of British Women in India before the Raj* (Pen and Sword History, 2017).

are beggars by their caste. They travel about from one country *(locality)* to another and are always well entertained, and they live upon what they obtain by begging, which is no great hardship since all the people supply them with the best they have. They are a tall, handsome, set of people; we see them by dozens with their wives and children. Their dress is the most beautiful; considered as picturesque as of any of these people. Many of the tanks *(pools)* and wells all over India are stained with a kind of red earth, and muslin being dipped in this, with the addition of some leaves, becomes a beautiful clear salmon colour. By the way, I must tell you that in these tanks, with these leaves, they wash nankeen, which becomes brighter by these means the oftener it is washed. Now these beggars wear a vast quantity of muslin, an under cloth of about 6 yards, an upper one of as much thrown over the shoulders in a fanciful manner, and a large turban in long folds. All this muslin is dipped in these staining waters, whether for men, women or children, and sometimes it is almost a rose colour. Over these muslins they wear these beads in great profusion; long strings of the largest sort are thrown over their necks and fall as low as the knee, and others of a smaller size in shorter chains. They have frequently a dozen chains round their necks, one lower than another, and in their turbans they twist them in all sorts of inventions, generally very gracefully, as milliners put beads in our caps, but a much greater number of them. The dark brown curved-looking beads lying upon the salmon colour has as fine an effect as you can imagine. These beggars have but a sad character given them by winter, but the Hindus hold them in great respect. They have special charge over the women, and are allowed to converse with them in private to give them advice. If a slipper of one of them be left at a door the husband is not permitted to enter till it be the pleasure of the instructor. It signifies to him that he is not to come near. Strangers, who have not the prejudices of the Hindus, are not ready to believe that they always make an innocent use of their extraordinary privileges. Without a doubt they have no bashful air.

I have met with a gentleman surgeon of the Monarch, East Indiaman, which sails from hence on the 20th, who is so obliging as to offer to carry something for me. I have therefore desired him to take the white long shawl for you: it has large sprigs, and EG, close in two corners. I have also sent the worked Bengal muslin for Lizzy, and Mary Thoburn, and Polly has stitched it upon two old body linings, without cutting, that it may not be taken *(impounded by customs)*. When washed it will, I dare say, pass. Polly desires you to give her love to Lizzy and begs she will take particular notice of the taste of making up, but desires she will not let the pattern become too common. I send by the same gentleman a mother of pearl snuffbox, in which you will find a china thimble for you, and another for Nancy Green, two pieces of crystal called here vellum stone for cutting seals upon, which are for George Samuel. The box is for Mrs Gwillim, and I should be glad if you will send it to her as soon as possible. I have likewise packed up an ivory fan for Nancy Green, which you will give her with my love. I wish I could have had an opportunity of sending her something better, at least bigger, but I could not get conveyance for anything larger and therefore bought a fan, the China ships being just come in here. I hope you will like your shawl. I shall send with this the remainder of a piece of gown shawl. I have cut off one square, which you will please send to my mother and the long piece is, they tell me, enough for three waistcoats. I wish you to send one of the three to Mr G. Samuel with my compliments, and tell him I hope to send him a better one when I get an opportunity. The other two I wish James to keep for himself to wear with his blue coats in the winter. Pray send the vellum stones with the waistcoat to G. S., and tell him I have got down one of his drawings and I am working away, after his manner, in backgrounds to my birds, but if I work much I shall have no colours left. I have searched and enquired in all places for the Indian yellow, but there is no such thing to be heard of, and I cannot think it is of the substance he imagines it to be. I should rather suppose it to be some preparation of turmeric, which is the paint the natives use on their persons, and I have seen a great deal, equally fine in colour, but not so finely ground and prepared. With so much as you have to do, I am sorry to trouble you with commissions but, unless you or Nancy Green will do it for us, I know not where else to apply to. I should not like to have too many things at once, and therefore must trouble you about twice a year to send to us little articles of dress. They spoil in keeping here, but the price of buying them is intolerable. Please to let us have six pair each of coloured kid shoes, and some green Morocco for me; six pair for each of us of white kid gloves, and twelve pair each of the finest Limerick gloves *(highly fashionable, very thin and made from the skins of unborn calves)* of a light yellow in colour will be enough or, instead of the Limerick, some pairs of fine soft yellowish grain kid. These carry and keep best: the brown ones spot and spoil sadly and do not wear at all well in the heat. Pray tell Mr Langston he must put each glove in a separate paper, for in the ships the leather heats, and all our gloves were sticking together. We were obliged to tear them asunder. They were gone like strings at the bottom of melted isinglass and, whenever a damp finger had been sewed, the silk was quite black. In short, they were almost all greatly injured, and the kid shoes the same, for want of separate papers. By the way, I may as well mention to you here to please let us have whatever lace is put to trim a gown or cap very white, and whatever is sewed minute should be done with dry hands, for whatever has been touched with sweat turns in the voyage as red as brick dust. The caps and bonnets I had worn in England could not be used here, but for making patterns, till they were washed and, what is remarkable, the best washed clothes that had not been much boiled, were the same several clean gowns I expected to have to put on in the ship, and which I found quite red in the wearing parts. I shall not want thread yet awhile, but a few needles would be useful for all I brought out were stuck together with rust, so pray do not let any more be oiled *(illogical?)*. They make nice cotton tape here: I want some shining French cotton for working muslin, but Pearson's is rough stuff; Butlers is the only place to buy it at, if you should think of it. I shall want colours and paper for drawing, but I hope you will have sent this. Pray send me a good many ribbons of all colours and widths; lilac and purple carry very well. My lilac crepe is as fresh as ever; white spoils sooner than anything. Made flowers are of the greatest use, but do not fear to send us anything you think pretty, and that is not expensive, in muslins for gowns, or cambric muslins if worn.[19] We can always get customers if we have too much of anything. Stockings do not wear out faster than at home, and I seldom wear silk. Silk gloves are quite disagreeable here; I never wear them. Mr

19 It is clear from these lines, and others in the letters, that the two sisters were familiar with making, or at least finishing-off and decorating, their own clothes. The darzee, or tailor, was on hand for the difficult work. Women would often copy patterns of new styles brought by someone into India in order to make, or have made, their own version.

Gwillim will want a dozen pair of silk stockings, with clocks a little ornamented, but as little open as possible, and half of them not open at all for the mosquitoes get in at the holes.[20]

Polly wrote to you to send me some more dishes the same as our dinner set. We do not want plates, but a great many dishes all sizes; one soup tureen, and it must be the best shape, the tall sort; salad bowls and vegetable dishes and some sauce boats. One plate for each person goes through the dinner here. This is laid out at first, but they all use china water plates which are set on the table, and thereon the water plates are changed. They keep kettles of water boiling outside the house to fill the plates constantly. *(double-bottomed plates; to keep food warm).* I want also, from Wedgwood's, two dozen plates to match my breakfast set, one dozen small dishes of different shapes for fruit, which is always set here at breakfast, twelve breakfast cups and saucers and twelve coffee cups with muffin plates, or any little things, but no chocolate cups. Several slop basins, and bread-and-butter plates too. I will draw a bit of the pattern, but I fancy they know it for I told them to write it down. I do not know whether Polly mentioned it before, but I want from the Derby China warehouse twelve plates to match my dessert set, and twelve dishes; the dishes must be four of each shape for corners. I should be glad to have a very clear handsome deep black veil of false lace and also about a dozen yards of white joining lace of a pretty pattern to put into worked muslin for veils here. Knowing how much you have to do, I fear it must seem a little unreasonable to request you to do so much for us, but as there is no particular time when it is to be done I hope between you and Nancy Green I shall be able to get my little marketings. When you go to any shop on your own account you can buy me any trifle you think pretty, and keep it till an opportunity offers. Pray send me some very hard toothbrushes. If Waite, or some dentist, could spare a few of these and some for the inside, I should be very

20 Clocking is defined as a short embroidered or woven ornament on each outer side of a sock or stocking, extending from the ankle upward. Although its origins are barely recorded, the use of ornamentation at the top of the gore area on stockings goes back centuries. Open clocks were gaps in the weaving, and they made the putting on, and taking off, of stockings easier in a hot climate.

glad, for the common ones are of no use at all to me and I cannot get any dentists' toothbrushes without giving a pagoda (eight shillings) for two.

The warm weather seems to agree with me very well; it is now getting as warm as is agreeable. We had a few fine showers a day or two ago, but we are not to expect rain till June, and it will be hotter till that time. The last three months have been the most delightful weather that could be imagined. I begin to get quite like a housekeeper, and to feel at home. At first I did not know how to order the dinner, however I find now that seasons are only considered in vegetables. Most of the fruit trees bear blossom and fruits at the same time. The plantains of all kinds are always growing; melons are not quite in yet. The favourite fruit of the country is the mango and the mango trees are now in full bloom, smelling very fresh and nice. The orchards look like walnut or pear trees, but the flower is a large spike of small blossoms like meadowsweet. There are as many sorts of mangoes as of apples, and as much difference between them. I like them unripe in tarts; they are like a fine green apple, but I fear I shall not like them ripe again as I was ill after eating them. We had been pretty busy, as you may suppose, before we landed; it was the very hottest time of year. The sun was right over our heads. That morning we came early onshore, while it was cool and pleasant. We breakfasted with Sir Thomas Strange, and to his house we had come two miles, staring all the way. After breakfast, as many people who came in the fleet wanted houses, it was thought expedient that we should look at such as were to be had, as soon as possible, and it was proposed we should go with a gentleman who brought his carriage for that purpose. We drove several miles; saw two great houses; and after that he would carry us to his house, which is what they call a bungalow. It is reckoned one of the prettiest things in the place, and he is a most nick nack man and keeps it in such a style as no man could who did, or thought of, anything else. It seemed perfect Fairy Land. I felt no inconvenience from the heat and he requested me to walk round the garden asking me if I felt the heat unpleasant, which I did not, so I continued to walk. The sheep were feeding; the grass was quite green; all the hothouse plants I had been used to delight in were in full blaze of flowers, and formed a large shrubbery. The tall cocoa palms were waving, and looked so cool, that I thought I could have walked all day. There was one immensely high tree with a hundred, at least, of the hanging birds nests upon it. With the sheep that were grazing were some beautiful little deer which came to eat out of our hands; the smallest things that ever were. When we went in we found a table of fruits and, among the rest, some mangoes for which he was famous, and of which he pressed me to eat. In shape and colour they were exactly like apricots, but as large as a small melon. The texture is like a very juicy plum, and the flavour much like melon, pineapple and apricots mixed together, and certainly very delicious, but too rich. I did not eat much, but I have never been able to eat any since. Whether it was from the heat or the mango I know not, or both together, but I got a most complete sick headache which lasted me two days and the poor man was so much censured for his imprudence that I believed he never would be free from the reproaches thrown upon him. I have been affected with the heat once or twice since, and am therefore now careful, but it is very odd that whilst one is in it one feels no inconvenience. I have begun a letter to my mother but I am just now told that the packet closes, so I doubt if I shall be able to finish it. I have written some long letters that I was obliged to write, and am very busy with drawing birds. We all join in duty to my mother; love to you and James and the child, and to all of James's family.

From Elisabeth Gwillim to an unknown recipient. Undated

When I came here I found the country in the finest verdure possible, and the trees in bloom, in which state they have remained ever since, and it is now six months. This climate is lovely from November to March. The mornings are cold, or else it is much like a pleasant summer in England, and the corn fields and hedges look much alike, but it is rice, not wheat. I have in my own garden plenty of turnips, very good; carrots rather short, but sweet French beans, very good; and a sort of bean of the country, eaten shelled. The country greens are a very nice vegetable. English cabbage with poor hearts, but sweet green peas of a small sort, but extremely good – cucumbers; endives, quite white; parsley, mint - besides which we have celery; excellent spinach; mustard; cress; small lettuces; sage, and almost everything but broad beans, cauliflowers and broccoli, which do not do well here yet, for gardening has not been attended to in this place till lately. I doubt not but everything would grow. I fear all the rest is to be held the whole year. Potatoes grow in the North, and we have many vegetables of the country. The oranges are very fine; the limes in abundance; melons; pineapples, are very good. Grapes do not come until April and May; the plantains are a nice fruit. The pears and the guavas are a good pick. Some think they have the flavour of a strawberry, and so they have, but they have a forbidding smell on the outside, like onions. The mango of the best kind is large, and of the colour, shape and texture of an apricot, but juicy and rich with a good deal of the fine apple flavour, but almost too rich for me. With the green ones, they make tarts, which well exceed the worst of apples. There are here also various fruits of an acid kind; not good for eating, but excellent for tarts. Some are so like a gooseberry, but with the advantage of a fresh taste. Raspberries, strawberries and bilberries are most esteemed here. English pickles are very valuable. We pay 3/6 per bottle for English vinegar, but I only give it to company for I think the country vinegar just as good, which is made of toddy in Arcot, a liquor drawn from the cocoa palm tree.*(See note 7, 1801, page 23)*. The fatted beef is too rich for me; the lean sort is sweet, but small and not tender. All sorts of poultry are as fine as in the London markets, and we have sea and river fish in great profusion. The sole, the mullet and the skate and eels, are all like the English; indeed the shell fish, oysters, crabs, shrimps and prawns are large as the tail of a lobster, and very fine here as are also some other kinds. Veal is very reliable, but small pork and roasting pigs very good, and the China bred (China hams) are good and they make good bacon. The mutton, when fat, is very nice, but you must feed it yourself; they have no wool but short hair. They are very full of meat, and very fine grained. You may buy a mutton sort of sheep, alive, for about three shillings. We have no woodcock, but snipe, wild duck and teal every day in the winter season, and some people must catch the teal in winter and keep them all the year. Hares are very cheap and good, but partridges are but the name, for they are as dry as a stick. They make the bread like French bakers and it is as white as snow. Muffins, and whatever can be made of milk and eggs; custard, trifles and all sorts of pastry, is in perfection. The butter is fresh every day, and is very nice. They take very little pains to beat it up as it comes crumbling in general but, for table, and all people who make their own butter, they have it as fine as in England and, indeed, are very ostentatious in displaying it, for they have their table butter made into a kind of model with leaves turning back like a pineapple, or cabbage.

Nothing can be a greater mistake than the general idea that, in India, ladies have nothing to do. It is an absolute labour to explain anything to the servants. They speak so little English, for if you explain they cannot remember. The men are the best. It will not do to try out notions too delicate here, for they come to you in all places and in all causes; you must write notes about everything. We have two women; one whose whole business it is to sweep the kitchen and to make curry, for a man never cooks that dish, nor ever sweeps. The other sweeps the rooms. I have a maid waits on me who is, as all are without any exception, without any idea of shame, a W *(written as capital W – perhaps wench, or could it even be whore)* and a tippler, and chews betel all day. She is dressed according to custom, with rings on her toes and hands, and bracelets, earrings, gold chains and necklaces, and she could not stick a pin in your handkerchief, thread a needle, nor care for your hair, nor help you on with one bit of clothing, and she is a story teller, and stupid. I do not know if she be a thief. There is neither hairdresser or milliner. We must wash ourselves, and make caps, hats etc. You will wonder why such maids are kept, but they wash your feet, and drive out the mosquitoes and such trifles. Women of caste are very good, but they never go into service, so one only has these sheep who act for one. The wives and daughters of the man servants would not wait on anybody, and their daughters are married about ten years old, though they do not live with their husbands till 13 or 14. These women are very chaste and good and never marry again if they lose their husbands.

From Mary Symonds to her sister Hetty. 18th March 1802.

I sit down just to write a few lines for my conscience sake that I may not have to accuse myself of omitting to write by every opportunity. I have little to say, Betsy having monopolised all the subjects except the descriptive ones, which are so many and lead to such long letters, that I have not ventured on them at present. Besides want of time, I am beginning to grow diffident in those matters as she does them a great deal better than I. Mine did well enough to fill up the time when she was silent, but now she writes such long letters I am a little jealous I can tell you, and am fancying you won't have much respect for my performance. Don't say this is all out of laziness. I think you can guess how happy your letters made me, particularly the account of the dear little boy. God bless him: I hope he is well, and be sure to tell us all about him in your letters. I must tell you how I spend a good deal of time; it is owing to a new acquirement which has brought me into great request here amongst my female friends; I am becoming a miniature painter (don't laugh). I have finished one lady's portrait and have two more in hand, and twenty parishioners praying to be drawn, but I don't undertake gentlemen for if I did I should not have breathing time. I thought to have sent you a specimen of my performance (in that way) by these ships, but I have not had time to do any of our own family, except myself. I drew myself first, as a trial, and it was thought like me, but I have had the misfortune to lose it. I believe it is stolen by some of the servants. I shall be much obliged to you if you will send me a dozen glasses for miniatures, of different sizes, and let them come by the first opportunity. Our friend G. Samuel will tell you where to go to get them; I can buy plenty of ivory here, and have got some charming brushes and white paint from China. Pray tell G. S. that I expect he will write to me and give me some information on the subject, and I desire he will let me into all the secrets he can find out about it, for I cannot get any instruction here. I hope you have thought of my wig; and Betsy's. I shall want it sadly by October; one's own hair does very well in this dry season but, during the rains and when the damp sea wind blows, it is impossible to be comfortable without false hair. I suppose Mr James would give me a wig *(wigging)*, as the sailors use the word (if he were near one) for talking of wearing such a thing. At sea a wig signifies a scolding. When you buy bonnets or caps for us, remember what suits you will suit me, and Nancy Green's head is exactly the thing for Betsy. We expect this fleet to sail tomorrow, but I shall be certain about it this evening, as we are to meet the Postmaster General at dinner: his wife is my very particular friend; Mrs Bowley. All the regiments at this place have lately been revised by the Governor and the Commander in Chief. The men are so very gallant here that the officers have always thought it necessary to give invitations to all the ladies in the settlement to breakfast with them, under tents. This is very pleasant, as they begin at daybreak and sit down before the sun becomes uncomfortably hot, and some of them have very good bands of music.

I have sent by the surgeon of the Monarch three small bags of beads. I don't know if you may like them, but I think they will look singular and pretty in England for bracelets and necklace. They are worn here by the natives; sometimes they have them set in gold like acorn cups at each end and connected by a little gold link. If printed cambric muslins, or any light-coloured things, are worn which will bear washing, I should like to have a few sent out frequently, as they are not common here, and the few I have are much admired. I don't altogether object to things which will not wash, as they are very pleasant in the cool season, but one don't want many of them. We are much obliged to you for your kind thought of the apricots and other sweetmeats. Whenever you can conveniently send things of that nature they will be very acceptable, as will a few bottles of different coloured sugar plums. You will get a great variety of those kind of things at Tringhams in Holborn. He will sell them very cheap if you get Dick Hodges to order them for you at the wholesale price, or he will sell them so to you, I daresay, if you buy them in John Gwillim's name. *(John Gwillim is either Henry Gwillim's father, d.1818, or his brother, a surgeon in Hereford; more probably the latter as he is shortly referred to again in a context of illness).* You need not fear overstocking us with them as they are much admired here, and are always put on the table when there is any company. I suppose you will think it strange, as we do, that our two companions should be appointed registrars: Mr Temple is Deputy Registrar to the Supreme Court. He is very well off for one who has been here so short a time, but there is no realising the golden dreams people have of this country. Pray give my love to Jemmy and tell him that master Harry has got a stick which would make him a little jealous: it is a fine bamboo, as thick as my wrist, and mounted very finely with silver. He has got a spade, and a hoe too, to work in his garden when the weather is cool enough to permit him to take so much exercise. Besides these, he has a fine family of live playthings which he takes great delight in: peafowls, jungle-fowls, turkeys and a fine cassowary, which is a curious bird you may have seen at Exeter exchange *(Royal Menagerie)*. It is shaped like an ostrich, of a brown colour; the feathers resemble hairs, and the wings are so small as to be useless. He has also a flock of sheep, two bullocks to draw manure for the garden, and his stud of four horses. There are two carriage horses, one fine Arabian which he rides, and a nice little piebald pony for the chaise, or bandy as it is called here.

Mr Registrar Clarke has got acquainted with several families and spends his time pleasantly amongst them. We accept of separate invitations, that is to say Richard is frequently asked out to male parties, and I am often asked to spend the day with young folks without Sir Henry and Betsy, but they are never asked without us. Richard and I are often at dances too, without them, as people who have young girls living with them sometimes get a little music from the regiments, when any of the officers dine with them, and so make up a dance without much formality. To be sure Richard has a little lead in his heels and we can't often persuade him to dance, but he is very fond of going amongst mirth of that sort and is a great beau at handling the ladies: this he does with a great air I assure you. I do not think you would know him if you were to see him; he is grown so tall and so stout. If you get the brown beads from the India house without any trouble I wish you would show them to Mrs Toussaint and tell her that I think she could introduce them very prettily for Court. They look beautifully with yellow or pink crepe; they are very cheap here so, if she should think them worth sending for, she can have them in less than a year from the time of writing, and I can send her a bag full at any time. I hope Lizzy and Mary will receive their two long-tailed gowns safe. I stitched them up without cutting the muslin to cheat the Custom House officers.

From Mary Symonds to her sister Hetty 1802

We are unexpectedly favoured with an opportunity of letting you know that we are all in the land of the living. It is not usual for ships to leave this place at this time as they generally experience very bad weather off the Cape, but the Commander of the Anna is the chief owner and is unwilling to lose time. Richard Clarke complains sadly of writing by her, and almost wishes she had not called here, for he does not think it fair to write two letters for one, and we are in hourly expectation of the fleet from England by which we hope to receive large packets of good news. We are as you may suppose all on tiptoe. Since I wrote to you we have changed our house. That we were in was in a low situation, and at a good distance from the sea shore, so we found it too warm for this season (April May and June being the hottest months). The house we are now in is a mile further from the Fort than the one we left; it has a good garden, and it commands a very fine view of the sea and all the ships as they go out or come in. We came to this place the beginning of April, and since we have been here I have not been at all oppressed by the heat. Betsy has been so much better than she was in the cool weather, and we are all in very good health. We have not yet experienced much of the land wind that is reckoned the most unpleasant, but it is by no means unhealthy. It is a hot dry wind, instead of cooling. When it blows upon you it feels as if a hot iron was passing close to you. It makes one's hair curl like a fuzzy,[21] and one's skin feel like old parchment. When these winds set in, they are quite regular, blowing from four or five o'clock in the morning till four or three in the evening, when it changes to a fine refreshing sea breeze. The land wind season does not last above a month or six weeks, in general. Richard and I walk out almost every evening, sometimes on the beach. It is very fine sand, but not so hard as the sand at Barmouth, and consequently not so pleasant, for it fills our shoes and, as our feet sink, it induces the fatigue very much, which is no desirable thing in this climate. We dine at four o'clock, and live just as we did in England only we go to bed, and rise, a little earlier and have half a hundred black men about the house, who do not wait upon us quite as well as two maids and a man would do in England. When I have teased my brain with explaining something or other in black English, (which I assure you is a very different language from that you speak) and, after an hour's hard conversation, the man I have been talking to still seems attentive and desirous of acquainting himself with the subject. But then he tells me, at last, that he is not a proper person for that business, and it must be

21 Fuzzy by itself might just mean furry or frizzy. When preceded by an article it suggests reference to an entity, perhaps to a black person because of their hair. The term fuzzy-wuzzy came much later in the 19th century and was used for the fierce warriors in the Sudan admired by the British soldiers.

another man that he brings, if mistress pleases, and then she can explain. I have got a shoemaker at work for me. I will tell you how I am forced to manage him. In the first place he must have money advanced to buy the last, and the leather. Now, if I were to trust him out of my sight I should never catch him again, so he sits under a mango tree in the garden, and boils his pot under another (that is his rice), which he is allowed 2 fanams a day for. His task is to make two pairs in a day, which he can do with ease as they are wretchedly slight, but that is of no consequence for it is only the white leather that is wearable, the black has an odious smell, and the other colours they dye so ill that they are not fit to be seen, except one, which is intended for red, but does not resemble that colour in the least. It is however something between a brown and a purple, which is not ugly. I do not think it worth your while to send us any white shoes for, though these do not keep the shape very well, they are so cheap that one can well afford to change them often. We get five or six pairs for a pagoda, which is only eight shillings. When you send things, a few pieces of narrow satin ribbon will be very acceptable, particularly white, for making shoe roses and such sort of ornaments. It is very dear here, and we are obliged to make all those little things ourselves. They do not carry well when made; the white roses lose their colour but the ribbon comes pretty good on the block. Coloured, and particularly figured, shoes we shall be very thankful for. I'm sure you will say I am a troublesome correspondent, for you must have a great deal of trouble to read my writing and, when you have made it out, it's all a budget of commissions which you are to have the trouble to execute and, and not only that, but you must have the trouble to transcribe them before you can forward the letters to my mother. Well, have patience and go on, for I have some trouble on your account. Let me tell you, it is a hard case enough when I have accompanied you in all your executions, assisted you in all your employments in the nursery, in the pantry, etc etc, to have some cross grained notion come into my head and tell me that my plan of the day may be quite wrong. I desire you will not think yourself quite alone when walking in the poplar walk. I pop in there too sometimes, and imagine you having got into the dairy with a large piece of bread, stealing the cream off the pans. If you eat such a quantity of cream after the custards you had yesterday, and the mulberries and peaches you ate this morning, you will be ill, and then you must send for John Gwillim, and he may be engaged with some fine thing of his own for aught I know by this time. This is sad prattle to send so far, but it may give you some idea of the occupations of my mind. I have been spending a week with my friend Mrs Roby at Bevedere *(the name of her house)*. It is not above 2 miles from our own, but it is the handsomest place near Madras. The house belonged to the late Nabob: it is very spacious and highly ornamented. The grounds are well planted and handsomely laid out with a great variety of fine shady walks. A river runs through the grounds which makes it cool (as the winds are always cool when they blow over water, whatever point they blow from). The house commands a fine view of the Palicat Hills *(possibly Pulicat, well north of Madras)*, which are very handsome in their form.

I do all the gossiping, visiting and most of the housekeeping here; all the other members of the family are becoming very learned in the Oriental languages. Betsy is studying the Gentoo *(Telugu – see note 11, Chapter 1801, page 29)*; Richard the Malabar *(probably Tamil[22])*; and Sir H. the Persian; what use they may make of them, when they have acquired them, I do not know. Richard will indeed have sufficient use for the language; it may be a great advantage to him. For my own part I have very little time, and no inclination, to attempt any more of them than the few words I pick up in my conversations with the servants. As I have never yet been able to acquire any knowledge in my own tongue, it would be great affectation in me to attempt to jabber in the Eastern ones.

If I draw a few plants and insects which differ from those of Europe you will be glad to see them, and I shall be much gratified of an opportunity of amusing you. I am going tomorrow to spend a few days at General Trent's.

22 The use of the word Malabar as a language is confusing. The Malabar region equates to the southwestern part of India, particularly coastal, and much of it in Kerala. Malabar Tamil was a variant of Tamil promoted by European (Portuguese) missionaries in Kerala, prior to the promotion of Malayalam. It seems to have been misapplied to East coast Tamil up to the early years of the 19th century. It is clear that when the letters refer to Malabar, they in fact mean Tamil. Yule, Henry, *Hobson-Jobson: A Glossary of Colloquial Anglo-Indian Words and Phrases, Etymological, Historical, Geographical and Discursive* (London 1903; Oxford 2013).

I have a great many of these kind of invitations and, when the family are all well and things seem to go on smoothly at home, I think I may as well accept of some of them, as it serves to make a little variety in our amusements. I believe you do not know that I may probably have a companion by the next fleet from England. Mr Strange applied to Sir Henry to receive a natural daughter of his. She was to have come out to Lady Strange if she had lived. Owing to his connection with Sir Thomas Strange, Sir Henry thought himself bound to receive her. She is a half-caste, or what you call mulatto, which two thirds of the girls who come out here are. *(and see note 14, page 68)* Some of them look pretty enough when they first arrive but, when they have been here a little time without the dancing master, they become as round backed as the natives, and they get several shades darker when they have been a little time in this climate, even though they keep themselves entirely out of the sun. They are generally wretchedly educated. Strumming two or three songs, and dancing a reel, is called accomplishment. You cannot imagine what wretched useless beings most of these kind of women sink into when they have been married a few years.

I am now getting to contradict the first part of this letter. The Anna did not sail when I expected it would, so I laid by my letter and it will now be sent to you by a frigate, which will be in England much sooner. This is shameful paper, but I have no better. I do not think I shall write to anybody else by this opportunity as I have only just heard of it, and must send my letter tonight, but I shall endeavour to write to everybody by the Anna. I have paid my visit to Mrs Trent. I was there six days, which I spent very pleasantly. She is a very mild, good, kind of a woman, but she has no children. They intend going home next year. The General is quite a Cockney, but a very good-natured man and has been 36 years in this country, except one visit of three years in England, which delighted him so much that he has never been contented in this country since his return. I cannot keep this to say more, but I shall write again by the same ship if she is detained.

From Elizabeth Gwillim to her mother. 16th July 1802.

Perhaps our last packet of letters was as much as you expected from us, and quite enough to tire you, but if the ships had not sailed sooner than we expected you would have had more. I expected to have heard from you again by this time, but no ship has arrived that could have brought us any letters. I have nothing therefore to answer to, and can only say I hope you all continue in health and that you have got over the winter well. The warm weather has been very agreeable as yet to me, and I have been a good deal engaged in visiting here, but I shall leave the White people to Polly and tell you a little about the Black people. The Hindus are a most extraordinary people, everybody exclaims, and indeed so they are: every day I am more and more surprised at their firm adherence to customs so ancient, and so unlike those of any other people. Subdued and oppressed as they have been by so many different nations they admit none into their society, nor do they vary any of their habits in conformity to their conquerors. Alexander the Great entered the upper parts of India to compel the payment of tribute money customarily paid to the Persians. It appears, therefore, the Persians had visited this country for the sake of its wealth long before, and the followers of Alexander describe the habits of these people, in the little they have said on the subject as it appeared at that time, with the only difference that they governed themselves at that time, and were rich beyond all conception in gold and jewels. Before this period the history of the Hindus is involved in fable. The antiquity of the nation is indisputably proved, and the unchangeableness of their manners, but nothing more is known. They say that God created the four elements, and a fifth of which the Heavens are made. That he afterwards created a Being imbued with perfect wisdom, called Brahma, and commanded him to make the world. Brahma, having made mankind, divided them into four tribes, the Brahmin, the Kittri, the Bise and the Indra *(sic)*. The Brahmins were to be priests and to direct men in the ways of God: the Kittri; Kings and soldiers: the Bise; merchants and cultivators of land and the Indra; tradesmen and servants, which division is most strictly kept to at this time. The Hindus have an idea of there having been four ages of the world. The first, or golden age, when the Tiger fed alongside the deer, that in which virtue was on the decline, and the iron age we now live in. The arrangements of Brahma seem to imply, however, by the necessity for a priesthood, that the people were not quite so perfect as to need no warning. One must suppose force was sometimes necessary to keep them in order. Some historians, rejecting all these fabulous accounts, say that a great King of India had a vizier of the name of Brahma whose children were so much more wise and learned than the rest of the people that the king, who they say divided the people into the four castes, ordained this family of Brahma to be astrologers and priests. However they first came by this high employment, they have had the wit to retain it to this day. Neither are they in danger of losing respect by the folly of individuals amongst them, for they have continued to possess the people with a notion that there is a certain portion of the Divinity in all Brahmins and, therefore, however weak, mean or wicked they may be, they are to be treated with the greatest respect, for fear of committing any offence against the deity who is supposed to reside in them. The Hindus are supposed to have worshipped the true God till the Persians introduced amongst them the worship of the sun and of fire, soon after which they fell into idolatry. In this state they have continued so long that divine nature is seldom thought of by them, however they have a concept of what being, superior to them, they might adore. Some writers have consciously remarked lately that their religion contains an idea of a Trinity, and thence suppose the notion of a Trinity to have been originally taught to all mankind. Whether that be the case, or that it proceeded from a natural consideration of God in his threefold capacity of creator, preserver and destroyer, cannot easily be ascertained. But their most ancient sculptures, and they never have varied from those modes, represent the figure of Brahma as a threefold deity; three upper parts, ending in one at the loins. The middle figure is called properly Brahma the creator; the one side is called Vishnu the preserver; and the other figure is called Shiva the destroyer, or avenger. Besides the sculptures that represent the deity in this threefold manner, they are represented separately, and the worship is divided. Brahma, who is the principal, has no temples erected to him though he is, as I have described, carved in them all. The temples, or as we call them, pagodas, are all either to Vishnu or Shiva and are somewhat differently constructed. All the Hindus are divided by this means, without regard to their castes, into worshippers of Vishnu or worshippers of Shiva. At first it is to be supposed it was a matter of choice, but it now continues in families, as they hold each other in no great esteem. The followers of Vishnu suppose him a benevolent being, who by prayer and supplication, or rather perhaps by an observance of ceremonies, will accord them what is desirable, and their rites have been always cheerful and innocent. But the followers of Shiva suppose him to be a being of a malevolent disposition, ever ready to avenge the smallest faults. Their worship is wholly dictated by fear. To appease this angry deity they formerly sacrificed their children and, when human blood was no longer shared on his alter, beasts of all kinds were slaughtered. Even at present the feasts of Shiva are said to be more disorderly than those of Vishnu, and are seldom attended by the Vishnu people. Besides that, these gods go under a variety of names in different places. They have wives and families, representations of which persons they keep in what they call swamy or sammy houses. The Pagodas in this part of India are very frequent, but these swamy houses are everywhere abounding. They are generally small oblong buildings, some as small as Thomas à Becket's tomb, and not unlike it. Others are as large as a small room, and there are many finished on the top in the manner of the Pagodas. They are generally much enriched on the outside but, like the pagodas, they are all dark within except the light which proceeds from lamps hung round the God. On particular days these swamy houses have the doors thrown open to show the God to the people, but none enter except the Brahmin. The stones of the floor of the building, and the walls, are quite black with the clarified butter which is poured over the God daily for, being Gods, they are attended with all the care that animation could require. On certain festivals their clothes are new, they are bathed and anointed regularly according to the rules prescribed by their religion, cookery and fruits of all kinds are placed before them which, however, are eaten with great respect by the people. When the gods are carried out of the swamy houses, they are attended by bands of musical Brahmins and dancing girls, a certain number of whom belong to each Pagoda and attend to the Swamies. Scarcely a night passes but there is a festival of some kind or other, and they go to a considerable expense. Their music, which to our ears is intolerably loud, is constantly to be heard during the night, at which time they hold all their ceremonies. Fireworks are the great part of their amusement or, as they say, ceremony. When I first came, I was so much occupied that I could not go to their feasts. I mentioned to you in one of my letters one feast for sacrificing before the instruments of iron. This lasted a fortnight, and was a general one. It is called the hunting feast, and formerly was probably about hunting wild beasts. At present it consists only in putting down a poor hare out of a basket. I went one evening to a choultrey near us, where the god stays, for when they are taken out of these swamy houses to go in a procession, they stop at every choultrey, even if these occur every hundred yards. The gods are mounted upon a carriage, but they have on this carriage a variety of ways of travelling. On this occasion he was put upon a large horse like a Pegasus, carved in wood and gilded, but the whole carriage, and horse and God, so covered with wreaths of flowers and finery of all sorts that his person was scarcely discoverable. He had however a golden face, ill enough carved, and was about the size of a large doll. The choultrey in which he waited was dressed with flags, and wreaths of flowers in a beautiful style, and the dancing girls performed a long time before him to our great amusement. The people dressed us with chains of flowers and gave us beetle and fruit, for they are always pleased if you attend their feasts. A great quantity of rice was brought out, boiled, and greedily devoured by the attending crowds after which, with great shouts, the God came forth on his horse, and the hare was let loose, but this God was turned round suddenly, and a great part of the crowd separated to pursue the hare which would belong to whoever had the good luck to catch it. This part of the festival was all I saw, and it was by daylight, but the same ceremony was performing in various parts. As their feasts are kept during the night, I have not been at any of them until lately. There was one feast, a few weeks before Christmas, where for many days the women appeared with their hair plaited, and within the plait the flower of the wild bread fruit, from which I told you in a former letter they make hedges. This flower is cut from the heart of the plant, like a rush flower, but as thick as my wrist and about half a yard long. Like seeds and grapes, it is clusters of minute flowers that are full of powder (farina). It has a fine but strong smell, which is the quality they esteem in flowers, for they use them for perfumes and always fold them in the hair. This plant is called Pandanus Odoratissimus.

Just after Christmas, in January, they have a feast called Pongal, the preparation for which lasts several weeks. This feast celebrates the return of the sun to the northward, or as we should say, the turn of the year. Besides the usual ceremonies at night, there are many others observed on this occasion, some of which I could not guess the meaning of. The ceremony from which the festival takes its name of Pongal, which signifies boiling, is the chief. For some weeks the bazaars, which are kept in places like the Parks in London, present just what an English fair would if it was kept in those places: roundabouts, and Up and Downs and suchlike sports, with stands of trinkets and sweetmeats. The pots they use are of red earthenware, and on this occasion the red ware is spread on the ground in profusion. It consists chiefly of large pots or vases from five to 20 gallons in measure. The parents, or elder relations, give to the younger ones on the occasion one of these pots filled with rice, green ginger, turmeric and a large quantity of sugar cane, fresh-cut. The green leaves hang out at the top of the jar, and round the neck of it is tied long wreaths of flowers of a golden yellow, strung together in their way. These yellow flowers are the ornament for three months of the year. It was curious to observe for some weeks, whichever way we went, people carrying these large pots so elegantly adorned with wreaths of flowers. On arrival to where it is to be presented, the wife takes the flowers and dresses her head with them; the children take the sugarcane, and the rest is for the boiling, or Pongal, which is rice, milk and sugar in this new pot. It must be performed with great care, and the rice well picked, cleanliness producing the best chance of good luck. If the pot is well spread with a mantle, and rises high and white, it is supposed the year will be favourable but, if the boiling is checked, or the scum appears discoloured, nothing but ill is ours. Not "How do you do?" but, "How was your boiling (pongal)?".

During these days, there is a custom of dressing up all bullocks, which are taken to a particular place to be exhibited. We keep a pair to draw sand for the garden, and I was applied to for a rupee for fresh sugarcane, and ginger and coconuts to hang about them, and flowers for their heads and necks, just as you see them in an ancient sacrifice, their horns being dyed either green or red, and the cart painted in red and white stripes. The common bullocks are of a light red colour, very pretty mild-looking animals, with long white horns, a hump between the shoulders, and a very long dewlap. But the bullocks kept for hackeries, or bullock-bandies, which are the carriages of the natives, are generally snowy white, and of the same form but larger. Their horns are generally encircled with gold or brass rings, and tipped with very delicate ornaments. When these white bullocks have their horns dyed a bright coral colour, and are dressed with flowers, they are extremely beautiful, and when drawing the bandy, which is like a little throne, one cannot help thinking of a carriage in some romance. I must not forget to tell you that this feast, of the return of the sun, is the season for renewing all things. Every house, from the best to the meanest kind, is entirely cleaned out, painted and whitewashed. Nothing could exceed the gaiety of the appearance of the streets in the towns and the villages. The devices on the Brahminy houses having been almost effaced, were all renewed and those, who could not afford better paintings, striped their houses with broad stripes of red and white. The rage for cleanliness is carried farther, however, than is pleasing to my taste, for even the trunks of the trees in front of the doors are painted to look like twisted columns, with red and white, and along the walls of granite that enclose the pagodas, and even the steps down the tanks, are striped in the same manner. Fortunately, this colouring is removed by the first shower of rain from these kind of places, which are much disfigured by it when it is fresh done.

There has been lately a great feast kept at St Thome, where we have been three evenings to see their ceremony, which lasted ten nights. It is in honour, as far as I can learn, of the marriage of Shiva. The God is carried out each night in a different way; one night he rides on a bullock, and on each side of him one of his wives, also on a bullock. The next night they ride out on horseback; a third night on elephants; a fourth in European carriages, and so on. On the last night he is carried out without his wives as a Pandaram, or religious beggar. I believe I have mentioned the village town of St Thome to you before. I frequently go there, as I much admire it. It is very large: one part is quite a Brahminy town. The streets are very broad, planted on each side with cocoa palms, and on the occasions of festivals they always hang festoons across the street from tree to tree, at the distance of every fourth or fifth house. There are sometimes pieces of silk, or cloth made in a kind of fringe, which has an excellent effect from a variety of colours. Sometimes they are of leaves strung together, and lamps of transparent paper as clear as glass, with paintings, and otherwise richly ornamented. These lamps and lanterns are of all varieties of form, and very handsome and rich. The houses are all illuminated with innumerable such lamps until it is a blaze of light. The great square at St Thome is about the size of Lincoln's Inn Fields. One side of this is a wall enclosing the pagodas, which are very handsome in appearance, and the other three sides are Brahminy houses with frequent openings into the countryside. Before this wall, and these houses, there are cocoa palms in two rows, then a broad driving way, and then another double row of cocoa palms at the edge of the tank, the whole square being beside one fine piece of water. This tank has a curb stone round it, and steps to the bottom made of granite. It must have been an immense work, as many of their tanks are. They are not flights of steps at intervals, but the whole sides are steps from one end to the other. It is so deep that a little temple, or pagoda, which is in the middle is now covered, and will not appear till after a long dry season. At present about eight steps brings you to the edge of the water. The illumination of this large tank is the prettiest thing of the kind that can be imagined. I cannot describe the appearance without drawing it. The lamps are placed on each step up and down in a wave down to the water's edge, and each lamp has a tremulous reflection in the water. They are very strongly lighted, and the reflection is like a pointed fringe of fire hanging in the water. The trees across the driving way are connected, as I have described, and at the four corners of the square what they call pandals are erected. These are temporary buildings, and are only a set of cocoa palm trees, very straight ones, set in the ground for columns of about 50 or 60 feet in height. These support an awning, which is either a large piece of needlework, representing the stories of the gods in patchwork, or else fine carpets with flowers of gold or colours around, and generally five immensely clear transparent paintings for lanterns, hanging from this awning. Under these places the gods rest a short time under this panoply, with the dancing girls performing all the while.

In order to see this sight, we set out about half-past 10 o'clock having 3 miles to go. The roads were crowded with men, women and children coming from all parts. We went to a choultrey in the street near the square, before which choultrey there was a pandal erected, it being near to the entrance of the pagoda from whence the gods were to set out. They brought us sweets and fruit, garlands of flowers of a kind of white jasmine around our necks, and from a silver ewer sprinkled our handkerchiefs with rosewater, giving each of us a ball of the same flowers as the garland to hold in our hands. These were like our cowslip bells. They then brought some of the best dancing girls, who are very richly dressed. Their hair is combed smooth, parted in front, and sweeping round the corners of the forehead with a fringe of fine work in gold and small jewels edging this sweep of the hair, and lying on the forehead. They wear a conspicuous piece of jewellery on the middle of the forehead, and various ornaments in the nature of clasps. One piece of gold, like a small saucer, finishes the back of the head and, between this and the front ornaments, wreaths of coloured natural flowers were twisted several times round. The back hair is plaited, and hangs down to a great length, mixed with gold and pearl tassels and flowers. Their ears are covered with ornaments; as many as possible hung in the ears themselves, and others are suspended from bands in the hair. The necklaces and chains they wear are very fine and cover their necks. Their arms have bands round the middle of the upper part of the arm, and bracelets on the wrists are innumerable. These jewels are sometimes false but, though very showy, are not of the value they may be supposed to be when real, as they are only table diamonds, and so thin as not to be fit for cutting. These women wear no shoes or stockings, but an immense weight of gold round their ankles, in strings of small bells which sound as they dance. Their dancing is very little like ours; they never step upon the toes but keeps the knees bent, and tread on the outside of their feet and move in a very small space. Sometimes, when they sing as they dance, they advance very forward in a straight line and, but at other times they dance for an hour within the space of a sheet of paper. The feet, however, are all the while in constant motion (I am speaking now of the dancing of a single person). The striking display of their skill is in the motion of the hands and arms, and the air of the head and the expression of the features. In these they excel and, indeed, the upper parts of their figures appear to me to be better formed than the lower. They are not like Grecian figures, but are short from the waist downwards, and dancing with the knees so much bent, and feet kept near the ground, seems to increase this defect.

The action of the other part of the figure is extremely graceful. It is sometimes voluptuous, but never affected. They dance, whether they recite or not, to two or three very loud instruments of a most piercing sound, one of which is a piece of metal held by one hand, and struck by another piece of metal held by the other hand. The man who plays this keeps his head close to the dancers and, with a kind of eagerness, seems to direct her in every motion, for he constantly repeats it. We had this evening a long performance by one dancer, and she was only once relieved by one of the girls in the background. It was a story of Shiva, one of their gods, who in the habit of a pilgrim of great beauty, set all the women in love with him. Some Brahmins at the back take up the chorus.

About 12 o'clock notice was given, by the loud reports of fireworks, that the gods were setting out, and we went to walk round the square of the illuminated tank with them. They were on three carriages, very large, drawn by numbers of people, Shiva in the middle, and a wife in each of the other carriages, which were a little smaller. The carriages were like large thrones, with many carved figures of the horses supposed to be drawing it, and coachmen in carved wood, and most gaudily painted and larger than life. Besides many angels and lions, the whole was dressed up with hundreds of little flags and wreaths of flowers. In short, the ornaments are so profuse that one can hardly be sure, even after much prying, that one has seen the face of either God or Goddess. After these shows, the ornaments of a theatre would look very miserable. The clear moon above, looking pale with the glare of fireworks and lights, the profusion of which you cannot guess at. It is a constant explosion during the whole tour made by the procession. If it were not almost profane to say so, these things really seem like a god. Thick darkness goes before them. The great clouds of smoke roll on before the carriages, and conceal everything but what peers at them from above. The great waving leaves of the cocoa trees which receive the light of the fires and of the moon, and mango and other trees covered with white clusters of flowers. The glare of fresh fires upon the volumes of smoke, and the showers of fire from different fireworks, whilst rockets thrown up unceasingly, twenty, forty, a hundred at a time, seeming to pierce the skies, have altogether such an effect as could hardly be conceived. The noise of their instruments is most tremendously piercing, but I think a little use would make it not disagreeable. The dancing girls preceded the cars and, when they stopped, perhaps twenty of them danced standing, as ours do, but dancing in their usual way, only advancing now and then to meet what we should call their partner, and then retiring. They are all women. Vast numbers of Pandaram men and women follow the cars, dancing in their own way. There are no other carriages allowed; the crowd all walk. Thousands attend, and they are the great beauty of the picture, for the dress is so graceful and so clean, the white muslin, turbans and drapery, and the order and tranquillity of their behaviour give great solemnity to the scene. One can hardly be surprised that they are unwilling to give up their shows for a better religion, the fruits of which do not appear very good in the examples our people give them who come out here. After we had walked round the tank, sometimes resting on the verandas of some houses where chairs were set, we came back to the Pandal under which we had sat. The God was taken to the pagoda, and some of the Pandarams entertained us with a kind of buffoon dance. Some boys, having on tigers' masks, showed some little activity around us in the art of tumbling at a fair. During these feasts the great cause of the tranquillity is the sobriety of the people. Those of caste never drink any kind of spirit, or fermented liquor, but besides this they are naturally very mild in their disposition. Drunkenness they detest to a degree you can hardly conceive. Their shops are just like the stalls in Covent Garden with ranges of fruit in some, and in others confectionery, which they make very pretty, and in a great variety of shapes, but with little variety of flour, and also sugar, clarified butter, cashew nuts in the way of almonds, and sometimes cardamom seeds, like sugar plums. The worst is they are fond of mixing a little arrack which is to us intolerable, and generally the best sort are covered with silver leaf, although all are very greasy. The shops of flowers are much like the flower shops in Covent Garden, but more like artificial flower makers because they hang up ready-made wreaths and bunches. It is surprising what quantities of flowers are sold in wreaths; eight months in the year they are of a sort of double white jasmine, the rest of the year yellow flowers, but all are occasionally mixed. All these shops sell betel leaf, which looks exactly like lily-of-the-valley leaves, and I used to take the little bundles to be some flower of this kind rolled into the leaves.

I wrote you all this account of Indian ceremonies for the amusement of you and little Tom, and had expected to send it with a letter Polly sent about the latter end of May, or beginning of June. She had also intended to write several other letters, as did Mr G., and that one letter I hope Hetty has had. It was sent by mere chance. We were disappointed in sending the others; nothing can be so teasing as watching the opportunity of sending letters disappear, the vessels frequently sailing without any notice. I have just now heard that the Swallow packet is going to sail, which has been lying here nine months, and is to be ready to sail at 24 hours notice. Whether it may now sail in a few hours, or be here some months, I cannot guess, but reports says it is to sail, and therefore I shall pack this off to acknowledge the receipt of a letter from you, and one from Hetty written from Tupsley, January 14th 1802. Mr G. had a few letters on business, and from some friends, but not one from any relation of his. I expected a box of preserves, and a box from Mr James, because Mr Temple's father said he had enclosed some books in a parcel for his son, which was going to be sent by Mr James, and which I expected would be with some gowns, caps etc etc. Mr Ware wrote to Mary that he had sent us some porter, but does not say how it was directed. We have received none of these things, and all the ships have come in for the season except one, which is not expected till August or September. The ships destined for China and Bengal have sailed from this place and we have made enquiry without effect, the letters not mentioning what has been sent. I fear our things are gone to China, by which means they will be lost or go back to England, but one of the mates of the ship, the United Kingdom, and who dined with us, tells us he thinks it likely the boxes are still in England, as unless some person delivers them, and takes a receipt from the officers, they are frequently left in the warehouses. Therefore, if the preserves and Mr James's box were sent, we shall be glad if he will enquire where they are. It is a little disappointment to me, but not worth talking of. I can go on if they come a few months hence, only I have no caps, and I cannot trick out in flowers like the young misses; a few handsome caps are therefore very desirable to me, and also a little false foretop of hair, that is in the fashion, could be sent now and then. Everybody, young and old, wears them here as we have no hairdressers, and the hair does not keep curled by reason of the perspiration, and damp of the air. I shall want both evening and morning caps, and this foretop of false hair, for the sea air takes out all the curl from our own, and there is nobody to dress it.

As for this false foretop, I have mentioned it in all my letters, and expect Mr James will be a good deal diverted at such a hue and cry after a lady's wig. Everybody here uses them, though Mr Gwillim inveighs against the custom most bitterly, and vows to burn mine if he finds it.

The months of April and May, which we were taught to think would be very hot, were to me delightfully pleasant, particularly in our pleasant house on the sea. Mr G. was also well at that time, but in June had a great many boils of which he was very impatient. They are a complaint that neither black nor white people often escape at that season. Richard Clarke has had plenty, but he did not much regard them. Mr Gwillim was really very ill with his for five weeks, and took up all my attentions for, though not alarming, they are extremely painful. I had three, which made me very ill for some days. Richard's were many, but small; ours were large. Polly has no ailment, but I lose her very much as she is frequently out for a fortnight or three weeks at a time, and has many invitations. At present she is away from home. I drive out on Wednesday to fetch her home. The last six weeks have been the hottest weather we have had, just as it was when we arrived. The land winds have prevailed, which are very disagreeable if they continue all day, but have nothing baneful in them except that by drying up the skin they check perspiration bringing boils and prickly heat which is exceedingly teasing. We have no mosquitoes in this house.

I shall conclude this with many thanks to you and Hetty for your letters, which I hope you will let us have at all opportunities.

From Elizabeth Gwillim to her
sister Hetty. San Thome, Madras 3rd August 1802

At this distance from you, I always imagine that it will be more pleasing to you to hear all you can of us, and our goings-on, than that I should regularly answer all the chitchat you are so good as to send me and, therefore, I do not answer to every particular item, many of which may have escaped you before your letter reaches me. Nevertheless, every line of your letters is a treasure to us, for you seem to bring us home by the description you give us of every person, and every action, and we think you little less than a good fairy that transports us through the air to our native country. A letter, which I lost an opportunity of sending some months ago, and at the time little regretted, has been kept by me till a few days ago, there having been in all that time no opportunity of sending it to England. I took the first chance to send it, and I find it has been put on board a Hamborough ship,[23] by which I fear it may cost more than it is worth but, as it may arrive after a long interval, you may not be sorry to have it as I have added to it a later part, with a short account of our goings-on at present. The ship I intended it to go by does not go at all, after nine months delay. In short, I have been so often disappointed in sending letters, and we have so often lost chances by waiting for what were esteemed certainties, that I shall never again presume to promise myself when a letter may go. This is intended to take a chance only, and will not for that season be long. I sent by the Monarch, in March last by favour of the surgeon, two pieces of muslin, a shawl and some pieces, and some seeds which I hope you will receive in August or September. I expected many opportunities before this, but they have all failed. Polly wrote a letter on the off chance of it going by the Anna; a country ship *(i.e. local)*. I believe she told you we had changed our house for one which I think you would like as well as I do. It is by the sea side, and the two months we had been taught to dread, April and May, turned out to be the pleasantest I have felt in this situation. We had a sea breeze almost constantly and, when that blows, we never feel too warm. About the 18th of June, however, it began to be extremely warm and, with the exception of a few days, we had six weeks of land wind which is reckoned to have been the severest season for 20 years and upwards, and has been in truth very disagreeable. This wind has in it nothing unwholesome but, by blowing over a long space of land heated by the sun, and by bringing with it a quantity of fine sharp sand, it gives a burning to the skin just like the effects of a sharp frost in England. The extremes of heat and cold seem to produce nearly the same effects. This wind sweeps with great violence and is dangerous for this reason, that the heat and sharpness of it produces boils and prickly heat, when exposed to the wind. For this reason we wear shawls, and guard ourselves from it by shutting the windows, as we do from cold. We have now had, even whilst the land winds blew, showers most days, but we have not had so much rain as could be wished for the sake of the country and the gardens, and everything will be late. When we came here on the 26th of July last year,

23 Probably Hamburg.

we found the country perfectly verdant; a verdure indeed beyond what I had ever seen. The grass was tall and fresh: it is now only just beginning to look green except where it is watered. The trees look fine but have an autumnal appearance: many leaves of the cocoa palms look copper coloured, and all appear red or gilded on the edges so, if one may compare great to small things, some of the smaller groves look like baskets of filberts, as for use with oil paints. They are extremely beautiful, and my view of the sea through them is perfectly beautiful. The rice is green in the fields, and the flowers keep blooming on, as they do not depend immediately on the rains for preservation of things of that kind. The tanks and rivers do not fail, and they cut channels in every direction, which they easily fill and then water every part. Mr Gwillim and I have been great martyrs during what is called here the Griffinage, that is the first year. I trust in God we shall do better the next, for I fear you will all think me very idle, though I have in reality been very much otherwise. We have both had boils and terrible prickly heat which, to a person so irritable as Mr G., is a perfect misery. It is indeed so to me, though I have tried to bear it with patience. These disorders are like the gout, and thus they excite no pity, but are very distressing. As for the prickly heat, a real fit of it (of which I have had three and Mr Gwillim two) is worse than I know how to describe. Every part of back, breast, arms and hands is covered with a thick scarlet rash that itches worse than the Scotch fiddle, and it would require a hundred hands to rub every part that itches. As for Mr Gwillim, he had four pair in constant employment besides his own. I have not been able to sit out of doors to draw, but I am very deep in Hindu learning, and am learning the gentoo language which I can write pretty well. *(See again note 11, Chapter 1801).*

Mr Gwillim bore the death of Mr John Yorke very indifferently *(sic)*. I never saw him more afflicted: he was low with his boils and, when he heard it, he cried a whole day. The death of Mrs Buller, too, the bishop of Ely's last daughter, was a most distressing circumstance. We had a most kind letter from Mr Carew, who married Mr John Yorke's only daughter, with a circumstantial account of his illness.[24] My mother says that when she has had

24 John Yorke 1728–1801 was the 4th son of Philip, 1st Earl of Hardwicke. He married Elizabeth Lygon, their only daughter being Jemima 1763–1804, who married the Rt. Hon. Reginald Pole-Carew MP. John Yorke's younger brother was Rt.

our letters from here, and hears of us having hers, she shall think nothing of the distance between us. I am sure if we had been much acquainted, before we came here, with people who are in the habit of coming here, we should none of us have thought so much as we later did on seeing people who have been here 10 or 12 times and who, when they are going to England, talk of returning here immediately. When I look out of my house and see the sea beating against the shore, and think that from the time I left I saw only the same appearance, I can hardly think the space between us so great as it is. Polly is writing to Nancy Green and giving a full account of our receiving, by this fleet, only a box of books from Butterworth; no caps or gowns, no preserves, no porter, nothing we were due to have. I fear they are all gone on to China, or else they are still in England and have been put into no ship, which is the best hope. We may still have them by some other vessel.

If letters come from one of us, and not another, you need not be alarmed because we think it best to divide them, because ships so frequently change their destination. In days when the heat is extreme by the thermometer, we feel no loss of appetite. On the contrary, people eat exceeding well. The land wind is much like our oppressive days in England, and takes off the appetite but, on the fine clear days when the sea air is extremely warm, a hot dinner, though large, has not the disgusting appearance it seems to have in England. With so many doors open and windows unglazed, one thing is that we are not distressed by the smell of the meat, as in England in closed rooms. I do not know if I ever before remarked a trifling thing to you, which is natural enough, but we were not aware of it during the summer months. When the air is hot we can see no steam or smoke from any dish, nor even from a pitcher of boiling water, by which means we have frequently burned our mouths, and I have been very near scalding my hands by plunging them into basins of hot water. In the monsoon we see the steam as in England.

We have one great comfort, I feel, by coming from the fancy servants in England, which is the attention and tenderness of these people in illness

---

Rev. Hon. James Yorke 1730–1808, Bishop of Ely, who married Mary Maddocks, daughter of the Bishop of Worcester. They had a daughter Elizabeth who married a John Buller, who evidently had a first cousin by the name of Templar, who is mentioned in the letters as correspondent and friend of Mary Symonds.

or difficulties. Even those who beat them and abuse them acknowledge that their care in illness is beyond all things. It is a religious principle with them never to be made angry by anything that an old person, or a sick person, says. They are patient and forbearing under insults and provocations of all kinds, neither do they bear in mind these affronts. I wish you knew my gentoo man Saamy. He is but just 19, but has a large pair of whiskers. Mr Gwillim is very fond of several of them, but he is our great favourite. He has the exact face of little Tom James; most beautiful eyes and eyebrows, and a face full of mildness and goodness; his skin, like most of the gentoos, a deep Devonshire Brown. He has not a thought beyond the house. We have two Malabar, and two Gentoo, men of caste. *(See note 11, Chapter 1801, page 29)* The gentoos I like best: one is extremely handsome. The people of caste are all delicately clean, but the gentoos are neater, fairer in their skins and handsomer than the Malabars. The gentoos are chiefly Vishnu people, that is they go to the pagoda of Vishnu who is a mild and benevolent god. These servants of caste will not do any menial office, for which they are frequently insulted unjustly by Europeans. The truth is that they hire themselves out for no such purpose, and would sooner die. They consider themselves as gentlemen and hire themselves in the same character as Dubashes, that is interpreters for when the Europeans first come to this country. Till lately, it was only these well educated people who could acquire the English language.

There are thousands of Pariahs who are a lower order of people, and will do all things, and those people who complain need not employ the better quality men. They find, however, that they are the only people to be relied upon. They will come behind a carriage, carry an umbrella, and always take things from the hands of the lower servants to give us, for they wait at table. If you go into a shop, they go with you and assist in choosing the things, and settling the price, and assume a character like the servants in old plays; a sort of companion to the Master. They will not dress hair, nor shave one, and neither will they do those offices for themselves it would be thought degrading, such as to cut their own nails, which are always nicely cut by their own barbers. If a man was to cut his own nails, he would be called barber, a term of such great reproach that he would never get clear of it. At five years old they begin to clean their teeth, which are beautifully kept. They never eat without washing their hands, feet and teeth, and always wash the hands and teeth perfectly after eating. They do what they call 'wash head' once a week, that is they are well scrubbed, one doing it for another, with a paste made of eggs and lime juice, and pounded vetches like an almond paste, and plenty of hot water. They are extremely agreeable in one respect in that they have no offensive tricks, which they abominate, and have a great contempt for Moor men who always indulge in them, and for such Englishmen as also do. They never scrape their throats, nor sniff with the nose, nor pick their teeth or fingers, nor make any odd noises, nor do they ever scratch their heads or, in short, do any trick that can offend delicate eyes or ears. I own I have often been not a little ashamed to hear one of my own country's people swear at them for beasts and dirty devils, who in ten minutes has committed ten things that would disgust these people. One thing, however, though they certainly equal the desires of Lord Chesterfield in niceties of this kind, they pay perhaps too high a price for this delicacy.[25] In their sacred books these regulations are mixed together, and a point of cleanliness, or manners, stands beside one of religion or morals, and is pressed upon them by equally forcible language. Our vulgar old proverb says cleanliness is next to godliness; they have made it at least equal, if not exceeding it.

Received your letter by the Admiral Aplin which has turned our sorrow into joy. Drank your health in great glee with our friends at our table.

From Elizabeth Gwillim 14th September 1802

I know not when any vessel may be likely to leave this place, but flattering myself that you may be as glad to hear of us as we are to hear of you, I shall begin a letter, and put in a few lines as I find myself in a humour to write, for when opportunities are so scarce I do not like to lose any chance of writing when a sudden one offers. Another ship, the Britannia, came in from England, the last but one, and not one of our things arrived.

25 Philip Stanhope, 4th Earl of Chesterfield, wrote a number of letters to his son which are celebrated for their wise aphorisms.

What is worse, not one line from any soul, except a short letter from Temple's father, to him, saying that in April 1802 Mr James's family were well. I hope to God it was so, and that they still are so, but a line or two would have given us great satisfaction. There is now but one chance more for our things, as the ship called Admiral Aplin is not yet in. I have not yet bought any things, but some mere trifles. It is therefore of no consequence, as long as the things are safe and we can trust you are all well. The heat of the weather has abated here now, and my garden is in good order. I have four large beds of French beans, but not yet in flower, and they are to be sold in the bazaar. However, the reason is that the people were busy with the building, and our gardening was not begun till late. Our building is now almost finished, but not dry enough to go into. I do not know whether Polly told you that we are so much pleased with this situation that the landlord has made an additional building to induce us to stay. The new building is connected to the original one by a curved veranda, or gallery you would call it, and it consists of one large room, two bed chambers, and a veranda to each, and all front the sea so that the breeze blows in very delightfully. The building has been some amusement to us, as I think it would have been to you. I intend to tell my mother a great deal about it as she understands these matters.

In my letters I have told you so much about the black people that I am afraid you will either not have time to read them, or that you will be tired of the subject, and yet there are a thousand things I have not said and would tell you about. I am always curious to enquire about their customs, and here there are so many different peoples that it takes a long time to distinguish one set from another. The Hindus, with all their different divisions; next the Moor men, with the Nabob at the head of them; then the remains of the Portuguese, and various low people whom they have converted to what they call Christianity. Besides these, the Armenians, who are all Christians of another kind, and have their churches and chapels, besides our own people, many of whom are as great curiosities as the strangest. I was in the garden of a Portuguese Chapel to see the ceremony, one night in Passion week, when the procession passed. I was amused with a little English boy crying out "Run: that Swaamy (that is: idol) is coming". It was a representation of our Saviour, as taken from the cross, and so shockingly represented in wax, as large as life, as to be very distressing. He was carried on a bier, with a canopy over, as if to the grave. Before his image walked a number of boys dressed in brown frocks, with borders and large painted wings on their shoulders as if to represent angels. Each carried a waiter (or salver) with some instruments used in the crucifixion; one had the nails, but of an immense size that they might be better seen; another the hammer, and the nippers; and another the crown of thorns. Behind the bier the women were carrying Mary, and Mary Magdalen, each as large as life in wax, and dressed in fashionably flounced black silk, and gowns with headdresses like Portuguese men, and with beads in their hands. These figures had their feet upon the top of a pole, which raised the feet as high as the heads of the people. Many other things were carried, besides innumerable attendants in ridiculous flounced dresses of coloured silks and gauzes, which the larger angels wore, much in the style of masquerade dresses. A great part of the procession was made up of people in long robes carrying candles, besides which the whole garden was a blaze of light. I thought the chant of the priest extremely fine and solemn and, ridiculous as the procession was, the effect of the voices was beyond anything of the kind I ever heard. These people are all dark; as black as the other natives; very few of them being really Portuguese, and those few have been so long in the country that they have become dark. The smaller angels had a quarrel, and were kicking one another as they went along, to the amusement of the spectators. In short it was a most unnatural mixture of solemnity and absurdity. We followed the procession into the chapel, where indeed I have been at other times. As many others are, this was very rich and it surprised Mr Gwillim, who had seen hundreds. There are not indeed any paintings, but the ornaments are very fine and extremely expensive, and the place is quite clear of people. This church, or rather chapel, is the only one I have been in. It is a large apartment, like the parish churches in London, but with no gallery on the sides. The chancel is very large, divided from the principal part and, before you reach that, on each side there is a chapel, each exactly in the style of the great altar. The design is an immense gilded sarcophagus, with many images and gold candlesticks, and lights in abundance, in all the niches and little hollows which in our churches are, in such parts, filled with dust and cobwebs. The figures also are fresh, and richly dressed, whether large or small, and they are numerous. Neither the ornaments nor the buildings are correct, being everywhere a mixture of Grecian, Gothic and Moorish, but the newness and brilliance of the gilding, the rich effect of so many small parts, and the lights dispersed in every such part, gave a delicacy of effect that I should not have guessed at by seeing a dirty monument in Westminster Abbey, which is the same kind of thing. These chapels are hung with damask of different colours, that is the colours are changed on different days. The roof of the chancel I thought particularly beautiful, with long pieces of satin of two colours in long strips about a yard wide at the top, and sloped to a point at the bottom. These were laid over each other around the cornice, all the points taken together in one knot in the centre of the ceiling, and the middle hanging hollow. It appeared the most beautiful top of a room I ever saw. You will judge what immense quantities of satin must be used when I tell you that the chapel is very high. During the whole of Passion week, all that passes in that week is acted over day by day as it originally occurred; the entombing, sealing and, on Easter day, the resurrection.[26]

2nd October.
I wrote a sheet to you one day, since when the ship Admiral Aplin has come in, but without bringing anything for us. I wish indeed I had my preserves, those I brought out having been very useful, but now gone. A cap or two, I also feel the want of, my head being rather disordered. I am not much inclined to turn to millinery having so little time to do other things I want to do. Lizzy Thoburn and Nancy Green have I presume forgotten us. I particularly told, I thought everybody, that we should

26 St Thomas is effectively the patron saint of Christian India. Christians number about 2.5% of the Indian population and the religion goes back a long way in Kerala and Tamil Nadu. It is said that when the Portuguese arrived in western India, bent on converting the local people they were surprised to find that the religion had preceded them. They nevertheless promulgated it, through the south particularly. According to tradition St Thomas travelled outside the Roman Empire to preach the Gospel, and reached the Malabar coast in modern Kerala in AD 52. He was eventually allegedly martyred on St Thomas' Mount in Madras and interred in then Mylapore, now St. Thomé. Both sites now contain catholic churches, the latter being a cathedral.

expect to have a few lines put into the India House once a fortnight, by which means we should always hear by every opportunity, and without a farthing's expense. I must beg of you not to put letters in parcels, but always in the India House, by which means I shall have them so much the sooner and more certainly. You must think we feel it a little hard to have had at this time no news from England of a later date than January 1802, when everybody in the settlement have had letters in every month from January till the fifth of June, just half a year later, during which time we have not heard how any of our friends are. I do not mean to reproach you, who have been almost our only correspondent. However long letters are great treasures. We do not ask for more than three lines, sometimes from you, and sometimes from my mother or Nancy Green, which could tell us how you all are and save us many painful conjectures.

We have had the most severe season ever remembered, and have as yet had no rains. We expect the monsoon to set in very soon. The heat of June, July and August was excessive; the land winds blew with great violence. Polly and Richard are in high spirits constantly. She has told you what a party we have, so I shall say nothing on that subject. Thank God Mr Gwillim is now very well, as ever I have seen him. I have just heard that Captain Marsh of the General Stewart is arrived here on his way home. I shall send after him, and will write by his ship to you and Mrs Shepheard: I shall therefore say little more now. We received a letter some weeks ago from Mr Edwards. It was written in a hand scarcely intelligible from tremor, and very confused. He said in it that he was recovering very fast, but I had not heard how ill he was, nor in what part of the country. By this letter, he said he was coming down to Madras: I am much concerned on his account, poor creature. It was very imprudent at least, if not cruel, to send him to this country.

It is in vain for me to conjecture how you all are, and what you are doing: I shall therefore say nothing on that head, but will try to hope for the best. I sent you by a Mr Prosser of the United Kingdom two Palampores *(bedspreads)*, one of which I wish you to keep, and I will let you know to whom I wish you to give the other. I was glad to get the opportunity of sending them, though he went to Bengal with them. I packed some pieces of muslin to show you what the women wear for their cholis: each choli takes half a yard. I also sent you a Moor woman's veil, curiously dyed. You will be surprised at the coarseness of the muslin but in this bright sun they look very well.

3rd October.
Although I wrote lamenting last night, the Aplin has been in one week. Today Captain Rogers called on Mr and Mrs Hargrove, and produced out of his pocket your packet; your nice long letter, James's letter and yours to Mr Gwillim; altogether of equal value with so much gold. I cannot now have time to write this over again, so you must excuse it. I have the greatest joy in hearing your dear little child is so well; I pray God to preserve him. I am sorry to hear you become so thin; I fear you walk too much; I hoped to hear you were got a little fat. I fear you are mistaken about Mr Thomas Gwillim's being a Post Captain[27] . I suppose it must be Master and Commander, however I hope it may be Post Captain, and shall have great happiness to hear it confirmed. Pray give our best wishes to him. You need not hurt yourself in fear about your letters coming safely to us. I have had all that have been sent as yet. Oh that I had those that are soldered up in the tin case; pray never put any in boxes again that are of any consequence. By the packet they are sure to be safe, and I pay nothing.

I hope that I shall have my seeds by the beginning of December. My French beans are almost all dead for want of rain; never was such a season known. I am glad you brought me some confectionery. That which I brought out with me answered amazingly well. Candied and sugar plum things are sold very dear here. A pint decanter of candied almonds, or caraways, are two pagodas. My tolu lozenges and mint seeds have lasted until now, and I shall be glad always to have tolu lozenges sent not in boxes, but from Tringhams by the pound. They have been most useful to me, and the mint seeds. I have also some black current drops still, that have kept extremely well and are very good. I owe you a thousand thanks for thinking of them: I hope you have long before this received a white shawl with large sprigs I sent you, and two pieces of muslin for Lizzie, and Mary Thoburn. These I sent by a Mr Long, a surgeon, who assured me he could land them. The surgeon

27 Thomas Gwillim was a probable brother of Henry Gwillim's but, if so, he was 14 years younger. The known brother of Henry was John, surgeon in Hereford, who inherited the family estate.

is the best man in the ship because he can lock up things in his medicine chest. Whatever you paid for your shawl, pray let me know, as I do not like it that you should be at any expense. I hope you have had a shawl sent by a Mr Chalmers, a lawyer, for Mrs Holland. You told me about the great muslin gown for Mrs Holland, and what came of it. I had it worked in black before I left England. Tomorrow Captain Marsh dines with us, and Captain Rogers: I hope they will carry some things for me between them. Mr Templar has also promised to carry some things for me.

I pray constantly for your health and happiness and we all talk continually of your kindness in writing so much to us in all your difficulties. I am glad you know Mr Livingstone; he appears to me a very attentive good young man, and is the very particular friend of a Mr Dove, a surgeon who came out with us and is up the country. I will send his letters describing the country to me soon, for yours and my mother's amusement in leisure hours. May God bless and keep you all safe till our return. By the time you have this, two years will have nearly elapsed - so time flies.

From Elizabeth Gwillim to her mother. 2nd Oct 1802

I have an opportunity of sending a letter by a gentleman who sails in a fast sailing Hamburg ship tomorrow, and will not let him go without a line to tell you we are at present all well after this very hot season we have passed which, though it set in late, has been most severe and considered as more so than the oldest Indian *(Indian British settler)* remembers. The weather now gets cool and pleasant. I trust in God you are all well, and shall not tease myself with conjectures, but the last letters I have had were dated January 1802 and every other person in the settlement have had two letters every month since that time till the 5th of June, some ships having come in *(only)* three months from England. I must entreat of you to write a letter, you or Hetty, and have it properly directed and put in the India House once a fortnight by which means we should hear. The monsoon is now expected to set in, when the flag is struck, and we shall have no hope of hearing from you again till February. This will be a long time to look forward to, and very mortifying. I have written several letters to you and Hetty, and hope within this month to write several others to you. This will therefore be very short. Polly is remarkably well having had no sort of complaint since she came. Mr Gwillim has had a letter from his father *(John Gwillim)* dated March which seems to say they are in health, at least nothing to the contrary. I find Mrs Squires is dead of a dropsy; no unexpected thing I suppose from her size. The building of my new apartments is nearly finished, and I think you would admire it very much. We are in the pillory for, beside the front of both buildings, a long curved gallery joins them in which I think they have put two pillars, where one would have done. It looks however the better, and is a very whimsical white marble palace, now it is all quite fresh.

Lord Clive opens a magnificent banqueting house on the 7th with a ball for the whole settlement. His house, and this banqueting house, altogether is extremely beautiful and looks like a palace for Priam and his fifty sons. We have continued reports that he is going to leave us, which I hope are not true. He dines with us on the ninth, and therefore certainly does not go at the time talked of. We shall be very sorry to lose him for, though he is not showy in his manners, he is very good-natured and not at all high. He has been extremely kind and civil to us, and I do not think I should like so well the persons intended to succeed him as Governor. It was a disappointment that Lady Clive and her two daughters had left this place, as they also were very free and agreeable. She delighted in this country, and made large collections of curiosities, which indeed any person might easily get, but there is great difficulty in preserving them from the ants, which are perfect scavengers and carry away every crumb left on the ground. They certainly have great merit in cleaning the house on behalf of any dirty servants, and are most expeditious in their work, the only inconvenience is that they sometimes take us for rubbish, and begin to remove us by biting us in a very sharp manner. I have had a bird eaten up in one night.

I hear nothing of John Gwillim's marriage, which you told me of *(see note 27)*. Mr Gwillim had a very pert witty letter from Dick Hodges - he is to go to Oxford. Richard Clarke is much improved, and grown surprisingly. He goes in a bandy, that is a one-horse chair, to the Fort every day and Mr G. goes in a palanquin. They return to dinner at 4 o'clock, and Richard has the evening and the morning till 11 o'clock. At first he had no great desire for the balls, and the company of the ladies but matters are much changed. He and Polly, and a few more, have so much business of that kind that I cannot enter into the spirit of it, and indeed they are so rampant sometimes that I cannot get any good of them. I am quite glad to have them do this part of the business for me, for the going out in hot and cold places does not agree with me. I get cramps and slight rheumatisms. We have a gay party in the home at present.

From Mary Symonds to her sister Hetty 2nd October 1802.

I sit down to write a few lines to you, as I will never miss an opportunity, but I think you may probably receive other letters before this (which will be sent by us some days hence), as we shall then have a charming opportunity of sending by the King's ships, which have been stationed here the greatest part of the war, and are now ordered home to be relieved. The gentleman who carries this is a Mr Samuel. He is an attorney here, and the editor of the Madras Gazette. He had the misfortune to marry a sister of Mrs Wills, the actress. She has behaved very ill in England, it is said, and it is whispered here that the purpose of this voyage is to get divorced from her, and to bring his children out here who have been educating in England.

I have the satisfaction to say we are all pretty well. Betsy is always a little nervous, as she used to be in England. We have at present a very pleasant house, and quite full of company. Mr and Mrs Edward Hargraves, and Mr William Hargrave, who just arrived by the Admiral Aplin: the gentlemen are sons of Mr Hargraves of Boswell Court. The eldest was in this country five or six years. He went home for his health, and then met the lady he has married for the consideration of, some say 7, and others 17, thousand pounds which she possessed. By the help of rouge and false hair her face looks pretty enough but, as the song says, she is 'badly warped in the back'. She was a Miss French of the city. I dare say James *(Hetty's husband)* knows the name. She has been at a ball last night, and I got her acquainted with plenty of smart young men for partners, and she seemed quite delighted with Indian gaiety, and Indian gallantry. I wrote to Nancy Green, a little time since, and told her a great lie, viz, I said I had sent you some drawings and a letter by that same ship, and I had intended to do it when I wrote to her, but unfortunately I sent them too late. I shall send them to you by a very charming young man who is now on a visit with us. He is a Lieutenant in the Leopard; Mr Templar. He is a nephew of Judge Bullen's, and a brother of a Mrs James Bullen, a sweet pretty woman who lives in Sarl Street: I knew her a little in England. He calls himself my brother, and I really love him as if he were so: he insists on my writing to his sister. I am not quite sure that he would not prefer being loved in another way, but I keep him to brotherly love on account of his youth, for he is not quite 20 and, as I have an utter aversion to inequalities, my heart is quite safe. If I were 16 I believe I should like him better for a lover, as he is very good and sensible, and exceedingly handsome. I am writing you an idle prattling letter, but it will convince you that we keep up our spirits pretty well. It is a fine thing to be in a place where a little beauty goes a great way. I am very handsome here, and very clever, and the Lord knows what. If you cannot believe it you may blot it out, or burn the letter, or whatever you like.

Tomorrow is Sunday and your birthday. I shall not forget to drink your health in a bumper. God Almighty bless you and send you many happy returns of it.

From Mary Symonds to her mother 3rd October 1802.

One of the happiest girls in the world is now writing to you. I have just received a packet of letters from Hetty, which has made me so. I finished a short letter to her yesterday, but it will go in another ship and I expect this will come to hand long before it. I have but a few minutes allowed me to write this, not being aware that the ship would sail so soon. Thank God we are all in good health and spirits. In my letter to Hetty, which I sent by a Mr Samuel, I mentioned my fears lest the parcels she sent us were lost, but I find by her letter that we may expect them some weeks hence. Indeed it may be some months, but that is not material so long as they are safe, and when we hear that you are all well we are quite happy. Hetty mentions Mr T. Gwillim being made a Post Captain, but that I suppose must be a mistake as he was not made a Commander when we last heard, and such rapid promotions are not usual. Whatever his advance may be, I sincerely wish him joy of it and hope I shall see him with two epaulettes when we next meet,. It would have been very gay for me if my finery had come by the Admiral Aplin, as we are to have a most splendid ball at Lord Clive's on the 7th, which he gives in celebration of the peace,[28] and on that occasion he opens the new banqueting house which he has just finished building. I fear poor Edwards (who came out when we did) is very ill. He was sent up the country to an employment soon after he arrived, and we heard nothing of him till the other day when Sir Henry received a letter from him, written in a wretched trembling hand, saying that he had been very unwell, and was coming down to the coast in the hope of recovering his health. Since that time he sent some books to be taken care of for him, but himself is not yet arrived. Poor creature, it was a shocking thing to send such a man into this climate, for by all accounts he was scarcely himself all the voyage.

I cannot bear to let a ship sail without some scrawl or other on it for you. I am afraid you will think my letters very trifling, as I give you no description of the country, but I think Betsy does those things better than I and, besides, I shall convince you soon that I am not negligent of those things when you receive letters, and descriptive drawings, of my performance. I should do more for you but, as Betsy has not the strength to bear much racketing, I am obliged to do the visiting for all the family, for Sir H. will never go to any balls and would rather take his evening nap than pay visits to the gayest ladies here. Indeed, it does not agree with him to be put out of his way. At first I contested the matter a little, because I did not like to go out without him, but I have given up now because I see it teases him, and now that I know every lady here I am never in want of a companion. No less than three ladies of my acquaintance have fitted up rooms in their houses for me, whenever I choose to spend a few days with them. Indeed, I find myself a great favourite here, but I don't know why, and I endeavour to be obliging to those who are civil to me. To be sure, the girls who come out here are for the most part ignorant, pert and bold, and receive all attention as merely what is due to their beauty, though God knows there are not three in the place who have the smallest pretensions to

28 The French wars ended in 1802, but restarted in 1803 as the Napoleonic wars.

it. I have filled this paper with nonsense and must now conclude, wishing health and happiness to all my dear friends

From Elizabeth Gwillim to her sister
Hetty Madras 18th October 1802

I intended to have written to you by the ship General Stewart. Captain Marsh dined with me, and promised to take a parcel to Mrs Shepheard. I hoped he would have later called on me but he did not and, finding it grow late, I sent yesterday everywhere to find him and had but just discovered his retreat, when a gun was fired from the Fort to order every person to go on board, and the vessels to sail. The north wind, or monsoon, set in suddenly with some strength, and a storm was expected. Before this intelligence could reach me we could see the ships underway from the top of the house.

I had bought a piece of muslin for handkerchiefs for Mrs Shepheard, and packed it up ready. Also, Mr Gwillim, in a great fit of gallantry, has bought you a pearl necklace and I fear neither one nor the other can be sent. However, the night became perfectly still, and the vessels appeared in the offing this morning. Orders have therefore been posted up to say the packet is again open, but I fear we shall not be able to send anything but letters. I am much concerned about the handkerchiefs, and Mr G. is in much distress for you to be adorned in his present. They are small pearls, so you must wear them often when you get them. I have been too much busied with company to write to you as I intended, or to Mrs Shepheard. The wind is very rough now, but the surf is not very strong. Mr Templar has been with us, whose family I think you must know. He is a nephew of the late Mr Justice Buller, and a first cousin to that Mr Buller who married Miss York, the bishop's daughter who died lately *(see note 24, page 105)*. He is a young man about 20, and extremely good-natured. He wished so much to call on you that Polly has given him letters, which I also hoped to have done. You will probably have this before you see him, as the king's ships are not so hasty in their movements. He is very good-natured, or else we would not have sent him to you as I am very cautious, lest I should give you troubles in your business. I have sent by him a small sized Palampore for Nancy James. It will be large enough for their beds; and also a piece of book muslin which is the manufacture of this country. I sent also, with the Palampore, one of about two yards size for your son if, please God, he lives. It is as coarse as straw, but is painted with fine lions in the style of the country: eyes and teeth in perfection. I think you will laugh when you see it. I have also sent a piece of chintz to line it with, with pretty Lori birds all over it, for such he may admire. These pieces of chintz are made no longer, being painted on purpose for one petticoat only in each piece. Polly had a present of a pair of shawl stockings for my mother, to which I have added a pair of shawl gloves. I had no chance to send to you these by Mr Barrol, not much liking to trust anything with one so wild. He dined with us twice: I daresay he will see you and tell you what passed. He behaved, I thought, more quietly than formerly, but said he was very anxious to get some appointment to come out again. I told you, I believe, I had a letter from poor Edwards, since which I hear that he died on his journey to Madras. Whether he was robbed or not by his servants, I know not, as he died at a great distance from here, but it appears that he was very ill-provided for and had scarcely any necessaries. It is said that he was not well off, and had very scanty provisions. I am very sorry for his wife, but it was a dreadful thing to send the poor man into this country. The surgeons, when first coming out, are particularly exposed to unhealthy places.

I have not written to Lizzie Thoburn, which I intended to have done, though she does not deserve it, but I have wrote a long letter to G. Samuel. We send by Mr Templar a jar of preserved nutmegs for you, and two jars of ginger done at home, but I'm not sure you will ever have them, for the jars were all upset in the surf of the sea, and some broken I understand. With these jars I sent some for Mr Templar's use, two pots with trees for Mr Whitley, and some seeds, but I find the pots were broken and I fear the trees destroyed, and the seawater has probably spoiled the seeds. Mr Templar promised me he would try at the Cape to get some seeds, and would add them to those I sent, which were but few. All these things were to go on board an hour or two before Mr Templar set out himself. One of the poor Hindu men, who are the greatest cowards in the world, had a great fancy to go with these things. Not one in a thousand has ever been in a boat, nor had he, but he longed to see a ship. He would not sit in the boat, but on the edge and, as soon as a great breaker came, it washed the poor man out of the boat and made all this distress. The worst of the matter is that it washed away Mr Templar's sword, which he had given him to carry; a Persian blade; part of his trophies from Egypt.

I am very sorry to hear of Mrs Thomas James's illness *(relative of Hetty's husband)*. I hope she will recover. I have heard of the death of so many I have known of about that age lately, that it makes me quite low. I had almost forgotten to tell you that Mr Templar took a piece of Bengal worked muslin, which you are to give to Nancy Green for a gown, with my love. Lord Clive has sent me 10 yards of the finest flannel from his estate near Welshpool. I shall do very well without my parcel therefore. I hear the Skelton Castle will go to Bengal before it comes here: by that ship I may expect my things.

I desired Richard Clarke to write his father a letter by way of giving him a taste of the outlandish words we use here, and I believe I must give you one, for I find myself writing them frequently. Tope for grove; tank for a pool; a Master for a pattern of anything; a cot for a bed; a godown for a kitchen etc etc. The beauty of this fantasticalness is that the words belong to no language used here. The natives say they are English words. I believe they are corruptions from various languages, but they are always used. Some are diverting; as this is a dirty letter and only to be seen by you, I may tell you. A chit for a letter; and as the natives constantly sound ch- like sh- it is a vast amusement to Mr Gwillim to hear the Butler say 'Madam: please to give chit - I want Mrs's chit - I can't leave without Master's chit - Sir, please to make chit'. Some pronounce words oddly enough: a bad woman they call a beach woman, because they wait about the sea beach, and this they call bich; and young they call hang: one hang gentleman talking to one bich woman. The Portuguese are the great writers of English for them, and they write papers and petitions to Mr Gwillim and, on various occasions, they pick up all the hard words they can string together from some old romances or novels, thus their papers are perfectly diverting, because in the midst of the grandeur are some words of the very lowest kind. They sent a paper the other day describing a man who had destroyed himself and, meaning to say amazement, they said they broke into his room and found him hanging to their very great amusement. I sent you a curious paper, copied by my man, saying it is an account of two great ladies who burned themselves, with their husband, last March.

This is an idle scrawl and I must send it off to Mr Gwillim, who has gone to the Fort to see if he can get any opportunity of sending the things on board to Captain Marsh.

From Mary Symonds 18th October 1802

Betsy has told you about the fate of the things for us which you put on board the Skelton Castle, but we think it better that it should be mentioned in both letters, and therefore I have opened mine to put in this slip of paper. Captain Pitman says he had them on board, but they were sent without an order from the Directors *(Court of Directors of the East India Company)*, and therefore he was obliged to put the things on shore again by an order from them. At first he said he had written to give notice of their being landed, to the gentleman who put them on board, but afterwards he said he believed he had written, and was not sure. The Captain of the Ameriques, which has arrived since, says he saw the cases in a warehouse at Gravesend. Should you ever recover them, and they are not spoiled, you may send them yet as fashion is of much less consequence here than with you. In your letters, you allude to some things they contain, and we are very much obliged to you for the trouble you took in procuring them, particularly the jam. We have received your letters by the Eliza, one dated September 4th, by which we have the satisfaction to hear that you have been very fortunate in recovering the things we sent to you, but I shall answer your letters more fully by the next ship. At present we have very little time, as she is to sail tonight and we send the letters 9 miles to the post. I have written to Mr Clarke, and John Gwillim, and their letters are enclosed for you to seal and send. I doubt they will not afford you any amusement in reading them, but I leave you to judge for yourself, or to be determined by your available leisure. All I can say to my friends is, if they wish to hear from me and will take the trouble to say so, I am quite ready to write letters enough, such as they are, for I have no pleasure equal to writing to my good friends, except reading their answers. Indeed, you are our best friend in that way, and I know not what I should do without your salutary epistles.

We were all at a grand ball last night which was given by Mr Oakes. He is a great man here, being the President of the Board of Revenue: he is a fine old fellow and a great beau of mine!!! The Lord love him.

Christmas, in many respects, is kept in Madras as May Day is kept in England. The temperature of the air, and the fresh verdure of the grass and trees after the rains, together with the flowers which abound in this season, enables them to do this. Indeed the whole country appears extremely like England in a fine warm May, but with the advantage that they have many ripe fruits. The houses of the Europeans are built in the style of Italian villas. The entrance, if the house consists of more than a ground floor, is a sort of piazza with an open gallery over it with columns and, if on one floor, it is sometimes a Piazza and sometimes a portico with columns or, as all these open apartments are called here, a veranda. At daybreak the arches of the piazza are dressed up by the servants. A plantain tree is set on each side of every arch (or opening, if it be a colonnade): these trees are stripped of the lower leaves and each forms a white ivory-looking column like a very large elephants tooth *(tusk)*. It may be about 7 or 8 feet high and, so far, it runs straight. Here therefore, very much resembling a capital, are fastened on large bunches of the plantain fruit; above these the long leaves, springing out, bend over and, meeting each other at the keystone of the arch, are then bound together with strings and bunches of flowers. These columns are then bound round with narrow wreaths of flowers, of which they provide at least 100 yards, and the tops of the arches are filled up with them by hanging them in festoons, crossing each other in various ways, so as to produce an agreeable open blaze of lines. The floors of the verandas and halls are strewed with flowers and small leaves, so as to make almost a carpet. During breakfast time the servants of the family, their children, and all people who are employed about the house, come in with presents of fruit and flowers. Everyone brings something, however small, but flowers always make a part, if not the whole. They never gather flowers, as we do, with stalks and leaves but completely take off all the green, for they esteem nothing but that which smells finely. Their nosegays are therefore very stiff and formal, being the heads of the flowers bound upon sticks in various fancies, like the flower pots made of wax or paper and cried about the streets in London. However, they often produce very rich effects, sometimes by contrasting colours and sometimes by disposing of rich tints into the softest gradations. A nosegay for each person of the family, with a lime or an orange or two, is a present from a menial servant. Those of the higher orders bring wreaths of flowers to wear round the neck with shaddock or plantain fruit. The Nabob sends us a letter of congratulation on the return of the season, and a large present of the finest fruit with wreaths of flowers. A relation of his also sent us a variety of fruit, with long wreaths for the neck according to the common way, which are about 2 yards long, and short ones of a purple flower like violets. These flowers were threaded (as they all are for the person) by a needle and thread, like beads, but pressed close together; and these purple ones are particularly beautiful. For the top of the flower is of a strong rich purple, and the under part has a pinkish or lilac tint, and the flowers being all threaded one way, as the garland is turned about it looks changeable, like a dove's neck. To relieve the purple, at distances were put in two or three white flowers, and a kind of tassel of the same white flowers was fixed by way of a solitaire. Each garland has a pair of bracelets to match. The carriage horses have their heads dressed with garlands, as those of state carriages are with ribbons. The coachman is adorned, the palanquin boys put flowers round their necks, and they twist the wreaths in their turbans with so much taste that I do not at all exaggerate when I say our best milliners would be improved by seeing them. For four or five days after Christmas Day, a set of people who call themselves Portuguese or Christians go about in the manner of the Morris dancers in England. In the note relative to the painted window represented in Johnson's Sheakspeare,[29] it is said that the hobby horse was frequently forgotten in the Morris dance.

It does not appear to be introduced in the Morris dancers here, but the Caffree, or Moorish king, riding his hobby horse with his horse-keeper, hookah bedar and grasscutter, form a party who go about separately. All people who ride in this country have a man to run by the side of the horse called the horsekeeper, and the great Moorish princes have, besides this, a

29 Samuel Johnson edited Shakespeare's plays, and they were published in 1765.

grass cutter to go with them, for the horses are here all fed by grass cut by women. Also a hookah bedar, that is a man who keeps his hookah lighted and runs behind him with it. When the great prince wants a whiff of his tobacco, this bedar kneels down and holds it whilst he smokes through the long leather worm. This farce therefore represents a Moorish king riding out in state. He is attended by pipers and tabourers *(drummers)*, who play whilst the others dance and, in dancing, offer grass to the horse and the pipe to the King, whose horse is meanwhile kicking and prancing to the tune. The machinery is so well contrived that, at first, I really thought it was a small horse, at a distance, for the Moor men frequently ride little ones. They are then almost as much covered by the trappings and the profusion of draperies, of various colours, which the Moor men themselves delight in wearing. The contrivance referred to is a large hoop, covered with trappings, into which the man gets and, tying it round his waist, he spreads his long robes over it. The neck of the horse is made with springs, so that the man pushes it up and down to represent a spirited horse. The head is well carved, painted white with red marks, probably intended as crosses. They are adorned with flowers, both man and horse, and a great deal of rich silk and linen draperies. The Morris dance is a distinct sport and, besides pipers and tabourers, consists of eleven persons, and is like a tolerable burlesque dance at the play house. There are three principal dancers, the King and, as they translate it to us, his two secretaries. These people are very richly dressed, particularly the King. It is a curious mixture of Christianity and paganism, for the King wears a crown, like the Spanish, very large and rich and all of gold, and with a large gold cross on the top of it. His hair is puffed out in great abundance under it, and he wears robes of various colours over each other, so contrived that you see them all when dancing. His upper robe is of purple gauze fringed with gold, and he has a sceptre in his hand.

Letters of 1803 and Commentary

Commentary

Once again, the first surviving letters date from February. One is just beginning to detect in Mary a hint of stress from the existing social balance. She refers to the tedium of repeated dinners and balls, especially meeting the same people constantly, and the tension this causes within the community. She notes also the extravagance and ostentation, which often cannot be afforded. In this first letter there is also the interesting reference to confrontation between the civil administration in Madras and the judiciary, as referred to in the Introduction and detailed in the final chapter and which would become a continuing problem.

At this stage there is the first description, by Mary, of Elizabeth's approach to ornithological painting, and how this was often from life, the bird being held and cared for by an ancient retainer who clearly had a skilful way with them. The garden is also full of birds of various sizes, temperaments and strangeness. Depicting them is clearly her passion, and her goal. Both women regularly write home for supplies of pigments, paper and even brushes, having found the Chinese ones mostly unsatisfactory.

There appears at this stage an entertaining interlude where Mary is trying to find out about the credentials of a young army officer by asking her sister Hetty to research his brother in London. One must presume he is a potential suitor and she, being suspicious of his worthiness, is probing for faults. She justifies her suspicions by pointing out the dissimulation by so many of the community in Madras, where people of apparent quality have shady backgrounds, or are unqualified for their position; even the existence of unordained priests. Her exclusive position in that society encourages her deprecatory tendencies, and almost immediately she lets fly at the young and single British women who are there in the hope of catching a worthwhile man, and who are described as shallow, acquisitive and uninterested in everything else. They are of course in sharp contrast to the Symonds sisters themselves, and undoubtedly to others in the community, and yet the temptation for a girl to pursue a husband so actively can only have derived from the oppressed existence they were expected to live, with complete dependency on the male sex for future support.

Elizabeth wrote more or less simultaneously, but in a rather different style. She first commiserates with Hetty James, her sister, on the loss of a child. In all probability this was a newborn, as we know that Thomas, although sickly, was born in 1801 and being written about in 1803, and Mary was yet to be born, arriving on the scene in 1804. Typically her style is to concentrate on detail, rather than make airy statements like her sister Mary, and much of her correspondence in this year reflects the need for items of food and clothing, and especially hats, to replace those that were running short, wearing out, or out of fashion. This subject is repeated at regular intervals throughout the correspondence over the six years of their stay in India. On one occasion, the surprising request for a fender and fire irons was made, which might seem superfluous to many who know Madras and its climate. In March of the previous year she had asked for additional items of Wedgwood china, being rather proud of her already large collection, which was almost the only one in all Madras. It arrived almost a year and a half later in August 1803. There is an enjoyable reference to the delights of receiving and tasting potted strawberries, and how this reminds them both so much of home. More fascinatingly, Elizabeth notes how some of the young English men who had come out as boys, probably as Company writers at the age of sixteen, had never before tasted such a fruit. Otherwise there is the ongoing business of sending presents home, particularly the much-coveted shawls. She continues to confess her desire to involve herself in a multitude of projects, her mind clearly running ahead of her actions.

Elizabeth being the older, married, sister reports back to her mother on Mary's love life or, more particularly, the situation with respect to the train of suitors that are presenting themselves. There is mention, in a later letter, of an army captain who one must imagine is the individual that Mary herself was earlier researching, via her sister at home.

In a letter of August of that year, there is an interesting single sentence comment from Elizabeth to Hetty which reveals, or emphasizes, her husband's irascibility, a character trait which must have influenced his developing relationship with the governing echelons of the Madras community. 'Mr Gwillim is sometimes full strong in anger and I think not a little ill-natured.'

Another interesting point of discussion reveals the disorderly arrangements by which passage on a ship to India were made. The captain had complete power over price, and storage of goods, and there was obviously every opportunity for deception, and extraction of larger prices than anticipated or quoted. It seems that the Gwillims were subjected to this, although the captain may not have chosen his victim wisely on that occasion.

In September, shipping was coming and going, as were boxes of goods and packets of letters, but by then they had learnt that war with France had flared up again, Napoleon having prepared for an invasion of Britain earlier in the year. From the top of the house in St Thomé the sisters' young friend Richard Clarke, one of Sir Henry's court registrars, could use a telescope to spot shipping arriving to his front, and read the signals from the fort to his left, excitedly chattering to the ladies below in anticipation of the arrival of letters, which will nevertheless take another two days to reach them. This passage in the letters somehow emphasizes the isolation the two women must have felt from all that was home and England. The coming and going of shipping, and the letters they may contain, was the only thread that bound them to home and family. It is no surprise, therefore, that the advent of war caused anxiety about its effect on the transfer of correspondence; even its loss. In that same month there arrived in one of these ships the new Governor of Madras, Sir William Bentinck, and his wife.

That month there is an interesting description of a farewell ball given for the outgoing Governor, Lord Clive. Although the effect a major electrical storm had on the proceedings is entertaining, particularly apposite is the knowledge that the party-giver, a Mr Cochrane, had given another ball the same week for a niece who was about to be married. The expense implicit in those two events is inconceivably massive; something like tens of thousands of pounds in the money of that time. This underlines the enormous wealth accumulated by some individuals in those days, mostly from private trade. This may have been a Basil Cochrane who had earlier been military paymaster to

Lord Clive, and more recently his assistant.[1] This latter position may have carried some responsibility, if Elizabeth Gwillim's assessment of Clive in October 1803 is correct, in that he was a man more interested in gardening and animal husbandry than administration *(see note 3 to 1802, page 43)*. Having made these statements, she immediately launches in the same letter into a wondrous, but completely unconnected, description of traditional Indian medicine. This is inevitably fascinating, but the most striking description, and one which has such logic and simplicity, is the setting of fractured limbs with potter's clay, much as one might with plaster of Paris.

There follows a brief, but entertaining, account of the problems faced by men with a multiplicity of wives, as was then the case with the Moorish, or Islamic, people. She takes the opportunity of briefly touching on the subject of keeping troublesome British husbands in order.

Drawing and painting continues steadily, and Elizabeth is complimentary about her sister Mary's portrayals of Indian people in their own surroundings. She then moves on to a description of her own specialty, Indian birds. She summarises virtually all the birds she has painted, describing each in turn as much in terms of its behaviour as its appearance. She is obviously particularly fond of the Brahminy Kite, and altogether readily reveals her ornithological abilities.

It is October, and the letters of 1803 are about to cease.

Letters

From Mary Symonds to her sister Hetty 7th February 1803

We have received by the Skelton Castle, which arrived here on the 23rd January, Mr James's letter containing a mixture of good and ill news. I must own that from the earliest accounts I received from my mother

1 Basil Cochrane 1753–1826 was a successful, devious and seemingly uncompromisingly acquisitive Scots supply contractor, and administrator, who accumulated great wealth in Madras. See Wikipedia.

and you of the dear little boy, I never flattered myself with the hope of seeing him. He was too delicate from the first. Let us not unreasonably lament the loss of such dear little creatures, since the most fortunate of human beings must acknowledge that he who dies early escapes from more sorrow than all the pleasures this world can bestow, and would reward him for enduring.

We received at the same time two very pleasant letters from Lizzie and Mary Thoburn, and a basket of seeds from Regi. He has been at his old wag's tricks and lettered all the bags of flower seeds with an imitation of Chinese characters. In return for his kindness I have written him a letter in what we call black English, that is precisely as the servants and all the natives speak. I think he will have a little trouble making it out.

What in the world put it into your noddle that Mr Thos. Gwillim was made a Post Captain. Sir Henry received a letter from his father with a very different account of him, and this puts me in mind to give you another wigging. You have had a smart poke at me for not dating my letters in your last one, and that very letter you date, incorrectly, May 16 1801. Now I have you, Mrs Saucy Lass.

I hope you will have seen my friend Mr Templar long before you see this. I wish much to hear of his arrival, and his fellow passengers the Rudgeons. If the climate of England does not alter him you will find him a most agreeable acquaintance, but young men sometimes get their heads turned with too much attention, particularly coming from this country where all favours are conferred by the ladies. I beg you will be particular in telling me how he behaves to you; you will see what familiar terms we were on here by the ridiculous stuff I wrote by him. The last fortnight he was with us was all spent in romps and play. To be sure I ought to have been better employed in writing long epistles to my friends at home, and collecting things for their amusement, but as such a friend as Templar will not often be met with, nor so much mirth be likely to be repeated, I do not much regret it, for the gaiety and show of India *(British India)*, which one hears of so much in England, have very little variety in them. The amusement always consists of a great dinner at eight o'clock and a great ball in the evening. At these one always meets the same set of people who do not care one farthing for each other, and the one half of them are wishing each other hanged. One hears the same scandal of all, and in general one sees the same fine clothes, and there are some ladies on whom you would think it snowed pearls, and rained diamonds, yet when you learn their secret history you find their husbands are over their heads and ears in debt, and that they have half a dozen children at home *(England)* whom they chose to be separated from, and to leave unprovided for, rather than to abate of some ostentatious extravagance which all their acquaintances know they cannot afford, and therefore condemn them for indulging themselves in. What folly is this.

There has been a fine hue and cry this last three months. Some of the foolish people about the government chose to oppose the authority of the judges by military force, but they have brought fear upon their marrow bones, and I believe no such attempt will ever be made here again. It has however cost poor Sir Henry, and Sir Thomas Strange, a great deal of anxiety and fatigue, but nothing can be more complete than their victory. We are all on tiptoe in expectation of a new Governor.

The present Lord Clive is a very good-natured man but in the affairs of the government he is a mere child and knows no more what he is doing than I do. He is extremely fond of gardening, and the natives, who have a good sense of humour, call him Gardener Maistrie, just as the people at home call the king Farmer George. Mr James made a great mistake in the time of celebrating Sir Henry's birthday, but that is no matter, he may keep it right next time. It is the 3rd of July, but all days are equally proper for a good jollification, and the kind intention is everything on these occasions.

Poor Betsy is never out of trouble, for if she gets dead subjects to draw from they become offensive before she can finish the work to her mind, and when the birds are brought in alive they stare, or kick, or peck, or do some vile trick or other that frightens her out of her wits. Sometimes she thinks the birds look sick, that is whenever they stand quiet, and then in a great fit of tenderness she lets them fly before they are finished with, lest their sufferings should be revenged upon her, or their ghosts should come flying round her and, flapping their great wings, scare her to death. These are serious troubles I assure you, but we do all we can to remedy such evils, and have now got a venerable looking old Moor man who catches a bird at a time. He holds them in proper attitudes and feeds these miserable captives in a proper manner, for her poor conscience's sake. Now you will think all must be right, and the drawing going on bravely, but it is no such thing for when she is prepared, and the drawing implements are all arranged, this wicked servant and his kind are wishing they are perhaps retired to some distant nook to smoke a pipe, or drink a little arrack together. For my part I think this world is quite full of trouble!!

We have a large old kite, who was caught last night and is kept in swaddling clothes. The old man has a curious method of securing their wings, and their claws. He takes a round piece of cloth and makes a hole in the middle of it, big enough to thrust the bird's head through, and then gathers the edges of this garment together round the bottom of the bird's body and ties them close with a string. Besides this we have six or eight large cranes, and storks, fastened by their legs in different parts of the garden. These great long-legged things are three or four feet high. They eat fish and frogs by hundreds. The bird catchers always bring them blindfolded. Then there is a cock and hen pheasant of a curious kind, who occasion much sorrow and trouble by their disorderly behaviour, for basically the cock pecks his wife and uses her so ill that Betsy has at last been obliged to have articles of separation drawn, and each has now a house or establishment to himself. But this is nothing, we have blue pigeons and green pigeons, partridges of different sorts, two quails, a great cassowary and draped skins of birds in all corners of the house, but I suppose you will see all their pictures in time if we have the good fortune we hope for, as I assure you that is her principal motive for taking all this pain to collect them. I sincerely hope she will have the health to go on with this kind of amusement, as such an employment will make the time we are absent from you seem much shorter. But as I am about it, I think I ought to mention the rest of our house stock. I believe I told you of our dog, Tipu, who is an exact resemblance of him *(Tipu Sultan)*. I have now another, which was given me quite young by General Trent, and have taken great pains to keep it. Indeed, it promised to be very pretty, and they told me it would not grow very large so in compliment to Mr Templar, when he went away I called its name Tyger but, I suppose owing to too much care in feeding him, he is grown so large, so prodigiously ugly and rough, that he ought more properly to be called Bear. However, all the servants are supremely fond of him and say he is good company, and we have no cats. They are very scarce, of no use, and very ugly. We have two bullocks, which are very useful as they carry heavy burdens to and from the fort, and bring manure for the garden and do abundance of business. We have four fine cows in our stock, which a gentleman has been so good to send Sir Henry from the Northward, and as they are all in the family way we may expect an increase of calves heads and, if it please God to send me an increase of brains, you will not think it amiss. I am just told that the packet will close tonight and therefore must close this, and I fear if this is really the case I shall not be able to write to any other friends, though I wish it very much. However, I hope soon to be able to take up the pen again, as several ships are expected round from Bengal, but they are particularly late this season.

Remember me a thousand times to every kind friend, except George Samuel and John Gwillim. They are two scrubby fellows who never take any notice of us. I beg my kind love to Mr James, and Ned, and Mr Thos. James, and I commission you to give them twenty kisses each at convenient opportunities. You may say anything you please to Mr George Samuel, but pray let his reward be proportional to his commitment. If he has written to us, say a great many pretty words to him and you may add a kiss if you have no objection but, if he has not written, scold him well and give him a thump on the sconce, for Betsy wrote him a long letter and I wrote him an absurd prim quizzy one. But that was the first, he shall have a better next time. Betsy sits opposite me drawing, and the old man is employed to turn about in proper attitudes an extraordinary kind of animal which was killed yesterday in Dr Anderson's garden. Our noses are terribly regaled by the scent of it, but it is very curious, so we must have its picture. Tis something like a dog, and something like a cat, and something like a mouse. It has beautiful black fur and a long tail. Half a dozen doctors have been consulted, and five hundred books hunted over, but no one can discover the name of this wonderful brute!! But everyone rejoices in his downfall, as he is known by the natives to be a sad devourer of local nuts and other fruit. I shall sit scribbling on till it is too late to send my letters, if I do any more, so God bless you all, and grant you health and happiness that we may one day meet together and talk over all these matters round a cheerful fire

Postscript. As the Wellesley did not sail as soon as was expected, I availed myself of the opportunity to add a few more lines of scribble. Notwithstanding the disastrous fate of the things you intended us to receive by the Skelton Castle, I hope you will not be disheartened from sending us a few things at convenient opportunities; a few articles of millinery, some trinkets which are not very valuable, a few gloves and, above all things, some shoes, but not white ones. You will be so good as to send some white ribbons of different widths, each time, as it is very much esteemed here but will not keep. I shall be obliged to you to send one or two cakes of Reeve's Carmine, one of Gaul stone, and a few brushes. We cannot get any brushes here that are useable. G. Samuel thought that we should find the Chinese brushes and colours useful, and therefore we sent for some but they are quite useless. One or two straw and chip brushes will be very acceptable. They will work inside each other, and take little room. I am wretchedly in want of a pair of earrings. I am very much obliged by a request you made me to send you my picture, but there has not been any artist who painted miniatures for a long time, and when any one comes, though he be thought but a bungler at home, he expects an immense price. Therefore, I believe I must beg you to wait till I am clever enough to do it myself. To be sure it is not easy to know oneself in any respect, but in general our own representations are as good as any that are made of us. At my age I cannot be expected to improve in my looks, nor do I think myself one bit handsomer for a great many very fine crow's feet which are added to my face since I left you.

A Captain Ashton has lately become very intimate with us. He introduced himself to Sir Henry as having known that part of his family who settled in Lancashire. I believe he is from that county, or Cheshire. He says he has a brother who lives, I think, in Wood Street and is something in the house of Vines and Co in Cheapside. I wish you or James would make a point of finding out what he is, and get acquainted with him if you can. His name is Arthur Ashton, and I wish very particularly to know all you can possibly find out about his commissions. His brother's name is Richard. He is a Captain in His Majesty's 12th Regiment. I suspect he has been a great pickle but perhaps, if you get acquainted with the one in London, you may find out the whole history of this one. I beg you will not neglect this request, and let me know something about him by the first opportunity. In this place one's acquaintances consist of God knows who. There are some very fine folks who talk very magnificently, and hold their heads vastly high yet, those who have been in England and made a point of enquiring, tell such curious histories that you would be much surprised to hear them. Some of the great men have been strolling players, and some have run away from their creditors and some, I believe, have run away from something worse. Here have been parsons who were never ordained, and some of the barristers came out common soldiers, and these are the sort of people who give themselves the greatest airs, and puff most about their families. One of the ladies who is at the head of this society is the daughter of a tailor, another, who gives herself the greatest airs in the place, came forth from a gin shop and, I do assure you, their manners are not at all superior to their former state.[2] You mention Mr Livingstone's brother. We did not even know he had a brother. Pray, what is he? Mr L. was only introduced to us by a letter from one of our ship mates, of whose history we know no more than his, only he appears to be one of the best creatures in the world. His name is Dove, a Scotchman and a surgeon on this establishment. He was particularly kind to Betsy during our voyage, and she has continued to correspond with him ever since. His letters are extremely entertaining, giving an account of all the countries *(local)* through which he has passed. He has been chiefly in Mysore country. Betsy preserves his letters with an intention of sending them home some time or other, as they will afford some amusement to you and my mother, and give you quite a history of the places you see through them. I only intended to add half a sheet to my letter, but one thing seems to spring out of another and I could go on for ever, just as if I was chatting with you, only I feel rather depressed when I consider how long it will be before I hear your answers to my wise prose. I have been very busy drawing some more fine figures as I sent you by Templar, but this set is for Sir Thos. Strange and he has requested me make him some little sketches from a book which

2 India was a land of opportunity for many. Equally, for many it was a refuge.

was translated by Sir William Jones.[3] He is going to send it home as a present for his sister-in-law, and so I have had the presumption to undertake it. I had made some, which he saw and admired so much that he begged them. Sometime or other I shall send you something of the same kind. Indeed, I give away all my things as fast as I do them. When I am improved a little I shall send G. Samuel something, but I am quite moved at myself for not being able to do skies and backgrounds, and it is very hard work to find things out without any instruction.

The girls who are educated for this country either learn very little or, when they come here, they think of nothing but husbands, for none of them do anything worth looking at or are capable of giving one the smallest assistance. I do not see anything they do well except dancing and making watch ribbons for the young men, who give them pearls and diamonds in return and many of them have no more decency than to accept of them. I have seen a girl here, whom I have been very slightly acquainted with, sit down and tell me that a string of pearls and a diamond locket she had on was given her by one man who made love to her, her diamond brooch by another, her bracelets by a third, one emerald ring by a fourth, and a diamond ring by a fifth and so on as far as a nine or ten. I know that some of the young men who gave them to her are nearly ruined by extravagance, and have spoken with regret of the sums they have expended upon this girl. This method of making the most of themselves occupies most of their attention, but this attitude don't look quite so genteel to old-fashioned eyes as to those who have had a proper education for the situation they fill.

I suppose that Mr Temple *(father of Sir Henry's registrar)* calls upon you pretty often as he always mentions you in his letters to his son. I assure you Temple is a very fine young man and I really believe as good as possible. Here are very many who have not been so well educated, or have in any respect such proper notions. I hope he will get on in his profession, and be a comfort to his father who is as honest and good a man as ever breathed. Richard Clarke has not yet received any letter from his father. You would be very much surprised to see Richard. I do not think you would know

3 Celebrated former judge in Calcutta, linguist, orientalist, polymath and founder of the Asiatic Society.

him at all, he is grown such a tall, stout young man, but his face does not look fat in proportion to his body and limbs, but that is owing to his fine long chin. The servants all call him Chinner Darah *(cinna means little in Telugu)* which signifies little master, or young master, but we think the name, as it sounds, very appropriate.

Our gardens are at this time in perfection for vegetables. We have every day an abundance of green peas, french beans, young potatoes, very fine salads, carrots, turnips and several sorts of greens. All this you will think very fine whilst you are choking over a dirty coal fire and glad to put up with a good pease pudding, or a dish of mealy potatoes, but our sorrows come on as yours go off and, in May and June, when you are refreshed by rosy bounteous flowers, and fine temperate weather, we are scorched up with a burning land wind and have scarcely a blade of grass left in exposed situations. It is in June we have fine fruits to relieve us, and the trees are always green, but most people have their skins not only scorched, but covered with that skin tingling disorder the prickly heat, and great boils. I think myself the luckiest creature in the world never to have felt any of these teasing complaints, and I am quite singular in not having had had any fever or any disorder whatever, by way of succumbing to the climate. I am however very thankful for any good fortune and am not so presumptuous as to expect to escape for ever. There are some instances of persons who have come here with very good constitutions, and have taken good care of themselves, who have lived here to an old age without a day's illness.

How are all the young ones, and is any increase expected? I suppose you have soldered up all this kind of news in the tin case. Once more, God bless you all and goodbye for this time.

From Elizabeth Gwillim to her sister Hetty 7th February 1803

I understand a ship is to sail in a few days from this place, and I shall not lose the opportunity of acknowledging the receipt of a letter from Mr James to Mr Gwillim which came by the Skelton Castle. The unhappy news it contained of the loss of the dear child, of whose engaging ways I had just before read so much, lowered my spirits very much. I never would allow myself to dwell too much on my expectations and indeed, for fear of what might happen, I have forborne to speak on the subject in my letters to you.[4] So much so, that I was almost afraid you would imagine you and he were not in my thoughts but, when a distress of this kind has happened, whatever has been written in the joy of the heart, is read with great pain. I shall dwell no longer on this painful subject but hope to hear a good account of your health, and James's. Besides Mr James's letter we had a most pleasing letter from Mr Gwillim *(Sir Henry's father)* by which it appears that he is well, and Mrs Gwillim better. I pray constantly for the preservation of the old people through the sharp winters and, what is worse, through the severely cold summers that I hear of you having. I have had a basket of seeds from Mr Whitley, which appear to be very good. They are sown in all ways and places. I shall write particulars to Lizzy, but I mention this as it is possible I may not have time to write by this ship to them. I have been frequently disappointed by the ship's sailing in a hurry. The moment the government dispatches are put on board they hurry them off. I hope you will not grieve yourself about our disappointment in not having our things by the Skelton Castle. I conclude they will be safe and that they will come soon. We sent to Captain Harrow for them and he answered that they had been put on board his ship but that the directors had ordered these, and other packets sent without a regular order, to be unshipped. This is a new regulation, amongst many others lately made, which it would seem is hardly worth their while to make. They have increased the difficulty of sending things so much by pinching part of everybody's former allowance of room, and in other ways. I fear

4 In St. Helen's Church, Bishopsgate, near where Hetty James and her husband Richard lived, is a plaque remembering their two children Richard, died 1800 age one year nine months, and Thomas died 12th June 1801 aged one year and one month. This Thomas will have died whilst the sisters were at sea a month before landfall in July 1801 and it is inconceivable that Hetty would not have mentioned it in one of her letters written in 1801 or 1802. It cannot have been the Tom James, referred to throughout the letters including those subsequent to this one, particularly that in February 1806 referring to his education, a nephew, and son of Ned James, close relative of Richard's. Furthermore there are baptismal records of another Tom James from Bishopsgate with parents Richard and Hester, baptised a day later, on the 13th June 1801. Perhaps it is this death referred to in the letter.

I shall not be able to have the trifles I want, unless I can get some arrangement made. The captains and mates of the ships make their money by the sale of the investments they bring out here, and therefore they do all in their power to discourage people from sending things out, so that they might feel obliged to buy from themselves. However, they shall find it difficult to stint me into compliance with the usual demands. It is now two years since we made our marketings, and I have only laid out one pagoda which was wantonly done for a flower, and besides I have not spent a sixpence in any European articles of dress. Neither can I be said to be in want. I should have been glad of a cap or hat, or two, because I do not like to give my time to make millinery, otherwise I have many materials remaining and could go on for a twelvemonth rather than pay 10 or 20 pagodas for a fright of a cap very little better than my own making. Indeed, a desire for variety and fashion is the chief foundation of wants of this kind, for the air here is so perfectly clear that nothing spoils that individual cap which I bought of Mr Toussaint to go to Court. I have in two years worn it a hundred times, changed a flower, and sometimes a feather, and both cap and plume are as clean at this moment as when I bought them. I have two straw hats never begun upon, but I know not how to trim them, and have not a bit of ribbon left. I have given all the world watch ribbons and shall now be begging. I have but two pairs of English shoes left and they must be treasured, for the country ones are poor things and lose their shape directly. I have still a great many gloves left but Polly has not, and they are very dear here. Mr G. has plenty, but he is hoping you or James have sent him some shoes, and a hat, as these articles are here dear and bad. Eleven pagodas for a cocked hat. I really believe Sir Thomas Strange's has been worn ever since he came here, and his round one is worse. Mr Gwillim's was a new one, but in the rainy season, in our first house, everything was damp and the poor hat was mouldy all over several times. In the dry season the spiders and ants took possession of it and some pouchies (as the black people call insects) have eat various holes in it. Some of the most conspicuous of these, the old tailor (whose picture you have) has sewn up with black thread. Such as it is, it is always worn on dress occasions. On common days he has a beaver-coloured one bought here about a year ago, the sea spray having spoiled the black one.

This much for eastern magnificence but, in other respects, Mr Gwillim is particularly neat, as he is never ragged and his linen particularly neat, but the washermen beat out the clothes so hard that rags are no disgrace here. The six winter months he wears the usual dress of the place except that his coat is generally black, an English cloth coat, and white waistcoat and breeches made of a cloth called izzerry, a sort of fine white nankeen, as white as snow. In summer he wears for dress, and in court, black coats of China taffaty *(taffeta)* and a coloured one of a very pretty China manufacture of silk and muslin in very small stripes. They are very pretty and look, when new, just like a silk coat for court. They soon get shabby but they cost only about three or four pagodas. In the mornings, and all day indeed at home, he wears white jackets of the same izzery. All men wear this dress in the hot season having it all clean every morning. Being so often beat upon stones and dried in a broiling son you may easily guess how soon they fringe out. I have tore up several of my Scotch muslin gowns, and they were just tinder.

We are at present in one of the sweetest houses you can fancy for a gentle country habitation. It is a house lent us by an Armenian at a place called the Mount; properly St Thomas' s Mount. The village of that name being near our house, this place is 6 miles from my home, and nine from the Fort. The road from the Fort to this place is said to be the most beautiful and interesting in India. The place is very charming and a great change, it being reckoned very cool at this time of year. About 3 miles before you come to this place it is a sort of forest scenery with roads wandering under the groups of trees in various directions all constantly filled with travellers and droves of cattle of various description. This place is such a place as one of the villages about London; perhaps Clapham Common is most like it. English soldiers in barracks with their musters evenings and mornings. There are about 40 or 50 villas in the Italian style, enclosed in gardens of most luxuriant foliage. The greater part of it is tolerably level, but yet the Mount itself is a hill of considerable height, though rising from the flat. About a mile further on, the mountains begin a country almost like Wales, except for the constant circumstance that the hills rise from a flat country. They are all like the Mount, but higher, composed of huge pieces of hard dark-coloured granite, as rough as any of the hills we see in Merionethshire. At the top of the Mount there is a chapel and some fine banyan trees, and amongst the rocks are several homes belonging to the padres. The Catholic religion is here in its glory. There is a broad staircase partly cut in the rock, and partly of granite, steps wide enough for six or eight to walk abreast, with seats on each side.[5] The view from the chapel is fine, but the fatigue of going up, or rather coming down, very great. However, all their processions pass and heathen, as well as Christians, go to see St Thomas carried out. They call him the God. I have the pleasure of hearing their bells which I like much. This place has altogether just the air of a beautiful English village, and we walk here a great deal. The soil is fine, and therefore I have sowed my seeds by Dr Anderson's orders. He has put some in his ground, as have many of the good gardeners. I have sent some to Lord Clive yesterday. Several of the flowers are come up though they have only been sown three days.

This is the first ship in a few days, and another goes shortly, and I imagine for some time we shall have opportunities of writing every week. I long to hear from you, and now look for the Devaynes, a Company ship, with great anxiety. May God bless and keep you all. I hope my next letters will bring me one from my mother written at your house. I am very anxious to hear how my poor little Tom James is.

From Elizabeth Gwillim to her sister Hetty 22nd February 1803

I have wrote you one letter, and now must again trouble you with another, but first let me wish you good luck and let me hope you will be well when you receive this. I will presume to hope no further. If any other good luck be added I trust I shall be grateful to God for it. At present we are all well, and thank God have been so all the cool season.

On the arrival of the Skelton Castle, we sent to Captain Pitman for our boxes according to Mr James description of them in his letter, which we received by that ship. In answer, Captain Pitman sent a note saying that he had had our boxes on board his ship, but that the Director had thought proper to order those, and some other small parcels, to be unshipped and sent to the India House, as they hadn't agreed an order for their shipping. He had given

5 This staircase is still in existence, and virtually unchanged.

timely notice of this to the gentleman who sent them, but he had to regret that his sailing orders had arrived before that above had been regularly arranged, and that he had only a basket of seeds for us. This note was dated by him Jan. 25th 1803. We had heard by chance that many packages had, by new regulations, been unshipped because they had been sent on board without an order. Many things will be spoiled, if the whole be not lost.

We had heard that such severe measures had been taken with respect to captains who had ventured to take some parcels, so that they were all too much intimidated to take any, and therefore things could not be sent until a packet went. From this I conjecture that Captain Pitman was either this captain spoken of or, that he being afraid, had them put on shore anywhere out of his ship, leaving them to chance, and probably only telling someone to give notice of the fact, who then never did so.

We have laboured to get what information is to be had about our boxes, but can obtain very little. Captain Pitman is so ill he cannot be seen and is unable to speak, and I think is very shy of the subject. The Captain of the Devaynes says he saw such boxes directed for us in a warehouse at Gravesend. I therefore cannot help thinking that Captain Pitman, seeing harsh measures used towards other captains, landed what he had in his fear at the first place he could get rid of them out of his ship. We cannot find that they are liable to be seized and should hope, if lost, Captain Pitman will be liable to pay for them, and for this reason I imagine he does not like to say much on the subject.[6]

6 **The shipping of goods**. Throughout the letters there are references to the difficulty of transporting goods to and from England. Anything imported from abroad was subject to duty and so smuggling goods ashore from arriving ships was common practice, although the 'smugglers' exacted a heavy fee. (See letter of 7th March 1804). The best policy was to have items and packages carried by an acquaintance who was going home, or who was a ship's officer, and surgeons were popular as they could conceal items in their medical chests. There was also a problem in taking goods out to India as the space available on board ship was decreed by the captain, and charges were made which were fairly arbitrary. There was competition from ships' officers who wanted space to take goods out to India, which they would then auction to make additional income. There were also East India Company regulations for outgoing as well as incoming goods that were tortuous, strict, and often changing, and the Gwillims' boxes fell foul of these.

I am also very happy to hear that you have had all the things so regularly from me, but am sorry you did keep Mrs Holland's shawl for yourself. The only reason we had for putting that aside for her was that she is in mourning, and that it had less show of colours. Yours is much the finest shawl, but hers is newer. Do not be surprised, but none of the white shawls are new, at least not one in hundreds. The Moormen, during their power in this country, engrossed the whole trade of shawls. Tippoo's palace was full of shawls, and were served out to the merchants as from a warehouse, and all such ones are worn by the great Moormen. When sold, they seldom part with the new ones. They wear a different pair, one on the waist or as a cloak, and one on the head, every day. At night it is folded up and perhaps does not come again until the next year. Some are so worn, or eaten with insects, that one seldom sees a white one without many defects. That shawl of yours, if quite new, would cost three times the finer of Mrs Holland's. Hers is not so fine. It is the fineness and thinness that are esteemed because such ones are light. I hope you will be able to send me some hats and caps, for my head is a great fright and I want handsome morning caps badly, but they must be trimmed ready. Handsome caps for breakfast, for dinner, for balls and one or two bonnets will last an age.

I write in a great hurry as the salute has fired and I fear the ship is going. *Additional note.* The pleasant part of the weather I have this year enjoyed exceedingly, not having had even a common cold. The house we lived in on the plain was damp, and surrounded with trees. Plantations too near the house are not good in this country. Nor have the servants been ill this year, as they were last, by reason of the different situation of the homes. Mr Gwillim has enjoyed the weather, and Polly never has had any illness. Her quiet way of sitting down is just calculated for this country. I am too much of a bustler for this hot climate, and often get reproached for it. However, I begin to grow a little more lazy, which is highly necessary, only the worst is I am but little the better for it, for the more at ease my limbs are the more my head is at work, and I am thinking of a thousand

---

Shipping permission had not been signed off in time for Captain Pitman to sail, and so he had to discharge them hastily.

things I want to do in this country, and have so many plans in my head, that like many other greater projects it ends in doing nothing.

I am very anxious to hear from you. Indeed, I hope somebody will put a letter once a fortnight into the India house for there are private ships, and various ways by which we shall get them if they are so sent. I long for a ship to bring me letters. The last ship was six months, a most annoying long time, and I have been so long without letters that I really tremble to open them. I have been again disappointed of my things but, from what I hear, I hope they will not be lost. I fear my sweetmeats will be rather ancient and it is a great amusement to Mr Gwillim to talk of our new fashions, which we have heard of so long and are not yet arrived. I made a great bustle to provide myself when I came out, and it was well I did, for I have never repented of anything I brought with me. We eat the last of the great Cheshire cheeses a few days ago and the last bit was better than the first. I wish I had two other such. I also wish I could get better opportunities of sending to you, but the regulations are so strict, or either so paltry, that one cannot send anything to please a friend. This is a very bad place for shawls. We can seldom get any square shawls, and all are dear, and frequently old compared to other places. If I could get opportunities to send them, I have some ready now. I have no heart to write to you until I hear more from you, which I hope you have provided for.

I close this in great haste as the ship is sailing directly.

From Elizabeth Gwillim to her mother. 7th May 1803.

Sir Henry has undertaken to write to poor little Tom, and therefore I address myself to you. I had the pleasure of your letter with his, and one from Mr Gwillim senior, and indeed the most charming packet I have had since I came into this country. Until now we thought ourselves almost forgotten. Thank God the good news the letters contained found us all very well. I will not dwell on the loss of the poor children for, distressing as their loss is, their lives are too uncertain to be depended on. I was extremely happy to see a letter from little Tom. I had been calculating his age and I flattered myself you would set him to write. I have the happiness to hear from everybody a very pleasing account of the mildness of his disposition, and his attention to his learning. I am sorry to hear that his health is at all impaired as, after all, that is most material to him. I have no doubt but he will learn very well if he have time and opportunity given him, which is as necessary as instruction. I hope now to hear from him by every opportunity. I am sorry it is not in my power to send from hence all I could wish. It is only by the favour of anyone that we can send things, and I have hitherto had many such things to send to various people who might think me negligent and, therefore, until we get an opportunity I hope you will not think we have forgotten you. Mr William Cann gave a letter to Mr Prosser and, as his ship was calling here, I have sent by him the half of a white shawl with a narrow border for you. The other half I have kept for myself. I have also met with a square shawl with green spots and sent it to Mrs Gwillim, as I know she always longed for one like Mrs Shepheard's. It is old, and not fine, but certainly if one can get them these are the best for England. I promised Mr Cann two waistcoats, but the gentleman would only carry one. I have therefore sent another, and one for Mr Gwillim senior.

I could never learn any particulars of the death of poor Mr Edwards. It was very improper to send to this hot country a man afflicted with insanity. He died many miles from this place. His effects were brought down here to be sold, and Mr Gwillim would have brought some little trinkets of hair to send to Mrs Edwards and gave orders for them to be purchased, but they were given to her by the creditors and I hope she has received them, though they must be a melancholy sight to her.

Mr Gwillim Senior desired us, in his last letter, to show what civilities we could to two of the Hathaways, who were in this country. They were not of this settlement, but of Bombay. I am sorry to say the letter was too late, though indeed I believe neither of them were in the habit of coming here. I did not know they were in the country, but about a fortnight before we had the English letters, Sir Henry had a letter from one of them, who was an officer in the artillery, saying that he found himself very ill and under the necessity of getting out to sea for his health, and that he was little able to bear the experience, but that his brother who had died somewhere in these districts had, he believed, left some property and he requested Sir Henry to enquire into the business. He answered the letter, but it did not arrive till the day after this young man had also died. Poor Mrs Hathaway has lost three sons in this country, but as the girls have died in England, and all of the same kind of decline, I should imagine it would not be by the climate. This young man I find is a great loss. He was remarkably studious and his death is attributed to his close application. He was one of the first Sanskrit scholars and understood also the Gentoo, Maratha and Canara languages. *(Note 11, Chapter 1801)*. From what I have heard, he was not worth much and, indeed, though probably he might have risen very high, he was too young to have acquired anything. His studies too must have been very expensive. What he had, he left to a black woman whom he kept, and by whom I fancy he had children. He had some Sanskrit books which were of considerable value, and many commissions were sent from Madras to purchase them, but they were sold to a Brahmin, a minister to a Rajah of that country, to the great regret of the English gentlemen, as they sold for 800 pagodas, that is between three and four hundred pounds.

Your daughter Mary is still Miss Symonds, and where she may be otherwise I cannot say. There have been several suitors, but they are not approved of. Sir Henry had orders to dismiss one in a great hurry, and he certainly was too much of an oddity, though certainly very droll and entertaining, besides a Colonel, and very rich. There is one that appears to be a very great favourite, and has been for this twelve month but, though his person and manners are more agreeable, I fancy the purse falls rather short. He is a Captain in the King's service and I believe in as good circumstances as any young man in the army can be. His father is a Lancashire copper miner and he has been chosen, without leaving his profession, for his knowledge of the process to work a copper mine, lately discovered by the Company. Should it succeed, he may become very rich, but the affair is at present unsettled. He appears to be a great favourite and, I think, a very tender-hearted man, and certainly very good-natured. He is certainly very much like Mr Thomas Gwillim, but smaller featured though quite as brown. I think him very handsome but here, as brown approaches to black, it is not a fashion to admire it. However, I believe he is thought handsome. He is but 28, which she seemed to object to, but I think the objection does not seem to stand. I shall let you know from time to time how it goes on. She is to manage the whole affair herself for I think she is old enough to judge, and I should not wish to interfere; indeed I see nothing to object to. The very wealthy matches made here are generally girls of 15 or 16, to men of 40 at the youngest, lately a 15 year old to a man of 54, and this does not seem to be approved of and, besides that, the lady is past the age to please these gentle youths.[7]

I was very sorry to hear of Mr Thomas Gwillim's illness, and also that he had not been promoted, which after such long service is very hard, when one sees young boys get on as they have done. I am rather surprised neither he nor John have written to their brother. As for Hodges, the account Mr Gwillim gives us of how he is going on is really shameful. He says the impediment in the boy's speech is worse, yet the father perseveres in making him a clergyman. It is very grievous to hear such an account.

Every sort of English vegetable grows here in perfection, except Windsor beans, cauliflowers and artichokes, and these grow in Bengal, but the natives do not understand the culture of our things and therefore it is only where the master of the house understands, and watches the garden, that things are good. We are but just beginning to understand it. I have a vast array of fine cabbages, but they are not yet fit to cut. They grow short and close, and so fine, and bloom upon the leaf that they cook quite comfortably. Indeed, we have so many screeching birds to pick up every grub and fly that our vegetables have never a bitten leaf. We have no trouble with washing off insects. I forgot to tell Hetty to send me bags of herbs from Covent Garden, constantly. Mint grows here well, and so does sage, but it is not exactly like ours, but thyme and marjoram I have not tasted since I came here. I will beg of her therefore always to put me up a small bag of both, and a little parsley and basil. I like the lemon thyme best, but both are good.

It is odd enough to write to you about what I want Hetty to do, but I should be glad if she would get made for me a very small pair of tongs and a fender, and indeed a poker and shovel would be as well, if they were smaller. The fender must be brass, and so must the tops of the tongs, for nothing of steel will keep here in the sea breeze. The fender must be 3′5″ long, a little bowing out, and a little sloped out, as the chimney is in a circular part of

7 See Introduction. The age of consent in England at that time was 12.

the room. I have got an old marble table to make a hearth stone, and my chimney is much admired, but I believe the bricklayer has forgot to make a hole at the top of the chimney for it smokes most horridly in the room, and I never could hear of anybody who saw any smoke coming out at the top, on the outside of the house. However, it is to be altered before the monsoon, as it is a great comfort to me during the monsoon.

From Mary Symonds to her sister Hetty. 7th May 1803

The ship is to sail tomorrow but the wind has been so high that Richard, to his great mortification, has not been able to go over the surf. No boy has been to or from the ships these two days. To go to a ship is his greatest pleasure, and he has risen at 4 o'clock these two mornings to go down to the seaside, but could not go. They have travelled twice to the beach in the bullock cart. The surf is tremendous.

I yesterday had the pleasure of seeing several agreeable epistles from English friends. Sir Henry received them by a ship which arrived here from the Cape. The letters were put on board her by an Indiaman which was detained there. Amongst the letters is a very short one from you, in which you mention poor James's illness. We are happy to find, however, that he is in a recovering way. Alas poor Billy *(Hetty's husband or a family member)*, why would you be so hasty to swallow plum stones? I know he has a good digestion, and therefore hope he is recovered, but I sincerely pity you, who having been confined to a bed chamber attending an illness which could not be avoided, were claimed and fatigued by one so foolishly obtained. Betsy has the pleasure of receiving a very lively letter from my mother, who appears by her writing to be as well as we could wish her.

Poor Richard has no letters. Indeed, they do not write to him as often as they should, considering how anxious he is about them, and how good and regular he is on writing. He could not help crying yesterday when he found he had no letter, but it is his aunt's silence he complains of most because, he says, she is fond of writing and has not so many engagements as his mother. I wish you could see with what glistening eyes we all meet round a packet of letters.

I hope you have received some representations of Indian dress. I have now sent some specimens. I promised Nancy Green the cholis *(bodices)*, and I have added to them a piece of muslin which is called the cloth, and forms the other part of a Hindu lady's dress. I have also collected some of the ornaments worn by these lovely damsels, and I think the bracelets will give you a fine idea of jewellery, however they will never help you in forming a notion of the smallness and delicacy of the hands over which they pass some of these. They are the largest size they make, and yet I doubt if amongst your friends you find one who can put on and off a pair of them. The young girls fill their arms half way with them, but they have a great many more varieties. One sort, which they are fond of, is made of glass, like the rings which were worn in England a few years ago. They have them of every colour. These are not the ornaments of rich people. They are only worn by those who cannot afford a sufficient quantity of gold, silver and jewels.

Betsy intends sending more shawls to be divided amongst her male friends for waistcoats. I think you will like the pattern of the shawl and it will have a good chance of arriving in proper time for the winter. Betsy has sent a little box with some small bottles of attar, and my friend Captain Ashton, who helped her to pack them, has written his own name on one of them, from which perhaps you will imagine him to be a pretty little fellow but I assure you he is no such thing. He is as tall and stout as John Gwillim, and just such a rattle brain. Mr Templar knows him, but he is grown vastly steady since he has been appointed to the copper mines.

You asked me in one of your letters what sort of pickles would be most desirable and I assure you Mr James's notion was very right for I have never seen a red cabbage since I came into this country. I have been told they grow in India, but it is not hereabouts. Walnuts, cauliflowers and mushrooms are never to be had here, except what are sent from England, and capers must always be sent out.

I am very happy to have the pleasure of telling you that some of the things you have had the trouble of sending are arrived. The box of millinery sent from Mrs Toussaint is all come in perfection, everything as fresh as when it was packed. We find it a very useful supply for I assure you we were become very shabby in the sight of all our company. The box contains two cloaks, two turbans, two undress caps, and bonnets, some flowers and a set of green combs. Such valuable ornaments as these are very acceptable to me. Betsy likes a good cap, and so do I now and then, but these things make a variety, and look light and pretty. Betsy says I look better in them than in a more formal dress. She is praying and wishing just one wig had come, but here I do not agree with her, for if only one had come it would certainly have been torn to pieces in scrambling who should have it. One's hair is such a torment here; it will not curl. We were quite surprised to see our old acquaintance the wire bonnet come into fashion again. I look at Betsy in pins and fancy myself in Harriet Place, as it was just what was worn when we were there.

I am very greatly obliged to you for your beautiful long letter of the 6th October 1802. It gave us all great pleasure, for your letters are so satisfactory as from them I was always knowing exactly how you are going on. Pray tell James he is a scurvy fellow to think I shall marry a black man, when here is such a choice of white ones to be had. However, as he has set his heart on having some little black nephews, I will try to accommodate him with a few for, if I ever marry, it is more than probable there will be a few ready, who shall be sent over for his amusement. Without loss of time I will enquire into the matter very soon.

I shall send you an arrangement made of flowers which I have dried in the sun. If it falls to pieces, it cannot be helped for they are only intended for one evening. The natives send them to us almost every day, with long garlands to wear round the neck, and bracelets for the arms.

I don't know what James will say when I tell him that your picture gets many a kiss from my beaux, and so do all the others. I have one beau who kisses it every time he calls, and sometimes he pays his respects to my mother in the same way.

Your allspice necklaces, which you mention, and all sorts of cheap ornaments of that kind, are very desirable to us if sent out when they come in fashion, for we are at parties almost every day. We generally meet the same people so that, if one has an expensive thing of that kind, one gets tired of wearing it often without a change. Even those ladies who have the finest of pearls and diamonds are quite glad of those things for variety.

I hope you will understand the curious drawings I send you. They are all sorts and sizes, but if they have no other recommendation they are true representations as far as they go. I send you all I have coloured, and will continue to do so, for they will entertain you and your friends, and I know you will take care of them. Betsy begs you will not give any of them away for, slight as they are, we may be glad to look at them when the original subjects are no longer present. I have not done any of the miniature paintings a long time, partly for want of materials and partly because it took up so much time. Sir Henry said it was a nonsense to spend my time drawing a parcel of foolish conceited girls instead of drawing the natives, and other things of this country, which my friends at home would want to see.

From Mary Symonds to her sister Hetty 14th August 1803.

Betsy is now writing to you, and I have no doubt but that she will say all that is necessary in regard to acknowledging the receipt of the parcels and letters you have been so good as to send us. But as you express so much pleasure on receiving letters on any subject, I will not let slip this opportunity of sending a few lines. At the same time, I do not think it is a very certain conveyance, as we have at present every reason to think you may be at war with France before the ship can get to St Helena, in which case she is very likely to be picked up, as she is not able to make much resistance, and will sail alone. She is, however, commanded by a very brave man whom you may have heard of as he was much talked of for a very gallant action off the Cape in the last war. His name is Gordon.

I have been vastly gay ever since the arrival of the packages by the Cumberland. Mr Livingstone was very kind and attentive in getting them all on shore for us, and I have the pleasure to say they were all in high state of preservation, both eatables and wearables. I admire your choice of gowns very much because they are neat and useful. The plain muslin frock with lace down the front has been lent out to half the settlement for a pattern. My shoes fit very well, but Betsy's were a little too long but she has had them very ingeniously altered. Her maid told her one day that, if she pleased, she could send for the shoemaker to cut a piece out of the middle. Betsy did not much like the notion of it but, as the girl was very solicitous, she told her to give him one pair. He did this very well by opening the shoe all round and then cutting a piece out of the upper leather, between the vamp and the quarter, and then sewing it together again. The gloves you sent are the most beautiful I ever saw but, I am sorry to say, they are all spotted except the white ones, but that is always the case with all but Limerick gloves, unless you could get any friend to promise to keep the box with them in his cabin, for it is owing to the damp of the hold. The flowers and ribbons, and indeed every unmade article, we think most beautifully chosen, and so are the turbans, but I should have been glad to have found what one may call useful things, such as neat straw or chip bonnets, much as you and I used to buy in the spring. The jewellery, I will fairly own, is not quite the thing except the peppercorns. We were very glad of them, as they were quite a general fashion, and everybody had them. But poor Miss Innis's little red beads are quite too pretty for this place. The pearl necklaces are made up too fine, but the ropes are quite beautiful. I wear mine with a gold chain, and the other beads of the necklace I shall use to mix in my hair. They are very handsome for that purpose.

Poor Templar! It was surely very hard to be detained after so long an absence from home, and he is such a warm-hearted, good young man, that I am sure he must have felt a great deal on his arrival. I suppose he will be gone to sea again before you will receive this. However, should you see him, remember me in the kindest manner to him, and tell him that his friend Ellis has been back again at Madras in the Trident. He has been to dine with us once, and we took the old walk, in the evening, to the bridge and then to the swing, which I had not visited since he left us. And also tell him that little Toppy Dodson was to have been married yesterday to Captain Cramer of the Navy, but she met with a sad accident as he was driving her out in a curricle *(sporty two-wheeled, two horse open carriage)*. They met another carriage with troublesome horses, which took fright and ran up against them, and the pole of the carriage struck against her side and broke two of her ribs, and otherwise hurt her so much she was carried home quite lifeless. She is, however, likely to recover in a short time, and then the wedding will be celebrated. This, you will think, is quite enough of people you are not acquainted with.

Mr Lane, whom you mention, is arrived in the Wexford as surgeon of the Earl Howe. He was in the Earl Howe last voyage, and he is now living with us and is a very steady sensible young man. He gives the same account of young Barrett as you do, but he blames him very much for going out to India at all which, he says, was only occasioned by his vanity, as his father offered him a share in his business. This would certainly have been a much more respectable situation than any he could hope to obtain here. Mr Lane has a great deal of pure Herefordshire humour, and he entertains us all very much with his droll stories. He has not the least idea of affectation, or of finery, and I think he would amuse you. I don't know if shall send anything to you by him as he is going to China, and therefore will be a long time before he arrives in England. I hope to have many opportunities of sending things soon, as several ships are waiting here for the arrival of the new Governor. I have sent you an example of a poor woman's dress, quite complete. I say quite complete, but it wants one garment which I thought was not worth sending, as anybody may know how to make it, being only a pair of full trousers of red silk, which I do not think you would be tempted to try on if you had it. I have drawn three women very badly, but they will serve to show how the veil is worn. I wish you would send Mr Temple a good scolding. He has shaken the table, and knocked down the ink pot. In turn I have sprinkled him a little, but he will not be quiet. He is inclined to be lazy, and wishes me to be so. Richard is reading aloud at the same table, some stupid play that Colonel Trafford has written. I tell you this to account for the blunders in my writing.

All the sweetmeats you made are remarkably fine. I never saw any so beautiful, and so are Mrs Whitley's apricots. The flavour is just as good as when they were first done I am sure, and not the least fermentation. Your strawberries, and in short all your preserves, have kept their flavours the same as the first day. I hope you will not mention what I now say but, in truth, Mrs Whitley's raspberries have fermented, and lost their flavour for want of sugar, but the apricots make amends, for all they are just as my mother used to do them; quite clear and firm. Mrs Chamber's damsons came remarkably good, and I must not omit to tell you how acceptable your two bottles of gooseberries were. They were quite a treat to me. I have brought out only one bottle yet, and made two tarts with it for particular company.

I must say you are the very best housekeeper I know. Your pickles are beautiful, as well as your preserves. Indeed, all your things are the best, for poor Mrs Chambers has been cheated in her walnuts. They are too old, and have hard shells, but yours are in perfection and your cucumbers are as green as a ribbon. Be so good as to tell Tringham to pack all the sugar plums in glass. If he puts them in tumblers and corks them, or covers them with bladders, they will come dry and, furthermore, the tumblers will be very acceptable. Don't put them in decanters because they are of no use here. The damp of a ship is too great to send them in boxes as many of them were all run away, and others were stuck together in lumps. The almonds were all in one such, and so were the barberry sugar plums, however they are just as good to eat, though not so handsome for the table. I think it is not so worthwhile to send capillaire *(Maidenhair fern syrup)*. It is too sweet to be grateful in this hot country. The raspberry vinegar is much admired, and a few bottles of brandy cherries would be very acceptable, as also a few bottles of negus and cherry brandy. The negus *(a port and lemon cordial)* Betsy bought at Gunters in Berkeley Square[8] and has been very much admired. You could order half a dozen bottles some day on your way to Brompton.

I have little to say of our own family as, thank God, we are all quite well and Sir Henry has borne the hot season very well indeed. The land winds have been remarkably mild, and we have lately had fine showers every evening which have cooled the air and made everything appear green and pleasant.

From Elisabeth Gwillim to her sister Hetty 14th August 1803

The expectation of a war has kept all ships here, and nothing can sail until we receive news from England, which of course is waited for by us with the greatest anxiety. We have had news by an American ship[9] so late as

8 **Gunter's Tea Shop** in London's Berkeley Square had its origins in a food business named "Pot and Pine Apple" started in 1757 by Italian Domenico Negri. Various English, French and Italian wet and dry sweetmeats were made and sold from the business. In 1777 James Gunter became Negri's business partner, and by 1799 he was the sole proprietor. In the nineteenth and twentieth centuries Gunter's became a fashionable light eatery in Mayfair, notable for its ices and sorbets. The shop continued at a different address into the mid 20th century.

9 American ships were often favoured, where available, as they were swift and usually cheaper. See Elizabeth Gwillim's comments about them in her letter of 6 March 1805.

the 6th March, obtained from a ship she saw come in to St Helena as she was about to sail to this place, and from that there was nothing decided of peace or war. The Castle Eden, which brought our things from Mr Toussaint, has been detained all this time in order to take home Lord Clive, and every day we have been in expectation of a new Governor. The Cumberland, the Lushington and the Harriett all arrived within a day or two of each other. Such a profusion of packages to open; such letters and papers to read, my head has hardly recovered from it. Such a rarity to talk to people who have seen you, and could give us an account of your looks. This was the first pleasure of the kind we have had, and we much enjoyed it. As for the papers, Sir Henry has not yet got through all the Gloucester journals, though he has particular times, at least once a day and sometimes more frequently, when at least one is read. At first, he began to read in bed of a morning, as soon as a ray of light came, instead of going out to ride and, in this way having skimmed over all the news, he has more carefully perused it at such opportunities as I have above mentioned. This may possibly have contributed much to his health, as he is certainly induced by them to give a sufficient time to his activities.

I am sorry you had doubts about sending Mr Waite to us. Such things are all in the way here and, as being at an inn would overburden one of those young men. We asked him to the house, which is always an easy thing to do here. For young men they put sofas out in the porticoes and galleries, as you would call the verandas, and they use neither sheets nor blankets. He stayed with us six weeks, his ship being detained all that time, and then proceeded to Bengal. He is the quietest and most orderly being I ever had in the house. His brother has taken great pains with him, to instil in him good and decent notions, and sent with him a present of brushes and powder, but we are four of us and use a great many. Besides the insects eat all the brushes; it is difficult to keep them out.

My cases of china, and of Wedgwood, came without any fractures and my sets are now very full and complete. All your sweetmeats are the finest I ever eat. You have no idea how pleased the people here are to smell strawberries, including such numbers of people who came out as boys and have never seen any. I never was a picker before but really, when I eat those strawberries I feel as if I was back in England, and it is such a pleasant fancy to indulge now and then that I frequently rob the pots, though Miss Mary, who by the way begins to be a little Tabitha-ish, warns me that things will not last for ever and desires me to recollect that I cannot have my cake and eat it.

We had the Governor and his train at dinner, soon after the good things came, and I assure you his Lordship did ample justice to all my varieties, and begged particularly to know where and how I came by such excellent things, the like of which he had never had the good luck to come at, at which he seemed a little pained till I explained to him what good friends I have to do such nice things for me. Since when, if anything is very good, he asks me; "Well Lady Gwillim; have you got sisters to do this for you too?" The poppy syrup is as fine as possible, and I had some in the middle of one night and Mr Gwillim boasts much of having prescribed it for me.

Sometimes, when the weather is very hot, we have no proper appetite and are sometimes tormented with such a gnawing pain, as if of hunger, that we cannot sleep. But above all things, the herbs you sent me are most agreeable, and been the occasion of my eating many hearty meals that I would have gone without in this hot weather. I was almost longing for some knotted marjoram, and if you had desired to favour me ever so much you could not have given me such a treasure. The marjoram retains its flavour so well, as if it was just picked, but the thyme has scarcely any taste, but that need not prevent you from sending both lemon and orange thyme another time. The sage loses its flavour so much that we are obliged to put a whole handful into a duck. What flavour it retains puts us in mind of home, whereas the sage that grows here is the tree sage, and has a very different taste. All the herb seeds Mr Whitley sent me I have tried in all ways, and given them to other people, but I never could get them to grow, nor ever hear of one that did. However, I do not despair and hope to try again in the monsoon. As for mint, I used to have great difficulty with it but I learned at the Mount how to manage it by cutting it down short, frequently, and now I have it as large as your dining room, as green as grass through all this land wind, and I think it is nearly as well flavoured as in England. I am quite amazed at your skill in pickling; such charming green cucumbers. It is very extraordinary, but we have none of those small cucumbers here.

A few large ones are produced, and the roots are burnt up. Yours are very nice indeed, and I value them much and very rarely give any out.

Mr Prosser is very good natured, at least I think so, and gave me the sweetest canary bird that ever was. It was his companion coming out, and I think it a great compliment. If you should see him, prey tell him it is in the veranda of every bedroom and sings from daybreak to sunset. I never loved any little bird so much.

Mr Gwillim is sometimes full strong in anger and I think not a little ill-natured.

I had your letter by the Wexford, one from Lizzy, one from my mother, the boys' drawings which I really think very pretty, particularly one soldier, and the book of the loss of our poor old ship Hindostan which I was glad to have. This puts me in mind of Captain Millett *(Captain of the Hindostan)*. I certainly would have wrote to him at St Helena as he desired, but the ships had sailed to that place the day before I received his letter, and there was no other opportunity for many months afterwards. I understand from reports here that he was coming out again, and therefore I did not write, indeed we have been in constant expectation of seeing him. I was much pleased with his conduct in many respects. The ship was clean, neat and orderly, and had many comforts I never thought a ship could afford which, however, was only our want of knowledge. Sir Henry is not pleased with him. He was certainly parsimonious to a degree, and did many selfish and Jewish things. In the first place he affected great liberality about the price of our passage and would not fix the price till every ship was filled and then in a hurry named nearly double we were taught to expect we ought to pay. Since coming out we find it really was at least three hundred pounds more than anybody has paid for the same. He also said that he had made a favour to Mr Gwillim by taking his money here, so that Mr Gwillim would save £100 on the exchange, but we found that instead of rating the pagoda above the market price, they had put it under, so that instead of saving he paid above £200 more than he ought. Upon the whole it was a complete bad concern. The agents appear to have been the friends of Captain Millett, instead of doing properly for their employer Sir Henry. Over and above this they made a mistake in drafting the costs and put down 2500 pagodas instead of 2250, which was exactly £100 more than the proper sum. The whole was left to the agents, as we could know nothing of this, but Captain Millett must have.

Our luggage was not in his agreement, as the Company gave leave that an unlimited quantity could be placed in the gunroom, a dry place, but he put our things in the hold, where they became very damp and injured, in order to get that other place for himself. On account of our going with him, and having so much of the gunroom allocated to us, he was allowed to take only half the number of cadets the other ships took. This is a great advantage, as the price allowed for them is less than the cost to the Captain. Also, when we got on board, he gave us only sherry and bad port wine, and excused himself by reason that if he put it on the table the cadets would drink it. However, he never sent a drop to our cabins, which he might have done. We understood none of these things at the time, but we since find that all the other ships had Madeira constantly, and claret always sent into the cabins, and occasionally brought forth.

Now all these things being explained, you may suppose Sir Henry is not a little angry and, as he is not apt to conceal his opinions when he has formed them, I dare say it will come to Captain Millett's ears, which is of no use, and therefore I am not desirous it should. Sir Henry has written to the agents to apply for the return of the money. As it stands at present, we have paid £300 pounds more than we should, by mistake.

From Elisabeth Gwillim to her mother. 16th August 1803

As a most unusual time has elapsed since we have had any opportunity of writing from this place, I avail myself of the first opportunity to write a few lines to you to let you know we have been very well this summer. Thank God the weather has been unusually mild and we have not been a day without showers. St Swithin's has the same effect here as with you and, although the natives are not acquainted with the name, they know that rain at the end of June and beginning of July is generally followed by a long season of showery weather. I should much like to know if you also had a rainy summer. The apprehension of a war has prevented any vessel from leaving this place for near three months, just at the season when we expected to have had opportunities of writing every day. We have Mr

Lane of Hereford with us at present, who is surgeon of the Wexford which came in about a fortnight ago. It brought me your kind letter, which was a great pleasure to me. Mr Lane has kept Mr Gwillim, and indeed all of us, laughing constantly with Hereford news. We are yet in a state of uncertainty whether we are to have peace or war. The last news was 30 April and then it was peace. Should there be war, I think it like enough that they may catch our ships and if Mr Prosser's ship should be taken (the United Kingdom) you must all be content to lose your presents.

The French ships came to take possession of Pondicherry, which is a day's sail from this place, down the coast, but our good old Admiral Rainier did not to choose to let them take possession 'til we knew whether we had peace or war. The French ships were lying at anchor before the place when a corvette arrived from France. What news it brought we did not then know, but in the night they all cut their cables and ran away, leaving some money and some ladies whom they had landed. We all concluded the corvette brought notice of a war, and supposed they went to the Ile de France.

I shall write further if I have time.

From Elisabeth Gwillim to her sister Hetty 3rd September 1803

With one of your nice pens I have the pleasure to tell you that we have at last received our six cases, and the further pleasure to say that all that was material was uninjured. The earthenware is all whole, and the books unhurt, the gowns, caps, hats, ribbons, flowers and everything of that kind just as you put them in the cases. Such delightful packing I never saw. The gloves alone were spotted, and some pieces of white ribbon were turned so yellow that we could not use them, but this I attribute to their being made of bad silk for other pieces, being in the same paper, were quite white.

The drawing and writing paper you sent is also quite good, that is the paper directed to me, but Mr Gwillim's packages of letter paper was very mouldy and many quires only fit for common notes or exercises. Three gammons of bacon appeared indifferent, being so much rubbed as to have nearly lost the outer rind, but on cutting two of them we found the meat perfectly good, and as red and white as ever with, as you may suppose however, a considerable loss of soundness on the outside. The ham seems quite dry, and will I hope be good. The worst account I have to give is of the sweetmeats. Impatient of so long a confinement two or three pots had broke their prisons and escaped. The jam in the pots had lifted up the tops of several pots, but it is not bad. Two bottles of capillaire *(maidenhair fern cordial)* had fermented, and the corks had flown out. A few of the lozenges are pretty good, and some of the lemon and barberry drops, but the sugar plums presented the most dismal appearance. All their colours; red, blue and green, in a stream like the appearance of a marble-paper cover of a book. Richard Clarke was very happy as he was freed from the usual constraints upon the arrival of sweetmeats. He now had no charge given him but not to make himself sick.

I fear you do too much. The immense trouble you must have had to collect all these things for us, and pack them, must have been a dreadful fatigue. I can only say that they are most admirably chosen, but to enumerate all the particulars would be almost endless. There is a very elegant lace cap with yellow ribbons, quilled between the rows, that is quite becoming to Polly. She looks better in yellow, I think, than any other colour. The green round hat does very well for me. The shirt is most beautiful, and was sadly wanting as we had no good pattern for it. For my part I contented myself without it, but that did not suit Miss Mary, who made herself some imitations that are by no means beautiful. Mr Gwillim, who has as you know a great aversion to seeing women wear anything like a man's dress, is constantly reproaching her with their unbecomingness. The muslin cloak and bonnet I have taken to, and I never had anything more becoming than that calash bonnet *(a hood-like bonnet, protective from bad weather)*. It is so nice and so white that it seems as if it had been made without hands. Even Mr Gwillim praises that bonnet. I did not much like the muslin bonnet as it was made upon a wire and stuck out, leaving the back of my long neck bare.

It is great luck that we have all our new things to receive the new Governor in.[10] There is a great importation of finery for the occasion. Her ladyship has seen nobody yet. We are to go on Monday, but the Governor has received the gentlemen. Mr G. has just now gone to call upon Lord Clive *(retiring Governor of Madras)* who has taken a house in our neighbourhood. Let me not forget to thank you for the jewellery. The two pair of earrings of enamel and pearls are very pretty and acceptable, and so is the little gold chain, as mine is quite spoiled. Polly has a very handsome one which was given her. I would not like any jewellery of a kind inferior to that, as one pair a year is quite enough. The amber necklace we are very glad of. I shall I suppose know on Mr G.'s return when Lord Clive sails. They say very soon. The Union arrived, and the Wexford, about a fortnight ago. On Sunday night the Walpole came in, and brought intelligence that the Governor had just put back to Rio de Janeiro but, after this intelligence had been bandied about, and put everyone off guard, the very next day at about 11 o'clock in the morning, the Governor arrived in the Earl Howe. We had notice that the ship in which he came was to put a flag at the masthead, so we have been looking out a long time for this signal. The Governor did not land until Tuesday morning, and I hear the Lady has been very busy ever since. He says she is not very well but my man, who is a relation of their servant, tells me she is very well but more than busy all day to see all the boxes open. He also tells me she is a very good-natured lady, and that seeing the carpenter sweat very much she desired him to eat some fruit and then go to rest until he was cool. My man went to look at her yesterday, according to their custom, by favour of his relation. I asked him how he could think of going to stand in the room with her so long. Suppose, said I, she had asked who that servant is, what would you have done. "Ah, says he, she can never find face so soon, besides great many will be going to room all day. No, she can never find face so soon. After 10 days we be going." All these creatures make their visits to the bedrooms and dressing rooms, and I dare say she is not a moment without 100 eyes upon her.

The weather has been very moderate this summer, till the middle of July, but the end of that month, and August, has been very severe, at least

10 The arrival of the new Governor of Madras Lord William Bentinck.

to me and many others, but Sir Henry has been better than usual. Indeed he has, thank God, been the support of the court, for Sir Thomas Strange has been laid up with boils for two months. We have had slight showers all the summer which gave a dampness to the air, and the weather has been like our dog days in England. It is in vain to dwell upon melancholy subjects, but we all received a great dampener from the death of Mr Bethel. I endeavour to forget as much as I can, but the loss of a person whose company we have so often enjoyed is not without pain. I am extremely concerned for Miss Bethel. I wait with great anxiety for another letter from you. There are yet three more ships upon the sea, and I think that you must have written, and suppose your letters are in those.

Our house is most beautifully situated for seeing the ships come in, and it is a sight so interesting to us that, if a sail is spied, we are all out in a moment. But we feel so anxious that I do not know whether it is not more pain than pleasure. I do not know whether I ever described this shore to you. We have no hills nor rocks nearby, but the coast is formed something like Aberystwyth. The fort, which is a large tower, stands out as the castle there does. Then we may fancy the Black Town to be just where the bar was, or where all the little vessels used to lie, and so just the same as it is here. All the ships lie in this part, except the King's ships which anchor more out, and near the fort. Then on the other side from the fort, to my house at St Thomé, the shore only has gardens and if you were in a house so situated you would just have such a view of the sea. The flat place here is a sand marsh, in which a river winds very prettily, and is a lake in the wet season. Cocoa palm groves shut us out from such a view of the sea on right and left, but leave us an extensive opening so that if we go upstairs we see the fort and the signals on one hand, and on the other the vessels coming in from England. They keep close by us, and when they come near the fort, anchor and salute. Richard gets up on top of the house and we all squeal out from below to know what signals are seen through the glass. After all this, perhaps we have two days to pass before the letters are delivered. It is about three miles from the fort to the end of the Black Town on the one hand, and the same to St Thomé on the other.

I did not consider paying Mr Livingstone 10 pounds as very dear for the freight of the boxes. They were very heavy. He made a sort of apology to me, and told me he thought it very high as formerly he could get things out for 3 pounds the ton. I regret the trouble you had for I dare say the boxes would have cost as much if they had been sent by land from London to York. We shall not in future want such heavy packages. Two guineas and a half on the shawl is rather more than it was worth, but I wished Mrs Gwillim to have it soon, and that is the usual price given to the smugglers. The two orange-coloured shawls I sent for you and Mrs Gwillim cost 40 Pagodas, although 25 Pagodas is the regular price. A pagoda is worth 8/6d to 8/9d. I bought a shawl for 8 Pagodas from a Gujarati man who is my great friend, and lets me have things at my own price. It is lucky enough if one knows anybody going on a ship, in order to give charge of any parcels. They are frequently better taken care of, or at least sooner delivered. As you had so particularly said there were six cases on board the Union, as soon as we heard that the ship was arrived, we sent a man on board to know if there were these said boxes for us. The answer was that there were no boxes or packages of any kind, and this intelligence affects us much. Mr. Gwillim got a gentleman who was acquainted with the purser to write, and by that means we at last learned that they were all on board, but we did not receive them till 10 or 12 days after the ship arrived.[11]

I have this moment heard that an overland dispatch arrived last night bringing news from England, dated 17 May, that war is declared, and bringing also the King's speech on the occasion. Lord Clive is therefore most likely to be detained to travel in a convoy. However, he called yesterday to take leave of us as he has resolved on going without a convoy, and they sail tomorrow. All communications will now be very uncertain for some time. I hope you will get the things we sent with Mr. Prosser, but I think it likely that the ship will be taken. There is a shawl for Nancy James which you will forward, and a muslin gown, for which you will have to pay 25% duty. There is also a basket of seeds for Mrs Davies

I think it likely Mrs Davies may call upon you. Therefore I shall tell you who she is. Her father is Mr. Penrose, Surgeon Extraordinary to the King. Her mother is dead, but her stepmother was a Miss Lucas of

11 See note 6 page 143. This paragraph further indicates the difficulties and frustrations of receiving and sending boxes and packages.

Monmouthshire. She was rather an old maid and very good humoured, and is said to be very amiable in her disposition. I think you can hardly remember her as you were then very little. Mrs Davies is a large woman but was, when I came here, extremely handsome. She is very genteel and well bred, and has been in good company. Lady Blount, Sir Richard Symonds sister, sends her clothes, and she appears to have been much time with them, and many high families.[12] It excites the curiosity of all people here, and I confess mine also, to know how a beautiful young woman, very fashionable, showy and well-educated, came out the wife of a disagreeable-looking little man with one short leg, and of course quite lame, excessively vulgar and low in his manner. He is an assistant surgeon, though not tied to that profession and in ability, as I hear, knowing nothing about it. Lucky is Mrs Davies! He reports himself to be the son of a clergyman, and I understand she has one child living with her father, and one with his. Davies is quite a Cockney, and his friends live in or near London. The report here; true or not I cannot say; is that when Mr. Davies came out with his wife he went to Mr. Samuel, editor of the Madras newspaper, and was a kind of head devil or scandal writer for the newspaper. How he came to get out as an assistant surgeon, and how he came in possession of a woman of that kind, is a matter of astonishment. She was slightingly spoken of at first, but has since been extremely well received everywhere, and indeed her conduct and manner are amongst the best here.

You will see by the papers what prizes have been taken in these seas. The Admiral is an excellent old man but we have no great force here, and we hope you have sent us some. I wish Tom Gwillim could get a ship and come out to us. Naval officers have a good life here, and these seas are without danger.

The pens here are so soon spoiled, that I feel this writing will be worse than any before. The land winds split them as you write, and this sheet is one of the best of the paper you sent me that I have so far tried, and yet the damp has taken the size out of it, and the ink runs badly. This war will make us very anxious to hear from you as often as possible, but write all

12 It is possible this is Sir Richard Symons. If so there is a portrait painted by Joshua Reynolds in 1770. There is nothing to suggest he was related to the Symonds sisters.

about yourselves, not what may be in the newspapers as we have all that sooner. For the same reason, I shall omit to tell you of things here because you get that news sooner in the overland dispatches.

I rise at eight in the morning. Breakfast, and the accounts, take my time until 10. From 10 till 12 is all the time for writing, learning or drawing. Only two hours out of 24!! And yet more often than every other day people come and take up those two hours. At 12 o'clock comes luncheon time or, as we call it, tiffin; we are ready to faint for food. Indeed, if I have been detained, I often do in the extreme heat. After this meal, we are so oppressed with heat that it is quite a force to do anything. At this moment I am writing after tiffin, and at three o'clock we dress, and at four we dine. We sometimes sleep a little between tiffin and dinner, but I never do it if I can keep up. Between five and six we go to walk about the garden to see it watered and seeds sown, or else we go out 'airing', and this is all the exercise we have. If we walk in the garden we drink tea, and go out at eight o'clock to make visits, and as the places are so far from one another we do not get home till about 11 at night. If we go for our airing at six o'clock, we have sometimes a little time for writing in the evening, but it is not to be depended upon. Visitors may come in, or we dine out, or we have company large or small is an equal hindrance, or there is a ball. In short, if I get my two hours in a day, it is all I expect.

From Mary Symonds to her sister Hetty 10th September 1803.

I have already written one sheet this letter but by some untoward accident or other I have lost it, and at present I assure you it is very considerable loss to me. Though it contained nothing very material yet it is provoking to lose a letter, and at present I am amazingly busy with some curious subjects for my pencil. I have got an old woman to stand for me, and a moor man to sit, both of whom are so handsome that I should be very sorry to lose the opportunity of drawing them. I am obliged take them when I can have them. They promise to come three or four times and sit for me, but after the first or second time they go away up the country, and I can see no more of them.

Betsy has written you an account of the safe arrival of the long looked for parcels which came by the Union. One of the gammons of bacon was dressed on Monday last for a very large party (all the gentlemen of the profession, to whom the judges give an annual dinner). The bacon was admired beyond anything at the table and they all said they thought it far preferable to the finest ham. The sugar plums and caraways had suffered from being packed in paper instead of glass. Henceforth you will have them put in tumblers and covered with bladders.

This is some of the new paper, but it writes so greasy that I fear you will not be able to read it. Almost all the paper that is brought out to this country is either greasy, or else it blots. I am quite charmed with the collection of millinery and dresses you have sent us. I am sure it must have been an immense fatigue to you and poor Nancy Green to buy them and pack them. I can perceive that these things have been made at some fashionable place, and though they have been kept a year in bondage, yet I prefer them to the newest fashions made at any common shop. Mr Cochrane has given two grand balls this week, the one to his niece who has just married and the other as a farewell to Lord Clive. This last was meant to be most magnificent. He had prepared a great many fireworks and transparencies in compliment to Lord Clive, which were to have been seen before supper. The supper was in a remarkably fine style. The tables were all laid in the garden under an awning erected for the occasion. At about 11 o'clock we heard a violent noise outside the house. Some people supposed it to be the fireworks beginning to be let off in the garden and ran to the door to look out, but many of the doors and windows began to slam to and fro, and the thunder roared and the lightning flashed with such torrents of rain as you cannot easily imagine. All the fireworks were extinguished and, what was still worse, the supper and the building which contained it were washed away. There was poor Mr Cochrane at the head of about a hundred black servants trying to save something from the wreck, but they gathered up custards, whipped syllabub, sandwiches and bunches of flowers, all mixed together. At last it was discovered that a great deal more supper had been prepared than the tables would hold and with that, and the first which was not injured, they made one handsome table inside the house which was quite enough, for all these things are just for show as nobody ever eats.

Lord Clive stayed until four o'clock in the morning and they finished the evening, or rather the morning, very gaily. I hope all our friends will get safe home who sailed from here in the beginning of the year, but it is much to be feared they will (many of them) be picked by the French. In the ship United Kingdom I sent many things for you, and letters, and in two other ships a great number of letters. The two last we have very little hope of as we have heard they were at St Helena before they could have heard of the war.

From Elizabeth Gwillim to her mother. 20th October 1803

We have not failed to write to you by every opportunity and I hope you have had letters from us by the United Kingdom which sailed the 18th of last May. We have since written by the Walpole and Castle Eden, both of which sailed in September, the latter having Lord Clive on board. It is a most wonderful thing that he should, with his immense fortune, have chosen to stay so long from his wife and children, his native land and fine estates, filling a place of great emolument so much to be desired by many noblemen of smaller fortunes and greater fondness for public business. He was extremely good natured as a private gentleman, but his whole time was given up to his garden and the fattening of veal and beef, leaving other matters to the care of a few people who contrived to hold him in a sort of thraldom, and lead him to their purposes, worse people than many of them you cannot conceive. Lady Clive is said to have greatly desired his return. I imagine from what I hear on all hands that she must be a very clever woman, and could not but see with pain that he was losing that credit which the name of Clive ought to claim in India. Such an influence had the few people about his house gained over him, that he does not seem to have had courage to support the very few that he brought out with him, who were all obliged to return to England disappointed. He never made the least provision for them, though offices of the most lucrative kind were poured upon most unworthy people. He does not seem to know anything of botany. His gardening was chiefly for culinary purposes, except such collections as Lady Clive had desired to be made. Indeed, the study of plants would have been esteemed highly by the natives, though their mode of studying botany differs from ours.

Such respect have they for vegetable dishes, that many of the more useful plants are venerated as divinities. Their books and descriptions are exactly in the style of Culpeper. This reminds me of giving you an account of the medical skill of these people, which I have been several times going to give Mr John Gwillim but, as he has not written and you tell me you communicate all useful information, I shall leave it to you to propagate whatever may be beneficial to the world that can be drawn from this source. I must first observe that they begin with a firm belief that every created being bears in the inside of his skull the handwriting of Brahma, in the Devanagara or sacred characters, and that the time and manner of his death are distinctly written. These letters, they assure you, are all visible on the pieces of the skull which they collect after the burning *(cremation)*, and bathed in milk. Medicine is sought merely to relieve pain, and not with the hope of prolonging life, and thus the conscience of an unskilful physician is secure from any deep wound, and much slander is prevented, as they never form much of an idea of any natural cause of diseases, but that they are the effects of sin, or of an evil eye, or fiends, so they can expect no remedy in the natural qualities of things and conjuration is therefore peculiarly depended upon. However efficacious the charm may be, the manner of administering it is very extraordinary to our notions. For example my maid, being much afflicted with the colic, gave a month's wages for about half a pound of lead which, having been properly prepared by incantations, she wears at the pit of her stomach, rolled up and fastened by a string round her neck. Many other remedies of the same kind might be mentioned. A servant, for whom Sir Thomas Strange has a great affection, had several fits of a sudden and dangerous nature upon which the doctor, instead of sending a couple of bottles as one's own would have done, sent him two young black dogs, and a bit of red gum, or earth, with an order, whenever a fit came on again, to cut the ears of the dogs and, having procured a little blood to rub the gum in it and apply it to different parts of his body, repeating certain texts.

As for female complaints, such as hysteria, nightmares, fainting, disturbed rest and the like, they are constantly supposed to be the consequence of unclean spirits having possession of the patient. She is therefore conveyed to Manaswamy (a God whom the Brahmins disown) who, with bell, book and candle, terrify her into convulsions when the fiend is supposed to quit his hold. But although they readily expect supernatural effects from their herbs and roots, they also find real ones, and have many excellent medicines amongst their vegetables, which they apply frequently with great success. Indeed, there is a knowledge of plants even amongst the lowest of people that shows a great attention to the productions of nature, although they have formed no notion how the qualities of vegetables act on the human body. They divide all diseases into hot and cold, and certain plants are supposed to be suited to cool, and others to warm but, from what I can learn, an English physician would neither agree with them as to the nature of the disorder, or the power of the herb. However, as their experience is better than their reasoning, their patients are relieved. As I am upon this subject I must not omit an account of their surgery, of which however there is little to say. Their employments are less dangerous than ours, and therefore accidents less frequent. When wounded or bruised they soon recover, even from such wounds as would destroy an European, for they neither drink spirituous or fermented liquors and live almost entirely on vegetable food. Their blood is generally in a poor state. They have a great abhorrence of the use of a lancet, and rarely open anything, and never bleed but with leeches. Almost every tree yields them fine aromatic gums, and also seeds and oils in the natural state, which they use generally for salves. Many trees on the roads have had the smooth bark so frequently wounded to procure the gum, that they appear spotted, like a leopard skin, by the small cuts drying into round spots. Their unskilfulness, however, makes many disorders fatal to them, which are easily cured by us. If a limb be broken, it is not the office of either physician or surgeon to cure it, nor yet is the conjuror called in, but wisely considering that men are but of clay, they send for the potter. These potters make their wares of the same kind of red earth as our garden pots are made of, but of a finer kind. They first set the bone as well as they can and then, taking a quantity of clay, enclose the limb near the fracture, and for a considerable way above and below. Having done this, they lay it over a slow heat, as great as the patient can bear, and the clay being thus baked around the limb, there is no danger of the bone being displaced. By practice they know very well how long a bone will be in setting firmly, and when they suppose it to be safe they break the pot which surrounds the fracture, and the cure is performed.[13] The surgeons say that, for simple fractures, their extraordinary method succeeds admirably well, but doubt much whether it would as well suit an European constitution, subject to inflammation. If a limb be much shattered, their method is not so likely to succeed, and they never amputate.

Wars, and rumours of wars, keep us in such a state here that we have had few opportunities of writing, and no previous notice. The packet for the Union closed suddenly yesterday, before I had time to send my letter, which was all I intended to send as there is the greatest reason to suppose she will be taken or, if not, that her passage will be very tedious. Our weather is become pretty mild and pleasant, and the monsoon appears to be approaching very fast, which is the reason for the ship' s sailing so soon. The rain generally begins the latter end of October in a good season, and the Brahmins say if there be no rain on the 15th a long season of dry weather is to be expected, which here is a terrible evil. St Swithin was as liberal here as in England. We had showers every day for two months which has made everything extremely verdant. We had dry weather for about three weeks, and now the rain begins again. My house is so well secured against the rain that we felt no inconvenience, thank God. I have the happiness to say we are at present all well. I only wish I could hear as much of you all. It is extremely unfortunate that we had not one letter by all the last ships. I fear now we shall hear nothing till February or March. A summons is just arrived, and therefore with love to all and a thousand good wishes to say that I am ever your most dutiful daughter etc.

From Elizabeth Gwillim to her sister
Hetty (incomplete) Oct/Nov 1803

Bombay is the place for shawls. I shall not send them frequently, only to my own family, or particular friends. That yellow was a gown piece which I bought and cut in waistcoats for different friends. I am obliged to cut

13 The word pot is still used for plaster cast in some parts of the world, notably Yorkshire, England.

them here for convenience in carriage. I have bought another, which is very fine and I think a great beauty. I gave 30 pagodas for it and it makes six waistcoats. Mr Gwillim ventured to send you some pearls which by now I hope you have received. He sent them in a letter. I also sent Mr Prosser a small tin case containing some small bottles of sandal, jasmine and rose. They are very valuable. I wish you to keep these for your own use . The rose is the most pleasant to Europeans, and also the most valuable. Some of it I received in presents from nabobs, and some from the Armenians. It should be put in the sun frequently, in the hottest place you can find.

Mr. Toussaint sent a letter to Polly desiring her to send his mother's things by a Mrs Anderson on board the Castle Eden, which she has done; 6 quart bottles of Masulipatam snuff, and two large and two small palampores. Besides this, I have sent by Mr Prosser three pieces of coarse chintz. They are the petticoats that Portuguese (as we call them) wear. I sent them that you might see how you like them. I think they would make up well in furniture. Tell me which you like best, and I will have some painted. I have sent, besides some seeds, a great number of trees for Mr Whitley, but he would grieve to think, as I do, that most likely none will be alive. However, Mr. Prosser is extremely good-natured in offering to take them, and therefore I send those most likely to live. However, the ship will have to pass the Cape in the depths of winter and most likely all will be washed overboard, as Lady Clive's were.

Polly has drawn some plants slightly, and on that paper I have written some accounts. The papers are rolled up with some drawings of hers. You must not give them away for, slight as they are, they are by much the best things I ever saw to give an idea of the people in the streets or roads here, in crowds, and so various in their dresses. You will see, in one, a group of young pandarams in their salmon coloured muslins and their brown beads. They are a very handsome caste of people. I wrote you a particular account of them, I believe, in the letters I sent by Mr Mackay, one of our doctors. I am extremely angry that he should have kept the letters three months before he put them in the post. I could have sent them in the packet to you, and you would not have had postage to pay, but he pressed me so much that I thought he would be hurt if I did not give him a letter or two to carry.

I have learned a good deal of the Gentoo language. *(Note 11, page 29)* I could write you a letter in it. It is difficult, but I could not get answers to my enquiries without learning the language and this labour must account for my not writing as usual.

We had a charming time of it for three months, the weather lovely, but this season has commenced very severely. The heat is extreme and long shore winds violent. Hot sun and cold winds give a constant headache to everybody. In one year we have only had 11 days rain. This came altogether, and it never ceased. It began soberly, but at last the wind rose and the last days were all storms of thunder and lightning and rain for 20 hours. That was no possibility of sleeping, and yet not the least danger, though the lightning was as bright as noon day, and not a moment's interval between the flashes. We want rain badly, but what is surprising is that the country looks quite verdant. The roots of the trees go so deep in the earth, and the grasses are all runners that cover the ground, though they do not rise an inch, and live on the dew. It is very hot, and you must not expect much from us. To keep ourselves alive is business enough for the next five or six months. I wish you had some good Moringas to eat *(Moringa pterygosperma – Horseradish tree)*, well stewed, or could see the tree, a lovely object, waving light as air with sweet flowers. The long pods we stew, and they are as nice as asparagus, not that they are alike, but as much to be longed for.

You will find, in our next package to you, some nuts like gingerbread nuts, which I know you were fond of in former days. They are the natives' perfumes. You must take one of these nuts and, with rosewater, grind it on a plate with the rosewater just as you would Reeve's colours and, when you have got enough, to please rub it over your hands and breast. It will look like dirt you will say but, never mind that, as it is cooling and gives a fine smell. The natives are very fond of them.

I have a beautiful cockatoo which I will send to you if Mr Prosser will take charge of it. At present it speaks a few words in three languages, but none in English, but probably the sailors may make it more entertaining by their teaching.

However unfavourable our domestic arrangements may be, I have not turned my mind yet to think well of taking an assistant wife. You tell us you are almost tempted to wish the men had a plurality of wives, in which thought you are much more Asiatic in your notions than I am. A Moor man, who is living in London has, I see, given in the Asiatic Annual Register a very exact account of the Moorish families, concluding by observing that a man might as well live with two dogs as two wives. I could, from what I have seen, give an account by no means more favourable of the domestic happiness of such families and, I assure you, I think the men who indulge in such liberties have no great thing to boast of for the women are extremely fond of their respective children, but they altogether much hate those of another wife and, as to the husband, he certainly has no part of their regard. Whether he be fondled on, or scolded, it is only to obtain particular advantages, without any respect to the state of the husband's fortune. Our English husbands tell us a great deal of their liberal treatment of us, and the deplorable state of the Asiatic woman. This I assure you is a fine story, and I think they would be a little astonished if they were to hear an eastern lady harangue. The rapidity of utterance is beyond me to describe, besides which he may get his beard torn out by the roots, and his ear bitten and, after all that, he is obliged to watch and humour the lady for fear she should jump into a well, or a tank. Nay, he is afraid to have many trees of the prettiest flowers grow in his garden lest she swallow a handful of roots, or leaves and, either by water or poison, put herself out of the world, which would be the most dreadful disgrace to him. I can tell you a great deal more some time or other. In the meanwhile, you may believe me that there are more ways of keeping husbands in order than you can easily imagine of.

You accuse me of not having given you an account of the birds of this place. I think, as a contrast to the last subject, I may as well tell you how the days here are nearly equal in length, and how morning breaks out suddenly. With the first ray of light, exactly at the firing of the guns which gives notice of daybreak, the crows awake as if they were really called by the guns and having, as I suppose, by the noise and confusion settled with difficulty their places for the day, they disperse, and the king crow, or cawbird as it is called, begins to call with a loud and very severe note. It has but two notes but these are frequently repeated. It is much like the blackbird, and is very pleasing from the top of the mango trees. It is of the same size as the blackbird, and colour, but has not the yellow beak. "The ousel cock so black of hue with orange tawny bill" *(Midsummer Night's Dream)*. However, though it is not so ornamented as the blackbird, it comes nearer the crow altogether. I think you would like it easily as well. The power of voice and sweetness is very charming. It has a remarkably long forked tail and sits, as our magpies do, on the cows' heads, and on the sheep, from where it takes its name, and it is a great favourite with the natives. It continues to call the greater part of the day, but chiefly morning and evening and after this, if the morning be pleasant, numbers of birds begin to sing, many of as sweet a note as ever I heard, but they never go on to any warbling. It is just a little song like a wren. There are great numbers of these little beautiful creatures for ever moving on the blossoms of the trees. We have a bird called a dyal, with a fine note. It is black-and-white, and also Bulbuls, or Indian nightingales. I cannot say their note is much like a nightingale. It has no strength and it is, besides, confused and almost too sweet and exceedingly hurried, like the noise people make with a cork on a bottle to induce Canary birds to sing at night. They are very pretty, some with tufts on their heads. These are rather better singers. Others with their tails up and wings down like a domestic cock; they are constantly running under the rose trees of an evening. I have drawn none yet because I have not had time to acquaint myself with the distinctions with all these singing birds and many others. You will suppose we have a fine concert, but the numbers of chatterers and screamers and croakers are so continually making noises that one has seldom a possibility of hearing them individually.

The crows here are of the sort called hooded crows, and so familiar that they come to the rooms and take biscuits off the sideboard. If the breakfast is laid, and the servants go out of the room for a minute, they are on the table eating the butter and the rolls. Loaves they take up, but not being able to fly with them they drop on the floors. A hundred times I have come to breakfast and seen the loaves carried out and lying on the pavement, and 20 or 30 of these miscreants flying away in a dreadful fright. Yet the natives are extremely fond of them, and never kill them. Indeed they never kill anything. The poorer sort of people, who have no courtyard within their houses, do all their cooking out of doors. It would amuse you, I think, to see half a dozen crows sitting within a yard of the pot watching the process, and conversing. Occasionally the natives brush them away, only with their hands, as you would a hen that came in the house, yet they are extremely quick and will not be caught. The natives sift their grain of various kinds in the streets, and lay it on mats or sheets to dry. A set of crows are constantly eating away with the greatest composure. Occasionally ravens come with the crows. The natives, who are perfectly superstitious, hold these in the utmost detestation. They are called Pariah crows. Whatever is superior of its kind is called Brahminy, and whatever is inferior is called Pariah, and thus we have the Brahminy Kite etc. The Pariah crow set up a croaking on the house top, or in a tree. The servants express the utmost anxiety. Owls are still more dreaded, notwithstanding the fact that they are very common. They scream much of the night and are in everybody's garden. I had one given me alive, which I drew, but I really believe there was not a servant in the house but what was perfectly miserable the whole time it was in the house. They begged, and entreated, and even one of our horses dying from eating wet grass was attributed entirely to the owl, and we were thought to have come off very lightly.

Here the cuckoos are held in high esteem, and to be lulled to sleep in the shade by the notes of Cokillas is the favourite idea in poetry. I have drawn three very handsome birds of this kind, differing much in the plumage from ours. The notes I am not sure that I have heard, for in the cages they are silent, and I do not know the call. It is generally disliked by Europeans, and just as generally admired by the natives. I presume it is somewhat like the notes of ours, as all the names have the same first syllable. Indeed we speak of the cuckoo with delight, as attending us in a pleasant season, but from Chaucer and Milton it appears that it is a bird of ill omen in love affairs. The contrary of which is here the case. Green parakeets are here very common, and the Coracias Indicus certainly the most beautifully coloured bird I ever saw. It is known by the name of jay by Europeans. However beautiful these are, I have no pleasure in seeing them in the garden because the notes are so abominably harsh. We have two kinds of bee eaters which are very common and bright green with fine bent beaks and long feathers in the tail, very little larger than the hummingbirds. We constantly see kingfishers. They are very numerous and here of three kinds; one large green and chestnut coloured, one black-and-white mottled and a small one the same as the English, but smaller. As for the sparrows, though very common, I never see them but in pairs, and they build their nests within the houses. They come through the venetians and build on the mouldings, or on any bookcase. They are slender in their form, in which alone they differ. I have seen no house without them, but never saw above one or two pair in a house. We have vultures in the open parts, common kites and hawks of a great many kinds. The Moor people are very fond of hawking and, as a man in England goes accompanied with his dog, so these people always carry on their fist a trained hawk. I have seen seven or eight men standing to talk together in the street, each with a hawk on his hand. They also train partridges and quails; the latter are to fight, and I believe the partridges also. I have met people on the road with a partridge running behind them, just as a little dog would follow a man. There are numbers of other birds which it would interest you to hear of, but many as yet are very little known to me. I saw no swallows for sometime after I came here, perhaps on account of the season, but we have many in some places, but they fly higher than with us, and are by no means so numerous. I have seen none that make nests in any buildings. I daresay you have heard, but perhaps not, of the hanging birds nests. They come only to particular trees in the next garden to mine, on a date palm, the leaves of which are very high and on which hang many of these nests. I sent you a nest by Mr Templar, which I hope you received. There is a chamber within for the family, and a perch across the bottom for the young birds to sit on before they can fly.

But the pride and delight of the Indians is the Brahminy kite. It is a small eagle, about the size of a common kite, well-shaped and of a bright chestnut colour. The head and neck are snowy white. They go in pairs, and a pair attend many gardens, but mine is not so lucky. The natives feed them with great care and consider them as gods. They must see them every Sunday morning before they eat, and whenever they see them make to them what they call dunnamooloo *(sic - origin unknown)*. A salaam is a salute to a master, a dunnamooloo is to a God or a Brahmin . It is holding the hands up closed, as we do in prayer. In the garden we had at the Mount, on a mango tree, the Brahminy kites had a nest, a peculiarly fortunate circumstance, and here on a Sunday morning the natives came in order to make their dunnamooloos, accompanied by a short prayer. Notwithstanding the Brahminy kite is held in such veneration, they are by no means numerous.

Peacocks are wild in the woods of India and are brought to us by the people who live in the woods, and who have manners and customs peculiar to themselves. The same people as the gypsies in England, part of them admire birds and beasts and are wonderfully ingenious in imitating the cries of different animals to entice them. Part of them gather leaves used in the curries and bring them into the towns exchanging them with the inhabitants for rice instead of money.

I think you know I would not tell you anything I did not see, but the things these people do are generally disbelieved in England and, indeed, after the jugglers here you would despise ours. Their feats of activity are equal to their sleight of hand. They also charm snakes, and I think Polly sent you one of her sketches, in which is a man in his fanciful dress with a Cobra Capella, that is a large hooded snake, reared up and dancing to the music.

Letters of 1804 and Commentary

Commentary

Again the first letters are dated February. Mary starts off the year, full of delight at the contents of the boxes received from England. Various new clothing styles and fashions cause great confusion, but equal pleasure, but what is so charming is the casual and expansive chatter of writing to a sister, as opposed to the somewhat stiffer style more appropriate to a friend, or especially a journal. Reading such letters gives one a glimmer of day-to-day life two hundred years ago, ungilded and unexpurgated.

The subject of the French war is now infusing the correspondence, as there are numerous privateers in the Bay of Bengal. The commission that has to be paid to smugglers to take goods ashore at the other end of a voyage has mounted, and all East Indiamen are now sailing in convoy, usually with a Royal Naval ship in attendance. Whether or not letters will arrive, or might be lost if an Indiaman is taken by the French, becomes a subject of some concern. A very short letter seems a waste of a voyage, as exemplified by Mary's reaction to a six-line letter from her brother in law.

At about this stage they express their awareness of the health hazards of that part of the world. Sir Henry is not coping with the heat, which is hardly surprising when he has to attend court in waistcoat, tailcoat, gown and full-bottomed wig, and is inclined to irritability anyway. A young man staying with them has the flux with blood, probably dysenteric, and the young clerk, Temple, dies very suddenly of an acute febrile illness, perhaps malarial, which Mary describes in some detail in the next letter. Two points are worth underlining in this letter from Elizabeth to her mother. One is the awareness of the brevity of life, and the fragility of health at that time, anywhere, and she expresses the terror they feel on seeing ships arrive, having not heard from her mother for ten months. The other is the perceptive, but completely unrelated, point about the value to men of learning Latin towards the better understanding of their own language, even though it itself has no practical use. Women, she comments, had to do without this advantage: they were not taught it.

Once again Mary indulges herself in the pleasure of dissecting the personalities of visitors. In doing so about a certain McMalliss, she touches on a subject which the sisters comment upon elsewhere in the letters, and that is the prevalence of Scots – 'who have hundreds of the same sort of ragamuffins come out every year fresh from Scotland and, like him, they all pretend to be great men'. The truth is certainly that there were large numbers of Scots employed by the East India Company. In the 1770s and 80s, 47% of writers were Scots, and almost 50% of doctors. (See also the letters of 16 Oct 1804, 6 Mar 1805, 11 Feb 1806, 28 Feb 1806 and, particularly, 24 Aug 1805). Of the much-prized free merchants' residence permits issued by the East India Company, which allowed trade in the east, 60% were to Scots. Half the royal regiments that garrisoned the Indian provinces in the 1700s were Scottish. This has to be seen in the context of a Scottish population that was only one-tenth that of England.[1] At about the time of the sisters' letters a major influence on the appointment of Scots personnel was the presence of Henry Dundas, Lord Melville, as President of the Board of Control of the East India Company, himself a Scot.[2] Three of his brothers served in India, and two died there. In October 1804, Elizabeth mentions that she had been at a ball where she and her sister were the only two English-born people. How, she wonders, did an Englishman have any chance in that environment.

In the letters of October there is further discussion about Indian eatables, fruit in particular, and an impression that the two women have learnt

1 Devine, Tom, *Scotland's Empire. The Origins of the Global Diaspora* (London, 2012).

2 Henry Dundas, 1742–1811, 1st Lord Melville, was a Scottish lawyer who entered the Westminster parliament and became friend and adviser to William Pitt. He early on became Home Secretary and, among many other interests, involved himself with India. His family never became nabobs although they sent sons to the east. Three of Dundas's brothers went, and two died there. He was a major architect of the India Act of 1784 which created the Board of Control of the East India company in which he was initially pre-eminent and later became its president. At that time he smoothed the path for the appointment of many young Scots to employment in India. See Oxford Dictionary of National Biography, ref:odnb/8250

a lot about their value and their flavour. There is then, by Mary, the first rather cryptic reference to reports of Sir Henry's efforts to perform his duty, as he sees it, and which by then must have been questioned. This subject is summarised in the Introduction and in the final chapter.

There is an interesting reference to the hazards of fire in the largely wooden structures of the native quarters of Madras. The especial interest is her observation that no effort is made to put out such fires as they are seen to be preordained in Hinduism, and especially so by Parsees. Even more remarkably, some individuals subjected themselves to immolation, as this too was thought to be the concurrent will of God. Mary reveals herself to be far less tolerant of the religions of India, even Catholicism, than her sister Elizabeth and less inclined to attempt understanding them and yet, in her letter of the 14th October, she obviously feels it is appropriate to describe the poor opinion the Indian people have of the British and their Christianity. 'They despise us as being little better than brutes.' 'The name of Christian they hold in abhorrence, beyond even their own outcastes, the pariahs.' Not long afterwards she mirrors their attitudes by being more outraged than fascinated by some of their sacrificial practices, or their animal embodiments of spirituality, such as attributed to a large garden cobra that had to be destroyed.

In her letter dated 14 October 1804, Elizabeth Gwillim describes in some detail the place of the outcastes *(known at that time as Pariahs, see note 15, Introduction, page 9)* in Indian society, in the context of the immutable and rigorous caste system as a whole. Her description inevitably accords with the colonist attitude of those times, particularly that they were thought to be a people with low moral values. Whether this was the effect of misuse by all other levels of society, or to a presumptive primary factor in their make-up, is hard to comprehend. Inevitably it is all something of an oversimplification, but she at least demonstrates an interest in the subject. She goes on to describe touchingly the character and experiences of her own personal maid, who had been subject to much abuse, but who appears to have been entirely loyal, and obviously the object of her mistress's affection. There are similar references in an earlier letter of March 1802 and, in August 1802, she offers further gently appreciative comments about another servant, male on this occasion, and relates how, as a race, they are extraordinarily caring for any sick person. There follows a lengthy and comprehensive description of the huge variety of servants, and their various functions, including some of high caste and considerable learning. It was common at that time for any larger household to have upwards of fifty servants. Both sisters express a little concern in their letters about pilfering, the selling off of household produce and the overcharging for goods bought in the bazaars, the difference disappearing as additional wages. They are nevertheless impressed by the obvious cohesion in a Hindu family whereby each member has a responsibility to the others, especially to the children and the sick.

The cost of this number of servants was not inconsiderable. Fanny Parkes, writing in her diaries some twenty years later, records the annual cost for her fifty servants as being £290, and this was just in a relatively lowly civil servant's home. This is equivalent to about £28,000 per annum today, a not inconsiderable sum *(Bank of England inflation correction).*

Elizabeth was intrigued, even disquieted, by the negative reaction to celibacy amongst the Hindus, a state of existence that barely existed, such that children were technically married at the age of nine or ten, although continued to live with their families for the while. She explained how if a person died unmarried he was thought unable to enter heaven, and he was therefore denied the usual death-related religious ceremonies. This belief was to such an extent that a man facing execution might have to go through a sham marriage to enable the usual religious processes to take place thereafter.

During this October Elizabeth first introduces her friends and family to the existence of Dr James Anderson (1738–1809), apart from a brief earlier mention in February 1803, who taught her a large amount about horticulture. He became a good friend, who advised her repeatedly on gardening and botanical matters, and who appears at odd intervals through the letters. A graduate of the Edinburgh medical school he eventually became surgeon-general in Madras and, in those multi-tasking days, finally physician-general. He is perhaps best remembered, however, for his development of a botanical garden in that city, for the planting of European mulberry trees to start a local silk industry, and the cultivation of apple trees, American cotton and sugar cane. He was a man of great humanity who was known to support starving peasants out of his own pocket during times of famine. There remains a statue of him in St George's Cathedral, Chennai *(See note 8 from Introduction, page 5)*. In relating her experiences in his company she slips readily into a brief discourse on the trees of the region, such is her fascination with all things natural, and from that point on she described how the Indian people used the bamboo and cocoa palm for building their houses and, from there on, a little more about their life-style. So the detail rolls on. One cannot help but think that she was at that time very happily immersed in her Indian life, despite its distance from home, observing everything around her, and learning from it constantly. This exhilaration continues in the next letter to another close friend, Nancy Green, where she describes how a woman carries all her wealth about her person as jewellery, and how extraordinarily attractive they look under any circumstances. 'All of them have a graceful manner of walking beyond our best public performers. Their trinkets are disposed with great taste, and the large quantity of thin muslin which they fold about them without form or shape, without pin or string, or any fastening but the folds, has more elegance in it than any contrivance that needles and scissors could give. When a set of these women walks from the well, with their bright vases on their heads, they look more dignified than you can imagine.' Many would regard this reaction just as relevant two hundred years later, particularly in rural India.

The penultimate two letters of the year are to their sister Hetty. The first is from Mary who, as usual, gets directly to the point in explaining a misunderstanding about the protocol of meeting personal couriers. It was clearly felt important to entertain, at either end, those individuals who were carrying goods and letters backwards and forwards from India to England. Hetty and her husband had been told in a letter from Sir Henry that they need not spend much time with people who were hardly known to the family in India. Hetty seems to have reacted oversensitively, and Mary moves to mollify her and, in the process, enjoys the opportunity to emphasize the ordinariness of so many of the supposedly important people in Madras, relishing again the chance to itemize some of their more undistinguished backgrounds; several senior ladies being the daughters of tailors or innkeepers, or other socially inferior positions. The remainder of that letter is sisterly chatter, which is interesting if only because it so well reveals the preoccupations and concerns of women of that era and that class. It is then Elizabeth's turn. She returns to her fascination with botany and introduces us to Johan Rottler,[3] a French missionary and botanist, from whom she learnt a considerable amount, and with whom she returned a number of specimens to Europe. She then launches briefly into a feminist aside about the neglect of so many women in favour of the needs of men and, equally briefly, follows this with the ever enduring luxury of censuring doctors for their practices, which were admittedly criticisable in those days, at least by modern standards.

Her final comments again emphasize the liberty of expression that can be enjoyed by correspondence between two sisters, when she relates an entertaining scatological episode among the young men of the household.

The final letter of the year is from Mary to Richard Clarke's father in which she once more touches on the subject of older men allying themselves to very young women, not always with the discouragement of the women, who might look forward to profiting from the event. This is soon followed by a fascinating account of life in a Muslim zenana to which she, as a woman, had access, if invited. The description of bejewelled opulence and luxury sits uncomfortably with the obvious lack of cleanliness, the boredom and the cruelty to servants or slaves. This, she comments, is quite unlike the experience of English servants, although not Dutch. At that time slavery was common in Dutch colonies, but it is interesting to note that there were no British slaves in India at any time under the East India Company, which is in stark contrast to the situation in the West Indies. There are few descriptions of zenana life such as this, and they are all limited to women's writings, the other well-known description being by Fanny Parkes.[4]

3 Johan Rottler, 1749–1836, was a French missionary and botanist, mostly associated with the Danish mission in Tranquebar, but later moving to an English mission near Madras. He was an enthusiastic botanist who collected more than 2000 plant samples from Southern India and sent them to Europe. Many went to the great herbarium of King's college, London, but were later transferred to the Royal Botanic Gardens at Kew. Most of his collections are in the Royal Herbarium of Munich. He was awarded a PhD in 1795. Despite publication, his achievements were overlooked for many years.

4 Parkes, Fanny, *Wanderings of a Pilgrim in Search of the Picturesque* (London, 1850).

So ends 1804, and the sisters withdraw into the communication blackout of the Indian winter months eagerly, but apprehensively, awaiting the arrival of news in the early spring.

Letters

From Mary Symonds to her sister Hetty. 28th February 1804

Having this day enjoyed the great satisfaction of receiving two pretty little letters from my dear mother and you, I sit down to answer them by the return of the post. You will more easily imagine, than I can describe to you, the pleasure these two letters have given us when I tell you that the last letter received, before these, were dated April 1803. Also, that a ship had arrived here called the Euphrates, having left England 29 September, without bringing us a single line from any one friend.

The collection of things you sent us has been a constant source of amusement to us, besides the satisfaction we have in eating and wearing new things, we are every now and then surprised at a new discovery in unrolling a piece of ribbon. When we get off half the quantity, out pops a beauty of another sort which we never expected to see and, the other day only, I discovered a pot of 'mottoes' amongst the confectionery. To be sure they were a little mouldy from having lain so long under some fruit lozenges which were damp, but I set one of the little black boys to rub them clean with a piece of flannel and now they look quite fresh again. I am sure you would laugh enough if you could but have a peep at us, sometimes trying on the things, for you have no idea how stupid we are grown, always about putting them on. One of the caps, with a yellow Laburnum flower in it, was tried on with the hind side foremost, and indeed every side but the right one. We could make nothing of it, although it looked beautiful off the head, so it was given up until a lady happened to come from Europe with the same one, which we saw her wear. Ever since, that cap has been a great favourite of Betsy's.

Then there is a pretty cloak which was like to be lost, for it was packed inside one of Sir Henry's hats, and he of course chose to have the pleasure of unpacking those himself, which he did in a little side room and threw out all the contents of the box, except the hats, supposing it to be only waste paper. As it was very light, the wind blew it under a couch in one corner of the room, where it stayed till the next day, only discovered when the woman who swept the room brought it to light and we began to try it on, that is Betsy took it up to her own room to try. She and her maid worked at it for some time, but not being able to settle the matter she came into my room to know if I could find out the manner of wearing it for, says she, "I am sure it must be very pretty if we could but tell how to put it on." I patted it down on the back, and I put the strings under the arms, and then the other arms, and then tried them around the waist, but all would not do. The cape stood out behind like a shift, and the lace would not quite reach to the elbows, which gave it a very odd look, so at last she took it off in despair and I began to turn it about on the bed, and to lament over it when, all of a sudden, it came into my head to put it on another way. Then, to our great surprise, we found that we had been all the time putting it on the wrong side uppermost, and that the thing we took for the cape was intended to be the frill of a jacket, and very pretty it is. Betsy wears it often, with the bonnet made of the same muslin, which she calls her calash, and she is quite happy in it because it hides the sides of her face, which you know she always liked to do, being so much afraid of looking old.

I have trotted about society in your thick green shoes, not on the sea beach because there the sand is very fine, and also I thought the seawater would spoil the shape of them at once. I always go there in the old shoes made in this country as they are of no value, but the thick ones I brought with me rise to the occasion when we are in the same house we had last year at this season. From this place we frequently scramble about the hills which are very rocky, and everywhere covered with brambles and a variety of thorny plants. Betsy has been highly pleased with her pair of green shoes which you sent her, and she thinks they were not bought at the same place with the others as they had no maker's name in them. They fit her better than any of the rest, though indeed both hers and mine are in general a little too long, but she wishes some more of the same.

We were very much amused by your idea of the cotton in which the pearls were packed. I assure you it is not the wool you suppose it to be, though I think it a pity to undeceive you yet I must tell you it is nothing more than a bit of Bourbon cotton, the same as that which makes the shining French cotton used for working the beautiful satin stitch so much the fashion at present. We have sent Mr Whitby a good deal of the seed of it at different times.

Poor Sir Henry is very angry at the late arrival of the Navy, which is not to be wondered at considering how much this country feels the ill effects of it. It just served to give the French an opportunity of sending out a fleet which has been annoying our trade ever since, and they have contrived to destroy one of the Company's warehouses. Our troops have completely succeeded in driving all the French out of the Maratha country, which is a great thing for us as they are a mischievous deceitful set. An officer of theirs has lately been discovered corresponding with his countrymen at the Isle of France. He has lived with the English for ten or twelve years, affecting to be a true friend to them, but has been employing himself in finding out the weakest parts of the country and, lately, whilst one of the bastions of the fort was under repair, and we were engaged with the Marathas, he wrote a letter to the French Admiral telling him the exact state of Fort St George and advising him to bring his whole force there to a particular part where he would find very little to oppose him. This correspondence was luckily intercepted by one of our frigates. What should be done with the Frenchman I do not know.

Betsy intends to send a shawl if we can get anybody to carry it and, if we do, I hope it will have the good luck to escape the nasty privateers which are acting freely this season in an inconceivable manner. Great fears are entertained here for the homeward bound China ships and, if they are lost, you will lose some trifles which we gave to their care. You would know of the event soon after the receipt of this.

From Elizabeth Gwillim to her mother 7th March 1804.

How I received your letter dated the 20th August 1803, written in Bishopsgate, I know not. Hetty said in her letter that she had been to the India house, and had scarcely time to write by the Aplin. Now the Aplin was expected here for many days but, instead of seeing the ship, we heard the fatal news that it was taken by a French privateer, but that the Captain had been allowed to go to Calcutta. Sir Henry was most outraged against our ships of war in letting this come to pass, and we were all miserable with the idea of having lost all the letters we naturally expected by the Aplin. A few days afterwards, however, a packet arrived from Calcutta by post, containing yours and Hetty's letters alone. The dispatches, and the letters by the mail, we understand were destroyed, and one can only conceive that ours must have been put in too late for the mail at the India House, and brought by some private hand, perhaps Captain Rogers himself, who is a very good-natured man and spent a day with us on his last voyage.

Our old Admiral Rainier is an excellent old man, but whether he has too much to do for the strength of force with him or what, I know not, but the Bay is overrun with privateers. There are no less than thirteen that they know of, besides four that have been taken. Four Indiamen are now about to sail from this place, under convoy. I hinted something of carrying things, but there was no response and, indeed, in these dangerous times it is a favour too great to ask. We shall send one letter by each ship if time permits. I sent some things by Mr Lane, the surgeon of a ship, who spent some time with us on his way to China. He could not undertake this without me giving him 25 percent, which is what they give the smugglers to land things for them. For this premium, they undertake to land the goods whenever they may and, if they fail, are paid anyway. So much for honour amongst thieves, and I am told they always receive payment, even if they lose the goods. You are also obliged to put the full value on it for, if they think the thing better than the price, they retain it and say it was seized.

I fear the China ships will be taken, because the French fleet which came out to take possession of Pondicherry took a course eastward, and we have already heard that they went to Bencoolen[5] and did all the mischief

5 Bencoolen, or Benkulen, (now Bengkulu) was an East India Company residency in southwest Sumatra, built to protect from the Dutch what little of the pepper trade the British still had. Its central structure was Fort Marlborough and to be posted there was regarded as demotion, as it became a white mans' graveyard with a high mortality from fever. Thomas Stamford Raffles was appointed Lieutenant-Governor

they could, which was however of no great consequence, but they are in those seas at present and it seems more than probable they will take our ships. At least it is here generally thought so. I shall be sorry if Mr Lane, who was an apprentice with the 'Illustrious Price', is taken, as he once before lost all he had gained, and he seems a quiet good young man, with much dry humour.

I have been in India from the end of November 1801 till about April 1803, and we had only 10 hard days of monsoon rain, and one shower, in the intervening spring, and that was to me the pleasantest year we have had. It was the coolest summer and the country was quite verdant till just before the monsoon. Since that time we have seldom been a week without rain, and the monsoon lasted three months. The torrents of rain which have fallen are astonishing. One should have supposed all this would have cooled the earth, but on the contrary the heat has been insupportable. The two former winter seasons we were glad to shut the doors of a night and put a blanket on the bed, but this year the thermometer has never been below 82, which as far as I remember must be as hot as you ever see it in England. The natives are much pleased with the season for it is a season of plenty. Rain is their wealth and their glory. If we had not had such rains there would probably have been a famine and dreadful calamity everywhere, but for these poor people, who make no provision for the seasons, life is horrid beyond description. All the areas about this place, however dry in appearance, and barren since I came here, have been sowed with rice and other different grains. The whole place has looked like corn country in England, in June. They sowed in December, and now is the harvest. I suppose the greater part will be cleared in about a week, and the tanks, that is the reservoirs or lakes, are still well filled, and they will no doubt get a second crop. Their custom is to float the fields of rice, by which means the air is impregnated with damp and becomes to me very injurious. I suffered much with the same kind of intermittent ague[6] I had the first monsoon,

---

of Bencoolen in 1817, and instituted many reforms including the abolition of slavery. It was handed back to the Netherlands in the Anglo-Dutch treaty of 1824.

6 An ague is an obsolete word for a shivering fever (shaking chill), such as from malaria.

but I was so extremely nervous with it that I could not know what to make of myself. Dr Anderson ordered me to go instantly to the Mount which, being high ground, is like the Hampstead of Madras and I have been there six weeks. Thank God, I think I am now as well as before the monsoon, and as fat. I am much fatter than when I left England, but I change very often from fat to lean, but not violently either way. I am very fond of this place. It is like an English village. The bells knoll to church on a Sunday, and the church is at the top of the rock, but it is too high church in every sense of the word for us. There is a broad flight of steps in the rock, as high as to the top of St Pauls, on the top of which stands the church and some fine trees. Some of the priests' houses are at different stages. The religion is Catholic in its most superstitious form, but I believe I told you a great deal about this place last year, and am only making repetition. However it is a curious place, and I must tell you something more about it in order to prepare you for a story, which I have translated from the Telugu language, or as it is commonly called the Gentoo, and which I intend to send you by Captain Price, as I fear it will be too large for a letter.

I believe I told you that the village of Saint Thomas (called by the Portuguese S. Thomé) near which I live is an ancient and holy city of the Indians called by them Mazoora Pooram, or the city of peacocks. From that village to this place, and some way beyond, is what they call a hallam; a word that in some senses means only a place. In a religious sense it means something like a cathedral city, or a bishop's see, a place where there is a great pagoda with many others subordinate to it, as you will understand if you read the story. This is a sacred legend, for the Hindus have a legendary tale to every church, as the Catholics have of their saints. Shiva and Vishnu are the gods to whom alone they raise great temples (or as we call them, improperly, pagodas), but in every temple the god is worshipped by a different name, or rather epithet, which has made many suppose their gods numerous. Thus they say the Lord of the Rock, the Lord of the Soul, the Lilywhite god, and so on. Shiva is the god worshipped in this village and district. Now the worship of Shiva is the more ancient, but it is also the darkest superstition. The people are the prey of the Brahmins, who make their vices a source of wealth. The followers of Vishnu have better notions, but even their worship has little but outward form. Some learned people think the Brahmins are conquerors of the Indians, and come from a distant country. It may be so, but it is a dreadful religion these innocent people are taught. Their virtues are not from the growth of it, but from their gentle natures, and this false religion is some excuse for any of their errors. It seems almost profane to compare it to Christianity.

This village is believed to be the first place where Christianity was taught in India, and St Thomas the apostle is said to have fallen a martyr here. As I was learning the Gentoo, I thought it would be a good exercise to translate the sthala puranam, or legend of this place, and therefore desired the Brahmin to procure it for me. It is a poem in their language, as all these kind of works are, but it is not in their most extravagant style. If you can get over the hard names, I think it will give you a better idea of the religion of these people, and their customs, than anything I could tell you. As you complain so much of the difficulty of reading my hand, I have put a native writer to transcribe it. I have put a great many notes on it at the end, or perhaps they ought to be called memoranda, for as such I wrote them. They will explain to you everything you want to know, and you may read them or let them alone, as you like. You must accept this story as a letter when it comes for, though not in my hand, it was copied from mine. It took me a great time to write, and a vast amount of trouble enquiring into the various circumstances beyond your beliefs. You must endeavour to let me know if it affords you any entertainment, so that I may judge whether it will be worthwhile to send you anything more, or if you be not quite tired of hearing Indian history

I told you long ago that I left the white world to Polly but I do not think you would care much about knowing the greater part of the people here. Our scandal is not a whit more entertaining than that of an old ladies tea table. Instead of hearing that an old lady stints her maid in bread and butter, or gives the cold meat to the lap dog instead of a Christian, we hear of one who has hanged innocent polygars,[7] and another who is haunted by the ghost of a Rajah, and suchlike morning chat.

7 South Indian territorial and military administrators, who collected taxes, maintained law and order, ran the local judiciary, and maintained a battalion of troops for their regional king. They were often at war (The Polygar Wars) with the East India Company up until 1805.

I am sorry you and Mr Gwillim have so much trouble to read my letters. I wish they were better worth it, but this is a fatiguing climate and I write as fast as I can, and seldom stay to read over again what I have written, so that I fear it is strange blundering stuff.

From Mary Symonds to her sister Hetty 21st July 1804.

The Tigress having unexpectedly put in here today, I have the pleasure of writing a few lines by her. She was hastily dispatched by Lord Wellesley direct to England but, fearing her water would run short, she has just put in for a few hours only to take in some more. It is now three o'clock and the packet is to close at six. This I mention in order to prevent my other friends being offended by our not answering their kind letters. We had the pleasure of receiving some packets from you by the Marquis Wellesley, which ship arrived here the night before last, in company with the Lady Jane Dundas, Lord Nelson and Princess Charlotte. The Marchioness of Exeter left England with them, but was separated by a storm off the Cape so she is not arrived, nor do they know anything of her. I hope she will find her way here in time, particularly as we expect to receive several letters from our dear friends. We have been cruelly disappointed of letters from home since the war, one ship was lost off Madeira, in which you say you had sent letters, the Aplin too was taken, and her public packets thrown overboard, however we received one letter by her from you, one from my dear mother and one from Mrs Shepheard. Sir Henry has one from Dr Cam, and a ridiculous little shabby note from James, for which he may expect a good trimming when I have more time to write. This letter to come 15,000 miles consists of six lines of business, and two more of apologies for not making it shorter!!!

Poor Richard Clarke has a most melancholy letter from his mother, with a particular account of dear little Mary Anne's death *(his sister)*. Surely it was one of the heaviest calamities which providence can bestow, to lose so sweet a creature in such a sudden and dreadful way. Betsy is so much shocked and fretted by the account of it, that she cannot write today owing to a sad headache she has got by crying and grieving, and poor Richard is as low as death. In other respects, thank God, we are all pretty well. I am very sorry to be prevented from giving you more satisfactory accounts of your dispatches by the ships of this season, but it is better to say something than nothing. Four ships which left England before then have not yet arrived, but we are in hourly expectation of them and I believe there is no fear entertained for their safety, though they are so long coming.

Admiral Rainier has been on shore at Madras some weeks, and all the fleet have lately been here to victual. The Admiral was expected to stay some time longer, but he went on board yesterday morning and sailed before sunrise, quite secretly. It is reported here that he had some information of Admiral Linois,[8] having come out from Mauritius, and then went in pursuit of him. If so, I hope he will come up with the French fleet and that we shall have a good account of them all.

You say your pretty little girl was six months old *(This must be Mary James, known to have been born that year).* This is the first time we have heard of her existence and she is now (I trust) 10 months old. Pray let us hear of her as often as you can. We are much puzzled to find how she came by her blue eyes. My mother always accounted for my pug nose by her looking at Nanny Wiles; pray who have you been ogling? I might have suspected my friend Templar, but you have not had enough of his company to make any impression, or else I think he has a pair of blue eyes as well worth looking at as any I know. I have received two very kind letters from him, and I find by them that I have lost one of his valuable epistles. Those I have are very melancholy. He complains sadly at having so short a time to stay with his family after his long absence. He says the kindness and affection of his brothers and sisters, instead of making him happy, were an affliction to him because he knew he could not stay to enjoy their society. He is an excellent young man, and has a most feeling heart.

I trust you will not be long at any one time without hearing from us, as we shall have frequent opportunities of writing between this time and October, and we will make a point of missing none of them. Sir Henry was obliged to attend the court today and therefore has not time to write, but

8 Charles-Alexandre Linois was a French admiral who was appointed in 1803 by Napoleon Bonaparte to command the French forces in the Indian Ocean. Flying his flag in the 74-gun ship Marengo he was a constant irritant to British merchant shipping all the way to the China seas.

he desires me to say he is much surprised that James has not acknowledged the receipt of the money he sent home by the Wellesley. It was £200. He begs and instructs that James will not be so very concise in his letters. Do find some way of punishing him for it. Lock up his stick on Sunday, and don't let him have the newspapers for a month. I find I must conclude as it is now five o'clock, so God bless you.

From Elizabeth Gwillim to her mother 12th August 1804

I hope it is still the Prince of Wales birthday, not the King's *(meaning she hoped the King was still alive and not yet succeeded by the Prince of Wales)*

It is probable that we shall have only one day to write. We have just had notice that a ship is to sail tomorrow (the Glory). We all intend writing, but not so fully as by the next ship which will probably be in England as soon as this.

I have the pleasure to say that by the blessing of God we are all in good health at present, but we have had a very severe season. The heat has been beyond anything I had before felt, and I may say I did not know India till this season. The heat does not disagree with me, nor the land winds. They soon cured my spasms and ague-ish complaint, but they are very distressing to Sir Henry who has suffered very much for three months. The rains came on about a fortnight ago, and he is much relieved even by a single shower. We have had it very cool with strong rain every day and, thank God, I do not perceive that he looks at all the worse for his sufferings. To a person so irritable as Mr G., you may suppose these winds are a terrible annoyance, and not be relieved by any medicine. He has therefore had little to do with doctors, for they have all alike told him that it was the mere effect of the wind. When it changes he has immediate relief, but we have had four months of these winds this year, and during that time he has been unable to study, or take delight in anything. Thank God they are now abated.

We have at present a young man of 20 with us, who Mr Gwillim and Mr James introduced to us. He is a cadet, a Mr Biss, whose father I have a faint recollection of but did not know he was married, nor that he lived in Hereford. I feel quite an old woman. He is a fine young man and very well-behaved. Richard and he are great friends. He has been confined here for some time for, though he had not much the matter, yet the doctors will not to let them go to Tripasore to drill till they are in good health, and if they have a friend who will receive them. He has had a bilious complaint, which he had had on board ship, for they had a most terrible voyage, I should think from some mismanagement in the ship. We have, besides, another young man with us who is a very good and elegant lad. He is a brother-in-law of Mr Plumer, the councillor who is on your circuit. Poor boy, he has had the flux with blood -- we have also had for some time the assistant of Hetty's apothecary, who came out as surgeon of a ship, and he also was sick. In short, the season has been so severe that almost everyone that came out has been sick, but I have heard of none dying. The doctors have been cautious, because so many accidents happened during the extremity of the heat with young people being full of blood. I suppose you will have heard, before you receive this, of the loss of poor Temple *(Sir Henry's clerk of court - not to be confused with Templar)*. That stout young man was called away in a moment, almost when no person entertained the least apprehension. He died of health, if one may say so, for he has never had any illness except a little bilious complaint for a few days last year. He ate heartily, and took too little exercise which was his only fault, for he was a most honourable and valuable young man, and one upon whose grateful disposition I had had great reliance. Sir Henry had exerted himself much lately to serve him, and about a month before he died he had been made lawyer attorney, so that his three appointments were nearly £1200 a year, besides what his practice would have been, as he was just admitted an attorney. I grieve for his father, for he was an only child and well worthy of a good parent. He was, as you know, clerk to Mr G. which was 60 pagodas a month, that is about £300 a year. That appointment is now given to Richard Clarke, who is manly enough for the office and thank God has, like Polly, constantly had his health.

I think poor little Tom (who ought now to be big Tom) is now 12 years old, and I'm very happy to hear he is so good a boy of which I had no doubt. Mr Gwillim tells me that, in the course of correcting the boys exercises, the masters ought to correct the English as well as the Latin, and he therefore thinks that there must lately have been a great neglect in the school, for poor Tom's letter is not well spelled, and that with words which must occur in every exercise -- that is 'has' for 'as'. "He is nearly has tall has I am". Pray tell him gently of it, because when this answer reaches him he will doubtless have found his mistake and be mortified, and we attach no blame to him. It certainly shows a negligence on the part of the schoolmasters. In other respects we thought he had written very neatly and well. At the same time I thought it best to tell him that he might be careful in spelling, which the learning of another language, particularly Latin, generally makes people do. The want of that language makes us women so uncertain. Few professions require men to speak or write Latin, and therefore the greatest use of it is to help men know their own language well.

A silence of 10 months from the date of your former letters to the receipt of your recent one, is so long. The terror we suffered when we saw the ships come by after so long an absence was beyond all things. We feared to open the letters and, as our fears were, so is our gratitude to God for his preservation of you all.

From Mary Symonds to her sister Hetty 12th August 1804

I wrote to you by the Tigress *(21st July)*, which ship left this place about a fortnight ago. I had then the pleasure to tell you we were all well, and that we had received some of your kind and truly welcome letters by the Fleet. Since that time we have received the remainder of them, together with the packages you mention. The millinery, fire irons, and the pickles, ketchups and raspberry vinegars are all in excellent order, but the preserves I am sorry to say have suffered much. Mr Biss tells me the ship was constantly soaking and full of water, which was the cause of the sweetmeats fermenting. Many of the pots were broke, and others had lost their tops, but those which were put in stone jars, and corked down, came safe. The millinery (as you observe) is a small quantity but as we had such an ample supply last year, it is quite enough and it is remarkably pretty and very well packed, so that it all looked as fresh when we opened it as if it had been made that minute. We are indeed very much obliged to you for the great trouble you take on our account. God grant we may all live to meet again and that we may have the power to make you some returns. That this life is all uncertainty, and that we ought not to promise ourselves anything beyond the present hour, we have sufficient proof, but yet there are few, if any, amongst us who consider this sufficiently to keep their minds prepared to meet misfortunes calmly. We have very sensibly *(sensitively)* felt the weakness of our nature in this respect within these few days. Temple had an illness so short, and apparently so slight, that it did not prepare us for the sad event which has taken place and consequently it has been a severe shock to us all. He dined with us on Wednesday and Thursday the first and second of the month and on Friday he dined with Mr Disney, a gentleman in the law. He was quite well and in remarkably good spirits all the evening. At night, when he was going home, the weather was cloudy and threatened rain, and therefore Mr and Mrs Disney endeavoured to prevail with him to sleep at their house, but they could not. It rained very little however, that night, and we do not know that he was wet at all. The next day at about 12 o'clock he complained of a little sickness at his stomach, which Sir Henry mentioned to us at dinner time, but the sickness went off and Temple said he was very well again. However, the next morning being Sunday, Richard drove into the fort to church and he called upon Temple to ask if he would come out to dine with us, but he found him very unwell and with a good deal of fever. He had a Dr Scarman with him, who lived next door to him. He said the disorder was of no great consequence, and that Mr T. would be well in a day or two. On Monday, Richard and Sir Henry went to the fort to their business, and both went to see Temple, but at separate times. When Sir Henry called he had fallen asleep, and therefore he would not let him be disturbed, but when Richard called he found him sitting up apparently well and the fever had quite left him. He said he should come to Mount Thomas, perhaps the next day. This they told us when they came home, and we all naturally concluded that the disorder was at an end, but the next morning, Tuesday, Richard went to business early, it being his court day. He set off from home at eight o'clock, and when he got about 200 yards he met one of Temple's men, running, who desired him to make haste as his master was very ill. Richard drove very fast, but when he came to the fort gate (a distance of only 2 miles from the place where he met the servant) he saw a man running with a note towards him, which was from Dr Scarman saying that poor Temple was no more. He was taken ill at eight o'clock the night before, and Scarman stayed with him some time but he did not apprehend the least danger, nor think the illness by any means of a serious nature. He left him quite tranquil at night, and at six in the morning he called on him again and still saw nothing serious, but he applied a blister because Temple complained of a tightness on his chest. Mr Scarman then went out to prepare some medicine and Temple told his servant to pat his back as he felt a fullness, which he thought was a wind. The man did so, and T. then said "that will do" and laid down as to sleep. The servant sat down by him and in a few minutes Temple called out, "go and bring Dr Scarman back, I don't feel well". The man ran and returned with Mr Scarman instantly, only from the next room, but they came too late for his breath had passed away in that moment. Mr Scarman called in three surgeons, besides himself, to assist at opening the body, as he wished for some witnesses lest his credit should suffer. They found that his death was occasioned by suffocation from the quantity of blood and water which had gathered in the chest and which, it is supposed, was the reason he always expressed a disinclination to take exercise. His disorder is said to be extremely uncommon in this climate, so much so that Dr Scarman thinks his assertion would have been doubted had he not taken the precaution to call in three of the most respectable surgeons to hear testimony. What consolation you will have in your power to offer to his afflicted father I know not, for what can we say in such a case that has not been said a thousand times before, and without effect. He has lost his only child, whom he looked upon as the sure prop to sustain his sinking age, and who reasonably hoped to receive the reward of a laborious life in the credit and comfort you would derive from such a son. He will sink under the loss of his darling treasure and, if it pleases God to preserve his life through such a trial, will most certainly for the remainder of his days feel himself a miserable solitary being. For though he could not have parted with him to this distant country without knowing that the risk to his son was very great, yet I fear that the three years in which he had heard only of success and good health may have removed all his doubts and fears, and lulled his mind into a state of perfect security. How hard a task it is to awake it to such pain? Poor Temple was beloved by all who knew him, and I believe there never was any person more generally and sincerely regretted. The families where he visited lament him as a relative, but most particularly General and Mrs Trent, who I really believe loved him almost as a son. The good old General attended his funeral and Richard says, when they were returning, the General went up to him and pressed his hand, but was so much affected that he could not speak. I have since called on Mrs Trent and found her extremely low. They intend leaving this country in October, and Mrs Trent told me she had just finished a keepsake for each of the two favourites (meaning Richard and Temple) the day before poor Temple's death. I hope you will know General and Mrs Trent in England; she is a most charming sweet tempered woman, and though he is a little odd in some respects, yet I am sure a better man does not exist.

I send this by the Glory which, however, is not thought to be a very safe ship, being a very bad sailor, and the same in which so much wickedness and trouble happened on her passage out. Those disturbances gave people a bad opinion of her but, as the captain who was a party in those troubles is killed, and the others who were engaged in them no longer with her, I think it very probable that she may arrive safe.[9]

Mr Biss is staying with us at present, and will continue some days longer; indeed we shall part with him with regret, whenever he leaves, as he is so quiet and good humoured. The cadets who came out with him were marched off to drill a few days after their arrival, but Sir Henry procured leave for him to stay a little time with us, partly because we wished to have his company, and partly because he had a little bile on his stomach. We therefore wished him to be a little seasoned before he went to his own management. He seems to have very good health and spirits, and I dare say he will do very well here. He loses no time by staying with us, as we have masters of everything languishing about the house, and he is very industrious and studious from morning till night. I'm sure he will be thought a wonder, if he goes on with the same anxiety.

9 The Glory was an East Indiaman launched in 1802. She made two complete voyages for the HEIC and disappeared on her third in 1808. On the second voyage she arrived in Madras in February 1804 where her Captain, Thomas Taylor, aged 28, accepted a challenge to a duel from a Major William Davison and was killed as a result.

Your friend the Dr (as we call him) McMalliss is an extraordinary being; a true Scotchman. He has been very amusing to the young men by his pretending to understand every subject that is started, and he is as easy at first sight as if he had known you for an hundred years. He stayed at our house as long as he had leave to be on shore. One day he came to dinner in such a dirty shirt and stockings that Biss, who sat opposite to him, could not eat for laughing to see him in that dirty state, talking away as if he had been my Lord Duke. He puffed away about his introductions here and, when they came to be explained, they turned out to be a single letter from Miss Saunders to Mrs Floyer, a very vulgar woman, a Major's wife, who is over head and ears in debt. This Dr brought her out a box of goods, which procured him a dinner when he delivered it safe, and that was all. He is a curious fellow altogether, but not surprising to us who have hundreds of the same sort of ragamuffins come out every year fresh from Scotland and, like him, they all pretend to be great men. I have given him some Argos pheasant feathers for you, consisting of five papers done up with a set of feathers in each, that is a plume of small ones for the point of the head, and a long one to twist round as a bandeau. Those you may dispose of to any friends you wish to oblige, and when out and dressed a little, they will make very handsome ornaments. I think in future the quantity of made-up millinery you have sent this time will be sufficient at each time. You should send three dresses each, three caps and two bonnets, six pair of shoes and six pair of gloves, a very little good jewellery, and whatever you think properly made. The comb with Wedgwood ornaments is very pretty. The blue necklace, too, is pretty, and so are the earrings. I have copied the turban, which I think is very handsome, and the pink cap. I wish you always to send a little unmade material, as I can then copy them for myself and give up the originals to Betsy, who you know does not like that sort of business. I am sure Mr Prosser did his best for he is as good-natured young man as can be, but I know the custom house officers are very strict in their searches, and will never let a bit of chintz or shawl escape if they can help it. I have mentioned hats and bonnets to be sent. Pray let them be of the plainer form, that is work straw or chip, and as long as round hats turned up on one side are worn, I shall prefer them to any other, for our heads get so old-fashioned that we don't know how to manage anything whimsical.

At the same time we wish them fashionable, just what you or I should have bought for ourselves in the spring.

You say you don't know how to act about giving letters to young men. I will tell you; put all your letters into the public packet, and give them a few lines mainly to introduce them, and stress it does not signify when they deliver them. If they will take charge of seeds, and promise to keep them in their cabins, it will always be an advantage to send by them, and when you meet with one you can trust, like Lane or Livingstone, you can send gloves or such small things as will not keep in the hold, and request them to keep them dry in their cabins. Letters are certainly best sent by post, for however anxious an officer of a ship may be to deliver them, yet perhaps he cannot get leave to come onshore for two or three days after the ship has arrived, whereas all that comes by post is sent over to us immediately. We wish you to understand this clearly, as it is the greatest pleasure we can receive to see and converse with any person who has seen you and, as for Sir Henry, he is seriously delighted when he gets hold of a Herefordshire man that he talks to him all day without ceasing. Herefordshire people and Herefordshire news are his delight. Biss has delighted him, and the first night they entered upon the subject we had much to do to get him to bed at midnight, and Betsy says he began the subject again as soon as his eyes were open.

I begin to be very conscious of my paper for I have made this a long letter, and it is such a one as I hope I shall never have occasion to send you again. I am sure of tomorrow for writing, and I shall employ it busily.

From Elisabeth Gwillim to her sister Hetty 13th August 1804

In return for all the kindness you have shown to us, and the labours you perform for us in the midst of your own difficulties and vexations, I cannot help writing a few lines by this ship, although I am assured on all hands that she will not be in England before the rest of the Fleet, which is to sail a month hence.

Mr Biss has had a dreadful voyage, but being his first he did not know it, until compared with the accounts from the other accompanying ships. They buried their men two or three a day. They lost all their masts. They encountered an enemy who, fortunately à la francais, ran away and, above all, their ship leaked most seriously and they shipped heavy seas continually. Upon the whole it is a mercy of Providence that they came here at all. It is said that the captain will be severely questioned, but others say that the blame was not his.

I expect that the whole returning fleet will be received with great honour in England. We drank the health of Commodore Dance and his India fleet every day for three months.[10]

Sir Henry is in great anxiety for his pepper and salt, ladies-cloth, English coat. He says he wrote to James about it. I must beg to have, as soon as possible, two pieces of strong huckaback *(a type of weave)* Hamburgh towelling, for ours are in perfect rags and I cannot bear the calico. Our things are just what I could wish only, every time, I should like to have one half piece narrow, and one broad, of some white ribbon, and perhaps a figured one or two, for it does not keep. All mine that came out are spoiled. They looked tolerable last year but now I cannot use them.

I rejoice that you like your cockatoo, and pray do not fret if he dies. I will try and get you another, although perhaps not so accomplished. This one spoke Malabar *(Tamil)* like fury, which is the muttering you hear. He could speak no English when I sent him. What will Mr Prosser say when he hears that my canary is dead, after all his good natured kindness. I thought Mr Gwillim would have cried about it, and I am ashamed to say I thought of it more than I ought to about a bird. I must close here having had the message for three minutes *(before the letters were to be collected)*.

Dr Sims has paid me great compliments. I blush. Pray what can I send him, if anything I can do will be acceptable. I shall be very happy in the way of plants. I presume to know a little more about them, as we have some botanists come down now, and I am becoming learned. I should never have done otherwise.

10 Nathaniel Dance, Commodore of one of the East India Company's fleets, gained a knighthood, and much praise, for duping a French squadron under Admiral Linois, that was raiding British shipping, into thinking they were a naval force, and so steered a whole merchant fleet home.

From Mary Symonds, probably to her sister Hetty 10th October 1804.

I wrote to you by the Glory, a ship that sailed from this place seven or eight weeks ago, and in it I thanked you for the things you so kindly did for me, but that ship sailed so soon after I had unpacked them that I could not give you the account I wished. Had we opened the things that had not opened themselves on the voyage, we should have spoiled what was good, and I expected these would be but little. I have now the pleasure to say that all my pickles and ketchup came in perfect order. The ketchup is as fresh as a mushroom from the field, and we eat it every day with our fish. The sea runs close to us, and repays us for its noisy roaring in the night by fresh fish every day, which we see caught, or at least we see the boats that are employed in the business. I am very sorry for the trouble you have had about the currant jelly, but I find that I need not trouble any of my friends for preserves in future. As I become more acquainted with the country, I find the less need of them. The ladies who come to this country are often of necessity changing themselves to suit this place, but those who therefore know such things are often no longer here to tell us what they have learnt. I find now that the mango fruit, used green, makes the finest jelly I ever eat in my life. It will not keep above a month, but the trees bear more or less all the year. We therefore do not want currant jelly, for there is not the least difference between the flavours. For white currant jelly, we have Salaccas *(snake fruit)* for tarts, much superior to gooseberries, and several other fruits of the same nature, particularly one called Bilimbi *(tree sorrel)* and another called Ambarella, besides which the green mangoes make us apple puddings and pies every day. In puddings they are very much liked. I tell the young men, when they first come, that they are our Indian apples. They are like a codling *(type of unripe cooking apple)*, when it is very young, and the boys cannot tell the difference between the mango and the apple. The mushroom catchup *(sic - ketchup)*, and pickles, are of great value to us, as we have no vinegar that would make them good, if we but had the walnuts and mushrooms, neither of which we can get. The vinegar is excessively bad, except what comes from England, which is so valuable, and the country vinegar is so cheap, that the people always adulterate it with toddy vinegar, a kind of arrack vinegar which has a perfectly offensive taste. I am most exceedingly obliged to you for the trouble you have had, which I am now ashamed to think of. I am truly happy to hear that your little ones are so well. I do not doubt of their being well educated under your care, for I am sure you will not give them false notions of vanity on one hand, nor meanness on the other, and I think they are very happily placed in a school of innocent children. I am only grieved to hear you complain so much of your own health, which I had hoped was mending. I trust you are not over anxious about anything, since happiness does not depend on place, or riches, and an exalted situation is no certain mark of a noble mind, or a clear understanding.

I am obliged to you for being pleased with the credit Sir Henry gained in the affair you mention. We were utterly astonished at any account in the English papers. Who sent it God knows. I received it from three places. It was not quite accurately stated, but I assure you not more to his honour than he deserved, nor near so much so. He behaved nobly, almost unsupported utterly so, till the last. What has been the effect of an attempt to do his duty here can only be told when we meet. At which time I hope we shall look back upon these trials with satisfaction, but the worst is they have injured his health very much. The climate is more than he is equal to without precaution. He has had a fever of about three months this year, which had at one time reduced him very much. He has lately, thank God, been recovering very fast, if the business does not over set him, but our seasons have been very severe this year.[11]

If Captain Pendergrass comes here, I hope he will call, but I assure the favour is all done to us, for the captains are in such request in the different families here, and so much engaged in business disposing of their investments, that we can seldom see them however desirous we may be. I am obliged to you for thinking of us when you heard of the fire, which was a bad one and consumed a considerable quantity of grain, but it seldom happens that lives are lost in this country by fire, for the houses are never more than one floor above another, and every window is so like a door that it must be an extraordinary case if anyone was behind, unless by choice. As

11 It is unclear to what this precisely refers, but it is likely to relate to the disagreements on matters of principle that Sir Henry was experiencing with Sir William Bentinck, Governor. See Introduction and final chapter.

it happens, few English families live in the Black town and the families that do are Armenians, and wealthy natives, and their houses of stones and brick could not easily be burned. The great destruction in cases of fire is amongst the poor natives, but their houses, and all in them, are of hardly any value and generally only a ground floor. I said nobody need be burned but by choice, which may seem a strong speech to you, but it happens in India that people sometimes choose to. There are sure marks of the worship of fire amongst the Hindus, and we read in their stories of persons hoping to save their children by throwing themselves into the flames to deprecate the wrath of that angry element, which they look upon as a deity. They daily make oblations to fire in every house of pious Hindus, but this superstition is to be found to the utmost extent amongst the Parsees, many of whom inhabit the islands of Bombay. If the fire was to catch your gown there, not a servant amongst the Parsees (who are the attendants there) would put it out, nor even if it was his own. He would not offend the God by attempting to snatch the victory he had seized. Perhaps you might have read in the papers of a terrible fire at Bombay since that at Madras. It was of shocking extent and hundreds, as I am assured, suffered voluntarily; nay rushed into the flames. The admiral, who was laying at anchor near, sent the officers and sailors to aid in quelling the flames, but could not prevail upon the natives to act. They threw away the water out of the buckets given them, and refused to throw it on the flames, in spite of all threats. Their little shops contained bales of shawls, muslins, silks, spices and chests of gold. These were rescued from the flames, and their owners forced out of their houses and their rich merchandise given back to them. Yet so bigoted are they to their superstitions, that they carried them back and sat on them patiently waiting till the flames surrounded them when they, and their goods, were devoured by the fire. If you could but be here for about a week, how you would be amazed with your notions of reforming these people. Europeans of every description hardly make one in a thousand of the natives.

When I came here I thought it most awfully wonderful to see that we certainly ruled these people absolutely, yet not a boat of ours can touch their shores without being dashed to atoms by the high surf. The planks of the boats with which they land us are sewed together with threads of the coconut, and so are saved by yielding to the pressure, but yet they could not be used by us. Here we are masters of the soil, enabled by their disunions and distractions. Yet in this state, ruled as they are by us, and terrified even of a nod, they despise us as being little better than brutes. They would not taste anything we had touched; scarcely even that we had looked at. Indeed some castes will not eat what we have looked at. The Brahmins, who think that all learning and wisdom is centred in them, may not have their vests touched by our clothes without being obliged to go through a purification. The clothes in which they enter our rooms are stripped off at the door of their own. The name of Christian they hold in abhorrence, beyond even their own outcastes, the pariahs. The manners of the Hindus are exactly now what they were before Moses wrote, and are likely to be the same as much longer. The Musulmen are crushed by our power, but you know enough of the history of the Turks to judge that they are not likely to turn Christian.

The Portuguese are a wretched race; a mixture of those, and the outcastes of these people. The English are only here for a few years, as it is contrary to present policy to settle a colony. There can be no marriage with a native woman of any sort. We have great numbers of people who are offspring of the English by the lowest creatures. Some of these are bred up for fine ladies and gentlemen, and called English.[12] Great numbers of children of poor officers and soldiers, by these wretched drabs, are here to be seen. The company, and government here, have established two large schools for their reception; one for boys and the other for girls, and there are at least a hundred in each. They are well taught; the boys born to be writers, and the girls married to soldiers, and their offspring will in time be called English, a shocking thing enough, for they are a wretched race of evil disposition, and full of disease. The schools are not of long establishment, so what the boys may be is not easy to judge. The girls do not do for service, as was hoped, and those that have left have all been corrupted, and indeed the native mothers and relations will not hear of their being unmarried after 12 years old. A husband must be found, be he black, white, old or what not, to save the reproach of passing 12 or 14 years unmarried, which to them is an utter disgrace, and although they have an excellent clergyman to attend

12 See also Introduction, and note 11 to this, page 8.

them, who is indefatigable in his duty, such is the influence of the mothers on these children that the worst consequences would follow if the desire were not complied with. It follows that marriage for chastity is a virtue little known in this country, except amongst the people of caste, and these people are altogether careful of their person. They are sometimes led astray by Europeans, but not often. They are bad enough amongst one another.

The greater part of the people who call themselves Portuguese, but who are only low pariahs, are of the Roman Church, and I perceive no difference between their idolatry and that of the heathen. The heathen *(native people)* indeed have the advantage for, though they have no worship in spirit, all is more ceremonious. Their discipline makes them clean, sober and orderly, whereas the Christians of the Catholic Church, which is quite as much lost in ceremonies, has not the advantage of these wholesome restraints. The people who are of that Church are the vilest miserable wretches, drunken and abandoned, and their half-caste children the English government endeavour to reform or educate. It is not the approved policy to attempt to change the religion of these people. It would be impracticable to the people of caste, and the others appear so much worse for it that it is not done. Protestant missionaries make converts, and have got very decent congregations. They baptise great numbers annually and will, if their zeal continues, I daresay work a change at some stage to the advantage of these poor people, bred in ignorance and vice, and thought unworthy by those of caste to be admissible. They look on them as being without souls, and never let them enter their places of worship. All these unfortunates know is that there are beings of superior powers to themselves, some benevolent and some diabolical. The benevolent, they suppose to be sufficiently inclined to relieve and aid them against the malignity of the evil powers they dread. Their whole attention is therefore to sacrifice to these Demons, to avert their wrath, and to save them from devils and giants and serpents. Their great Goddess is the queen of the serpents of the infernal regions, for whom they kill sheep, and so much fear her that they can hardly be prevailed on to kill a snake, and never do it of their own will. We had an immense Cobra Capella, or hooded snake, killed in our garden. Two of the horse-keepers, aided by Mr Clark, assisted in the slaughter, but they so far feared the vengeance of the black goddess *(Kali)* that they burned the snake in entirety, as if it had been a man. The next evening, hearing that they were about to make a ceremony over it, I went to the end of the garden under the coconut trees to see it. It was a dark night, but they had abundance of torches, and the people were assembled round with all the old kettles and tubs, and watering pots, by way of drums which they beat incessantly to charm the Demons. The wives of the men had previously sat over the bones of the snake, and cried an hour. These bones were now washed with milk, tied up in a piece of cloth, and dressed with bunches and garlands of flowers. The men danced a kind of frantic dance, every woman and man clinging round each other's neck, and howling as if in an agony of grief. They tore their hair, and spread it over their shoulders, and addressed the snake, that is the bones, near which they burned incense. The making of their frequent addresses was as if to exculpate themselves. "Why did you come out of your hole. If you had concealed yourself we should not have been compelled by these people to kill you etc". There were half a dozen of these black things dancing, and the lights and trees would have been a good scene for a pantomime.

From Elisabeth Gwillim to her mother. 12th October 1804.

I wrote to you the particulars of our health by the Glory, a ship which sailed from hence some weeks ago, but which we are told will not leave St Helena till the fleet joins her. As I have nothing particular to say, I shall in addition employ my paper in answering some questions about the country, which you asked me so long ago that you have probably forgot you did so, and lost your desire for an account. I apprise you of the contents of my letter that, if you are not at leisure, you may lay it down till you are. You asked me how it happened that, whilst the manners of the people were so pleasing, the servants should be so bad. The reason is this. The people of this country, who are Hindus, are divided into four castes, or orders, as I mentioned to you before. Now there are, besides these four castes, a very large tribe of people called pariahs or Mala people *(South Indian outcastes)*. Whether or not these people existed when the Hindus were first divided into four castes is a matter of doubt, and will not soon be settled. Some say that they were a part of the original inhabitants of the country, and excluded from the four castes. Others suppose, at least the Hindus say, that there were originally only the four castes. If a man of the first caste did anything contrary to the rules of that order, he fell to the next class and, in the same manner, if he or one of the second-class was guilty of anything contrary, he became of the third and thus till, at the last, if a man of the fourth class designation offended against them he became a pariah or outcaste. He is a man held in the same degree of contempt by the rest of the people as a convict is with us. This sort of degradation amongst these people is similar to our transportation of fellows, but with this cruel difference, that the punishment descended from the father to the son for a thousand generations. All the guilty might be degraded, but none could on any pretence be restored to their original order. By these means, these pariah people have become so numerous, and are also multiplying so fast that, were they to contend with the others unaided by anything but bodily strength, the pariahs must of course be victorious. But they are bound by a tenfold chain and, unless the operations of Europeans work a change, are likely to be in the same state for ages to come; not only outcastes, but in the state of excommunicated persons, for they are not allowed to approach the places of worship, and are thought unworthy of instruction. If you begin at the third verse of the 30th chapter of Job, and read to the end of the eighth, you will have a perfect idea of these people. Not a word need be changed except the names of the plants. They bray amongst thorns, instead of nettles, and eat other roots and leaves than mallows and juniper. Their vegetable food is of spontaneous growth, for they cultivate nothing for their own use, that I have observed, in their nests near the large settlements. They are sometimes employed by the farmers in labour out of doors, but they must not approach the house, and are obliged to stand at 10 or 20 yards distance from a man of the lowest class. They are dirty, lazy, saucy, vicious and extravagant, for if they ever gain much money they live in vileness till it is spent. They sometimes make a formal marriage, but the bond is dissolved at the pleasure of either party. Chastity is a virtue they know nothing about. If they have any well-looking girls, they dispose of them to European gentlemen, that is the mother does, for they are like the beggar children in London, all fatherless. There are few exceptions to this rule. The money for which the girl is sold is sometimes considerable, and it is soon spent on meat and drink. The younger women, from 10 to 20 years old, are generally in the service of some person or other at somewhat better wages than could be obtained by other means and, as you may suppose, they sometimes get a great deal. They save none however; the family disposes of it all, and meanwhile the disengaged parts of the family bring forth other girls abundantly, to be disposed of in the same way. As to the boys, they become our servants and attendants from the first, as I shall explain to you hereafter. If a girl has had the good fortune to have been kept by an Englishman, a sergeant, soldier, or young officer, she learns a little English, and is by these means qualified to attend a lady when she is no longer an object much to be desired by the gentleman. Such are the maids we have to attend upon our persons. The lower sort are such as have not had these advantages, but are by no means more chaste. All we have of these are two women called water carriers. The one is called the house water woman, a filthy *(dirty)* creature and quite common, whose business it is to sweep all the rooms, which she does stooping down with a whisk, as indeed they all do their work (they never put a long handle to any broom or spade). She must also wash the earthenware bottles that hold the spring water, and carry it from the large jars to the doors of the rooms. The other is called the cook-room water woman, and her office is somewhat like that of a kitchen girl, except that she does no cooking but the curries, which are her business and the cook does not interfere. This woman we seldom see, as the cooking is performed in a place 100 yards from the house where we could not go in the heat of the day, and at night these two go home to their families. We are often obliged to see the house water woman as no man, however low, would sweep the floor of a bit of powder, or a few crumbs fallen down. In such a case, half a dozen go in search of this charming damsel, who is as hard to be found as a turnspit dog. As to the ladies' maids, few of them can sew. Those that can call themselves Portuguese, though they are the same pariahs and have nothing to do with Portuguese. What they do is not worth having, and they are always the worse for their knowledge, and abominable thieves, whilst others are not. None of them are of the least use in more than hemming a towel, and cannot stick in a pin. It is astonishing how simple they are in the midst of all this vice. It shows that it is the fault of wicked men, for in what they have been taught they are strictly accurate. I cannot give you a better idea than telling you the history of my damsel, which you may read or not as you like. The girl I brought out with me was never sober, after she had received her money. I took another petticoat-wearing Portuguese lady, and she was a thief. Therefore, upon the advice of wiser people, I requested to have one brought who wore the country dress. When Poppa was brought, she said in reply to my questions that she had learned a little English by being with her mother, who was a water woman, and had amply improved it in other places. She was about 21, at which time the downy fineness of their faces is a little worn, and this is their chief beauty. Her face was plain, but her teeth and eyes very fine and the most delicate form I ever saw, of the lightest kind. I asked if she was married and she said very simply she had been married twice, that her first husband was a Dutch Captain of a ship, who had bought her for two hundred pagodas when she was ten years old, that her second husband (the Captain having gone to Europe) was a steward to a gentleman in Madras by whom she had a son, whom she had put into a charity school, but that this man had now taken another woman, the ladies maid of that family. He gave her nothing, nor took any notice of the child, wherefore she came to seek my service. After some time, I used to question her because she agreed to have leave to see her child once a week. "I suppose", says I, "you were very sorry when this man took another". "No", said she, "what should I care for him. I care only for my child and I do not wish to go again to any gentleman. Some servants have been to me and wanted me to come and live with their masters, but I like ma'am's money better. It is true they will give me five pagodas a month but if I go to one of them, in a few months he will leave the place, and I cannot leave my child for I shall die if I do not see my child." She has accordingly lived with me two years and ten months, I believe in perfect innocence. The only trouble she gives me is asking frequently to go to see her child, but a refusal occasions no resentment. She is honest in the strictest sense of the word, sober and not guilty of falsehood. She is extremely useful to me in some respects, as all the servants go home of a night, except one or two who are in a distant part of the house, and leave us with all the hundred doors of the house wide open, with jackals and pariah dogs howling round. Owls and bats enter at pleasure, and the bed curtains are bestrewn with grasshoppers that stun one with their cry, to say nothing of the frogs that in a rainy season prevent all sleep by their croaking chorus. Poppa sleeps upon the hard stucco floor in the room next to mine, in the same apparel she wears all day, her muslin dress and her gold necklaces. Mr Gwillim calls three or four times every night to bring toast and water, and she always jumps up in good humour and appears in full dress, as that requires nothing but shaking herself. She never lays even a mat under her; the only indulgence I have seen her use (though there are carpets at her command) is to bring a couple of bricks which she uses as a pillow for her head. Even this is a luxury she seldom takes the trouble to bring in. At five in the morning she smokes her saroot *(sic)* of strong tobacco and, when her work is done, reheats it and basks under a tree asleep on the ground in the best clothes I can give her.

All our servants, who have any labour to do, are of this description of people except the butler, and the Dubashes as they are called, of which we each keep one to attend us. These are young men of caste, very neat and clean, who always read and write two languages, or generally three. They are frequently the sons of wealthy people, who send them to these services from which they seldom depart till their master leaves the country. In this way they rise to employment with the Collectors and servants of the Company, in which they can get richer than their masters. These men, being of caste, would not do any menial office but are quite necessary to us, as the others are not to be depended upon for anything. I will give you a list of our servants, and their offices, which will serve for any other family in Madras and, though we have fifty, you will see there are not many for the domestic business. We have, in addition to all others two chubdars allowed by government to attend Sir Henry when he goes out, and wait at the door when we are all at home, and carry letters etc. These are always Musulmans, or Saracens we may call them, in the Moorish dress with large tall silver sticks in their hands. They never do anything in the house. At the head of the family is the butler, who does all the work of an old housekeeper and butler, but both very badly and, moreover, he cheats most abominably. To him we give four pagodas per month, besides which he takes heavy customs on all he buys. This man has two pariahs, his matys, who wash the plates and dishes and glasses, clean the plate *(i.e. silver)*, lay the cloth and bring the things from the kitchens to the hands of the dubashes. Then there are two masalchis, pariahs who clean lamps, rub furniture, dust the house, clean knives and shoes, and carry lanthorns and run before the carriage of a night; a thing of absolute necessity here if you dine out, which continually happens seven or eight or twenty miles off. They run with the lights (for we dine at seven o'clock, when it is always dark here) to the house and back as fast as the horses can go. This custom was very distressing to us when we first came, but these people suffer nothing by doing it and are much less tried by it than the horses. To the matys, we give each two pagodas a month. To these other men, one and a half, that is three shillings a week, out of which they each maintain a woman of some sort, children, and any old people belonging to them, for the money is a common stock amongst the young and the old. They never save, but they never spend more on themselves than on their relations. In youth they work, and in old age they are fed by the young. This indeed is the case with those people of all descriptions in India. But to proceed, we have a pariah man as a cook, and he has a maty. They kill, and they skin and feather, and do everything in a strange way. They cook immense dinners, all in earthen saucepans and earthen frying pans. They have everything to prepare, and not one convenience. They keep some naked pariah children, who turn the spit and are paid by scraps. The cook has four, and his maty two, pagodas a month. My maid has three pagodas a month, and the water women one pagoda each a month. And now I have come to an end of the servants who do anything in the house. Being four of us, we have each one dubash, and one old Moor man, a tailor, who does all the sewing. His picture you have seen, as also my maid's and my man's, and I take some credit to myself that they are the best in the family. The gentlemen's dubashes dress them, give their clothes to the tailor, and sit to watch him whilst he mends them, which is no small work, for the washermen beat it on stones and English linen is of no use. My towels were fringed the first washing. Hetty sent me out a stock of shirt buttons to last me a year, all of which the tailor sewed on the day I received them, for he had embroidered the old ones over and over till they were as round as balls, and worth a shilling apiece for mere labour. Mr G would not hear of having the country *(Indian)* buttons without wires, because he fancied they hurt his throat. Fancy goes a great way; the old ones were as hard as bullets. In short, the clothes come home in such a state from the washerman that it is a great economy to make one tailor mend for two men, with the servants to watch him.

As for my dubash, and Polly's, they never leave us, and work enough we have for them; to carry orders to the cook room, to translate to working people who speak three or four different languages, all of which they know, to receive a thousand idle messages from the natives who, as they do nothing themselves, send continually a flower or a bit of fruit with compliments: tedious to hear and laborious to answer. By the way, I must mention that nobody, who has not been in a country like this, can imagine what immense time is spent for want of language. Translations by a translator imperfect in the language are fatiguing always, and how can any man be perfect in them? Instead of one dubash, we ought to have half a dozen. These men, as I have said, generally write three, but speak four, languages. Four are absolutely necessary in this country - English, Moorish, Malabar *(Tamil)* and Gentoo *(Telugu)*, to all of which the characters and mode of writing are as different as Hebrew, Greek, Chaldaic *(Chaldean)* and English; and how can we expect that boys sent out to service at twelve or thirteen should know these things perfectly? It would require a deal of birch at home to do it. I am surprised at how much they learn, and yet our lads that have come out knock these fellows about if they make the least mistake, and call them stupid, ignorant, degenerate savages, and all this to other lads of their own age who sit down and correspond in three languages, and translate in four, whilst they cannot even correctly write their own. The rest of our servants ought to be called by some other name, for they are not used in the house. There are nine palanquin boys who, according to the custom of this place, do nothing but bear the palanquin. They live in a hut of leaves at the end of the garden, and receive eighteen pagodas a month between them. They live upon a quarter part of it, and save the rest. They are a fine handsome set of men of the Telugu, or Gentoo country, to the north of Madras. They come here to carry palanquins, as the Irish or Welsh come to harvest with us. When they have made 30 or 40 pagodas they go back and, with that capital, become rich farmers. These are all men of caste that would not eat our food; they are clean in their cooking, and eat out of brass bowls as bright as gold. One of them is cook, and eight only run with the palanquin. The cook goes once a week to a neighbouring wood, and there cuts down as many firesticks and boughs as will last him a week. He makes them up into two immense faggots. They are very light boughs and, running a stake through them, he shoves one to one end, and one to the other, and puts the stake over his shoulder and looks like a walking wood.

They eat but little meat, except when we give them a rupee for a sheep. Their food is chiefly plain rice, the water of which, or rice gruel, they drink. It is called Canchi; they season it with tamarinds, capsicums and onions. When they have leisure they fish, and are very expert at fishing. They make their own nets and are generally employed in netting. Indeed, they are never idle, unless you should call their attention to their persons idleness, but the Hindus think no labour vain that improves beauty, or is for cleanliness to their health. They go into the tank in a morning to wash, and there they scrape their teeth for half an hour. If they wait for their masters at a door, they take out a bit of looking glass and examine their faces, taking out every superfluous hair from their eyebrows, and shaping them in the neatest manner. They eradicate also the hairs of the nostrils, and any others that grow round their faces, with the utmost exactness. Such appearances would be as disgusting to them as it would be to us to see our nails grown to claws. Their nails they also pare very neatly, and are indeed very clean in every respect you would be, and cultivate a bit of our garden for their own use, for capsicums and sour greens.

We have a head gardener, and three or four or five men under him, who are all people of caste, but very poor and low. They are Malabars, who are not so neat as the gentoos. What they are employed about might puzzle you to discover. They bring nothing into the house to eat but a few vegetables, that require hardly any culture. Their work is watering the trees, and cleaning the walks of weeds. The heat prevents us from observing them, and I believe they lie down all day, but we must have them to clean the place, and they will not do more unless they are watched. When they work for a native master they are made to do a great deal. We pay these men one and a half pagodas each, or two to the master. They steal and sell all the garden produce and, without constant scolding and threatening, we should never have a thing. We have sour oranges, limes, mangoes and guavas in abundance, but they think it hard to allow us any. There is a large fruit as big as a peck measure, called a jackfruit, which they sell for three or four fanams apiece. We had about two hundred on the trees last year, and I never got but about eight or ten. Between the butler and the gardeners, they were all disposed of. We have a coachman, who is always a pariah. Ours is tolerably good, but they are in general horrid bad. We pay him five pagodas a month, and clothes, which is more than twice what a dubash has, who is neat and clean and to be trusted. The coachman does nothing but drive. It is the custom of this country to have a horse keeper to each horse and, indeed the horses are so uncertain in their tempers, that it is necessary. These men always run by the side of the horse, whether in a carriage or otherwise. They clean the horses, and their wives bring them their food, in the horses' stable, and they and the horses all go to bed together, for they always sleep by the horse they attend, and this is all their labour but sometimes it is hard enough. It is painful to one's feelings to see them run by the carriages and phaetons, the horses at full canter in the heat of the day. Though we have no meadows nor fields where horses go to graze, there is a grass cutter to each horse; a woman, or horse keeper's wife, or some of their set. These bring home every evening a bundle of grass which they dig out from the dry ground, where paddy has been in the wet seasons; from the roadsides; from the borders of tanks and waters; from commons and places that look frequently so arid that you would little expect them to yield what they do. They are covered however with a most nutritious species of grass, called Agrostis linearis in the language of botany, and by various names amongst the people of India. It never rises far above the ground, but runs along it to a never ending length, and it takes root as it runs. The stems are white, round and sweet; the leaves small and fine, and abundant in its blossom. The women tear this up by the root, first cutting up the ground with little hoes. Each of these women receives a pagoda and a half monthly, as do the horse keepers also. They are of no use to us in the house; such wretched good for nothing people they are, and filthy beyond measure. It is amazing, when they see the caste people, that they do not become ambitious to be a little cleaner. It makes one half inclined to think, as opposed to the Hindus of caste, that they cannot be good. Sam, my sensible boy who died, told me when I reproached him that they did not instruct the pariahs, that it would never be of any use and that, though many of them were well featured to our eyes, they had Shani in their faces, that is the planet Saturn, who is their Satan. He is the great author of all mischief according to their notions, and they see his mark in all the pariahs. "How", says Sam, "should we make them good? If the parents have no sense, how should the children? They are false, and the children will be wicked." It was this speech of his that put me in mind of the passage in Job that I mentioned, and which is a description of those people more exact than I could give in other words. I fear I have tired you, but I believe I must finish my account of the family.

As we lie exposed all night, and the servants leave us, it is customary to have three or four sepoys to watch the garden gate. These are invalids discharged from the service, or any safe pariahs that can get a sepoy's dress. They receive one and a half pagodas each to take care of the garden and house in the night. They are never in the way, except when they are asleep, or pretend to be watching, and they may steal all they can get. They are a sad set. Besides these, we have a carter, who takes care of a pair of little red bullocks that draw a cart which holds about two wheelbarrows-full. He goes to fetch Black town mud and river sand for the garden, and gravel for the walks. He goes to the Black Town for the grain that is fetched for the horses, cows, bullocks, sheep, deer, poultry etc. He also goes into the country to bring straw; that is nice straw, which is the food of all the horned cattle here. The people do not strip it so clean, as we do our wheat straw, for they never thrash here. The bullocks tread it out and they do not "Muzzle the Ox." *(i.e. they are allowed to eat some of the fruit of their labour)*. These animals are half-starved before the harvest begins, but grow fat in treading out the grain. We give ours grain, as indeed private people always do, and our cows have, as all milk cows do, bran, Bengal grain, cotton seeds and a sort of grain called Natcheny *(Eleusine Coracana – a kind of millet)*. I do not know the botanical name just now. This carter is a man of caste, as also is the man who takes care of the cows. He feeds them, walks them out, washes them, milks them and makes butter every day. These men each have two pagodas a month; and now you will see that, although we have so many servants, we have no great enough numbers to wait upon us if you consider the heat of the country, which is enough to disable us. These sets of people cost us £500 a year;[13] a 100 pagodas a month; and one may faint before a glass of water can be obtained if the young dubashes are not present, and we often have no boy to help with our caps, nor to aid in dressing.

The pariahs eat all our food, which is a great deal, for we can never keep it above a day; yet these wretches have as much wages as the others who are not permitted to touch a bit. The people of caste never let their women go into service, however poor, though they might have immense wages if they could. But they are all married at nine or ten years old, but are frequently at the mother in law's house till they are 13 or 14. At all events they leave then, and the families live united. Widows of all ages continue in the family, at the head of the house. These people are better off here than in England for, though the wages appear low to you, every man's wage is enough to keep himself, a wife and children, and no man is unmarried. It is enough also to keep an old relation or two.

They have no conception that a man should exchange his labour for his own food, which is certainly a very improper notion, although we do it in England at times. If you hire a man here he says; "I cannot come for so much time; I have eight people, or I have 10 people, to keep;" seldom much less. The domestic business is all that is asked of them. The old women nurse the children, and they never sew; they do not know how; and yet they never require any sewing. Their clothes are all in one straight piece, and it is never in want of mending as it lies loose. It goes altogether, when it is over with. The husband's clothes are the same, and the children have none. They pay a washerman a mere trifle to wash for them; they never do it themselves, even the poorest. The dirty clothes are all sent to the river. Their women are much better off than ours, and in sickness are well attended, and so are the men, for these united families have many comforts. As to the state of celibacy, the Hindus know not what it is. Indeed they have all the utmost contempt for unmarried persons. If a man dies before he is married, they think it impossible he should go to heaven and they carry this notion so far that, if a bachelor dies, they do not trouble themselves to do the usual ceremonies, but look upon him as little better than the beasts that perish. The ceremonies ordered to be performed for the departed soul cannot be

13 Approximately £50,000 per annum in today's money.

done for a single man. There was here a Polygar, a man of high caste, hanged for an attempt to murder several people a Court of Sessions or two ago, and for actually shooting one. Not being married, the whole marriage ceremony was performed the night before his execution; the Brahmins attended; he was dressed in flowers and perfumed, like a bridegroom, and the family were up with him the whole night. His sword was adorned as if the bride. All this was done in order that the funeral ceremonies might be performed which are thought necessary to salvation. Upon enquiring, we found this was a common practice where a person is in imminent danger, which you must allow a man is who is going to be hanged. I suppose that this is an invention of the Brahmins to get the profits from such ceremonies, for all these things turn to their account.

You asked me, besides, an account of the buildings here or, if you did not, I promised to send you one. I shall, in another letter, but I fear my long scrawls, and three years' stories of these outlandish people, will have tired you out for hearing more about them.

Our monsoon has begun these three days, or at least it has rained incessantly, although the usual day according to the Brahmins is the 15th. Sir Henry, thank God, begins to get stout. I fear I shall soon begin to quake *(from fever)*, but I intend to be beforehand with the enemy and take some bark *(cinchona, i.e. quinine)* as a preventative.

We expect ships hourly with our new Commander in Chief and new Admiral. Our governor lives very quietly and Lady William *(Bentinck)*, his wife, is as plain in her dress and as simple in her manners as possible. On state occasions she wears a great number of jewels, and he has a fine service of plate, but in other respects they seem to set an example of economy that is followed by all the settlement. Sir Thomas Strange's brother, who lost all his fortune in that house of Walwyns, is come out here and has brought his wife, Lord Melville's daughter *(Henry Dundas's daughter)*. She is at least my age and very delicate in her health. She has been ill ever since she came, and is now pronounced to have a liver complaint.[14] She cannot return now,

14 A liver complaint was a common diagnosis at that time. It did not mean that there was actually anything wrong with the liver, which would then have been largely undiagnosable, unless jaundiced. A strong belief had developed among doctors that

but is to go back in January if the Doctors do not settle matters otherwise. I shall finish here, etc .

Part of letter from Elisabeth Gwillim to her friend
Miss Thoburn Undated

I spent yesterday morning with Dr Anderson. He is very attentive, and his garden contains all the useful plants that bear hot climates, and all the trees that are either useful or beautiful. His attention is wholly given to the fruit and forest trees of large growth. His great pride is having brought into this country the Bastard Cedar. It thrives here exceedingly, is found in every hedgerow and is certainly a great acquisition in a tropical climate. It is a native of Jamaica; it's verdure is very fine and the foliage most profuse, even after the greatest drought the country can experience. Its leaves are food for the cattle when scarcely a blade of grass can be obtained. I think it is more like a lime tree (but fuller of leaves than any tree), and is like that tree covered with flowers that have a honey smell. The natives, who have seldom any delight in novelties, are very fond of this tree. They have a superstitious respect for bees and, as this tree smells of honey, they set a great value upon it and, if they do not go so far as to be industrious in planting it, they take the greatest care in sheltering and protecting every young example of it they find springing up, either in the roads, or about their huts. Dr Anderson boasts that he wants no cultivation of it as he has the crows very active in aiding him. The fruits or nut of the tree have a smell by which they are attracted, and they carry them into all their retreats, and in such places they attempt to open them but the shell, being so hard, they leave and, after the rainy season, it springs up. We have a great many trees of it about our grounds, and one fine large tree that shades the whole side of the house, where Mr G has his study, its branches sweep to the ground on one side and spread over the veranda on the other

fevers had their origin in putrid bile, and thus originated in the liver. Consequently, and especially in India, a range of different medicinal therapies were introduced. The chief among them was the mercury compound calomel, which was used for almost every illness and was only much later recognised to be toxic.

so that, when one sits in there, one seems directly under the tree. The squirrels run up and down the branches all day. They are very pretty and very numerous all about the houses and gardens here. Dr A made me particularly notice one tree which is a great height and size, smooth sided, and is 18 feet in circumference. This tree is only 12 years old; this is no longer ago than that time when his garden had not a shrub, while at present it is a forest. This place has undergone an entire change within these five and 20 years. At that time the plain on which Madras stands was without any plantations, and it is now an entire grove, with roads cut through it in different directions. We have all the variety and beauty that wood and water, and works of art, can produce on a plain washed on the one side by the sea, and everywhere crowded with inhabitants whose natural grace exceeds what we see represented in the finest ancient sculpture. Here are frequent groves of cocoa palms. The heads of these form a fine shade whilst the tall stems leave the ground on which they grow clear for the purposes of the Indians. Under these, therefore, they delight to build their villages; they raise, in the more artfully constructed houses, about 2 feet of brick, which they cover with coarse mortar or chunam, enclosing one or two small rooms. In the corners they stick bamboo sticks, about 10 or 5 feet high, and these support a kind of hurdle or mat made each of a cocoa palm leaf, by turning down divisions on each side, and plaiting it into a sort of mat. The middle stem is set in the clay or mortar and this is the wall of the house. The roof is generally the same, but is sometimes of the palmyra leaves spread over each other like fans. A house, if it is to be raised from the ground, costs I understand six or seven half-crowns. A fresh built house looks very green and gay, but becomes brown almost as soon as a ribbon would fade. They look, however, not less beautiful when brown if they are kept in tolerable order. Doors, windows and chimneys I have not said anything of, because they know nothing of them. They use their houses as a shelter from rains and sun, and would consider any aperture, but that necessary to come in at, as an imperfection. Their cooking is performed without the house, where also they sleep on mats unless prevented by the rains and, for doors, they need not lock up their houses when they go out from home. They have no liquor but water, and their meat and rice is bought daily, and their wealth is always carried about them. What they acquire by labour they have in gold of the purest kind. They do not put it in bags or boxes, but send it to the goldsmith who fashions it into earrings, bracelets, arm clasps, better ornaments for the hair, nose rings, toe rings and bands with belts for the ankles, and ranges of necklaces. This gold is given to him in coin, and he returns it undiminished in weight, however fine the workmanship, but receives pay according to his labour. However moderate, their ornaments are their resource in misfortunes; they talk of them as money, and always tell you how many pagodas are in each. The youngest and middle-aged women are loaded with finery, but there is something very melancholy in observing that old women are generally destitute of them. They seldom (never in these parts, at present) burn themselves when they lose their husbands, but his sickness, funeral expenses and superstitious ceremonies take all their ornaments. A gentoo widow, if she be childless, which appears to be frequently the case, is as great an object of pity as can be seen. She has little left to make life desirable and is frequently compelled, after being unused to labour, to earn her subsistence by some fatiguing employment and, to add to her wretchedness, it is expected of her that she does not take any pains in cleaning her hair or person. They are clearly normal people, and consider dirt (as we humorously call it sometimes) mourning, and never permit their persons to be dirty except in affliction. A widow is not allowed to marry again, though her husband die when she is not more than five or six years old, and before they have lived together. An Indian village makes no appearance, no smoke or smell of cheerful hearth, to apprise you of it before you come to it. When you do, the little huts concealed under the trees would hardly draw your attention. The chattering in the bazaars, however, and the crowds of people that are employed about them, will give you a notion of the number they contain. There is generally a choultrey or two near each of these places. These are richly ornamented with carved work, but they are seldom more than a portico enclosed on three sides, the roof being supported in front by a row of columns from 6 to 8 in number. Some of these choultreys have back apartments and, if they are endowed, Brahmins live in or near them, and who boil rice for travellers. It is a religious duty for the rich to build and endow them. All the towns are full of them, as well as those frequently on the roadside, and they afford no earthly convenience in general, but a shelter from rains. A well of good water is generally near them. If the weather be dry, the travellers seem not to sleep within the choultrey; all the convenience any of these people require for sleeping is a bit of mat in which they wrap their bundle. This they spread under them on the ground and then, loosening the muslin they have wrapped round them, they spread it over their bodies and feet, and the same quantity of muslin which they wear on their heads is also in part let down, and wraps up the head and hangs down like a cloak. Thus protected, they lie down to sleep secure from mosquitoes or any other teasing flies, which are all they have to fear. Plantains one can hardly call trees, but there are innumerable sorts, and some are very good. They are like pears when you eat them; some sorts less juicy, but warm to the stomach. Indeed they are perfect food, which is an advantage of many of the fruits here. The rajah plantain is as fine a fruit as ever I eat. Oranges are dark green outside and are remarkably juicy and sweet; the peel has an aromatic flavour . The tamarind is a very beautiful tree and very high.

From Elisabeth Gwillim to her friend Nancy Green. Undated

This is a very pleasant country for those who are never tired of company balls and dinners, but we have no public amusements. It is a pleasant country, too, for those who have any curiosity to know the history of the world, which may be studied to advantage amongst the oldest nation of the world, now mixed with the most polished modern ones, or to those who delight as I do in the productions of nature. I have received a considerable degree of attention since I came here, and even the servants bring me whatever they find that has not fallen. I am sometimes tired with looking at novelties, till I wish sometimes they were less numerous. This extraordinary people, their habitations, the animals, the utensils and the purposes to which they are applied, are so new and curious and excite my attention as to the Hindus, the original inhabitants of the country. You will acquire the best notion of them from the Bible. The stories and descriptions there correspond with whatever these people do today, and it is pretty clear that they have not changed their manners since the time of Moses; possibly still older. The women dress in the same manner, and hold the same place in society. The wives and daughters of the richest people go to the well for water. In the morning they are less ornamented but, in the afternoon, when they fetch water for their great meal, which is always at night, they wear all their ornaments; frequently the weight of a thousand pagodas in gold. A pagoda is eight shillings, *(approximately £40 today)* worked into the most delicate shapes and mixed with pearls, rubies and emeralds, and an equal weight of silver on their toes and legs in rings, and strings of pearls, making a double fringe round their feet. Large bands worn on their legs leave pits with their weight. All of them have a graceful manner of walking beyond our best public performers. Their trinkets, except those on the nose for which I cannot yet acquire a taste, are disposed with great taste, and the large quantity of thin muslin which they fold about them without form or shape, without pin or string, or any fastening but the folds, has more elegance in it than any contrivance that needles and scissors could give. When a set of these women walks from the well, with their bright vases on their heads, they look more dignified than you can imagine, and the flowers they add to their dress any feast time gives them an air of gaiety that is very pleasant. As to the Moor people, as they are called, the Arabian nights will give you an almost exact description. They are more showy, delighting in the most brilliant colours. This taste in the wealthy Moor people is very admirable, and they produce very fine effects from their mode of dress, but the lower order look dirty, paltry and uncomfortable, whereas the very poorest of the Hindus look clean, even the caste that do nothing but mend the roads and are not allowed to live in the towns. They look neat and wear nothing but white, with a narrow border. Although it is coarse it is clean, and the bright sunshine of this country makes a brilliant clearness to all colours. These people are, I think, the handsomest castes, and are remarkably good, but nothing can raise the people from their original caste. The women are very pretty, wear a great deal of ornaments and, if they have not gold, content themselves with brass and beads. Their arms are covered with bands and bracelets. They work with their husbands; the men dig, or raise the work, and the women carry the materials in small baskets on their heads with a child in one arm, or rather riding on the hip. They will carry a load that a strong man cannot easily raise, however the men set it on their heads where they seem able to bear it, and they walk with infinite cheerfulness and spirits. When they arrive at the place the burden is to be set down, they put up their hands and shove it forward. They do not take long walks but merely carry the materials from the heap to the workmen.

From Mary Symonds to her sister Hetty, 14th October 1804

I hope you will receive my two letters by the Glory; one was a good long story and, to tell the truth, I believe you must think me a sad gossip for I am never so happy as when scribbling to my good dear friends. Now I am going to scold you like anything because you want to put a bridle in my mouth. I love to speak from my heart and tell you all that passes here, piping hot. Surely there should be no reserves amongst us. You must have misunderstood what Sir Henry said, but James and you are just as touchy. I assure you, Betsy and I have attacked Sir Henry soundly about what he said, and he protests he did not say a word that ought to have been taken up in the way you take it. He only meant, he says, that you put yourself to more expense and trouble than was necessary in entertaining people of whom we know nothing, and perhaps only see for an hour or two when they come out, before they sail home again. If he makes a wrong statement, I desire you will give him a lecture upon it. Betsy says you have no right to be prickly about anything he says, because you encouraged him in his sauciness to others. I assure you your letter put me in a grand stew, because I had just sent off my letter with some stuff about the Scotch doctor, which I should sooner have hid than written if I had known how you were fidgeting, but we all laughed so much about him that I could not resist writing. I am very glad you sent him, for if he had not been here we should all have been as dull as posts with all our correctness. An odd character of that sort, thrown in amongst us, is like the lemon juice in a bowl of punch.

I don't know what Sir Henry has said to you about the young men coming here but, this I do know, that he is always glad enough to see them, and most unwilling to part with them, and particularly the Herefordshire people. He would fain have persuaded Biss to be sick, or anything else, to have kept him here. To be sure he is a darling, so mild, so modest, a thousand times too good for this country. I own I am half in love with him.

I am very angry with you believing things not in my heart, and what stuff and nonsense do you talk about of your own inferiority. Not many come superior to you. In this place, I am sure there are at least half a dozen persons whose connections are half as good, and those half-dozen forced here by either wretched poverty or disgraceful conduct. If you would do us the honour, hold your head as high as your neighbour's. An honest man is the noblest work of God but, if you want instances, I will give two or three from the heads of our society. The first lady here, after the Governor's wife and Betsy, is the daughter of a Mr Douglas, the tailor who lived near Charing Cross. Two others, who hold their heads high, are daughters of a Mrs Goldfinch, a Hosier in Lombard Street. Here are five sisters, all well married in the eye of the world at least, daughters of an inferior Customs house officer who lives on Tower Hill. Two other great ladies are the daughters of an innkeeper at Hounslow; two more, daughters of a slop shop *(clothing store)* at Portsmouth. I have given you now all the heads of the place, the rest are all the bastards, black or white, of whom the former may generally have the pleasure of seeing their mothers fry pancakes, or sell fish, in the native markets. Now I think I have said enough upon this subject, and perhaps too much, but I really was worried about it because I know a month's residence here would set you to rights in this matter.

You will acknowledge that I spoil paper enough, when I tell you that my Indian *(British in India)* correspondents are as numerous as my English ones, and many of them so kind as to favour me with a letter every week. Biss is amongst the number of my correspondents, but he certainly does not trouble me too often. Poor fellow, he has not much time at present, he has been unwell with a bowel complaint since he left us and, as soon as we heard of it, Sir Henry wrote to desire he would come down here and be nursed, but he soon got better and, as he was afraid of losing time in his profession, he declined the offer. However, we are to have him for a few weeks before he joins his regiment in January. I am nursing a very pretty little terrier puppy for him, which I got from Mrs Trent. It is a beautiful little wretch, but so mischievous that he is a great plague. It is my constant companion night and day. We sit with all the doors and windows open for air, and the breeze blows everything about, upon which he scrambles immediately. He has eaten a fine flower out of my cap, and several bows of ribbon while I have been writing, and I hope he won't tell his master any of my secrets, but I must trust to his honour, for he has eaten two sheets of my letters.

I am very glad you like your friend the cockatoo. It is a hardy bird, and likely enough to live. I dare say he is entertaining enough in a winter evening, but I am surprised Thomas has so much patience with his impudence, and mischief in biting the chairs and things. We shall be glad enough to see Prosser back again. He is a kind man for carrying things home, and we always have some trifling thing or other to send for your information. Did the pickled coconut blossom arrive safe? Could you take it out of the jar to see it? It is a most beautiful thing when fresh.

I must tell you again about the things you sent us this time for fear my former letter should miscarry. A great deal of it came safe and good. We have picked out a few excellent strawberries, raspberries and white plums, and all the pickles, catchup *(ketchup)* and raspberry vinegar arrived without a crack. Betsy has never had such pretty caps to her head before, particularly the two white satin ones, one with a geranium flower and the other a net trimming. "It fits," and she looks quite comfortable in them but, as for fallalls *(ornaments for women's hats)*, she certainly never will understand how to stick them on. I have resigned every cap to her except that with the pink ribbon, and I took that because I knew she would make herself look like a cockatoo with that red topknot, yet it is a very pretty cap. I have worn it with great credit and lent it out, and out again, for a pattern.

My friends General and Mrs Trent go home in the same fleet which takes this letter. They wish to know some of our friends, and therefore I shall give them a letter to you. Mrs Trent is a good charming woman, and the General is a good-natured, well disposed, man as any alive. They don't wish to visit much with 'Indians' but to live in a quiet domestic way. Their income is about eighteen hundred a year as long as he lives. They will not be very showy, but I suppose they will keep a carriage and, if the money holds out, they will have two houses. He likes a good dinner, and is so much an Indian that the dishes must be pretty highly seasoned if they are homemade ones. You see I am giving you a hint and, to make it complete,

I will tell you that his favourite meat is grass-fed lamb. Should they live in London, it will be somewhere about Fitzroy Square. The General is flattered beyond measure by the attention of ladies and, if you attend to him and pay him a few compliments, he will talk to you a long summer's day, and give you a very good account of India, and many particulars about our family.

I cannot pretend to contradict your accusation respecting the dates of letters, but something may be said in excuse, which is this. I frequently begin to write a week or more before the time of a ship's sailing, which is always uncertain till the last, and I leave my letters without dates till then, because I think the later the intelligence the more satisfactory it is to you. Then, in a hurry at the last moment, I seal them up and forget the date altogether, but I will tell you how to find out without referring to my dates. You will always see what time the ship leaves this place in the papers, and you may rely that my letter is never sent off till then. You will hear from all hands of the loss of poor Temple, and I have elsewhere given all particulars of the event, which will afford you no satisfaction to hear, and that reason, as well as others, would give me much pain to repeat. I beg you will remember me in the kindest manner to all friends, and tell Mrs Shepheard that I wrote her a letter by the Prince of Wales, and I hope to God she will receive it before you get this but, at present, we are under great apprehension for the safety of that ship. She met with a terrible storm off the Cape and, as she had not arrived at St Helena six weeks after the ships which sailed in company with her from hence, it is feared she is lost with every soul on board.

From Elisabeth Gwillim to her sister Hetty, 16th October 1804

The Captain of the Glory, calling here and seeing the boxes of plants lined up ready under a tree, said he would get the Captain of the David Scott to put them on the poop. I am glad to accept the offer because there is, in one of the boxes, a large tree that is above 2 foot high, of the plant which the German Botanical Doctor has called by name and I thought, if it could be preserved, you would like to see it. He has sent some sprigs of it to Germany and I wrote the particulars to Mr Whitley in the Prince of Wales. We have the greatest fears about that ship.

I am learning botany seriously. A gentleman, lately come down the country, has lent me a large botanical library and Dr Rottler, the German *(actually French)* missionary, has given me a lesson once or twice a week. I am very proud of my acquaintance, and hope to be of use in time, for I have hitherto left things unnamed and meanwhile, Sir Henry, who has taken it into his head to be a great admirer of the animals of the country, tries to put upon me to draw them again and I have done drawings of sheep and goats for him, which if they ever get home you will like.

I had the ague, or something of that description, with such a something that they called nervous, that almost gives it me again to think of it; every morning about 10 o'clock, lasting two hours, and at three o'clock in the night the same. I fear it will distress me again this year, as I had a smart touch of it a few days ago, when we had some monsoon rains *(possibly malaria)*. I firmly believe that I caught it during that cold wet summer. I had never seen an ague, and I could describe it to nobody, but this is the same thing, only stronger. As soon as I went to the Mount I got better; the hot dry seasons cured me. It is the damp I suffer from, but I design to take bark the moment it begins this year, for last year I neglected to take care in time.

Before I go any further, let me put down Mr Gwillim's message. He begs you to write two lines to Mrs Edwards, *(See pages 120, 146)* wherever she may be, and say that Sir Henry begs she will call upon Mr Ware, N. Holborn Court, Gray's Inn, to receive her money. The Bills are Court of Directors Bills, and they cannot be paid for three months. I believe the money is £170. It is a good thing that the judges are here for, before this Supreme Court was established, there was no means of applying for, or of obtaining, these sums *(legacy after death)*. Sir Henry has got £60 for Mrs Hathaway. I wish it had been more, but men are very unfeeling to their poor mistresses and sisters, much the same as if the family money had been exhausted in the cost of sending them out to India. Young men waste their health and their money on filthy black things *(people)* whom servants of caste would not touch. One of her sons was a clever young man, and had books to the value of 500, or even 700, pounds but all went to one of these beings and her brats, a disgrace to society. How they can forget their mother and sisters, living upon bread and salt, and who have incurred no expense but sacrificed all to their son's connections, and fitting them out *(expensive)* for their place in India, is to me astonishing; yet so it is. This is between ourselves. It would be a pity it should reach the mother's ears.

Our doctors are shocking. They are sent out as raw boys in a ship, where they think only of selling their saddles and shoes and grocery. Then they become great Doctors. Those who have gained experience, by being here many years, will not attend to their people. God Almighty only knows what might have been done for Temple. I have heard, since it was too late, that profuse bleeding would have saved him but that according to modern practice, particularly in this country, the lancet is not at all used. He was certainly too healthy, too gross and ever had an aversion to any exercise. He never stirred out but to dine out. His companions laughed at him about it, though Sir Henry sometimes spoke seriously. I do not think it ever well that young men should grow so gross. He was an excellent young man, and his principles were honourable in the strictest sense of the word. He got his position in the court despite terrible opposition. There are good members of every country, and amongst the Scotch highly commendable and virtuous persons, but they being so together and so numerous here, and having so much command of this country, an Englishman has no chance. I have sometimes thought that they should either send out no English, or more. I have been in a large assembly of people, such as a ball, where there has not been an English born person, except myself and my sister. I dined out twice last week and there were none, although we were at one place twenty five at dinner.

Richard, as you will know, is Sir Henry's clerk, which aids his income. He is very innocent and good, and living with us is a great security for the young men lead each other into expenses and vices.

Young men think properly of themselves when they come out first, but when they come to be doctors or captains here, their heads are turned. I well remember telling you so before. Their heads are as much turned with the finery as the girls are with the flattery. We are all glad to meet those who know us, and the sight of a face introduced by you is always an occasion for a holiday, in which Sir Henry is chief. He received Longdale three times. We had three dinners almost on purpose, for the young men and he, and Longdale, were the greatest friends. If anybody turned his head therefore, he did it to himself. He lived at a man's whom I mentioned to you,

Davies, a lame man whom they here called Devil, first because he is lame, and next because I hear he was something of a printer's devil, or news carrier, for Topham's paper, which Mr Samuel conducted. He knew nothing of doctoring, but somehow or other he married and brought Mrs Davies out here, whom I told you of, and who went home last year. How such a match could be, God knows, but they continued to live with Samuel, and who has left him the whole profit and management of it, and a fine house while Samuel went home to be divorced.[15] The truth is that people make a sad laugh about it here, and Mrs Davies is not in great esteem on that account. She certainly was very ill when she went home and, had she not been so, her going home just after Samuel would have looked so bad that nobody would have mended their thoughts about the situation. What she is doing in London, or how going on, you may not know, though I own I should. She is a very fine woman.

We never dined less than ten, and usually nothing was unpleasant, but there was once this doctor who was dirty, and you cannot guess what a dirty Griffin *(newcomer to India)* looks like. Biss and friends came out to India clean, as they were well provided for, but this doctor, poor thing, was not, so the others lent him shirts. Some joke caught our ears and we asked what it was, and so we heard it. Mr Gwillim said to Biss, "Have you got all you lent back". "Yes", says Biss, rubbing his nose, "And more Sir", then they all laughed. "Why, what did you lend?" "A shirt Sir"; then another great laugh. I believe it was all following a scarcity of paper, and a disorder with which they were all troubled. There were three of them in the same state, only the others had their own linen and could do as they wished. This is a fine story to write about, but I am sure you would have laughed and could not have helped it. Mr Gwillim laughed most, and I believe would have been very glad to have them all round him again. Where there are several people, one of them will usually be the cause of a joke, and laughed at.

You have sent me more catchup than I shall use, although it is good. Your walnuts are excellent. Please get them as young as you can, for Mr Gwillim has no teeth and when he comes to a hard one he says "Hetty

15 See also Elizabeth Gwillim's letter of 3rd September 1803, p. 165.

has forgot about my teeth". We have not opened this year's, but must in a few days.

From Mary Symonds to an unnamed male friend,
almost certainly Richard Clarke's father 14th October 1804

I am greatly flattered by your kind letter which encourages me to trouble you again with some of my tittle tattle. I believe Sir H. Gwillim has written to you several times since the date of your letter to me, and I suppose he has given you his reasons for not writing before, if he had any, though I really believe he had none. Indeed a great allowance may be made for him, for he has suffered a great deal of pain and uneasiness in this country, and during the four months of the year in which the land winds prevail, he is incapable of doing anything from the extreme irritation of his nerves. Unfortunately he has not been able to avoid those unpleasant winds hitherto, owing to the absence of Sir B Sullivan, who has been at Bombay acting as Recorder since the death of Sir William Syer. I hope next year we shall go to Bangalore, which is a delightful climate, when the nights are so close at Madras that we are almost suffocating. We should there be glad to wrap ourselves in shawls and blankets. Besides the particular effect of this climate on Sir Henry Gwillim's constitution, the peculiarity of his temper or nerves (or whatever it be) is such that he seems incapable of doing particular things, except at particular times, and I have often known him very desirous of writing when some oppression of his spirits has made him unable to persuade himself to set about it. I was very much diverted with the humorous passage in your letter upon the difference between acting and thinking, but why cannot it meet the account of your own plans. Surely there is nothing unreasonable in a man's promising himself many years of enjoyment after your age (at least I hope there is not). What is forty-eight, with a good constitution? All your amusements are rational, and may be enjoyed at any time of life besides which, you are only returning to your former habits, not beginning a new way of living. I could show you a score of wise men from fifty to sixty years of age who have hitherto known no enjoyment, except what they derived from the hope of spending agreeably the trash *(sic - cash)* they have been scraping together, and in that hope have just taken to themselves wives of about seventeen. They talk continually of the happiness they shall have in returning to England. Good men! They forget what havoc forty summers have made in their own constitutions, and amongst the friends they are thinking to return to. They flatter themselves with the hope of enjoying the same sports and amusements which delighted their boyish days. Such men, you will say, are far enough out of the right way of thinking to perceive their error, and I believe this may be so.

I fear you won't like my morality if I talk so lightly of old men marrying girls of 16 or 17 to make themselves happy. However, many think the girls furnish me with an excuse, for I assure you I have known several instances in which they were not sacrificed by avaricious parents, but by their own sordid dispositions, which have made them prefer age and riches when they might have married men suitable to themselves in years and with fair prospects, but without much ready money. When this is the case you will allow tis no great matter. Don't you think me very impertinent to run on in this manner to you? I daresay you do. I shall therefore try to give you pleasure by choosing another subject, and by that means hope to divert your attention from the faults of the writer. I cannot expect to succeed better in this attempt than by saying something of our good Richard. He was greatly pleased with your last letter in which you proposed his returning home at the expiration of Sir Henry's term, and was in such excessive spirits about it, and expressed his joy in such a strong manner, that I (who never heard he had any particular dislike to this country) could not help asking him how it happened that he was so much charmed with this plan, which did not seem to offer greater advantages than those he had thought of before, particularly as he was disappointed in his favourite hope of procuring a Writership. He said it was true, he wished for that appointment because it would be a certain provision, but he had always thought of our leaving this country with great dejection, though he had not mentioned it, and had always imagined he should be solitary and uncomfortable when we were gone, and should have no one near him whom he could actually call a friend. I believe this painful reflection had arisen in his mind, or at least had been greatly increased, by the loss of poor Mr Temple, with whom Richard always lived in habits of great friendship. They met every day in their offices, and had

I believe a very great regard for each other. The sudden death of Mr Temple made a very strong impression on poor Richard's mind; perhaps it affected him more owing to the very afflicting news he had just received from you and Mrs Clarke *(the loss of their daughter, Mary Anne)*. I feel inclined to say something on the subject of your late severe trial, and I heartily wish it was in my power to comfort you in any way, but I am convinced it would be impertinent in me, ignorant as I am, to attempt to console you, who are so well acquainted with the source from whence alone consolation can be drawn on such occasions. It must be evident to every grateful mind that our benevolent creator always accompanies his heaviest visitations with some circumstances to soften and reconcile them to us, and for that reason (I am persuaded) He directed that your letter should arrive at the time it did, to soothe poor Richard's troubled mind with the pleasing prospect of seeing England, and yourselves, so much sooner than he before expected. Since that time he has been quite well and happy. I shall not trouble you by relating any particulars of poor Temple's death, because I know you will hear the circumstances of it from Richard, and I have already written it to Mrs James, but it is a sad task to write or to read it.

Richard has not yet given up the Tamil language, and he is also studying the Persian. His knowledge of the native languages gives him an opportunity of making himself so well acquainted with the customs and manners of these curious people, that I cannot presume to tell you anything about these men whilst you have such an excellent correspondent. The women, however, I may venture to speak of as they are so much kept away that no man can have an opportunity of describing the higher classes. The Hindus do not confine their women as the Mussulmans' do but, as every rich man chooses to appropriate a great many to himself, he is very jealous, and unwilling to have them seen, particularly by Europeans. He can have no reliance on these women's honour because he sets them so bad an example for, by the Shaster *(Shastra - Sanskrit word for a book of rules)*, he is forbid to have more than one wife and yet those who can afford it marry five or six, and keep twenty or thirty women besides. The Moorish ladies are never seen by any man who is more distantly related than a brother and, as I have had the honour of visiting two or three families of Moorish Princes, I will endeavour to give you some idea of the comforts of the harem, or zenana. The Mussulmen always live together in families, that is all the brothers in one house, and all their wives, concubines and female slaves in the Zenana belonging to it, which is a detached building with a small garden attached to it and bound by a high wall, which encloses the whole space allotted to the women. We entered in through a large, strong gate, from which we went into a narrow passage, and were then met by four of the ladies who took our hands and led us through a square courtyard, on the side of which the apartments are built. The eldest son's first wife is more honoured than any of the other women, unless his mother be alive, who is called the Begum, and though she be a widow she loses none of her authority. She is not, however, allowed to wear any jewels; all her ornaments go immediately to the eldest son's wives on her husband's death but, such is the respect paid to her, that none of the women, not even her daughters, are allowed to speak at the same time she does, nor to sit when she stands. Neither have they the same sort of seat in her presence, hers being a little elevated, whilst they must sit on the ground. This has two cloths spread over the mat for that purpose, the one thick, and striped with red or blue, the other which lies over it is white and thin, to show the stripes of the under one through it. These ladies have a great many cushions and pillows to support their bodies and limbs, as they throw themselves about in various attitudes, forming beautiful groups. They wear a great quantity of thin drapery, which does not conceal the person much. This dress consists of a pair of very full trousers reaching down to the feet, which are generally made of a very rich, crimson satin weave, and embroidered over with gold figures. They also have a little sort of waistcoat, made of silk and richly embroidered, but it is so small and short that the whole of the ribs are quite bare. Over this they wear a very full gown made of thin transparent gauze, or muslin, edged all round with gold lace. It is fastened at the throat by a single button only: some gowns have sleeves and others have none. In the latter case they half cover the arms with jewels. They have also a piece of thin gauze or netting as the veil, richly embroidered at the ends, and edged round with a broad border of gold, and it is about the length of a shawl. This they twist and throw about their figures, in a playful manner, as they converse, shading a small part of the back of the head. The only unpleasant thing in their dress is a large nose ring, which is worn by the married women by way of distinction. The widows, however young they may be, are obliged amongst other mortifications to give up this graceful ornament, which they think more becoming than any other.

One of the ladies we went to visit is sister to the nabob Wallajah. He is said to have been a man of elegant manners, and a very fine person. This sister is about seventy years old; her features seem to have been quite regular and beautiful and, if one may judge from her fine hands, and what remains of her form, she must have been a most delicate figure, though small. She is rather below the middle size. Her house contains about three hundred women and children, one of which is her daughter, a widow of about six and twenty. She herself is tall and strong, beautifully proportioned, and I think, if she had the European red and white complexion, she would be the handsomest woman I ever saw. Yet it is not the white we want in her skin so much as the red, for she is by no means darker than the Turks, but she is extremely sallow, as all the moor women are, owing to their confinement and the heat of the climate. Fifteen or twenty of the other women are the Begum's son's wives; forty or fifty more are their concubines, and all the rest are slaves. A concubine is not a contemptible person amongst the mussulmen, though inferior to the wives. She has many rights and privileges in the house, and is entitled to a part of the man's property when he dies. Every lady is attended by about eight women, constantly. One holds her betel box, which is a little gold square casket; another prepares the betel leaves, and presents them to her; a third holds a little gold vase, sometimes set with jewels, for their mouths are constantly filled with the red juice of the fresh betel, which they never swallow. Two more servants attend with fans to cool her, and keep off flies; a sixth holds her handkerchief; and the others give her water, which she is continually wanting to rinse her mouth of the betel juice, and which they keep in a silver or gold ewer, and present in a glass, or gold cup. This description will give you an idea of great order, delicacy and magnificence, and yet nothing can be more disorderly and offensive than a zenana. The fine gold and silver vessels are so dirty that one cannot distinguish the metal from old lead, and though the forms of them were very elegant, and the ornaments in a very good taste, they are beat and bruised with such savage carelessness that one can scarcely trace what they have been like. All the servants are so dirty, or so filthy, that no description can give a just idea of them. They smell of the various oils with which they anoint their hair and bodies, in a most odious manner, and they crowd into the rooms in immense numbers, and with a boldness that cannot be repressed. The lowest and meanest of the slaves obtrude themselves into the apartment of the great Princess without fear or shame, so that the heat is intolerable. But I think the worst of all is that the great, and apparently delicate, ladies are themselves in their hearts as ferocious as tigers, capable of shocking deliberate cruelty. They spend a great part of their time in quarrelling with each other, and a still greater part in idle childish sports in which the slaves and all join, sometimes dressing themselves with skins, and running about on all fours like antelopes, tigers etc. At other times they dress the animals in their clothes. A little time ago a Moorish lady dressed her favourite cat with as many of her finest jewels as she could tie about it. The cat made its escape from her apartment and got over the zenana wall, when somebody or other saw it and took care it should be returned without its finery.

The first, and highest, of the ladies occasionally assist in the business of the house such as preparing the food. They distinguish themselves from their servants only by the splendour of their dress, and make them feel their inferiority by very liberally bestowing blows and other punishments. The other day, when we were at the Begum's, an order was given to a slave by a very elegant looking lady, whose hands head and neck were covered with jewels, her dress a white gauze ornamented with gold, and a crimson veil forming a drapery about her beautiful figure. This lovely looking creature, observing that the girl did not attend to her order, rose up and, passing through the dirty crowd, seized the girl's ear giving it an unmerciful pinch and twist that must have caused most excruciating pain. This she did without speaking, or changing her countenance at all, and then sat down, and with the utmost composure went on with the conversation; indeed, I believe it was a very trifling punishment in comparison to those generally inflicted when they are offended. I saw a slave girl, belonging to one of them, the other day who showed me several large marks on her bosom which were made by her mistress who, being angry with her, walked into the cooking room and brought out a firebrand with which she burnt her. These things are practised even now and formerly, they say, the mistresses often killed their slaves for very slight provocations. I thank God there are no slaves amongst the English. Our servants are as independent as they are in England. There is no saying how people's hearts grow hard. I am told that the Dutch women in their settlements exceed even the Moor women in cruelty. If I should relate half the circumstances of this kind that we hear, I should swell my letter to an enormous size, and make it very disgusting, but I thought it right to give you one or two instances to justify the harsh expressions I used.

It is the custom with all the Moors, when a visitor is going away, to perfume her handkerchiefs and clothes with rose water, which is kept in an elegant case of little bottles made entirely of jewels set in gold. Without seeing it, one could not form a just notion of the mixture of misery and splendour which in England is called Eastern magnificence, and in which I do assure you no jot of comfort is to be found. The Moor women have, generally speaking, fine regular features, and elegant figures, but their countenances have an unpleasant expression, an almost horrible fierceness in their look when they are at all moved. I fear I have taken up too much of your time in trying to describe these women, who are a part of creation that seems to us to be very useless, to say the least. Of that, however, we must not pretend to judge. He knows best, who has permitted them to go on in the same way for so many ages, and has heretofore chosen to put so many creatures in their power.

We went to an entertainment at the Nabob' s Palace, which was all in the same style, and was dressed very fine with a profusion of jewels and gold, and so were the Khans or Noblemen who attended him. The room, however, was dirty and wretched, and the walls would have been quite bare but for the industry of the spiders. The servants crowded in amongst the company in the same ungovernable manner, and the men were not more clean than the women.

Our friends, General and Mrs Trent, leave us by this fleet. I think you and Mrs Clarke will like the lady for her mild, sweet disposition but, as for the General, you will at first think him rather to be endured than admired but, when you are better acquainted with him, you may see that he has a kind, good heart which he takes some trouble to conceal and, like many wise men, despises the virtues he possesses and wishes only to be admired for qualities not half so valuable. He was born a Cockney and, though he has been thirty six years in this country, he retains the language together with that agreeable lisp which is peculiar to natives of London. He also has a little stammer, yet he says he was born to be an orator, and that his talents have been misapplied and he wishes he had been bred to the bar. He might then have made a distinguished figure in the world. He is kind to his servants beyond description, and every creature about him but, when I have sometimes complimented him upon his tenderness towards them, he protests he despises the whole race of Hindus, thinks them inferior brutes and wonders the judges should befriend such a vile people. A great deal of this arises from the magnificent idea he has of himself, and of the English character compared to that of the Hindu.

Letters of 1805 and Commentary

Commentary

The year starts in February, once again, with Mary writing about Sir Thomas Strange, the Chief Justice, taking passage to England without much warning, and giving no clear reason. There is hence much speculation among the remaining British residents of Madras as to his motive for doing so, and what an extraordinary move this is, given that he would have served his time there within a matter of months. With the third judge, Sir Benjamin Sullivan, being on extended sick leave, both Mary in this first letter, and Elizabeth in a letter of August, emphasize the large increase in workload left on Sir Henry Gwillim's shoulders, and thus their inability as a family to get away to the cool of the hills near Bangalore during the hottest season. It would appear that he received no real warning of this, and no contingency plans were made. In Elizabeth's letter of March to her sister Hetty it is clear that the sisters liked Sir Thomas Strange, and he had always been very courteous and kind to them, and he and Sir Henry worked well together in the control of unruly elements among the European population who had been unused to legal restraint. She undoubtedly suspected duplicity, however, and was very suspicious that he had gone to England to obtain preferment from Henry Dundas (Lord Melville) who had just returned to power, and to the daughter of whom Sir Thomas Strange's brother, James, had just been married. Sir Thomas himself later maintained that he had sailed in an American ship because he had wanted to see America ever since his time in Nova Scotia which, in the event, was prevented by the return of hostilities between England and France. In her letter of the 24th August Elizabeth, clearly sensitive to the pressures placed on her husband, again inveighs against what she regards as the deviousness of the Strange family and the use of their links to Lord Melville, King's Minister.

During August of that year the Gwillims entertained all the lawyers to dinner on the anniversary of the formation of the Supreme Court. The following night the 'lawyers leavings' were offered to even more august company in the shape of the Governor, Lord William Bentinck, who had arrived in 1803, and to two admirals who became rather well-known, Sir Edward Pellew and Sir Thomas Troubridge. There is no mention of the new Commander in Chief, Sir John Cradock. It is interesting to note that the household had just received from England three gammons and one useable ham and yet, within a short time, that ham had been wholly devoured by the higher echelons of Madras society after four months at sea. It is little wonder that the letters are so full of requests for more shipped goods.

In the early part of the year the family were living in a rented house some miles from the centre of Madras which was more rural, cooler and pleasantly situated in Pammal, among the cotton fields to the south-west. Both sisters were painting, and reporting back to their mentor in England, George Samuel. Mary was painting landscapes, but also local architecture, although in a letter from Elizabeth in August she was reported to be painting a myriad variety of tropical fish. Many of these were lost in a ship home that foundered. Elizabeth is of course painting many species of birds, frequently from life, and always with their subsequent release. Both women suffer from a lack of materials *(E.G. to Hetty 6.3.1805)*, particularly paper, brushes and an array of colours with names still familiar to us today. In her letters of the 6th March and the 24th August, Elizabeth describes her fascination with botany and her desire to study it for its own sake as well as for its value in understanding Hindu. She also recounts her new interest in painting botanical subjects. All this is much encouraged by the flattery of the botanist Dr Rottler, who names a new species after her. Sending paintings and living botanical samples home is an anxious business because of the fears of loss, lack of care, inattentive couriers and unhelpful ships' captains. Dr Anderson had previously encouraged her to have native Indian copies of her paintings made, and to send those home, which was probably wise advice.

As Mary makes clear in her first letter to her sister Hetty that year, the receipt of letters and of parcels was exhilarating and joyful. Great excitement was felt upon opening a box containing a bewildering mix of shoes, hats, newspapers, peas, jam and cloaks. Although entertaining enough to a modern reader, clearly Sir Henry Gwillim derived some amusement from the event as well. Nevertheless, behind such jollity is the ever-present concern that there was an element of luck about the arrival of such cornucopias. The presence of French privateers off the eastern coast of India was a constant worry in time of war, although a way round this was to use the occasionally available American ship which, being neutral, was safe from predation. Such ships were also quite often used for passage home as they were cheaper and quicker, even though travel was via America. Clearly expediency had rapidly extinguished any loss of pride from British failure in the War of Independence, only some 22 years earlier. The other great anxiety was the loss of a ship in a storm which occurred with some regularity. In 1808–09 no less than fourteen East Indiamen went down,[1] the loss rate being less in other years. Such an event occurred to the Prince of Wales in 1804. The two sisters knew many of the people on board, including a number of children, and they lost in her many letters, documents, gifts, botanical specimens and paintings. Because she was felt to be one of the safest and best commanded, many people sent things home by her. Despite these various risks, there continued to be a constant stream of requests for locally unobtainable items and, in this year, Elizabeth asks for a diverse range of goods, ranging from the already mentioned painting materials to cloth for towels, with soap, yellow Limerick gloves, silk stockings and, for good measure, writing paper. She also wistfully mentions her lack of significant jewellery compared to her peers, perhaps implying that her husband was meaner than he should be, or just thrifty. It was in 1805 that the truth was revealed about the lost letters in the Admiral Aplin, taken by the French in 1804. Many of these letters were returned, which generated among the Indian British population a glow of warm gratitude to the French officers who had thus behaved in such a gentlemanly fashion. It was then discovered in the following year that the contents of all this

1 Parkinson, C. Northcote, *Trade in the Eastern Seas, 1793–1813* (Cambridge, 1937).

private mail had been copied, and published in French newspapers. The glow developed into incandescent rage.

A recurring theme throughout the letters was the concern the sisters held for young men recently arrived in India. One or two lived in the household permanently, such as the legal employees Richard Clarke and Temple, the latter having lately died, and others stayed there for months on end, such as William Biss. A number of others passed through, sometimes more than once, and all were much appreciated by Sir Henry. It seems they were much appreciated by the sisters as well. Mary amused herself with some light flirtation, and enjoyed the male company generally, and Elizabeth showed a maternal instinct and concern. Being childless herself may have enhanced this, but she also had an overworked husband who was falling asleep at 9.30 pm, and of an uncertain temperament at the best of times, so she may well have enjoyed a little youthful male company for its own sake. Elizabeth makes very occasional references throughout her letters to Sir Henry's temperament, and had previously commented on his tendency to 'ill-natured anger'.

In the letter to her mother of August she revels in the presence of a host of young men celebrating, as guests, Richard Clarke's coming of age. Their privileged family connections added to their attraction. Later in the same letter, however, she demonstrates her protective inclinations in expressing her fears for the risks young men undergo from cohabiting with local women; 'easy of access'; and the consequent risk of disease, and the perils of inebriation. She, and other women like her, would provide homes for young men that had been introduced to them as a means of safeguarding them, and helping them to avoid the hostels and similar accommodation where too much temptation lay. Both Elizabeth, and Mary in an earlier letter, emphasized the considerable financial burden that young men endured in paying for a passage to India, and the difficulty faced by young officers who were paid too little to cope with regimental expenses, particularly if they had looked forward to a life of ease, or as Elizabeth put it in a letter of August that year: 'a flashy life lounging about'. The road to debt was all too easy, and certainly perilous because of astronomical interest rates levied by local Indian lenders (see Mary Symonds 4 Mar 1805). Nevertheless, in a later letter, none of these concerns stopped her from encouraging more young doctors to come out to India because of a shortage, having played hostess to a young English surgeon who undoubtedly charmed her. In fact both women were regularly charmed by these young men: 'beauty-hunting Biss' sighing after the ladies, and the excitedly thrilling description of Richard Clarke, and friend, indecorously suspended from a hedge they had just attempted to climb. Elsewhere they saw the potential depredations that seemed to be consequent upon young men cohabiting with native women, and noted the risks to their health, and the waste of money which might have been better sent home to hungry mothers who had financed the travel to India in the first place. (Elizabeth's letter of 16 Oct 1804). For many, consorting with Indian or Anglo-Indian women was an inevitability, however. Many young men came out to India at the age of 16, as writers or cadets, and had no experience of English women, who were in any case scarce, being outnumbered sixteen to one. As already noted, something like three-quarters of young men kept a bibi *(concubine)*. There must have been a frisson of resentment among the English women living there at that time, especially any unmarried ones, but little more than this. Impoverished young English men were of no marriageable interest to them. Furthermore, they were used to the presence of large numbers of Anglo-Indians in Madras. As noted in the Commentary of 1802, and in Mary's letter of 11th February of that year, at least half the women they met were of mixed race. Despite any concerns, Elizabeth felt no qualms about singing the praises of a daughter of her friend Dr James Anderson, whose accomplishments and charm were doubtless a product of her education in England. Nevertheless, she was a natural daughter which meant that her mother was an Indian woman, and that her illegitimate existence had been acknowledged. Somehow she was not a risk unlike those others who threatened all Elizabeth's younger male friends.[2]

There are two other comments arising from the letters of this year. Firstly, Mary turned down another suitor. Any would-be husband had to be screened by the family for adequacy of means, for the very straightforward reason that a single woman in those days usually had no significant means of her own and

2 See Introduction, and also Robb, Peter, *Sex and Sensibility, Richard Blechynden's Calcutta Diaries 1791–1822* (Oxford, 2011) See also note 14 of 1802.

was absolutely dependent, after marriage, on the support of her husband. If such a woman did have some means, this became the property of the husband in any case. In Mary's situation the suitor in question failed the test, having been found to be heavily in debt following loans to native princes. Such debts were not uncommon and were often concealed from the public eye, hence the need for some surveillance. There is evidence of censure in Elizabeth's letter in that these loans were made at unreasonably high rates of interest to local nawabs who needed money to ward off their regional enemies, and to maintain their status quo, but were unable to service the loans after the battle of Sriringapattanam and the consequent acquisition of large amounts of their local lands and estates by the East India Company. She then comments that the latter were thereafter uninclined to make good such losses, declaring that they had outlawed these loans anyway. Soon afterwards these died out in any case. The point is further made, as it has been elsewhere, that the Company found these territorial maintenance costs burdensome and for this reason were reluctant to continue such acquisitions, a view particularly held by the Court of Directors but rather less so by the then Governor General, Richard Wellesley, to their significant discomfiture.

The other point of interest is Elizabeth's reference to the Dutch, not for the first time. She, and others of that era, regarded them with censure; 'a depraved cruel set'; continuing torture and slavery into the second half of the nineteenth century. The women were felt to be no better than the men.

Thus ends 1805, the last letter being late August. There were probably others, lost at the time, or since, but the next recorded communication is not until January of the following year.

Letters

From Mary Symonds to her mother. 2nd February 1805

An opportunity has just now occurred of telling you that we are all in existence and well. The ship by which I send this is an American, and it is supposed that the passengers may arrive in England by her two months sooner than those who will go by our regular Fleet, which will sail the second of this month. For that reason, Sir Thomas Strange has taken his passage in this ship, having some very urgent business to transact which requires his presence in England.[3] What his business is, he and his family keep a profound secret, but his sudden departure has put Madras into a general consternation, some conjecturing one thing and some another. It must certainly be something of an extraordinary nature, which could induce a man at near fifty years of age to risk three Indian voyages, particularly as he is within six months of having served his seven years, and by going before that term he would forfeit his claim to the pension of £1600 a year. He declares his intention is to return in a year and a half, but even that absence is a loss to him of £1000 as his housekeeping goes on here all the same, for his brother and sister live with him, and one person more or less makes very little difference in a house here.

I shall only write this one letter now, as I am obliged to send it by a private hand, there being no packet for England by this ship, and I shall direct this one immediately to you as I think you are best situated to inform our several friends of the state of our health here. All my chitchat I shall bestow on Hetty by the regular ships. Betsy and I are now living at a house situated about eleven miles from Madras. It was built by a gentleman who was in the company's civil service. He got a grant of lands, which are very extensive, for the purpose of planting cotton, and a kind of aloe which makes very fine strong ropes *(probably sisal)*. With these, he expected to supply the Navy. The ropes were tried, and found to answer very well, but it is said the agents for supplying the Navy being people in power, and finding that their income would be greatly reduced by the loss of that article, they strongly opposed the use of Mr Webb's ropes and he, needing the encouragement of Government, finds his speculation turned out very ill, and the demand for the rope so small that he does not think it necessary to reside on the farm. The cotton is taken care of by servants whom he keeps here for that purpose. The house he frequently lends to any family

3 His excuse later given for using a fast American ship was his desire to see America. This always seemed improbable given that he was only six months away from the end of his contracted term in India, and yet his planned round trip would take eighteen.

of his acquaintance who may wish for a change of air, or variety of scene. We were very glad to come here for a little time, as it is high ground, a very pretty picturesque country and, at this season, many degrees cooler than Madras. Betsy has been very busily employed in drawing birds, and the village people have been very good in bringing many curious ones to her. I assure you I have lost no time but have also been very busy in making drawings of the country and, well done or ill done, I take care to make them as much like nature as I can by colouring them on the spot, so that I trust in God we shall one day have the pleasure of giving you, and all our friends, some idea of this country and its inhabitants when you have our joint labours to aid our descriptions. We are here surrounded by hills and lakes, and the neighbouring villages and choultreys are situated in beautiful groves for, wherever the natives of this country build, they also plant; every man makes a screen for his own house to shelter him from the hot winds, and to shade him from the noonday sun. It is pretty to see the numbers of little girls who are employed in this cotton ground. They run about all day amongst the bushes with little baskets on their arms gathering in the ripe cotton, which they carry to others who are sitting down in rows and, with a simple machine made for the purpose, separate the seeds and clean the cotton. Sir Henry comes up to us in the cool of the evening, and goes down to St Thomé early in the morning. He goes every day when he is busy and, when he has leisure, he stays with us two or three days together. The exercise seems to be of service to him, as his appetite is good and he sleeps soundly all night, indeed he generally drops asleep by nine o'clock and at half past ten just hobbles to bed with his eyes half shut. We have had a remarkably pleasant season, and the weather much cooler during the last two months than I have ever felt it in India. I hope to God it will brace Sir Henry a little, and enable him to bear the land winds, as Sir Thomas Strange' s going home will prevent our going away from Madras to avoid the heat. It is indeed very hard upon Sir Henry to be left, I may say alone, with all the business of the Court upon his hands. For Benjamin Sullivan is an old man and, having been very free at living, he is infirm beyond his years. He has had two or three alarming illnesses lately and is, besides, so unused to business that he is quite alarmed at the idea of acting in anything.

Whilst we are here, there are three young men keeping house for themselves at St Thomé. Mr Richard as host, and Mr Biss and Mr Turton his guests. Their business and pleasures prevent their coming to us all the week, but citizen-like they come up on Saturday night, and go down on Sunday evening, or Monday morning. Mr Biss returned from Tripapore last week, where he got great credit for his exertions in the study of the Hindustani, and in his military manners and, in consequence of his good conduct, Lord William Bentinck has fixed him at Madras for one year; a member of a Society, which he has just formed, to be composed of only such young gentlemen as distinguished themselves at Tripapore. They are to be instructed in certain things which Lord William thinks necessary to their complete accomplishment as officers. They will we be immediately under his own eye, at a house he is fitting out for them in the Fort. Till that is ready, Mr Biss will remain with us.

We received a packet of letters from Hetty about six weeks ago, by one of the ships of the Fleet in which I knew Commander-in-Chief, Sir John Cradock, had sailed. That fleet arrived in the Bay during our monsoon, and therefore they were afraid to put in here and all went to Bengal. We know that the ships are safe in Bengal, but they have been detained much longer than was expected, owing to an embargo which Lord Wellesley *(Governor-General in Calcutta)* laid on these ships, in consequence of a report of several privateers having been seen in the Bay. The expense of land carriage for letters from Bengal is so great, that very few have been forwarded to Madras out of those ships.

I hope you receive all our letters safe, and then I think you will have no cause to complain of anything, but the trouble of reading them. To be sure, that may be trouble enough for you, as neither Betsy nor I can boast much of our penmanship. However, you can employ young eyes, and I'm sure it will be good practice for Tom to accomplish him in the reading of crabbed hands. What would I not give at this moment to know how you all are? Perhaps surrounded with snow a yard deep, or at best cold, dirty and slushy. If you could but give us your summers, or we could give you our winters, what a rare time we would make of it. We now have fine harvest weather; the evenings and mornings are very cool and pleasant, but from nine in the morning till four in the evening the heat is too great for women to venture out on foot.

Betsy will leave her post to me as she has now three curious birds waiting to be drawn, and her conscience is concerned in doing them as soon as possible for the poor things will not eat in confinement, so they are allowed to fly away when they have done sitting for their portraits

From Mary Symonds to her sister Hetty 4th March 1805

We have just received your two boxes by the Baring; the one containing a box of millinery, a piece of black cloth, and a full dress and black coat for Sir Henry. The other filled with peas, two pairs of nankeen shoes, a dozen newspapers, Mrs Grimes parcels and two pounds of jam. The millinery is a very nice little assortment, and very useful to us. Betsy is quite glad to see the blue hats, and I am equally so to find a neat plain chip hat, for I have neither had hat or bonnet that I could stick on my noddle for a whole year. You cannot form any idea of our stupidity in putting on fancy things and if, after standing an hour in adjusting some dashing hat, you were then to meet me in it, I dare say you would burst out laughing to see how completely I had mistaken the matter. Besides which, I assure you I don't look half so young and blooming as I did two years ago. The two black cloaks are very beautiful. We admire both the make and the materials very much. I willingly resign all the caps to Betsy as I shall imitate them, which I can do very well now you have been so good as to send such pretty materials. We have not yet seen the gentleman who brought the boxes, but he has written once or twice to Sir Henry. I believe he has not been onshore, for the Captains and Officers of the ships are very much hurried. They were detained a long time at Calcutta, and have now a very short time allowed them for lading their ships, for the Admiral is quite impatient to sail and, indeed, every day they are now detained may be the cause of their encountering a storm off the Cape.

I believe Sir Henry was a little disappointed on opening the boxes not to find a coloured coat, which he promised himself you had sent. He said you mentioned a pepper and salt coat, which you had chosen for him a long time ago, and now he is obliged to go on in his old long backed fashion, though (for aught I know) he may have intended to eclipse all the best in this place. I am sure he talks as much of it as if he did. I wish you could be in a corner when we are opening a box from you, it would entertain you very much to hear the observations. Sir Henry generally gives himself sport by laughing at all the things as they make their appearance; the comparisons and resemblances are beyond anything. Betsy has fallen violently in love with a blue quilted bonnet and he declares it is a piece of his aunt's old petticoat. A little time ago, Betsy had been drawing a small kind of tiger and, after she had done it, she told Sir Henry that she discovered a great resemblance in the tiger' s countenance to mine. She did not communicate the idea to me and, the next day, I made my appearance in a kind of military waistcoat, with loops of ribbon crossing the breast from button to button. As I sat down he began to titter, and then gave Betsy a jog to look at me. "Betsy", says he, "Look at old Tiger Pol;" "She has dressed herself in the skeleton of a man she killed yesterday."

When Mr Biss first arrived, he was quizzed and laughed at by us all. He was the first very short-waisted gentleman we had seen. Sir Henry used to sit laughing and making fun with him by the hour; his little waistcoat, his large shoes and boots, and his high collar and stuffed cravat, but I assure you he has undergone an entire metamorphosis, and is now quite reduced to a neat Indian Officer, and in his turn laughs at the griffins *(newcomers)* that are just arrived. The young men generally begin by reducing their neck cloths, which they preen and pose daily, like skinning an onion, and then there are those fine high collars and long sleeves that lead to the addition of a good crop of prickly heat, so that they gladly exchange them at home for a white cotton sheer waistcoat. Comfort becomes of so much value, that the dashing appearance is forced to yield to it in a very little time.

The paper you sent is very acceptable to Betsy, as she has had a fit of drawing lately and nearly used up all the old stocks. For my own part, I am trying to buy a little, but it is wretched stuff that is brought out to sell in general, and all matted up immediately. I have been, this cool season, at a place called Pammal, about 12 miles from Madras. The country about it is extremely pretty, and I have made myself very busy sketching, so you may now tell George Samuel, in answer to his enquiries, that I have got Pagodas and Choultreys and Montapums *(sic)* and Mosques and Moor houses, but alas no paper for landscapes. What we have brought out with us has entirely lost its sizing, and takes ink worse than blotting paper. I wished to give you an idea of our house at St Thomé but we had no paper. Betsy thinks it was very stingy to send only twelve sheets of the thick paper, so would you be so good as to double that quantity, and send with it about the same of such as will suit slighter drawings; that thick sort is only proper for very high quality finishes.

You are very good in mentioning everyone who is dear to us as, by doing so, you prevent our being unhappy in case we are deprived of their letters by any accident. Our good old Admiral will convoy this fleet all the way home, so we have a fair prospect of your receiving our letters in reasonable time. His successor has not yet been on shore here, so I know nothing of him but, as he is a young and active man, I hope we shall be more fortunate in these seas than we have been. Madras has been all show and finery for these three weeks, quite full of fine folks and gay folks, at least as far as external appearances go but, I believe with many, that is all. The civilians gave a dinner, and the Navy Agent a grand ball and fireworks, to Admiral Rainier prior to his departure, and the civilians gave a very grand ball and the military a very fine dinner to General Wellesley *(later the Duke of Wellington)* prior to his departure. Lady William Bentinck has given evening parties to introduce Sir John and Lady Theodosia Cradock *(the new Commander in Chief)*. I took the trouble of going to two of the balls in order to oblige Mr Biss and Mr Richard Clarke, but I am by no means fond of such hurly-burly, for it is all the same thing over and over again, and all the same people for the most part of the year. Just now, to be sure, we have plenty of new faces to stare at, and new fashions to laugh at; all the people who are come out by four or five ships from England, some for this place and some for Bengal, and all the people who are come from Bengal and going home.

Mr Biss, who has been with us this month, is indeed a very fine young man, and a great favourite with us all. I believe, like every other young man who comes out, he does not find India all he expected, though he really does not complain as everyone else does. In England they hear a great deal of the fine pay of Officers here, but nothing of the sad imposition they are obliged to submit to, the very great expense they are at in fitting themselves out with various necessaries which are unheard of in England, and the many hardships they are forced to undergo on their first arrival. When once their establishment is fixed, the pay is certainly sufficient to maintain them very genteelly, but it is impossible for any young man to join his Regiment without considerable assistance from his friends. This is a circumstance very little known in England, but very severely felt by all the housekeepers here, who have numbers of poor young men recommended to them, and whose friends think they have provided for them by giving them a good stock of clothes and paying their passage. Sir Thomas Strange told me he had two or three thousand pagodas[4] owing to him, not one of which could ever be paid, for the young men's friends would not remit the money, and he himself could not find it in his heart to note them for it, knowing it was not in their power to pay it without contracting debts to natives. They would charge an immoderate rate of interest, and keep them in thralldom for many, many years.

You write us very surprising news of your being at Clapham. I begin to think you have an eye towards the mansion house. Pray have you the honour and pleasure of Mrs Ravenhill' s acquaintance, or is she quite too sublime? I suppose you give yourself little care whose acquaintance you have, whilst you have your dear little prattler with you; I think she must begin to prattle now. I wish I could hear of her, and you, once a week; for now I don't like to think much about her, nor to promise myself pleasure which is at least so very distant.

From Elisabeth Gwillim to her sister Hetty 6th March 1805

Upon your nice paper, and with one of your nice pens, let me thank you for your nice care of all our things, and still nicer packing of them. It would have been as difficult to replace the various articles in the box, after we had satisfied our curiosity by looking at them, as to fold a rose back into a bud. Please except this fine simile in lieu of long letters which, by this fleet, I shall not have time to write. I wrote immense quartos by the

4 3000 pagodas at 8/6d per pagoda is equivalent to £1,275. Today that would be worth approximately £110,000 (Bank of England inflation calculator).

Prince of Wales. I liked Captain Price; his ship was reckoned the best, and he the best officer, but we fear that neither will be heard of more. I wish you may have better intelligence; there were sweet children in her, and everybody here is in great anxiety about her. I hardly know what I sent in her, and in such a case cannot think of calling them losses but, lest you should think me negligently missing my labours, I must inform you of what I recollect. Letters numerous: one of five or six sheets, and with it a translation of a Hindu religious history; a sort of legendary tale which might have entertained you; a similar letter and a copy of the translation for my mother, and some dried plants for Dr Smith; a plant, which Dr Rottler, the Botanist *(see note 3 – 1804, page 184)*, chose to give my name to, if it might be accepted; a large box of most curious plants for Mr Whitley; seeds, and small boxes with sandalwood trees. These were the fruits of my labours. The other things Polly tells me she has enumerated.

It has been a dreadful long time that we had no sort of opportunity of writing. Of the letters Sir Henry's father had, one was of necessity sent to Bengal at a great expense, and one he sent as a trial by an American ship not having any idea that it would reach England. He thought it would amuse his father to have a letter that had been in the four quarters of the globe, for the American ships touch at the Cape and carry their letters to America from choice, as there are little packets continually sailing there. These letters are sent to England and, as the Americans are a neutral power, their ships pass the seas without fear, and of course without any delay that it may occasion. The Americans have used this neutrality to good purpose, for they have taken many passengers from hence, and those persons being landed in America easily find a passage to England, and have arrived quicker, and infinitely cheaper, than by going in our own East India ships. Such was the case of the letter you mention. It was at that time quite a hazardous thing, but the Americans have been so punctual in dismissing to England all letters entrusted on board their ships, and they have arrived so punctually, that all the people are charmed with the scheme and, in future, I shall write to you by every American ship that leaves this port. At least some of us will; an American left this place about three weeks ago, by which Sir Henry and Polly, Biss and Richard wrote. The Americans not only do themselves a benefit in this, but us Indians also, for the East Indian Captains are, in particular, so enormously expensive in their demand for a passage home, that many people are mere prisoners in this place, and even those who have a little money are glad to get a passage in an American, and embark a second time from there rather than pay these enormous demands. I hope, therefore, that it may be some check on the Captains.

The last American carried home many passengers, amongst them Sir Thomas Strange, whose reason for visiting England has astonished everybody. I should have written to you on the subject before. When we came here, we went to Sir T. Strange's house as you know, and Sir Henry had a great regard for him from being at college with him *(Christ Church, Oxford; but two years later)*, and we have always been upon friendly terms. He is a most pleasing man in his manners, both attentive and kind, and has a handsome person with the accomplishments of a gentleman and of a scholar. But, he universally had the character of being intriguing in spirit and utterly deceitful. I have never been inclined to believe this report of him, for why should a man deceive, or flatter, or intrigue who, being placed in an exalted situation, may command all the honours of it, and do all the duties of it, by the plainest rules of morality. One thing was always apparent, that he was ambitious for grasping all the power and all the patronage belonging to this situation. However Sir H is not of a disposition meanly to give up his rights and, a little contention excepted, things have gone on marvellously well. The match Mr J. Strange *(brother of Sir Thomas)* made with Lord Melville's *(Henry Dundas)* daughter enhanced Sir Thomas's reputation, but his ruinous circumstances have been a great affliction. Sir Thomas's father was an engraver, as you know, a profession which nobody in high life falls into. However, he rose to great honours in it, and some wealth. At the same time there can be no pretence to family.[5] This match, which connected him with the King's first Minister, led to every ambitious hope, but had Mr J. Strange been content to remain quietly in possession

5 Sir Thomas Strange's father was Sir Robert Strange, who was a Scottish engraver of prints in both London and Paris, and had considerable skill and reputation. He was particularly known for portraits by van Dyck and Titian, and latterly worked under Royal patronage. Elizabeth belittles him somewhat, when correctly indicating that he had no distinguished background, but forgets to point out his ability, perhaps because the Strange family and the Gwillims were by then becoming estranged.

of his own fortune of seventy thousand pounds, it would not have led to the question how he might have risen greatly with such a match. There was everything to hope for with her interest. He has now got the leave of the Company to come here to gain a third portion, to the great discontent of the other Civil Servants, who must of course feel it a little hard to see one of the best situations given to a person who has been so well provided for. It has occasioned great discontent, but the interest is so great that he will probably be in the Council next. Sir Thomas has always exerted himself, with Sir Henry, in the suppression of all the violent measures of a set of people who, till the establishment of the Courts, were unrestrained by law.[6] Such exertions required a great and independent spirit and, now he has such a brother here, his task has become doubly hard. He has told us that it was his wish to prevent his brother from coming out but, be that as it may, he is come. His brother's wife makes a display of jewels more than all his debts, which is generally thought very indecent. So far from an easy temper, as you supposed, I believe she is most troublesome. I think I can plainly perceive that Sir Thomas has no love for her. Some say it is to avoid her that he goes home, whilst I think there is no doubt that he has gone home to use her interest in some way or other, whilst her father is in power. What his motives are, ought to be examined. Sir B. Sullivan is most offended that he has not said whether they are private or public. It is generally supposed that he goes home to solicit for himself some higher employment and, at the same time, to serve some friend and countryman by putting him in his own place over Sir Henry's head. [6]

If he should do all this to further his own interest, it would be a most abominable thing, but everyone has insisted it is so ever since we came here; that he is capable of all sorts of intrigue, and that his sudden going home just at the moment Dundas (Lord Melville) comes again into power, looks most extraordinary. His affection for me and Polly are so great, and so freely expressed, and his whole manner so full of apparent kindness, that I am unwilling to believe, and hardly can believe, such hypocrisy in human nature.

6 See the final chapter.

Besides ambition there is country. The Scotch hang so together that we cannot guess what they will do for one another, and an English Governor and Irish Commander in Chief coming out here has put them all on the alert. I am quite content with my present situation, but why should a younger person be put over Sir Henry's head when he has done his duty in a most exemplary manner. He has written home about it.

A sweet neighbour of mine had given me a pot of a curious light black ware, of value about a groat, but from the interior of India. Knowing it to be thin, I put it on the ground. I had not gone ten minutes out of the room before it was broken by Biss or Richard throwing a whip through the window, butt end foremost. I had reproached them so much for breaking the oil pitchers the Sunday before, they thought that if this evil was communicated it would go amiss with them. Hearing from Mary that I had received the pot from this lady, they determined to put a good face upon it and go and ask if she could give them another. But there was a difficulty in that I might see them going out, in the heat of the day, if they went out in front of the house. So two of them set out at the back, without waiting for the boys. Unfortunately they had a gate with wooden spikes to mount, which gate was about 20 feet high. The first misfortune was that Richard was caught by the back part of his small clothes *(britches)* and hung there till the nankeen gave way. The other, determined to be wiser, mounted the hedge which was higher but, as he is a Cavalry Officer, he hung by his spurs and could not be liberated without much difficulty. However, Richard covered his misfortunes with his coat and they set out and enquired for Captain Howe, my friend's husband. A black man said "He is in there Sir"; so in they walked. Captain Howe was writing at a little table and poor Mrs Howe in a state of undress, as Richard calls it. They had no idea that the room they were diverted to was the bedroom, and the servants never here think of such good form. Mrs Howe took such compassion on them that she ransacked the whole home for more pots, and her father, the old General, asked them all to dine with him on Wednesday. I shall send you the pots by Mrs Tappington in the Apsley Castle, when she sails.

Two years I was without Bristol paper. It came at last at the beginning of the heat. As soon as the sun got to the south of us, I began to draw upon what was sent, and have done more since that. All I have done since I came to the country is twelve drawings of different sorts of sheep and goats and above thirty birds, so that I was in a great fright that my career would be stopped, when the last little tin case arrived. Mary is still at fault for landscape paper, Newman's cartridge paper, and some other good drawing paper and, above all brushes. Many brushes, and varnishing brushes; good broad ones to wash over sketches; also Indigo, Lake, Umber, Vandyke Brown and Payne's grey, or Smith's grey. We cannot use the Chinese brushes. Send also some very large paper, both Bristol and common drawing paper, to do various points of the countryside, if it shall please God that we are able to. You do not know, and cannot guess, what a great botanist I am become since I have had one volume of Dr Martins New Edition of Miller's Dictionary. Dr Rottler praises me too much, which makes me lazy and turn my mind to other things. The truth is that I should not have put myself upon so new and difficult a study, but that without some little knowledge of botany it is impossible to read the Hindu languages. Their allusions to particular plants, which appertain to their different ceremonies, are so pointed that unless you know the plants, which botany alone can teach you, the merit of the whole passage is lost. After learning a little botany it seems almost impossible to stop.

No letters have I had from Brompton for nearly 2 years, but one, and I will not write again until they write to me, for I have written three for each one of their letters. I wish to have Bewick's second volume of British Birds immediately, which I see by the paper has now come out. Do not forget it, by the first opportunity.[7] I hope that my two pieces of Hamburgh huckaback, for the towels, is upon the sea, for our towels are more ragged than a dishcloth. Pray send a basket of writing paper whenever you can; about a dozen guineas, but let a little be gilt and ribbed paper. A pound of Windsor soap is a good thing to have, if there is room in a box, for it is very dear here; and white ribbon, both sarsnet and satin, is always acceptable. I cannot imagine what it is, in different ribbons, that some turn

7 Thomas Bewick, 1753–1828, was a celebrated English wood engraver and natural history author. He is best known for A History of British Birds in two-volumes, which became the forerunner of all modern field guides and is still admired for its wood engravings. See Oxford Dictionary of National Biography. ref:odnb/2334

yellow and others preserve their whiteness, but I think it is the clear blue whites, very clear, that keep best. You have sent one piece of broad, and one piece of narrow, and a threepenny width. Now the broad is as yellow as flax, and the other two pieces quite white. I should like half a dozen pairs of very handsome silk stockings, with large legs and small feet, for they bind them up in washing here. Let the clocks be very handsome, if they are present. A few short yellow gloves we should be glad of, and Polly says also a few yellow long gloves. She has none left, she says. They are called Limericks; they are best for this country. If you could get a pair of stays with single shoulder straps made of single India dimity *(a lightweight sheer cotton fabric)*, I should be glad of them, but remember I am rather fatter than I was. Next time you send things, I could wish to have a cap with a white plume of feathers, just by way of high fashion, to look distinctive when going to Government House and, at my age, I seem to want something of that kind, particularly as I have no pearls, nor jewels, like some of our ladies have. A cap with a flower is not dress enough. I do have some feathers, but they are not made up into plumes, and I cannot bear feathers unless they are well put in. I cannot do it myself, but Polly can do a thousand turns and twists however.

Biss wants eighty pounds to buy himself a home. If he borrows the money he must pay 10% interest, but he is going to have it from Sir Henry anyway.

From Elisabeth Gwillim to her mother.	Approx. Aug 1805 (Received in England Feb. 1806)

I fear you will have thought it a very long time since you heard from us before this can reach you. The ships have been detained; some of them for at least three months, and during all that time we have been in expectation of an opportunity of writing. They are at last about to sail, but I have been so hurried with company and visiting that I shall not, I fear, have time to write to you so fully as I could wish, having had so much to say to Hetty. Hetty's letters, all have arrived safe, as also did your letter by the ships which came in July, and all my packages of every description arrived in excellent condition. I have the happiness to say that we are at present all quite well, and that we have spent this year much more pleasantly than we have done any one since our arrival. The season has been so mild that the oldest inhabitants remember nothing like it. We have had rain every evening and this hot season, as we call it, has been much cooler than any part of the preceding year. Sir Henry has had no indisposition whatsoever, and he has done an unusual quantity of business being left the whole care of the Court. Sir Thomas Strange is in England, and Sir Benjamin Sullivan to the Eastward on account of his health. Richard and Mary are, thank God, always well, at least they have been hitherto. Mary has wonderful spirits, but she likes being here better than the countryside, but I own I liked the countryside best. You ask if Mary is married. I hope that you are not over anxious on that subject, otherwise you may be sorry to hear that she has refused another offer which was lately made her. The gentleman was in so good a situation here, and had been so long in a good one it was certain he must have accumulated large sums that, though he was somewhat older than what could be called a suitable match, it yet seemed improper that the offer should be hastily declined. Such is the fate of numbers of Indians, that they cannot help entering into speculations by which they lose all that they get. Upon enquiry, it turned out that about £40,000, which he had acquired, had all been lent to native princes, and that there was scarce a hope of any of its being recovered. In order to sue for it, he had been obliged to go to England and pursue measures which had embarrassed him so much that he must have considered himself unable to return in any limited time, and if any accident should happen to him he would be likely to leave behind him nothing but distress. The communication of his circumstances was truly surprising, as they were unknown, and communicated in confidence only. The matches made in this place sound very grand, and sometimes turn out well, but much more frequently it is otherwise, and therefore it was necessary to dive to the bottom of the affair. He himself is very sanguine in his expectations of recovering his fortune, or at least that it would be recovered by his descendants. Who could depend upon such a distant hope; what distress might not happen the meanwhile, especially when people live according to a fortune which may never be restored to them? Half the inhabitants of this place are in this predicament, living in splendour with a sword hanging by a thread over their heads. Here, there is a beautiful young woman of twenty-five, now going home with five children, from magnificence to poverty: it is a transition so dreadful that I think no state of moderate happiness should be changed for a chance of it. As to Mary I believe, indeed I know, she thinks so. I wish certainly that she were married, and that she were well and comfortably settled. Doubtless there is something desirable in having a house of one's own, but nothing can be happier than she has now with a mixture of company, and she is always in health. I believe she is satisfied with us, and most assuredly we are with her, so that if nothing comes to induce her to change her state, you must be content to have an old maid for a daughter, however I hope that will not be the case.

The way a vast number of people here have got rid of their money is just the same as the person I have mentioned. The native princes, to support their contentions one with another, have had recourse to borrowing money at most enormous interest, from 12 to 20 or even 30 percent, and this has been an inducement to those English who had acquired great sums, to lend it to them, by which great fortunes have been gained. Inasmuch as it strengthened these people, and served to increase their contentions, and for other reasons, the Company made an act to prevent any persons from lending them money. In the face of this act, however, they continued to do it till after the fall of Seringapatam *(more correctly, Sriringapattam)*, then the smaller places became entirely under the English Government. The Rajahs and governors of these places, having lost their countries, have nothing left to pay these debts, and it is not to be expected that the Company will pay them, although they have taken these countries, because they had prohibited the loans. Besides, they say truly enough, that the expense of keeping these countries in a state of submission eats up all their revenues, and that they have been, as it were, compelled to take these countries. Upon the whole, it appears that the money is lost to the persons who have been weak enough to lend it, and would take such usurious interest from the distress of others. Of this system there is now an end.

Amongst all the people going home, I have nobody by whom I can send much, as the ships are so loaded with passengers and officers returning home, that I can get nothing carried, but I am in hopes that I shall see some of the Bengal ships on their way home. I have given to a young gentleman, who returns to England for his health, a pint bottle of Caya Putty Oil; an infallible remedy for spasms and cold pains to be used outwardly, or in bad cases a few drops in water inwardly. Though I hope you will not often want it, yet I trust that you will receive it safe. It was a present to me from a friend who brought it from the eastward.[8]

Our acquaintance in India is more with the rising generation than the old inhabitants. They are, generally speaking, a much better set. Our great possessions here have induced people of the best families and principles to send their sons to India, and the society is very genteel and agreeable amongst the younger people. Last month Richard Clarke became of age, and we made a party, or at least directed him to ask all he liked. I never spent so pleasant a day. He sat at one end of the table, and Biss at the other, and we had to perform the parts of visitors. There were six or seven of the institution in which Biss is; they are to be called Guides, and the institution is called the Mathematical Institution. They certainly were picked youths, as only those who had been very correct were admitted to it, but I really never saw such a beautiful row of faces as down the table, so that one would think that beauty and goodness were united. They are for the most part sons of people of consequence: a very fine young man, who is the most eminent for his talents, is the son of Walpole the Ambassador and he is extremely beautiful. We had two very young ones, not more than 15 years old; the one is the son of the Admiral, Sir Edward Pellew *(successor to Admiral Rainier on the Indian station)*, and the other the grandson of the Duchess of Gloucester. He is a Lieutenant in the Admiral's ship, and these two are like twins; both very handsome, particularly Mr Seymour. His mother was a great beauty, as well as his grandmother. Mr Thomas Gwillim, if he be with you, will know whom I am talking of, for this lad's father was Lord Hugh Seymour *(a recently deceased English Admiral of distinction)* and Mr Thomas Gwillim was in his ship, and this lad was generally on board. We had a great many more; in all four or five and twenty. Richard and Biss sung like a Nightingale and a Thrush. Biss has such a capital voice that singing

8 Cajeput Oil – distilled from the leaves of certain coastal trees and used as a liniment etc. In Indonesia it is known as Kayu Putih oil. It is related to Tea Tree oil.

is quite the fashion with us. Richard's voice is very weak, but sweet, and he is so correct that not a note is ever out. However they all sang that day.

I intended this to be a short letter of three sheets, that it might be sent you by the post, but I perceive that in my hurry I have lost two sides by writing wrong, and turning over the leaves at once. I must therefore finish my account of our stay in the old chapel, which I told you in my last letter we had visited. We spent nearly 2 months there, and I saw more of India than I ever have done before. We had the building shaded on all sides with roofs of palm leaves, and the thick walls and roof defended us so well from the land winds, that I attribute Sir Henry's good health in a great measure to them. Covelong, or probably Comalam, was a settlement made by the Emperor of Germany *(a fishing village with an old Dutch fort, south of Madras)*, but the port and all were destroyed as the place was an object of jealousy both to the French and English, who have their Presidencies on the coast. The moors and rivers are romantic as Wales, though the hills are not lofty, and the place is abundant in rarities. It is particularly curious for fish; there are such fish to be found in no other part of the world and, had I not seen them, I could not have believed that such a rich variety existed. There is every colour; red fish of every tint; green, purple and yellow and striped like the most showy flowers; many as if wholly composed of rows of jewels, rubies and Topazes set in chains. Mary drew above thirty sorts, but that is a mere trifle. It would take an age to do them all. She intended to have sent home these drawings, but as so many things were lost in the Prince of Wales, Dr Anderson has entreated that she will let a native copy them before they go home, that they may not be entirely lost if an accident should happen. When that is done, you will see them. I drew many birds, so that I have now about a hundred birds altogether, and hope to amuse you with them some day. We were called from this retreat by Sir Benjamin Sullivan's illness and, since we came home, we have nothing but visiting. There was a round of visiting on the arrival of the Admiral, another on the arrival of Lord Cornwallis *(the new Governor-General in Calcutta, successor to Richard Wellesley, 2nd Earl of Mornington)*, and another on the arrival of all this Fleet *(Admiral Pellew's)*, and the second fleet with Sir Thomas Troubridge. Next came Mr North, the Governor of Ceylon, who goes home with this fleet. *(Frederick North, later 5th Earl of Guilford, and MP)*

He dined with us the day before yesterday, when Biss, as usual, performed aide de camp. Richard sits at the other end in that capacity. I think Biss looks a vast deal better than when he came out; his complexion clearer, and he is altogether better, but such a beau you have hardly seen; such an admirer of the ladies that we call him beauty-hunting Biss. He is terribly fickle; one beauty always puts another out of his head. He could not therefore be in a better place, for here is a constant succession. What is better, he has done his work so well that he has received the greatest praise from his superiors, and he has made a map of the greater part of the country on our side of Madras, and they say it is so accurate that any person must know it instantly, and done with such neatness as to equal anything that has been seen. He is to survey a large part of the country very soon. They are all extremely good in the Society, and very regular in their conduct. They are sober, and go to church every Sunday.

I am glad you visit Mr and Mrs Biss. I have received a very kind present from Mr Biss *(senior)*, whom I do not know, of two fine hams. I never eat any so good in India. We had them for our great dinners, two of which came close together. I used the hams first, because I know that the Gammons will keep. Three Gammons I have; the others were mouse bitten, and Hetty sent me something else in lieu of them. It will be a long time before I shall hear of you again. No ship will be here before February, at least I fear so. You seem to have been in a great fright about us in England. Admiral Troubridge could easily have taken Linois, but he was afraid to lose a moment, and the privateering wretch is still doing mischief.

I have had two very smart presents. The one was a cap for Mary, and another for me from Mr Prosser, who brought all our things very safe, and also three dozen of cider from his uncle, Mr Powell. The Misses Thoburn sent each of us a white chip hat, with a white feather, which make a pretty head dress, and to Mary they also sent a pearl ornament for the head, so you see our friends in England do not forget us.

It seems to be quite the fashion for you to send out your lads, which I am not sorry for. If they behave well, this Indian service is a very good one, but they are generally disappointed at first. They come out with a hope of having a flashy life, and lounging about as young officers do in a country town. Now here, they can do no such thing; they are almost always on some duty or other and, unless they absolutely apply to some branch of their profession, they will never get into good employment. The Artillery Officers are called upon to construct all sorts of buildings, and must be good architects, civil and military. Others have the country to survey, and all have one language to learn perfectly, but they ought to know more than one or two before they could hope for any employment that will make them respectable. For these reasons, the boys who are sent out should have a tolerable education before they come, and should be taught that they must not lead a life of idleness. They will have quite as much necessity to employ every hour of their time as if they were in business. Neither can they indulge with impunity in any sort of intemperance or immorality. Every irregularity is closely followed by severe suffering. The women here, who are very attractive and easy of access, are all afflicted with hereditary *(sic – possibly intends to indicate transmissible)* diseases which will be communicated, and cannot be cured. Inebriation is, in this climate, certain destruction and therefore we see that all Eastern law-givers strictly forbid every sort of spirituous and fermented liquors, rather choosing to let some perish for want of the support they may afford, than allow the use of such enticing mischief. Even the more pardonable follies lead to serious consequences here, for if ever so small a debt be contracted it is hardly ever got rid of, the interest is enormous and, before a young man can hope to pay it, the debt is doubled. Besides that, everything he buys upon credit is charged at double price.

I sometimes sincerely wish that Tom had a cadetship such as Biss has, but I have not the least notion whether or not they are difficult to obtain. If he could obtain it whilst we are here, our situation would make him respectable, and there would be no danger in his coming to this country whilst we are here to take charge of him for the first year. After that the danger is over. Boys learn how to take care of themselves, and see the consequence of an error in the sufferings of others who have no friends to guide them. Certainly I would never let a boy come out a cadet to this country without some friend at the Presidency to which he belonged, who could have an absolute authority over him. I should suppose there could be no great difficulty in obtaining an appointment for him, if you should like it, but I know not whom to apply to. Mr Biss, or Woodcock, or some of those who have sent out sons could tell you. It is possible the application would be forwarded, or at least not retarded, by his being Sir Henry's nephew. I should think it would be facilitated; the application for Temple was instantly granted.

Since I wrote the above, I find a boy must be 16 before he can be appointed to a cadetship. As to the expense of fitting him out, much is incurred for want of knowing what to do. The Scotch have the advantage of us in this for, till lately, they have had the whole, or nearly the whole, to themselves. They know everything that is necessary, and what they can do without. When young men come out so late, as Biss did, they certainly require a much greater expense, because they have to appear as men, but if they come out at 16 much less is requisite, and a very little to those who have friends.

I have this instant received notice that I must instantly close this, therefore give my love to the family, and whoever may be with them.

From Elisabeth Gwillim to her sister Hetty 24th August 1805.

I begin now with pleasure to write to you. A most unusual time has elapsed since I could enjoy that pleasure, for the fleet now lying here has been about to sail for three months, and yet is here still. It is said that they will sail on 1 September, but I have doubted this information, and therefore was unwilling to write. It will be many months before I can hope to hear from you again, but I will trust in Providence for your preservation. I thank God we are all well, and have known no ill health this year.

Captain Hudson's ship, and Mr Nicholls, arrived some time ago and all was well. By those ships I received all your kind letters, and very happy they made me. Captain Hudson never called upon me during his stay here. He was always considered a sorry crab, and he made such a fuss of carrying my plants that I almost repented of asking him to do it. I was obliged to say they were for myself, for he gave me to understand that he would not carry them as a journeyman. A drole man here, who knew him, pretended to read a passage from a letter, in order to laugh at me, as though it were written by one of the passengers on board his ship from St Helena, the half way place. He stated that the stingy thing had starved all my plants, and would not allow water to keep them alive and that therefore they were all left at St Helena. This really turned out to be true in part. Mr Nicholls spent what time he could with us; he was always welcome, for he was a great favourite of mine on board ship, and he is one of Richard's best-beloved of all the sons of the green waves. I feel great obligations to him for the care he took of the seeds, which came at a lucky time, and are now growing cabbage plants and, if they are not all stolen, they may become cabbages in my garden. Mr Nicholls made us a valuable present, too, for which I hardly know how to reward him. He softened our hearts with a cask of the nicest English beef that ever was bit by Indians' *(Indian British)* teeth. Here there is nothing but feasting; breakfast, tiffin, and supper. To this he added a cask of pork and, most admirable, a bag of split peas! All superlative delicacies.

We all admired Captain Price of the Prince of Wales very much, and never indeed saw a man so generally beloved and respected. He had such a character as a seaman that nobody chose to credit the loss of his ship till almost now. I fear, however, there are no hopes now. There were a number of lovely children on board, and Mrs St John with all hers, and she was almost the most beautiful woman that I ever saw. I have mentioned all these things in my two last letters, but I did not say so much as I wished, being ashamed to mention my trifling losses when so many poor innocents had perished. It is remarkable, such was the opinion entertained of Captain Price and his ship, that almost everybody sent their letters on board that vessel. I sent various little remembrances, some of which had cost me much time and some expense. I wrote volumes by that ship.

I hope none of my friends will think that I neglect them because they do not receive letters in due time, for I have been a most regular correspondent. But I must have lost many letters by the Aplin. What a vile thing that has been; exposing families. The French made copies of our letters, in the Isle de France, and then sent the letters on here, and now you send them back to us in your newspapers. The French admit that this is an infamous practice, but excuse themselves by saying that we began first which is, I fear, but too true. It is a sad, sad thing that we ever neglected to take Mauritius and those islands. It is astonishing how they annoy us from thence, and there is no hope of catching them, for the place is full of French, either thence or from Pondicherry, or Tranquebar. They know all we do as soon as we know ourselves, then pop out, take the ships, and run into their ports immediately. Besides, it is distressing employment for an Admiral, and a fine irritation to be watching a pilfering enemy whom they have scarcely a possibility of catching, and over whom a victory would yield no credit. You will see by the accounts from hence that Linois (Admiral), in one of their frigates, has had the audacity to endeavour to cut off one of these ships, and that somehow or other Sir Thomas Troubridge has let Linois slip through his hands. The Indiamen are blamed; I do not know who is at fault. *(Mauritius was taken by the British in 1810).*

Biss is quite well now. He has occasionally been a little bilious, and is a weak and nervous young man, but excessively beloved and very fortunate in being chosen into this society, for he will gradually become immured to the climate here, and learn how to manage his constitution before he is called into more dangerous climates. He spends every Sunday with us, and dines here generally once or sometimes twice in the week; so he considers it as a sort of little home. He comes on Saturday to dinner, if he can, and sleeps here on Saturday night and Sunday and goes to work on Monday morning.

With the last fleet came out a Mr Roberts; a young surgeon for the Bengal establishment. He is a Herefordshire young man; the son of a clergyman whom I do not know, but who has always lived in the county. He has been an apprentice with the apothecary of *(St)* Bartholomew Hospital and, since that, house surgeon there. I think him clever, and he is also a very agreeable young man; very modest and good-humoured. He stayed with us near a month; all the while the ships were here and, as he had no other friends, he seldom went out but with us. He knew nothing of us, except that he was acquainted with Mr Gwillim's family. Sir Henry fancied his face to be like that of Prosser, and never broke the habit of calling him Mr Prosser. I dare say 40 times a day he made this mistake, even to the last day. I never saw anybody more delighted and surprised than this young man seemed to be. He seemed to imagine that he was coming to a strange country to be buried, as it were, and suddenly found himself in a cheerful house, without formality, and all his county people round him. He appeared as though he could not believe it for joy and, when we rode out, the hedgerows and the trees were "Like England, and so luxuriant withal!"

His friends had been averse to this travelling scheme, or else he might have been here a year sooner, the loss of which time he regretted terribly. I was quite sorry to part with him, and I believe he was sorry to leave a place he liked so much to proceed to Bengal, but he seemed likely to be gratified everywhere, and rejoiced to find out at last that coming to India was not so bad as slavery. I desired him, when he thanked us for our hospitality, to tell his young medical friends what he thought of it, and not let them be afraid to stir from home, sitting down starving there, whilst the Scotchmen here were rolling in wealth. He told me he certainly should have done so of his own mind. Now I am on this subject, let me tell you that if you hear of any well taught young English surgeons who want to come out, that this is an excellent time to apply, for the Government have written from hence to insist on the Directors sending out eighty surgeons to complete the establishment or, as they say, not so much to complete it but because they can make no arrangement with fewer than eighty.

The Admiral, too, has been so distressed for doctors that he has been obliged to take a step of which there has only been one precedent, and that in some desperate time. He sent a press-gang on board all the Indiamen to press every surgeon's mate. I dare say that you know the Indiamen have generally a surgeon, and one or two mates. Now all these learned doctors, to many of whom you would not, I think, like to trust your cat, were all called out and hurried off. Never was there such lamentation; the Captains begging, and representing their dreadful state if the surgeons themselves should be taken ill; the young doctors weeping, their investments *(in trade goods)* to be disposed of how they could, and their future prospects all destroyed. The Admiral called out to the Captains, "Mr Such-a-one; I know what you call on me about, but I must, and will, have the doctors". Only two got off; I do not know who the one was, nor who prayed for him, but the other was the poor lame boy Charles Simpson who was come out upon his first voyage. Sir Henry was petitioned, and he was successful in his application to Sir Edward Pellew in the poor creature's favour. Mr Nichols made me laugh too, in describing the scene; "Only think", says he, "When by their profession they ought to be considered as gentlemen, to be called into a boat", and then comes the Admiral, and his Captains, staring at them, "Well Sir; you have something about your eye; I think that you will be of some use to us; get into the boat Sir". "Let me in Sir"; "no, I think we won't take you Sir; you may do for the Indiamen perhaps; I do not believe you can do much; you may go back, we don't want you". Miserable indignities!

Sunday, August 25th

I left off yesterday in order to dress *(for dinner)* and, before that was finished, there arrived Richard, with Biss and Mr Prosser. I have another young gentleman with us at present, who is here till he sails for England where he is going for the recovery of his health, which has been injured I think by over-application; he being naturally weak. He is one you would like; very clever, and very good and tender-hearted; a learned and genteel young man of about 24. We were all very merry at dinner. Mr Prosser brought on shore with him the little chip box with the pearl crescent and the beads, the paints and brushes, and a small box containing two caps; presents to me and Mary. One is lace and blue crepe, and silver with no feather; the other is white with a lovely pink feather, so beautifully curled I have hardly seen anything before like it.

Biss was extremely annoyed at their sending out red cabbage; "I wonder they could think of such a thing" says he. So, having found out about this, he is plagued all day. Sir Henry, reading the letters, protests he finds such passages as these; "Poor dear Billy (Biss) is so fond of red cabbage: I hope it will be sent to him wherever he is", then Biss; "I don't care, I won't eat a bit of it".

A serious thing was likely to happen, but it was stopped in time. The ship in which Biss and Richard's things are, took fire near the galley, just over the powder magazine, and Mr Prosser says burned for 20 minutes, and all the other ships at anchor were going to cut out, but it was fortunately quenched. This happened on Friday night.

You have no idea of Biss's grandeur and delicacy; he is such a beau, and languishes at the ladies and sighs like a Romeo. He is certainly a very pretty young man, and the young officers in the Society, of which he is one, are all the sons of people of some consequence, or young men of great abilities, and they dress in a high style, but they are a very innocent set I assure you, however much below their dignity. We are all rejoiced to hear of the red cabbage, and we tell Biss he shall not have to have a bit.

This is an odd thing of Richard: he has this appointment to the Company's service and he cannot decide whether to take it or not. He is dissuaded from it very much but, as his father has obtained it, it does seem proper that he should accept of it, for it is a most valuable appointment. But the death of poor Temple made a great change in Richard's circumstances. His own Court appointment, too, remains without change; that is £500 per annum, and his clerkship has been worth as much again, and while living with us he lays aside the whole for interest in the first two years. He touches one hundred a year to pay for his carriage, and those things which we used to pay for. Sir Henry would not otherwise let him break in upon it till it became a complete sum. All he has since gained is added to it, so that he has already acquired more than £2000. He could acquire a pretty fortune that would forward him in his study of the law. It does seem that he might be better off as he is, than by going into the Company's service. He would, if he stayed as he is, work at the law and at his Persian, and return to be called to the Bar, and there can hardly be any doubt but that he must rise very high in this country in the law; probably as a judge as early as could be. He would have such very remarkable advantages in his knowledge of the country languages, and his constant attendance at the Courts will make much of the business quite familiar to him. If he now enters the Company's service, he will only have £250 a year for three years, and he will be obliged to spend more than that in living, as he will be sent up the country and have to keep a house. After that it will be many years before he can make more than his present income, out of which too, he will have his establishment. He is just like the horse with two bags of hay; there is "nothing but calculations" all day. One thing is in favour of the Company's service: it is for life, and he will have his security on his own life, not on that of another, and when they rise in the service they may grow rich if they are not extravagant. The place he has in the Court for Small Debts, his registrarship, is in the gift of the Company, and we hear that Lord William Bentinck has already promised it to another young man if Richard accepts the Company's service. He is fully master of the subject himself, so we are not in a position to persuade him, and I do not know what I should do in such a case. He must give his answer soon.

I understand that you met with Colonel Strange[9] on your way to Vauxhall. He is arrived here, but I have not seen him. He broke his arm, or did it some injury, on board ship and did not go out for some time. Biss and Richard have met him, and they confirm all accounts I have heard of him. He is generally considered as half madman, half idiot, and is constantly drunk. He is by no means respectable, and this Strange, who is now placed in the Council by Lord Melville's interest, is said to be a quite useless person in the business of this country. He is a very weak man. The fortune he acquired was gained much faster than might have been expected from his salary, but the Collerton family *(a presumed family friend)* have had vast power. It is not so easy now to acquire great fortunes in so short a time, and he had lost one fortune before. He is now, by the interest of this match, put into Council but, as Lord Melville is now out of power, it is conjectured that the Directors will not confirm him. It really is to be hoped that some check will be put on the Scotch interest, for even they themselves (or at least some of them) are ashamed of the gross partiality. In this fleet we have a whole family of Dundas *(Melville)* relations. They are come out to form a settlement on Prince of Wales's Island to the Eastward *(now Penang)*, and the whole is to be composed of Scotch. I really do wonder how such a thing could be borne by the English. It is a complete Scotch job, as I hear it is called. All these people are in the ship Mr Livingstone came out in. The country they are going to is a fine one, and I believe we might have what we please to the Eastward, for the Dutch settlers are such a depraved, cruel set, that the natives would everywhere receive us with joy. We know nothing of these countries in England, and but little here. Occasionally, however, we now meet with people who have visited the Eastern Islands, and I am particularly acquainted with a man of learning who resided long

9 Sir Thomas Strange had two brothers. The first one, already encountered, was James Strange, 1753–1840, a former East India Company Factor, trader explorer on the Pacific Northwest Coast, and later a Member of Parliament. He incurred significant debts as a result of the failure of his bank, but married the sister of the renowned Henry Dundas, 1st Viscount Melville, through which he undoubtedly expected to obtain some advantage. He travelled back to India, and his connections gained access to worthwhile positions such as a seat on Council. The younger brother was Colonel Robert Strange, later Major-General, 1760–1811.

there, and who knows the language, and with a lady who has also been in various parts. It is there that you see nature in the highest perfection. The palm trees, and forest trees, of this part of India are said to look like mulberries to those who have seen those lofty woods. There the trees grow close to the sea; the branches bend down into the water and the oysters are found in clusters fastened to the roots and branches. The interior is rich beyond description, and every garden is equal to the support of the family, supplying it with food, raiment and firewood. If you would read Marsden's Sumatra you will get an idea of the people.[10] Besides what may be gained from that work, there is little to be known, because the Dutch have been careful to suppress all information relative to these places, from whence they have derived so much wealth. The present race of Dutch on the Eastern Islands happily join the rude manners of two or three centuries back; the licentiousness of the East and the cruelty of slave drivers. They are a disgrace to humanity, and the women are neither more chaste nor less cruel than the men. But, be this as it may, the country is delightful, and people who are ill go from this place to recover there, the air being always temperate by the constant rains. Sir Benjamin Sullivan is there now. He was in a very real state of poor health when he left this place, and despaired of his life, but has somewhat recovered and therefore intends to stay there if he can, but he expects to be turned out when all these new good people arrive, as there are few European homes and he will be obliged to give up that which he inhabits, unless they have the civility to permit him to inhabit it. Sir Benjamin was very nearly in the same state of ill health when Sir Thomas left this place, and who left us about six weeks afterwards. You will understand therefore that Sir Henry is doing the whole business, and has been throughout this hot season. I think you will say he is pretty ill-used, for Sir Benjamin Sullivan apprised Sir Thomas Strange of the state of his health before the latter set out for England. At no time, however, has Sir Benjamin been fond of business. He has not been accustomed to that sort of thing. All the work for a year and a half, therefore, has been

10 William Marsden, 1754–1836, was a scholar and orientalist who wrote the History of Sumatra. He was well-connected in naturalist and Royal Society circles. See Oxford Dictionary of National Biography. ref:odnb/18102

thrown upon Sir Henry. Meanwhile a man *(Sir Thomas)*, privately conniving with the Governor, goes away to make arrangements perhaps to suit their convenience. Never did so much falsehood appear.[11] Those who affected most surprise at Sir Thomas's going, found out after a month or two this and that which he was about to do. I hope that Providence will defeat all such dark intrigues; indeed I should suppose that the whole will fall to the ground if Lord Melville is not restored to office, for all was set on foot as soon as he first came into power.

Never was there seen such indecent exultation as at this event, nor such wretched despondency as at the account of his fall. You know that I have never told you much about the white people here, having nothing that pleased me to communicate. The English increased here much whilst Lord Melville was out of office but, as if it were the last hope, everything possible has been done in favour of the Scotch since he came in again. Mr James Strange being thrown back upon the Company's service by his losses, has I suppose induced Sir Thomas to take the step he has. The arbitrary proceedings here were always extraordinary, but at present I can give you an instance. You know, perhaps, that we have true newspapers in Madras; one is called the Government paper, being immediately under the direction of Government and receiving all their advertisements. Dr Davis prints the other, which is Mr Samuels paper, and there is a third: these are supposed to be more independent papers, but they are all subject to the control of the Chief Secretary who is Mr Bashan, (a great ass, if that be no treason) a nephew of Lord Melville. Now it is customary to copy in the Madras papers all proceedings of the House of Commons, just as the Gloucester or Worcester paper copies the London, and these papers are the only means of circulating such intelligence to the numerous English who are scattered over this extensive country but, because Lord Melville is a relation, every mention of the late transaction is struck out of the papers, and the printers are ordered to refrain from inserting a word about it. The reason, he states, is that Mrs Strange is in a family way and, in delicacy to

11 This and subsequent paragraphs hint at Elizabeth's disquiet about the deteriorating relationship between Sir Henry and both Sir Thomas Strange and Lord William Bentinck, and the increasing background of intrigue. See final chapter.

her, it must be suppressed. Meanwhile the said Mrs Strange receives visitors, whilst all the English papers relative to the affair lie before her, and she converses very coolly on the business. The people have growled, but all in vain. I should have yet seen no account of it, but Sir Edward Pellew lent me his *(English)* papers, brought out by Lord Cornwallis, and there I saw the whole. Had it not been so, I should have seen nothing all this long time till we got papers out of these ships. There were not above three sets of papers before in the settlement and, as the Governor's copies were not lent, I have much to thank the Admiral, who certainly had no desire to conceal his own, for he hates the Scotch. Now, do you not think that it is carrying things pretty far to forbid the publication of an affair interesting to the whole kingdom, and this whilst you in England durst print accounts of your own Sovereign, and every Sovereign in the world?

Monday, August 26.

All my party assembled yesterday after three o'clock, the greater part after church, but Mr Livingstone sent an excuse. He was sent for on board his ship, and he tells us that it has been discovered that his ship received so much damage from Linois' raking fire, that they are obliged to stay here several days to put all to rights before they can sail. I do not know how Sir Thomas Troubridge can excuse himself for not taking Admiral Linois. I am afraid he will have the laugh against him.

We plagued Biss about the pickled cabbage till we made him laugh along with us; nothing has been brought ashore yet. Mr Prosser went with Richard to breakfast at Dr Anderson's today, to see his garden and some young ladies. He was to go from thence on board, to return here on Wednesday to stay onshore. Yesterday he borrowed Sir Henry's palanquin to pursue the body of a woman, which was being carried to the beach to be burned: he witnessed all the ceremony there, and told us of it at tiffin. Very amusing, you will say, but I don't much mind it. Richard and Temple used to go often to see them throw cocoa leaves on the top to make a blaze. In the evening they all set out to see the people walk through the fire which is a sight, I think, enough to scare one, but they liked it. Customs differ, and the Hindus delight in such sights.

Tuesday 27th:

I saw several papers yesterday. This affair of Lord Melville is enough to raise a civil war in the country. The scum of the earth rise in triumph; all these profligates, who have been so long kept back, are glorying in his fall. He ought to be tried for giving them such an advantage, and distressing his party. Sir Henry says he does not like the proceedings and that, however guilty Lord Melville is, they have been too hasty, and that he does not think there was sufficient proof at the time of the vote in the House.[12]

Mr Livingstone sent me a box of seeds, with the catalogues I requested, which I am glad of as they give me much information. I have been dividing the seeds amongst my friends, and the colours and brushes I received before from Mr Prosser, and beg you will thank Mr Samuel. I hope you have sent me plenty of paper; I drew a great deal last year. I am sorry that I cannot send home the drawings of birds, but as I have now good, bad and indifferent I want to consult them occasionally, but I wish they were in your care. I think there are some non-descripts for I have two species, which I think are jacanas, not described in Gmelin.[13] I have drawn the plant which Dr Rottler has done me the honour to name after me. I hope it may be new and, if so, you may like to see it as Gwillimia Indica. I have taken great pains to send it home. The plant General Trent was so kind as to carry was, I hear, alive when he left it in the ship, and I hope it got there safe, but it was a cold time for a plant that requires sun. This was the fourth time I have sent trees of it to England. It is a very sweet flower, at least here; it has a delicate odour, but not strong. It came from Batavia and is there called Sampa Salacan, which means milk flower. It is very much like a species of Magnolia although seldom opens wide till it is near fading. I rather think that Dr Rottler wants this drawing, which I have made to be sent to Dr Smith with the dried specimen, but perhaps he will return it to Mr Whitley and if he does, the drawing is for you. If not, I will draw you another. The flowers

12 This refers to Lord Melville's impeachment for supposed embezzlement of government funds relating to the financing of the Navy. He was forced to resign in April 1805 after a vote in the House of Commons, and his impeachment went to the House of Lords in 1806, the trial commencing in April. By June he was acquitted.

13 Johan Gmelin 1748–1804: German Professor of Medicine, and natural historian, and also Professor of Chemistry, Botany and Mineralogy. He also published the 13th edition of Systema Naturae by Carl Linnaeus which contained descriptions of many new species, including birds.

are always larger in the early part of the year, but it flowers all the year and the leaves almost always appear scorched or broken at the ends, unless at the top of the branches. This I attribute to the strong winds we have at Madras. The air of Batavia and the Eastern Islands is all softness. The place is not the more wholesome for that; on the contrary, Batavia is a grave to Europeans. An expedition went from this place some time just before we came here, and every person who slept a night on shore died. This, however, is only the case at Batavia and the unhealthiness is in a great measure due to the dirt of the people. I am sowing my sunflowers in my walks today.

We had a tremendous thunderstorm last night; the thunder and lightning is not, as with you, at intervals. There are several flashes at once, and a continual rolling of the thunder. It is a concert of thundering; some piano and some forte; accordingly the natives speak of the thunder in the plural. The Gentoos say (that is my language) Wooramooloo - Wooratoonavi - the thunder's thunder. Almost all their words have a sound expressive of their meaning.[14]

I have a petition from a young man who is with me, and who is going to England for his health, to give him a letter for you, and I should like to do it if I thought it would put you to no trouble. He is one of the few whom I would call gentlemen that I have had the opportunity of sending to you. He certainly is one, in every good sense of the word. He is a nephew of General Harris and is in the civil service here, but I fear he will be obliged to give it up. His health is so dreadfully bad. His constitution appears quite broken, but not by his own fault. He is a young man of exemplary morals and very great abilities. He is first rate in Persian and Arabic learning, and if you wish to ask anything about the Muhammadans, the masters of this country before we came, he will tell you everything. I think you will like Mr Keene; he is very mild and gentle, and has no extravagant or flashy notions. He is extremely neat in his dress; well shaped, but plain, in his person. His face is, I think, expressive of a good understanding. He is the son of a lady left in unhappy circumstances, but she is now married to a Mr Mawley; Proctor in the Commons. He had been three years an officer, like Biss, in

14 Contemporary dictionaries give the Telugu translation for thunderstorm as 'urumulato'.

the Company' s service when General Harris, who is his mother's brother, procured him this place which he is now about to leave, I fear. Sir Henry and he take a composing draft every night, lately from your stone bottle. The poppy syrup is as good as ever and, on the strength of your having sent out two more bottles, the old stock is going very fast. Mr Keene is to ask you for a glass in return for drinking his health.[15]

I have seldom given you any account of the Muhammadans, first because I do not like them so well as the Hindus, about whom I was more interested and, secondly, because the language I have learned is a Hindu language and enables me to make enquiries relative to them, but not of the Muhammadans. I am now beginning to acquaint myself with their manners, and may tell you more about this in future. They differ little, however, from the Turks of Constantinople except that they are, I think, inferior in general. They are however a magnificent people, though their morals are bad. They have had fine poets and great philosophers amongst them.

Friday the 30th. Was interrupted; I could not do a bit more.

Since I wrote last, the things are all arrived safe and well, and are admired exceedingly. Mr Livingstone called on Wednesday morning to inform us that he had been on board the Preston to enquire of his brother for the package with Richard Clarke's coats, and Biss's saddle. His brother had informed him that he sent every day to the carriers at Portsmouth for the case, but that it was not come, wherefore he supposes that Mr James could not get it ready, and that Biss's things were not arrived in from the country. At dinner the party assembled and this news was communicated to Biss, who heard it with great emotion, and the disappointed beaux joined in lamentation and reproaches in which the other young friends joined.

15 Henry George Keene, 1781–1864, was a nephew to General Harris of Madras, and initially a young army officer in India who led the attack, with scaling ladders, on the walls of Sriringapattam in 1799. Following a deterioration in his health he entered Fort William College, Calcutta, and achieved first class honours in Persian and Arabic. He became a civil servant in Madras and was rewarded for writing a book on law in Arabic. He returned to England in 1809 and later entered Sidney Sussex College, Cambridge, eventually becoming a fellow and taking holy orders. Later he became Professor of Arabic and Persian at the East India College, Haileybury. He retired in 1834 and devoted his time to writing on ancient Persian history. See Oxford Dictionary of National Biography. ref:odnb/15249

Sir Henry is ravished with his shoes and boots. I never saw him better pleased, and his coat; he likes the colour extremely, and so do I, but it has not been put on yet but I will let you know how it fits.

I gave away a piece of white ribbon to a neighbour, and I shall send some to Mrs Stone, General Smith's daughter, a most charming woman who was my neighbour at the Mount, but are now removed to Visakhapatnam. I will enclose one of her letters giving an account of the place. It is on this coast, but northward, in the country of the Telinga people which lies between Bengal and this country *(on the coast, east of Hyderabad)*. The Telingas are the people vulgarly and erroneously called Gentoos. They have the country about Golconda, which you must have heard of. It is where "Diamonds grow". I longed to visit it, particularly as it is the language of that country which I learn *(Telugu)*. They are the finest people in India.

On Wednesday is the anniversary of the establishment of the Supreme Court, so we will have all the lawyers and all that appertains to the Court. On Thursday, the only day that could be fixed on, we are to have Lord William Bentinck, the Governor, and Mr North, who is at the Government House and just arrived from Ceylon, the Admiral, that is Sir Edward Pellew, and the other Admiral, Sir Thomas Troubridge, if he does not sail beforehand.

The chip hat is a great deal too small in the crown. My head is very large; I shall take out the wire, and I hope to be able to stretch it. I think I shall make it do with a little coaxing, and bundling up my hair. A clean white chip hat is such a rarity, and these are as white as snow. I delight in blue and white, but blue will never keep long. I am obliged to put it all up in the dark. I wish I had another blue feather, but I shall try to get them dyed here. I have some white ones, very long, and this is a handsome fashion. Whilst I think of it, be sure and send out fine large black silk stockings, two pair of dress, and two pair undress, by the first opportunity. I do not want any more pairs; the *(Indian)* people do not use them, so they are not much stolen and consequently last very long. I thank you for the brown velvet bands for the hair, for all the velvet we had is disposed of, and this came in time. The shoes and gloves are most acceptable and fit exactly. Next time you send out, pray send me two or three petticoats with little bodies, or shoulder straps, to wear under my gowns. They will serve as patterns for the tailor to make more. The old petticoats I brought out begin to get thin, and I like nothing so well as cambric muslin. I wrote to you in my last letter for 12 dozen pair of white silk stockings; very smart ones; as the open clocks stretch better and it is such a fatigue to drag on one's stockings in this country. After pulling on a tight pair one is in a perfect bath. The weather is very close and hot now.

I do not know whether Mary mentioned to you Mrs Young. She is a natural daughter of Dr Anderson; very dark, but extremely pretty. She was educated by Lady Dalling, and bred up within her family. She is extremely clever and very good indeed; she is a very sweet creature whom you must love; her voice and manner are just like Nancy Green. She is precisely such a brilliant as Lizzie Thoburn, and just as innocent and pleasant. I have no friend with whom I am a hundredth part so intimate.

I have two jars of ginger from China, which I want to send to you because the jars look to be pretty and the pair should be kept together. A Mr Young has given me two bark vests, such as the peasants in Malacca wear. They are made of the bark of a tree, beat flat, and they are fastened on to look like a petticoat. These ones are very coarse and bad, for they are sometimes beat so fine as to have all the delicacy of kid leather, and such I have seen. This is the sort of drapery mentioned by all Hindus as worn by their Rishis *(holy seers, or sadhus)*, that is their saints and prophets, who lived with their families in groves sacred to their religion, for the pious Rishis made no vows of celibacy. They are called in some translations woven vests of bark but, as you will see, that is a great mistake for they are only beaten out. It is in imitation of these that the Pandarams *(lower caste hindu priest)* dye their clothes with a salmon colour, for the finer vests of this kind are also brighter and clearer in their colour. The Pandarams are a sort of religious mendicant whom I have described to you before. It is they who wear the Rudraksha beads *(seed; originally used as a prayer bead)* which you call jaquier *(jackfruit)* beads. However, they are not properly called so as the jaquiers are religious, belonging to the muhammadans, and have nothing to do with these beads. I have sent also by Mr Prosser the peace of cloth wove round without any ends to it. It is made of the young leaves of plantain split into little threads, and also a palampore that is neither wove nor spun but beaten out thin, and I think you will like this. The shoemakers here make little boots for children very cheap and, as I thought they might amuse Nancy's young ones, I have had a few pair made and three pair I have given to Mr Prosser to carry. If he comes here again I shall give him more.

September 3rd.

Mr Prosser called here yesterday, middle day, and brought all the things we had bought of him, which was a great deal of wine and a barrel of vinegar. The ships were to sail to Bengal in the evening and I believe went off sometime last night. I sincerely hope that he will return here and, if he does, I shall send more by him. I have seen no more Mr Livingstone and I fear that I shall not. Captain Mackintosh of the Apsley Castle is so ill as to be thought in danger. In his ship there is a Mr Tappington; he is the second mate of the ship, as he was also of our ship when we came, and was in the Hindustan when she was wrecked. He has promised to take anything for me, and I shall therefore send him to you. His father is a wealthy attorney and has a large family by another, and also a second wife, and I believe does no great good to this one. He himself is very good, and very honest, and his acquaintance is with Mr Clarke *(Senior)* who, sometime when young, was curate of Faversham. I shall give you a list hereafter of what I sent by him.

I must now tell you about the eatables; the sweetmeats, or rather preserves, of yours and Mrs Whitley's, are all come quite safe and well; not the least accident, and they are super excellent all. The pickles are all right, but woe and alas there is no pickled cabbage. Biss has been laughed at so much and at the last not a bit of pickled cabbage for poor Billy. The confectionery in the tumblers is all come dry and good, but several of the tumblers fell to pieces, which is no great loss. The lozenges and almonds in papers are not safe; they are many of them shelled, and the candy is gone from the orange chips. They will not come out safe in papers. The three Gammons of bacon are quite firm and good and so is one ham; the middle of one is decayed by some accident, but the sides are tolerable. Tongues will not keep that way, and it is a pity to send them. They are one of the best things we are furnished with from the shops. They are brought out in little casks and are sold one by one, if you like so to buy them. A whole cask is rather too much to be eaten whilst good.

I will again repeat that you have sent me nothing too much, and the morning caps you have occasionally sent me I wear till they are quite threadbare. I had a very pretty one, lined in lilac. Once you sent it I put Poppa to wash it, and she starched it finely and hung it on a towel to dry. Down came a crow and, liking the taste of the rice starch, carried off my lace cap to the top of a cocoa palm tree, whence it was with difficulty restored to me.

My bustle is, thank God, over. Yesterday, and the day before, we had our two great companies. We dressed one of the hams, as the gammons will keep the best. It was cut neatly so we made it do for the next day; this was very saving, you may think, to give the two governors the lawyer's leavings, but it was the most delicate ham that ever was eaten in India. Those we buy are kept till they are so hard, and are cured so hard, that they have no flavour. The reason for this is that, when delicately cured, they will decay if put together and the middle of one of them, as I said, was decayed from damp or bruising. The gammons of bacon are quite good.

Biss is our aide du camp upon all grand occasions. He sits at one end of the table; Richard at the other; Sir Henry and I face-to-face in the middle of the table. This is the Indian fashion when we have such Officers of State. Biss is so solemn we laugh afterwards in proportion to the solemnity of the day. Such sniping on Wednesday; those were the lawyers; such state on Thursday. I had put the large creped white feather into the white satin hat and wore it. I assumed I looked ten years younger. I was almost afraid that I should be obliged to give up, and turn old woman with what grace I could muster, but I congratulated myself that in that hat I should be sufferable a little longer. You see what I owe to your taste, and that of the milliner, and I beg therefore that, wherever you bought that and the blue hat, you will buy me some more. They are so soft and easy to my head, and such nice rich satin, and as handsome a fashion that I quite admire them. Indeed, I have never had such an elegant assortment. The two of us hardly know what to admire most. The Hussar cap with the swan down becomes her *(Mary)*, and just fits her little head. I give her all the jewels, and most of the flowers, and she gives me the greater part of the caps observing, as I so spitefully have, that women who have no grey hairs do not wear caps much in this country.

You will find a pair of oval flat opals, and a pair of drops; you may send those with the string or not, as you please upon enquiry, but I wish you to enquire if opals are held in any esteem in England for at present I can buy them very cheap here and, according to the account in Chambers Dictionary, they have been held in great esteem. Opals are the stones which are imitated by the firestones; probably not well, as it is said that opals are the most difficult to be imitated. These are not so clear as the false but, if you lay them on your arm by candlelight, you will perceive the colours very bright, as indeed you do in some measure by looking through the light. Let me know of what value they are esteemed. I gave about 14 shillings for the row I send. I send you also some stones called Cat's eyes of which I have seen rings, and good ones are held in great esteem. They are a harder stone than the opal, and dearer. They may however be bought cheap sometimes. I gave a pagoda a dozen for these, which was I believe too much, but I want you to tell me if they are of use, or could be made into anything handsome. You will see in an instant why they are called cat's eyes, which is on account of the bright light which runs about them, and the brighter this light is the better the stones. I send a pair of agates, and the largest vellum stone I ever saw, to G. Samuel, and pray give them to him with my best remembrances and tell him he is very ill-natured not to have written to me. I should have heard from him with great pleasure, but he has rejected my correspondence. Tell him however that I thank him for all he has done for me, and that his drawings are more than ever the admiration of all beholders, and the best and most valuable, and most valued, furniture in my house.

Mr Keene has given me such an exquisitely elegant book. It is a manuscript; the length of the leaves is 2 inches and 5/8 of an inch, and the breadth 2 inches and 3/4. It is 5/8 of an inch thick and contains above 700 pages beautifully written on polished paper with broad margins, and nine lines, and borders of scarlet, blue and gold intermixed round every page, besides various paintings of Hindu stories. I cannot part with it. I wish I could read it that I might hope to explain it all to you. I am almost sorry to take it from him, and not be able to show it to you.

When will you be able to read such an enormous letter as this. I never wrote so idly before, for here is nothing to entertain you but all plain matter of fact. *(and so ends her longest letter; almost 10,000 words in the entire unedited version).*

Southeast view of Fort St George, Madras. Thomas Daniell 1797. (Author's collection)

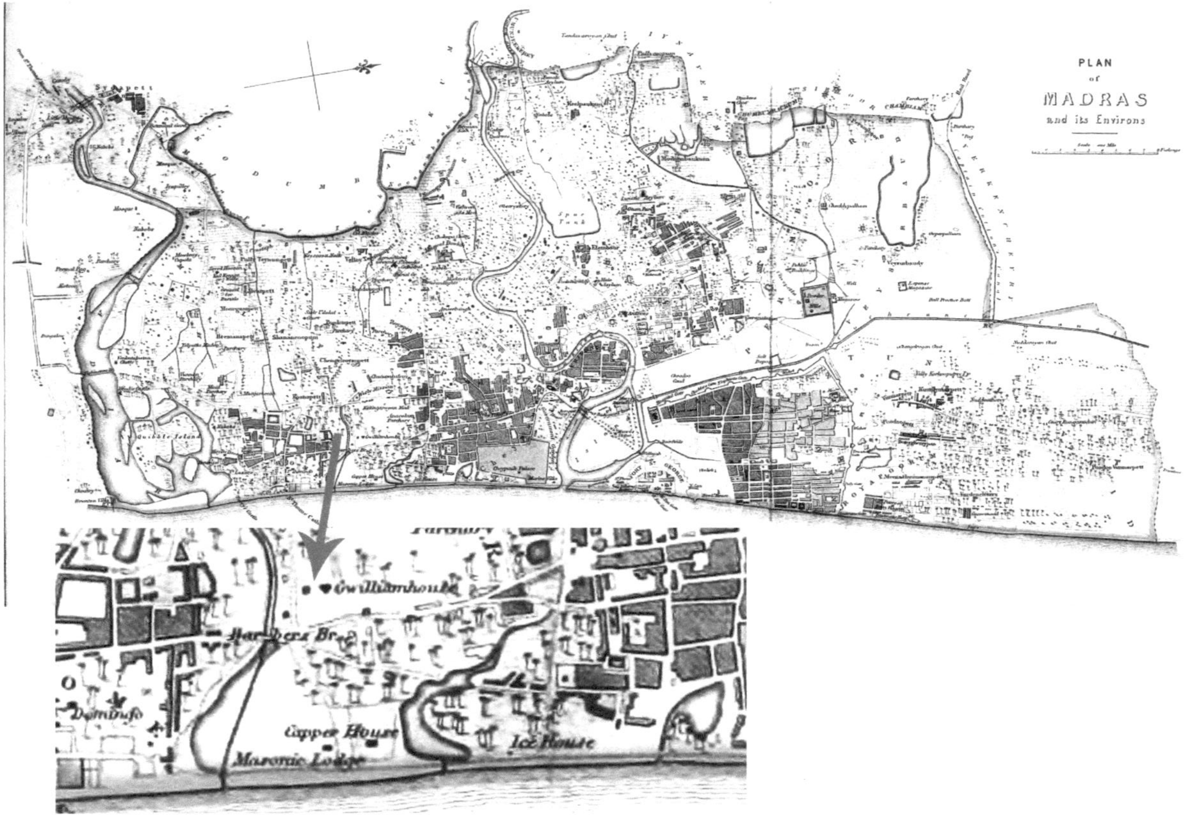

Map of Madras from 1854 showing a house still called the Gwilliamhouse, in very much the position of the Gwillim's house in St Thomé. (Author's collection)

The Gwillim house at St Thomé, by Mary Symonds. (Reproduced by permission of the SADACC Trust, Norwich, UK)

View of Mount St Thomas, Madras, 1804, after James Hunter. Which also demonstrates the then existing racial integration. (Author's collection)

Lesser Golden-backed Woodpecker, by Elizabeth Gwillim. (Courtesy of the Curator of Manuscripts, Rare Books and Special Collections, McGill University Library, Montreal, Canada)

Great-eared nightjar, by Elizabeth Gwillim. (Courtesy of the Curator of Manuscripts, Rare Books and Special Collections, McGill University Library, Montreal, Canada)

Indian paradise flycatcher, by Elizabeth Gwillim. (Courtesy of the Curator of Manuscripts, Rare Books and Special Collections, McGill University Library, Montreal, Canada)

Pheasant-tailed jacana, by Elizabeth Gwillim. (Courtesy of the Curator of Manuscripts, Rare Books and Special Collections, McGill University Library, Montreal, Canada)

Purple sunbird, by Elizabeth Gwillim. (Courtesy of the Curator of Manuscripts, Rare Books and Special Collections, McGill University Library, Montreal, Canada)

Red Whiskered Bulbul, by Elizabeth Gwillim. (Courtesy of the Curator of Manuscripts, Rare Books and Special Collections, McGill University Library, Montreal, Canada)

Hindu travellers, by Mary Symonds. (Reproduced by permission of the SADACC Trust, Norwich, UK)

Sir Thomas Strange, Chief Justice, the Supreme Court, Madras 1801–1816. (By permission of the Governing Body of Christ Church, Oxford. Ref. LP252)

The Supreme Court building at Madras from 1816 to 1862, thereafter the High Court until 1892. (Author's collection)

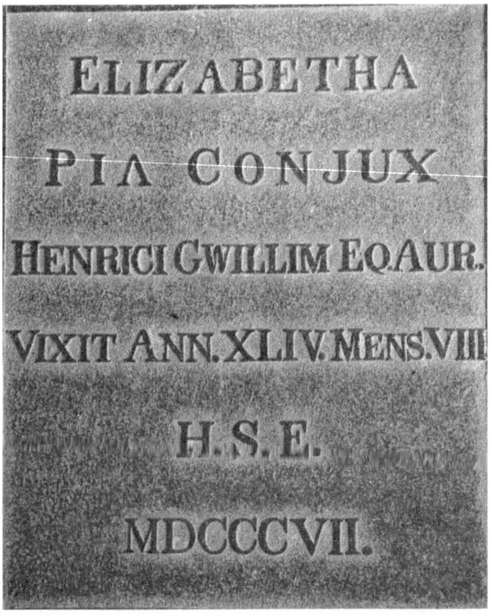

The stone marking Elizabeth Gwillim's grave, laid just inside the entrance to St Mary's Church, Fort St George, Madras. (Author's collection)

Letters of 1806 and Commentary

Commentary

The letters of this year start in January; a little earlier than formerly. The family have already moved to a cotton farm in Pammal, which lies about 4 or 5 kilometres to the south west of Mount St Thomas, which for a while had been their former home. That in S. Thomé was being restored and redecorated. Today the intervening territory is mostly taken up by Chennai International airport. Life here two hundred years ago was unimaginably more rural, and Elizabeth departs from her usual practice of painting live birds and takes the opportunity of using some local men to shoot some of her subjects. She had to paint these almost as swiftly as she did the live ones, who could not tolerate captivity for long, because within only a day they had deteriorated in the hot climate. This activity kept her away from her quill and paper, and much of the letter writing was left to Mary.

Both sisters are conscious of the pressures on Sir Henry, who was doing the work of three appointed judges, one being very ill and the other still away. He was absent all week, sometimes returning at 9 o'clock on Wednesday evening, but otherwise not until the same time on Saturday. He was up at 5 am and his only rest day, Sunday, was interrupted by strings of visitors so that his favoured reading, Cobbett, lay untouched. Also untouched was his wife, Elizabeth, in the sense that she saw very little of him. 'I do not think I have exchanged more private words with Mr Gwillim this year than I have written to you.' He was obviously conscientious about his work and, like so many of the judiciary in India at that time, was under pressures of all sorts. 'He has such a set watching him who hate laws and law makers, and love nothing but cash.' The two sisters were beginning to have serious reservations about Sir Thomas Strange, who was shortly to come back from England.

In her first letter of the year, Mary mentions the receipt of despatches recording the sailing of troops to the Cape of Good Hope. Britain had occupied the Cape from 1795 but handed it back to the earlier occupiers, the Dutch, after the Peace of Amiens in 1802. During the Napoleonic wars the Cape became part of the Batavian Republic, theoretically under French control, much as other Dutch territories, particularly Java. This was a significant threat to the British sea route round the Cape and, as Napoleon was in the process of sending troopships to reinforce the garrison there, the British decided to seize it. She also mentions the death of the Duke of Gloucester, leaving the King as the last of the brothers still alive, but it is quite interesting that nowhere in the letters is there any mention of the Battle of Trafalgar. News of this victory must have been reaching India at about that time.

One of her favourite topics is that of young William Biss, who at that time was a member of the team of military, who were performing the Great Trigonometrical Survey of India, starting in 1802 under the direction of the East India Company. This ambitious project was surveying India in stages, starting from St. Thomas Mount in Madras and using triangulation techniques to map the whole country accurately, and eventually to measure the height of Himalayan peaks under the great George Everest. This enterprise was at the forefront of early 19th-century technology, using highly accurate 100 foot chains, as well as theodolites, with forensically careful measurements and sophisticated trigonometry. The fact that the two sisters were so impressed by Biss's role further suggests their intelligent interest in all goings-on around them. He was popular in the Gwillim household because of the 'gentleness of his disposition', but one cannot help the suspicion that his manner betrayed a nature that was becoming somewhat spoilt. 'My gentleman is so touchy, so very tender, that it is high treason but to find that anything he does is not what you wish it to be' (March 1807). The other young man around the house, a more regular member of the household, was the aptly named Richard Clarke, Clerk to Sir Henry Gwillim, who was a close friend of Mary's and remained so for the rest of their lives. She described him as 'most wonderfully beloved, and is a proof that virtue must be pleasing to people of all descriptions .... his disposition is infinitely better than that of any young man I ever knew' (Nov 1806).

She painted a portrait of him for the benefit of his family, although she was somewhat critical of this work. She obviously admired him greatly. Nevertheless there was to be no matrimonial future for the two of them. As Mary explained to Hetty in January, she had not yet met anyone suitable as a husband, and that her age precluded many possibilities, as so many of the men were much younger than her. Richard would have fallen into this category. Apparently any further information was for Hetty's ears only.

At about the same time she mentions a drawing of the house in Pammal, which had been sent home and was evidently admired by Hetty and her husband. This may well be one of the paintings by Mary Symonds that are to be found in the South Asia Collections Museum in Norwich. At the same end of the year she is writing to request more drawing paper, there being constant pressure on its availability and, at the same time she presses for more paints, brushes, writing materials, pen knives, scissors and needles. For good measure she would quite like half a dozen pairs of silk stockings, and some gloves for Sir Henry. In the preceding paragraph, she prepared the way for these requests by thanking her sister, in a rather neat phrase, for all the 'internals and externals' sent to them.

Both sisters again lament the delays in receiving letters and packages, the French wars having made things much more difficult. Nevertheless that indefatigable shopper, Hetty, is ever at work and before long they are thanking her for things received, including coats and wigs, courtesy of the saintly Mr Prosser. On one occasion Elizabeth is surprised naked, or so she says, but probably not entirely, by the arrival of a packet of letters. As always, these lay greater claim than anything to their time and their thoughts, and she has to read them before reaching for a robe and whilst a meal grows cold on a table near her. She is frustrated by the scratchy writing, and yet hastening to get through them. 'What is more teasing than a puzzling hand when one is in a hurry?'

Elizabeth relished the rural surroundings; the turkeys, geese and ducks near the house, and the opportunity to go shooting in the morning, for the younger men at least, even though the heat of midday drove them back into the billiard room. It isn't long before she succumbs to the temptation to talk again about birds in her letters, and she launches into a detailed description of the Baya Weaver and its habits and life, having a caged pair herself. This is just another example of her fascination with natural history, especially birds, and her constant desire to expand her knowledge in so many directions.

Again Elizabeth rails against Sir Thomas Strange and his apparent deviousness in having avoided a direct decision on the promotion of Sir Henry Gwillim's highly regarded protégé, Temple (now dead), favouring his brother in law Anstruther, or some 'Scotchman', instead.[1] She is further amused to learn that Sir Thomas had found an appointment for William Linley, a moderately well-known musician and civil servant, and seems to have implied that this might have somehow enhanced Sir Thomas' personal status in local society, in his eyes at least, particularly in view of the fact that he had little taste for music. She continues by describing Linley's colourful family and background in some detail, little of which is complimentary.

There is now a gap in the correspondence until July, when Mary wrote in response to Hetty's painful news that their mother had died. Although undoubtedly bereaved, she responded pragmatically, saying how she felt she had already lost her when leaving England for India and, that even if she had been fortunate enough to see her again, she would probably by then have declined in health anyway. Of significant concern, however, was how to break the news to Elizabeth, who was clearly very closely attached to her mother. After rather clumsily tip-toeing around the matter, they realised Elizabeth had of course guessed and, although greatly affected, this was less so than they had expected. Elizabeth herself delays writing until September/October. Her expressions of grief to her younger sister in England are affecting, and both thoughtfully and considerately expressed, and best not paraphrased. They stand as a definitive testament to her feelings.

Both in July and September, each sister wrote about the mutiny of the sepoy troops in Vellore which occurred on the 10th of July. This was a major event, and the two sisters were undoubtedly anxious to convey knowledge of their safety to England, and the absence of a continuing threat, even though it was generally believed Madras would have been an

1 Sir Alexander Anstruther, 1769–1819, was Advocate-General in Madras from 1803. He was a Scot, who had become brother-in-law to Sir Thomas Strange, and who later succeeded Sir John Henry Newbolt as Recorder of Bombay in 1812.

eventual target. With her characteristic attention to detail, and desire for a complete understanding of any event, Elizabeth goes into considerable detail, and particularly castigates the Commander in Chief of the army, Sir John Cradock, for his brazen lack of concern for the religious and social sensibilities of the native troops. Her affection for, and understanding of, the Indian people clearly reinforces this attitude. She is also shocked by the severe reprisals dealt out by the English with those other troops who remained loyal. Mary gives her own considerably less extensive account in November, but with her typically forceful condemnation. To this letter she has attached a formal descriptive document of the events of the mutiny which resulted in the recall to England of the rather disliked Commander in Chief, Sir John Cradock.[2] Lord William Bentinck was also recalled, as it had been decided in London that he too should have been alert to the detrimental changes ordered by Cradock. The two sisters' descriptions of the events, although supportive of the sepoy resentments that underlay them, were inevitably described from the British point of view. There is also the impression that they were rather less sympathetic to any supposed role played by Tipu Sultan's family, who had been confined in the palace in Vellore since 1799. The degree of any such role has been the subject of debate, however. The commission of enquiry came to no definite conclusion, but there were witnesses who stated that Prince Muiz-ud-din fomented unrest, but others who implied that his attitude was no more than an acceptance of a successful outcome, should it occur. It is possible he was a catalyst where discontent was already brewing.[3] It is just as possible his supposed involvement was a rumour encouraged by the British.

2 Sir John Cradock (later Caradoc) was an Irish General, son of the Archbishop of Dublin and educated at Trinity College. Following his return to England he was embittered and sought an active role, becoming involved in the Peninsula campaign. He prepared the defence of Lisbon against Marechal Soult but was superseded by the Duke of Wellington. He remained bitter, considering that he had been badly treated on many occasions, but was made Baron Howden in 1831.

3 For further information on the Vellore mutiny see <http://www.britainssmallwars.co.uk/the-vellore-mutiny-1806.html>, and The Vellore Mutiny, Alan Cameron. PhD thesis submitted to the University of Edinburgh 1984.

The sisters were never of course to know that the Vellore mutiny was, in a sense, a dress rehearsal for the Great Uprising of 1857.

In her letter of November, Mary also reports the return from England of Sir Thomas Strange, and takes the opportunity of pouring a little more scorn on him. Firstly, she relishes the existence of the public letter of admonishment from the King for the judge's unofficial leave of absence, and she then summarily castigates both him and his two brothers. She finally launches into an enjoyable commentary on Strange's folly, at the age of 52, in marrying a young woman who, although a daughter of a Calcutta judge, was seemingly both frivolous and none too attractive. Her disdain may partly have been a result of the growing distance between the two sisters and Madras society, arising from the steadily worsening antagonism directed towards Sir Henry Gwillim by both Bentinck and Thomas Strange.

She returns to the usual subject of goods and letters sent from England, and it is clear that much was lost with the sinking of the Lady Burgess, East Indiaman, in April of that year off the Cape Verde Islands. Apart from the inevitable deprivation of letters, she expressed some dismay at the loss of the mourning clothes sent to them. Both women had had to make do with black dyed muslin, which was not only malodorous but stained their skin black. It seems inevitable that the irony of this must have been amusing to their servants.

Mary ends the year referring again to several young men staying with them, and the dangers they were subject to if living independently. They were exposed to all sorts of temptations, she believed, and describes how one young man had sunk into a state of advanced decadence and illness, and so subsequently died. There is the suspicion that young English women must have resented the apparent disinterest in them by such young men, in favour of Indian girls, perhaps forgetting that they were very much unavailable for marriage to men so young and impecunious. The importance of age is made clear by Mary Symonds in her letter of January 1806. Furthermore, many such young men survived such dissipation unscathed, deriving from it obvious, although self-indulgent, diversion.[4]

4 Robb, Peter, *Sex and Sensibility, Richard Blechynden's Calcutta Diaries 1791–1822* (Oxford, 2011).

Letters

From Elizabeth Gwillim to her mother (abridged) January 1806

Our house is being painted, and it has been newly stuccoed, or chunamed as we call it, and is of course damp and bare so that I cannot return to it, nor do I know anybody by whom I could send anything of consequence, so I must hope for better times. Sir Henry has so much business on his hands that I have scarcely any servants to my share. He comes up here one night in the middle of the week and on Saturday night he comes, and stays all day on Sunday when we have a party. This exercise does him much good, and this place has a fine dry air, but I am at a loss for news about the sailing of the ships, and am so circumstanced that I cannot well write. I came here five weeks ago and obtained by a favour the loan of a couple of shooting men who go upon the hills and collect me curious birds. When they bring them in I am obliged to sit down and draw them, for here if dead, they will only keep one day and, if alive, they cannot long be kept so and are suffering much. I hope therefore you will accept of Mary's letters in lieu of mine. She has written much to Hetty, and if the ships stay till Sunday I will write further.

For a whole year Sir Henry has had the whole business of all three judges. Sir Ben Sullivan, who is old and shattered has been absent ever since Sir Thomas Strange went. He left Sir Henry very ungenerously but, thank God, all the business has been done and no suit has been delayed. He has, however, not had a moment free but, I assure you, I think his health is all the better, for he has no contradiction from party or national prejudice, and his profession is his delight. He never has been so well, so long, since I knew him.

From Mary Symonds to her sister Hetty. 28th January 1806.

Our overland despatch arrived yesterday, giving an account of the sailing of the fleet accompanied by several men of war, and a great many troops, and etc. for taking the Cape, it is therefore probable they will not be here for some weeks. The same despatch brings an account of the death of the Duke of Gloucester. I suppose it must be much felt by the good old King, as he now stands quite alone; the last, though the eldest, of his brothers. He is an example of the benefits arising from temperance, and by his private virtue he becomes a public blessing.

I have the happiness to tell you that we are all in good health. Betsy never was better in her life. We are now at Pammal, the cotton farm that we wrote from this time last year. The weather is very cool and pleasant, and Sir Henry goes down to St Thomé every morning to his business, and returns to sleep at night. He thinks the exercise does him good, and the distance is not more than ten miles. The house at St Thomé is being repaired and beautified in our absence, and we are very glad to be out of the smell of paint. Mr Biss is now stationed about 4 miles distant from this place and (I suppose) for the first time in his life, being in his tent, he seems much pleased and is in remarkably good health. He has a companion at present, a Mr Walpole, who is a very elegant young man; sweet tempered and remarkably handsome. He is of Lord Orford's family, and son to the Public Minister at Lisbon.[5] They both spend their Sunday with us. I have no doubt but Mr Biss will give you a fascinating account of himself and his employment, as you seem to be a prodigious favourite of his. The twelve young men, who form the Institution of which Mr Biss is a member, are stationed at certain distances to make an accurate survey of this part of the country, and I believe they are to survey the whole of the country, and when the plans are completed the Governor says he intends to send them home to the Court of Directors as a proof of the ability of his Institution and of the particular merit of its present members. Biss does himself credit, wherever he is, by his industry and the gentleness of his disposition. His friends have nothing to apprehend for him but the delicacy of his constitution which, however, I hope will become stronger as he grows older. I do not think the climate disagrees with him at all, but on the contrary that

5 Probably the son of Robert Walpole, Envoy Extraordinary and Minister Plenipotentiary to Portugal 1771–1800, in turn the fourth son of Horatio Walpole (First Baron Walpole) who was a younger brother of Sir Robert Walpole, First Earl of Orford and former Prime Minister.

he is rather better since he came to this country than at his arrival, but he is of an extremely nervous habit.

I have not received a line from my kind friend Mrs Trent. I long to know how you go on together; how you like them, and how they like you. I am sure they must be much altered if you are not good friends. I have written much tittle tattle to Mrs Trent, which she will read if she has interest and a good stock of patience. Richard is more generally beloved than any man in the country, I believe. The sweetness of his temper and extreme modesty of his manners prevent his offending anyone, and the fairness of his principles and elegance of those accomplishments, which his father's excellent education has bestowed upon him, are qualifications so rarely met with here that they cannot fail to distinguish the possessor. This Sunday he and all my friends were treated with some raspberry tarts, but as the stock is getting low I am rather stingy. However, I am proud to say that my mince pies have been prodigiously admired this year; real orthodox mince pies. The party was all vastly gay, with the jam and some fine fat ducks, and two handsome dishes of green peas; there we beat you I think on the second day of February. We take care to keep the English season too, for as it was Candlemas day, which Sir Henry calls the last day of Christmas, we had a large Norfolk turkey and some mince pies. I think I am writing you a pretty nonsensical letter, but it is necessary you should have a familiar peep at us now and then, and I know that no one else will spend ink and paper on such subjects. Our party consisted of our own family only, with the addition of Mr Biss, Mr Walpole and a Mr Dalgaines of their Society, whose tent is pitched about 4 miles to the westward of us. Having thanked you in the name of the whole family for your kind attention to our internals and externals, I shall proceed to make some further trial of your friendship by requesting you to execute more commissions for us, one of which, of a new and rather extraordinary nature, you will find enclosed on a separate piece of paper. By some opportunity or other I requested you to send two plates of looking glass to repair the accidents which had befallen two dressing tables, but as you have never noticed the request I suspect the letter must have miscarried. I have not the proper dimensions here but will endeavour to get them before I send it off.

You will be so good as to omit no opportunity of sending drawing paper of all sorts, for Betsy finds she has acquired such a facility in drawing, and is so anxious to go on with her collection, that I can scarcely be allowed a bit of good paper to practice on less the stock should be exhausted before our fresh supply comes to hand. We are also in want of the following colours; lake, Prussian blue, indigo, light red, burned umber and gallstone, two cakes each; four or five dozen of black lead pencils, and as many brushes of all sizes. Pens and writing paper, with sand, coloured wafers and etc, as you kindly sent them before, will always be truly acceptable. Two good pen knives, and two or three pair of scissors, a few needles, some tape bobbin, both silk and cotton. Pray send a few pairs of gloves for Sir Henry, and a few bits of watch ribbons of cheerful patterns, but not over gay. If you are a little more liberal to us in shoes it will be no hardship, and be so good as to send mine a very little smaller than the last. If you send Betsy and me half a dozen pairs of good silk stockings each, I think they will be very acceptable by the time you can answer this.

I am by no means indifferent to your kind admonishments, but I cannot help but think it better to abide by an evil I know than one I do not. A dependent state is a perfectly happy one, but I could never think myself independent in being the wife of a man of whose conduct my heart could not approve. No, I shall wait patiently and remain ever as I am unless that happens, which however may happen, that I meet with a man in whom I find those qualities which I think necessary to my happiness though, amongst my numerous admirers in this country, I have not yet met with such a one. I think I cannot be accused of making any unreasonable demands. If I were some 10 or 12 years younger it is probable I should have married long ago, for I know several young men who would be most happy to take me such as I am, to whom no reasonable woman of eighteen or twenty could object, but as they are men twenty-two to twenty-five or six years old, I should think myself guilty of an unpardonable rashness in doing them the injury to accept them, and should deserve all the ill consequences which might naturally follow such a step. Perhaps you will think I make too much of this subject, but yet I could say more if you and I were together in a corner, but the distance and the uncertainty of the fate of letters must withhold my confidence till we meet when, or if, it shall please God to grant me that happiness.

The supplier of wearables you send us out every year is really very handsome, and must give you a great deal of trouble to collect but, my dear Hetty I should like very much to know what the expense of them is. You have never sent any account yet. Besides the pleasure of knowing how much I cost my friends, I should like to know the price of articles, as I am often asked for the sake of comparing mine with those bought here. You could perhaps send me the sum total of each year and, if it is not too much trouble when you are packing, will you be so good as to fix a bit of paper on each with the price of it. I believe I told you Mr Prosser had brought Betsy and me each a very pretty cap, and Sir Henry a hamper of most excellent cider. I scarcely ever saw him enjoy anything equal to it. He has had his glass full out of every bottle that has been opened; it is the only thing I ever knew him keep for himself, or use so economically.

This season of the year reminds me always of our little excursions to Brompton, when we used to open our eyes after a gloomy journey to look for some kind bud or blossom to cheer us with the promise of fairer days. When will such happy tranquil days return to us all? They are at least far off, but the hope that such may again be enjoyed, and that we shall find no diminution in that warm affection which was the real cause of this happiness, is the prospect which enlivens all my present hours, shortens the time of our separation, and smooths all the rugged roads of this careworn life.

From Elisabeth Gwillim to her sister Hetty 11th February 1806

I suppose you are about reading all the letters we sent by the fleet which sailed hence the 10th September, and yet the fleet which prepared to sail from England in May, a few months ago, is not yet arrived at Madras. I own I so much disliked the thought of writing before that fleet arrived, that I have omitted it till it is too late to write at all. I really long to hear from you, and this delay of the fleet mortifies me extremely. I rail at Bonaparte, and all the causes of the war which has so much interrupted our intercourse ever since we have been here.

I hope you have seen Mr Keene. By him I thanked you for all the last packets, which were so well chosen and brought so carefully by Mr Prosser. They have been useful, creditable and comfortable to us. Sir Henry's coat is very handsome, but he wears it only on dress occasions. He is very fond of it, and so am I, but he wants another without lining, of some neat brown or fashionable colour, but it must be a kind of frock coat, wholly unlined except the sleeves, which should be lined with sarsnet or silk serge. A ladies cloth, if it be of a fine close texture, is the best. As the pepper and salt coat was so long a-coming, he took a blue one of Richard Clarke's thin blue cloth, and that has been his undress country gentleman's coat ever since. It is now worn out, and we can buy none but heavy coarse cloth.

Thank God we have had no sickness in the house this year and a half, except that Richard Clarke had a cold with some fever for a few days. I believe he would have been well the day after he was taken ill but, finding himself relieved by the perspiration in the night produced by some hot wine and water, he jumped out of bed in the morning and washed himself with cold water, and by breakfast time became worse. He was then obliged to send for a doctor and put himself under our care. The doctor sent him a sweating draught, which threw him into one of those kind of sweats which Sir Henry calls a brewing. The first breaking out of it was so new to him that he really became quite terrified. However, in the morning he was relieved. He stayed at home a week to take care of himself. It was his first absence from his office. He was nothing worse a few days after, but the medical man ordered him to wear flannel waistcoats next his skin, as conceiving that he had caught cold not so much by any accident as by the unusual coolness of the weather. We have had 18 months of mild weather and some months indeed when the evening and morning have been very piercing to our tender bodies so long stewed in the heat.

The young men, of whom we have generally a good party, make out the day by shooting in the morning and billiards in the heat of the day. Richard is a famous shot, and a great lover of horses, in neither of which he takes after his father or uncle. You might see how busy I am by the bird skins, which I get skinned and he sends on to his uncle. The skins are not well cured, for I have only the cook to do them and, as I am obliged to draw them first, that is delineate them, they are frequently done too late and the skins become tender.

We have many amusements in walking or climbing about the rocks. Sir Henry went upon a pinnacle the other evening to pluck a Baya's nest *(Baya Weaver)* that was hanging to a branch of a tree, and he desired me to send it to you and tell you that he had plucked it at the risk of his life. I have a male and female Baya in a cage and I will send them on, and the nest, if Richard can find any interest to get them sent by one of the ships. There is a Mr Kennett who has offered to take some things. Mr Kennett was sent to us by a very respectable young man, who is purser of a ship, and who sold Sir Henry a pipe of port wine and offered to take anything to you. I suppose you know that the Baya is the famous hanging bird which makes its pendant nest at the end of the branches of trees which overhang any precipice or lake. The nest has two chambers, and the Hindus assert that the birds put fireflies in the nest to be a light. It is certain that fireflies are found in the nests, but it is probable only put there as food, for the birds eat insects and grain. Rice is their chief fare; rice in the husk; and their dexterity in catching the grain thrown up into the air is wonderful. They crack the husk and take the grain out with surprising quickness. I wish I could send you one or two trained birds, but that would be impossible, unless I sent it by somebody who would exercise them all the way. The bird is about the size of a sparrow, but the male has a yellow head; the female is the more docile, but both are easily taught. They learn every trick in a week, but the mischief is that the boy who takes care of my birds, and teaches them, sells them off as soon as trained and tells me they are dead, or replaces the trained one by a new one. Indeed, they very soon forget their tricks and do not perform them, but when hungry they will catch a bit of silver when thrown up overwater before it has sunk in the stream, and are made to catch all their food grain by grain thrown up in the air. I have seen one who would fetch a flower out of my hand, and put it to our master' s nose; beetle leaf, and put it in his mouth; money, and put it in his hand, and this repeatedly without any mistake but, after every service, it was rewarded with a grain of rice.

I have had two living porcupines brought me. They ate through their cages, however, and ran away in the night. The Polygars who catch them brought me one dead for the purpose of roasting, as they said it was the most delicate meat they had. I have heard many people praise it and accordingly I had it roasted. It was a young one, and fat, and looked and smelt like very delicate pork, or wild hog. The natives like it better than the common wild hog, and call the animal the thorny hog. A roasted porcupine was, I believed, a joke, but all agreed in liking it.

I have a notable farmyard here; turkeys, geese, ducks and fowls; they make such an abominable noise at daybreak that I cannot bear it. Sir Henry says it is delightful music. Mr Webb, in whose house we are, has another farm about 6 miles farther on where he tells me there has lately been a Bengal tiger which had killed nine sheep of a night. I have been drawing a beautiful tiger cat which a Captain Cleveland is taking home with him to England. If it should ever live to get there, it will be a great curiosity. I intend to send you this picture by the first opportunity.

Wonders will never cease. The ships were unmoored; the passengers on board; and an absolute order to be under way at four o'clock February 12th. I sent my letters from Pammal at five o'clock in the morning. I wrote little, because I hate to write when it is to answer nothing. Dull and downhearted, I spent the day in sullenness. When lo! Just when I was going to eat my roast fowl and Bengal potatoes; very watery and not much bigger than a jack stone, up comes the Chubdar Bob! *(staff-bearing aide)* "A large packet of letters from England. The ships are to stay till tomorrow". I am in my closet and cannot come out with no gown on. Obliged to read an hour naked, the fowl cold, and all uncomfortable, but right to the end I was obliged to go. Thank God they are all well. I will answer the letters the instant I have read them, but who can make out these letters? I cannot read half of them! My eyes are dazzled. "Get out boy; I don't care whether the dinner is cold or not". "The Chubdar must go back to his master this minute". But I can't send them to him till I have read them myself, and who can read this. Whether Mr Milburne sells swan quills or goose quills, surely he must sell something that can be written with. The pen that I have would be a disgrace to him, dear Hetty, where did you procure it? There were once a few good ones, but Mary keeps them all to herself. It is hard, for what is more teasing than a puzzling hand when one is in a hurry?

I shall hope for the letters tomorrow, or by Sir Henry tonight, as he is to come up if he can. This is Wednesday night, and he arrives at nine o'clock tired and drawn, or so has done, and goes fast asleep. With difficulty he is awakened to go to bed. He wakes at five o'clock in the morning and mounts his horse. He comes up on Saturday night at the same hour, in the same state. On Sundays he sits at rest, reading Cobbett but, scarcely is he sat down to read, but in come all sorts of visitors. Friends who have a mind to be kind, for this is his only leisure day, come to tiffin. Merchants, who can go out on no other days, and come to conciliate his favour and explain their grievances; Polygars, and all sorts of hunters and shooters. "The master has leisure today and so we come to make a vigil." Poor man, it is worse than all the other days of the week. Here are Mr James's kind present of books lying before me at this instant, and I do not believe he has made up his mind about these, or even got through them yet. It is not for want of taking them in hand. In due time you will hear all about them but, I assure you, I do not think I have exchanged more private words with Mr Gwillim this year than I have written to you. He is so anxious about his business, and he has such a set watching him who hate laws and law makers, and love nothing but cash.

I give you credit for perceiving Sir Thomas's flummery. It is sickening; he is a perfect joke here on that account. He has behaved towards Mary and me in the most tender manner, just when he was about to do the most ungenerous act towards my husband, and what for? Because Sir Henry tried to do right, and his duty. You know not how he fought it out about Temple *(Clerk to the Court who died)*, and he and Anstruther, his brother in law, were always pretending to quarrel with each other, and abusing one another to everybody, when they were otherwise proposing one Scotchman or relation of theirs after another, wholly unfit for the place that was suited to Temple, and yet saying what fine things they had written home about him. Sir Henry was delighted that the person he brought out should be so satisfactory, and concluded the thing done. At that moment Sir Thomas said no. He would not agree; he must have these Scotchmen, or he must have Mr Anstruther, his brother-in-law. It was base and bad; it opened my eyes, as I am ashamed to say they had been a little blinded by flattery.

But this is diverting, that you tell me Sir Thomas gave Linley his position! [6] Oh good God; a civil servant of as long-standing as Linley didn't need Sir Thomas, who cared not for him. I know that he despised his talents, which are indeed only those of a fiddler, but he was gay, and acted upon the stage, and played when Sir Thomas had friends, who praised it, but never listened to it, for he has no more ear for music than a beetle. Linley was inclined to scold his servants, abuse his wine, and make a joke of him. I may say without partiality, and I believe it causes no small degree of envy, Linley is, or has been, a pretty, lady-faced, man who learned music because he never heard of anything else in his family. He came here a writer, but with such a hankering for the orchestra that he left this fine employment in order to seek his fortune as a musician. He left the country, as they have permission to on pretence of ill health, and without giving up the service. He wasted five years in England; tried, as I have heard, to be the leader of a band but the talents, so flattered here, were of no success in public. He also tried a play, or farce, and it met with the worst fate from the audience. He wrote a novel, but who buys or reads it.

Old Mrs Sheridan, who was I believe the mother of Sheridan the orator,[7] and was a writer of novels, wrote The Memoirs of Miss Sidney Biddulph, and some oriental pieces which met with applause. One of the latter is called the Nourredin *(The History of Nourjahad)*. It is the story of a worthless fellow, being indulged by his patron with luxuries sufficient to provoke his vices till he grew sick of them, and then rewarded for so doing. It has much of the air of the oriental stories, as we call them, but more particularly to speak of Mussulman stories. Perhaps it was borrowed from some prints, but I know nothing of its history. Its merit is the depiction of

6 William Linley, 1771–1835, one of a talented family of society musicians, well-known at that time. He was variously composer, writer of musical theatre and author, but made no great success of these. He went to India twice, firstly as a writer and later in a more senior position as paymaster at Vellore and later sub-treasurer in Fort St George, Madras. He had rather more success with his music at this latter time, which coincided with Elizabeth Gwillim, who seems to have been witheringly unimpressed, unusually so for her.

7 Richard Brinsley Sheridan, the playwright and MP and, coincidentally, husband of William Linley's sister, Elizabeth.

a man, so vicious any Christian would think deserved to be hanged, but that Christianity lacked morality in so finding. This story, of all others, Mr Linley chose to change to an English history, and then happily got rid of all that had merit in its manner, and retained all that was immoral. To this he added a plentiful quantity of dullness and, if now you should doubt my criticism, please send to Mr Lane for the book called Forbidden Apartments, written by him, and Mrs Sheridan's Nourredin, from which it was taken. The truth is Linley is a pleasant, but weak, young man who fancies himself a scholar. Upon his failure in the public world he returned to his activities in India. He waited for some time, and he had been in India about four or five months before we came, and after three or four more he was appointed by Lord Clive as Paymaster at Vellore. But this was all in the regular course of things, and far from any favour of Sir Thomas's. His recommendation would have been a hindrance at that time. Linley lived there quite stingily, saving every six months, and acquired enough to keep a home, quite disliking this country. He left the place, and came down to Madras, with an intention to sail to England. He sang and played all, and amazed the public here. It is probable Sir Thomas might mention him for the position he now holds, which is no better than what he had left, but more agreeable to him than a solitary residence in the country. Still he hates India and, as to his position, it could be given to none but a writer, that is a company's civil servant such as he is. It is all routine, and that place was offered to five different people who all refused it. Had he refused that, he would have had another. It is his own pleasure to leave the countryside. The only favour Sir Thomas did was giving him a couch in his house, as we and he do to many.

Sir Henry is arrived and stops any writing. He says he thinks the ships will sail early tomorrow morning; that government will dispatch their papers to Ceylon where all the ships are to rendezvous.

From Mary Symonds to her sister Hetty. 22nd February 1806

When I arose this morning I heard a salute fired, which (being 12 miles off) I concluded was from the ships that were getting underway to sail for England but, to our great delight and surprise, about two hours ago

Sir Henry sent up a messenger with a packet of letters from you. They could be the ones we have so long expected, but must have come by some ship which has been despatched since, as they are dated September 1805. What is now come to our hands is a letter intended for Betsy and one from your dear self with a packet containing two wigs and several loose letters from Mr Biss's friends. I am very glad you received my letters with the drawing of the house, and that my dear James liked it. Pray tell him I will not let another opportunity pass without sending him views of all the houses we have inhabited in India, and such other things as I think will amuse him. You complain that I have not given a view of the sea with the house. Now, my dear Hetty, if you just recollect, I have told you that we see the sea from the house and therefore to draw the house I must necessarily turn that end towards the sea, which could not consequently describe it, but you shall have it in all directions, fore and aft.

Poor Sir Henry too; he has not acknowledged the books. I wonder at that too, but to say the truth he has little time for reading them. Mr Cobbett lies on the table by me now. Sir H carries them about with him but, poor soul, he has so little leisure he reads when he can, but it is not often. He has not been able to come up to us every night lately, as he has work to do, but stays down at St Thomé for three or four nights at a time during the session. When he does come, it is about nine or 10 o'clock. He is quite tired, and generally takes up a book after telling us the news, sits down on a couch and falls asleep in half an hour with no difficulty. With some difficulty we persuade him to go to bed. It is not want of inclination to read but want of leisure.

The fault you find in Tom James's education is a very general one. I know not why it is. Whether the Masters really pay too much attention to the dead languages and too little to our own, or that they think only of receiving their salary and neglecting their duty altogether, but certainly young men, of whom I see great numbers, are extremely deficient in the English language. I have known but few who were otherwise, and these were young men of high families and educated at public schools.

Sir Henry is come up; he says the packet has closed. Therefore I shall close this and let him take it down in the morning for the chance of a private ship.

From Mary Symonds to her sister Hetty 28th July 1806

You will see, by the public papers, an account of the shocking mutiny which has taken place at Vellore, I write a few lines by this uncertain opportunity just to satisfy your mind as to our safety. I thank God we are all well, and we have every reason to think ourselves safe. The disturbance was occasioned by an order being issued which directed an alteration in the dress of the Indian Army, and interfered with some of the aimless prejudices of these poor people. I cannot write you any particulars, having only half an hour allowed me to prepare and send this. The ship which carries it is an American, going to New York.

On 27th June we received your letters by the fleet which left England the first week in March. They brought us the sad, unwelcome, news of our dear dear mother's death. You have indeed a loss in her; her sweet consoling tenderness; her sensible good advice, and her innocent and virtuous example you will miss. I pray to God to protect you. I have wished to be with you, that I may endeavour to supplant her loss to you in some degree, by comforting and assisting you as well as I could. For ourselves, she has been long lost to us when I took my leave of her before I came to this country. I considered it as a last separation, and have sincerely suffered myself to hope for the happiness of seeing her again ever since I have been here, or if such a wish has for a moment entered my mind, it has been immediately checked by the recollection that I could only, at the utmost, hope to see her in a declining state, and to perform the last sad duties. We will write fully to you, on this and every other subject, soon.

Ships from England are hourly expected here, and in them I suppose we shall find packages from you. They will also bring us a new Governor, and Governor General, and we expect an entire change of men and measures which is much to be desired, for weaker or worse than the present can hardly be. God Almighty bless you and send us a happy meeting at the expiration of our time in this place. I think you need not fear its being prolonged. I have so many things to say to you that I know not how to quit my pen, but it must be.

From Mary Symonds to her sister Hetty 30th September 1806

I wrote a short hasty letter to you in the hope of sending it by an American ship, and I sent my letter to Sir Edward Pellew who had promised to forward it with his own letters. Unfortunately the ship did not touch here, and by some accident or other my letter was mislaid in his office till yesterday, when he sent it on. The first news I heard this morning is that the Sarah Christina is arrived here from Bengal and will sail again tomorrow. This ship was to touch here, we heard some time ago, but she has been so long on the passage, and there are so many privateers in the Bay, that we began to think she was either taken, or that she would sail from Bengal direct. She is going home with dispatches, entirely on account of the sad mutiny at Vellore I believe. I fear the French papers will give a dreadful account of that lamentable business, and that you will be apprehensive for the safety of us all. Thank God, the evil has not extended beyond Vellore, but attempts have been made at other places and a general massacre of the English was intended, and certainly would have been attempted had the orders of the Commander in Chief been enforced. They have been withdrawn, however, but I am sorry to say other people are now publishing, almost as dangerous, contrary edicts. Our blessed Governor is now, against all advice, making concessions to the natives which had never been thought of before and which, of course, will convince them that they have only to oppose whatever they dislike in order to obtain the opposite.

Betsy has written you a very long letter. She prepared it in order that she might not be taken by surprise, or miss any chance that might occur, knowing that you would be most particularly anxious to receive answers to your last letters giving us the melancholy account of the death of my dear kind good mother. Those letters were received on 27 June. The ships came in on the 26th, and Richard Clarke went into the fort early in the morning of the 27th in order to procure our letters, and I waited anxiously for them, and wondered much that he did not send them so soon as usual. At last, Sir Henry came into my room and went out again two or three times, without saying a word, and I then began to think there was something amiss. I questioned him, and he told me he had no letters, and that Richard had written him word that there was some ill news for us. I instantly summoned each dear, loved, friend to my recollection, and thought over and over whom I should endure to find myself separated from for ever, but could not determine it and, at last, was become so anxious and miserable in suspense that even the afflicting news I heard was a relief, being a certainty. The next trouble was to break it to poor Betsy, which Sir Henry did by showing her his father's letter, in which the sad event was not mentioned, but said that he had serious apprehensions from the nature of her disorder. Sir Henry tried to pacify her by assuring her that he had no further letter on the subject, and we all sat down together but, seeing me more depressed than herself she guessed the truth, and after endeavouring to reconcile her to the event by as much discussion as the case admitted of, we acknowledged the truth. She was of course very much affected by it for a time, but I am happy to say she has not suffered from it as much as I feared she would. Separated as we have been from her, and unaccustomed to hear her voice, or see her face, and to watch the regular change which time must have made in her, I think of her continually as I left her. Except when I am writing on the subject, or called upon by some particular train of thought, I forget that she has gone from us, and sometimes catch myself thinking what will be her opinion when she knows of this or that occurrence. But I have really no melancholy thoughts on the subject.

Her little property, or that which is my portion of it, I wish to bestow in a way in which I think she would have been pleased to see it disposed of. I will not now say how, because I fear I am not at present at liberty to dispose of it at all. Sir Henry wished me to accept of Betsy's share, but God forbid that even a farthing of it should be expended for my use. How dreadful would be my feelings if I thought it possible that I should ever be forced to diminish, instead of increasing, that little store for the purpose to which it should be destined. How should I reproach myself for a wretched ill spent youth? I have declined his offer, but have given him no positive reason for this. However, perhaps he may guess what my objections are. He tells me that, though I do not accept it, yet he wishes it to be in my name in order to save trouble and expense. To that of course I cannot object but, as I do not understand business of this nature, I cannot explain to you what the difficulties are which are to be obviated by this union. I have made you a small copy of our dear mother's picture, and intend to send it by the next ships.

I have three people standing by me and hurrying me to conclude, so I can say no more, but request you to make my kindest remembrances to my dear friends, and assure them I will write to each and every one of them by the regular ship. This is a very uncertain opportunity, and the ship, though a remarkably good sailor, is very likely to be taken *(by the French).*

From Elizabeth Gwillim to her sister Hetty — September and October 1806

I went on the top of the house to see them come in about sunset. Little did I think of the melancholy findings they were bearing to me. I have told you before that our home affords us this early opportunity of seeing the ships arrive. By many we are envied, but we have ever felt the interval between the arrival of the ships, and the delivery of letters, as the most painful period of life. The illness I had laboured under for some time, by enfeebling my body a little, was not a preparation for a severe trial. Had it come upon me in the height of health and spirits I might, and probably should have, born it more than I did. It may seem a great folly in me, to strangers, to call it a severe trial to lose a mother who had attained, nearly, the age of 74 but, having no children of my own, my pleasure consisted more in the hopes of delighting the aged than in the prospect of pleasing an unborn, or at least an unknown set of little friends. That I shall love those who are the offspring of others, whom I so sincerely and affectionately love, I am sure and certain, but I feel less satisfied in the hopes of gaining their affection, even if I should live to claim it. Besides I had to own that, in my weakness, I had flattered myself that I should have the happiness to cheer my dear mother's age. Her game constitution, free from all disease, induced me to form this hope. The family, too, have been for the most part long-lived, and the account of her vigour and sprightliness almost obliterated all my fears upon her account. The delicacy of her constitution occasioned me frequent matter of apprehension, and it is that which has at last been fatal to her. I am not, I hope, impious in my grief, but I mourn the event and feel it through all my frame, nor is the event forgotten by me morning or evening, or in the middle of the day. My chief grief is that I was not near her in her last hour. On this account

I consider the distance that separated us as a dreadful calamity. Formerly, I thought I fancied that it was productive of some little pleasure to her, and I had therefore infinite pleasure in collecting all sorts of information that I conceived would please her. I trust in God that our absence has neither shortened her existence by depriving us of the power of watching over her, nor by giving her extraordinary anxiety upon account of us. But my dear Hetty, I also grieve extremely for you who have not only had this great affliction, which you bear in common with us, but the additional pain of communicating to us intelligence so painful for you to write, and for us to receive.

Our principal reason for wishing to write to you one letter at least was not merely to acknowledge the recent one of yours of March 1806, but to ease your minds relative to us if any exaggerated accounts should have come to England by way of France of the late unhappy massacre at Vellore, a station near this place. It was doubtless the intention of the devisers of it that the inhabitants of Madras should share the fate of those at Vellore, but Providence in his infinite mercy to us, of which I fear we may not be worthy, preserved us. Mary's letter, I believe, detailed this affair as well as it was then known but, as the insurrection of the sepoys had been provoked by sad misconduct. I presume that you will have had in the newspapers, before you receive this, some account of the insurrection at Vellore, but as our Government here were in no hurry to communicate an affair likely to do them so little credit, I expect that you will have had accounts by the way of France, or from Tranquebar, long before any account reaches you regularly. As those accounts will doubtless be exaggerated by the French, I should not be surprised if you were told that we were all murdered, as I believe indeed it was intended we should be. This unhappy affair seems to have arisen entirely from the obstinacy and arrogance of the Commander in Chief, and the people belonging to him, but as his doings were not controlled by the Government, who had the power to control him and ought to have exercised it, they seem altogether equally blameable. By long residence in this country, the old officers of the Company became well acquainted with the habits and customs of the natives. They kept them in a state of strict discipline, but they never ventured to thwart these prejudices, of any kind. Above all, they regarded those of a religious nature, amongst which must be classed their dress in some parts, their marks and the cutting of their hair and whiskers, with many other particulars which may appear matters of mere indifference to an enlightened European, as customs that differ in every caste and distinguish them from each other. These trifling forms, which they daily observe, constitute the religion of the Hindus. A few of the Brahmins excepted, they know no other. When they go to the temples it is only to look at the image, or to celebrate some festival, and all they have to do is to follow the procession when the image is carried out. But the marks on their foreheads are considered by them as most sacred, and their whiskers are only cut as a mark of mourning for the death of a parent. The Musselmans have not these marks on the foreheads, but their whiskers are equally sacred, and to say to anyone I will cut your whiskers, or to offer to touch them, is an affront of the most unpardonable kind. Now the regiments of sepoys are composed of a mixture of Hindus and Mussulmans, and hitherto they had been most faithful to their leaders. They never have shown any inclination to rebel upon account of severities exercised on their persons, nor have they turned their backs in battle. A few Europeans led them, and they have ever shown great bravery in following them. But some of the gentlemen who have lately come out have been quite above any regard for their religious prejudices, and the present Commander in Chief formed orders that the sepoys should wear no mark on their foreheads, and should appear closely shaven. The sepoys were terrified that these orders, and those Mussulmans in the palace that was Tippoo's, and doubtless many others who must bear our yoke with great impatience, took advantage of this alarm and persuaded the sepoys that we were going to make them lose their castes. Having thus made them pariahs, we were to force them all to become Christians. But this was not all; they have a violent dislike to anything made of leather (I mean the Hindus have), and leather is absolute pollution. The Brahmins, when they wear anything on the feet, have a wooden sole fastened on by means of a stud which passes between the great toe and that next to it. How they contrive to walk with them I know not, but they would not endure a strap of leather, and the people of the other castes, or some Brahmins engaged in business with Europeans who have got rid of their prejudices so far as to wear the ornamented shoes made in the fashion of the shoes of the Mussulmans, leave them on the outside of their houses and wash their feet before they enter any part of it. Any person who uses leather in his trade is infamous. The shoemakers are the lowest outcastes, below the pariahs, for they make harness for horses, and they burn the dead, and are the executioners. They live nowhere near the other people; they eat cattle and horses which have died, and frequently die themselves in great numbers by so doing. The sepoys have from time to time been brought, without orders strictly for the purpose, to wear leather belts and various straps as necessary to their uniform. This has been brought about by the native officers who have great power with the sepoys, and act under the English officers. They love finery, and are certainly more fond of imitating us than is generally believed. They now copy us in all they consistently can, as they heretofore copied the Musselman, their former masters. All this has been done without threat or force. They have even gone so far in their civilities, and their desire to look regular and like the British troops, as to come to the parades without the marks on their foreheads. Then as soon as they go home they make their supplication, that is repeat certain collects which they are taught. In this they must first wash and put on their marks. This is at home, and for the sake of their religion they appear in their proper dress, but were well satisfied to forbear these customs when on duty. These late unnecessary orders, however, led them to fear that they were to be wholly prevented from putting on their marks, and thus be mingled together with sects bearing, like other religious sects, mutual hatred to each other. Nay, worse than that, that they should appear like pariahs, the utmost evil they know to dread. I am told by those whom I can trust, that no order was ever before issued for this compliance, nor was it thought heretofore prudent to venture upon giving one. Some time ago a native sepoy would sooner have been cut down than wear his drawers more than, or even as far as, halfway down the thigh, for drawers and breeches, or any clothes made up by tailors, are what they dislike. Their clothes are worn as they come from the loom. What we use as a pocket handkerchief, either checked or blue, is the Pallicat handkerchief *(Pallicat, or Pulicat, cotton comes from north of Madras)*, which is generally fastened by a string and is all the dress of the ordinary natives when they are at work (even though of good caste). By degrees they have been made to have their drawers approach nearer to the knee, and some of the regiments have got them below, like pantaloons, but this has all been done by hair breadth advances. You perhaps do not know that they wear no shoes or stockings. I have now been so long in the country that I have forgot what struck me at first but you would, I dare say, think it odd enough to see a field full of fine troops, elegantly dressed in all other respects, but barefooted. I used to think, as I saw them in the ranks, that they had black shoes and gaiters. Formerly, the Colonel of every Regiment dressed his own corps and, as he knew from what districts they were raised, he understood the honour that prevailed amongst them and acted accordingly. But Sir John Cradock, who came out as last Commander-in-Chief, and who is the weakest man I think that ever I spoke to, and as arrogant as he is weak, took it into his head to dress all the regiments himself, and to dress them all alike. Col. Agnew, the Adjutant General, is next to the General, and next below him (Deputy Adjutant) is Captain Pearce. Who he is I do not know, for I never saw him. But for the last two years have heard much of him and, from all I can find, he is a young man whose friends have mistaken his talents and made him an officer instead of a tailor, in which latter department he might have made a great fortune for he invents all sorts of new lapels and ornaments, caps etc. As those above him adopted his fancies, the sepoys have had innumerable changes in their dresses and cap. Here, unfortunately, the sepoys pay for these new whims out of their own pay, and they have been so expensive that some in the Regiment have been reduced to half their allowance by means of these abatements, and have been a good deal chagrined by it. The last unfortunate invention was a new cap of leather raised very high. The troops, upon first sight of these caps, objected to wearing them first as being of leather, which they liked not to wear on their heads, but chiefly on account of the shape which they said was exactly like that of a drummer' s. As the drummers are pariahs, they were induced to believe that the putting on of these caps was the first step towards overturning all their ancient religious practices.

The imprisoned sons of Tippoo, and their adherents, who are allowed a great sum annually, availed themselves of this ferment to bribe, and to persuade, the sepoys to rebellion, but it was naturally to be expected that such persons would exert all their influence to regain their former power, and such an opportunity ought not to have been given to them.[8] The officers of the regiments, who delivered out these caps, were in some cases hissed at and hooted by the troops, an expression of resentment which was quite new and unexpected but, if the caps had been wisely suppressed, and a few of the worst of the men punished, the affair might have ended. The commanders, however, did no such thing. They insisted that the caps should be sent to all the regiment. They were accordingly taken to another set who, one and all, took them off their heads and trampled on them. Nine of the ringleaders, as they were called, were brought down to Madras and passed publicly through the streets in irons, destined to receive the most dreadful military punishment, but as the commanders began to perceive that they were somewhat unlucky in their designs and, being unwilling at the same time to admit their mistake, they did, I think, the worst thing they could do. They ordered the offending regiment to march down, and put them on duty in the Fort (to keep guard, as they do about the Tower or St James's Park). There they appeared all day, in every part, without their caps, and with red handkerchiefs round their heads. This was designed as a measure of mortifying them but I fear that, on the contrary, it was the means of creating in their minds a horrible disgust of us, and to lay them open to suggestions from those who are our enemies. A thousand Hindus for one European pass each gateway of the Fort. All these men are bound by the same prejudices as the sepoys are; indeed they are the same people; brothers or fathers may be, and their firmness in rejecting such badges would be to them a matter of triumph rather than regret. Here, however, these men remained for a long time but, meanwhile, their accumulated grievances; some real, some fancied, stirred them up to a fury producing the horrible affair at Vellore, of which you will have doubtless heard too much before you read this account of its rise.

8 The contribution of Tipu Sultan's family to the mutiny is debated. Two well researched Indian PhD theses give opposing views, that of Maya Gupta; *Lord William Bentinck in Madras 1803–1807* (1969 & Capital Publishers 1986) being in favour, and that of P. Samuelraj; *The Vellore Mutiny and Related Agitations 1806–07* (1971) being against. See references in note 3, page 297.

The fate of the Regiment made to do duty in this disgraceful manner at Madras, and the nine men in irons awaiting a most severe punishment, was made use of by the sons of Tippoo, who have been kept prisoner in the Palace at Vellore since the taking of Seringapatam *(Sriringapattam)*, and served to ripen a design that had long been formed. A conspiracy was formed by the sepoys to murder all the Europeans and take possession of that fort. One of the sepoys gave information of this conspiracy to some of the officers, but they were so overconfident as to distrust the information. They called a few of the native officers up, and enquired of them into the truth of the affair but they, as was natural, denied it. The informer told the officers that it was denied by the native officers because they were themselves concerned in it and they, in return, said that this poor man was mad. Their words, by some infatuation, were trusted and no precautions were taken. On the night of July 9, after the officers and everybody had retired to rest, a dreadful howling was heard and this was followed by firing in all directions. Some of the officers rose and went out; others, in despair, hid themselves, and the women and children ran across the place whilst the shots were flying in all directions. Colonel Fancourt, a mild, religious and worthy man who commanded, was covered with wounds and died. Two other officers, merely by accident passing through the town, were shot through 20 times over in their palanquins. The Paymaster and, in short, all the Englishmen that could be found were killed. Two young officers were shot in a bath where they had concealed themselves. They fired into the barracks where the English soldiers (the 69th) were asleep and, in short, spent the whole night in murder and plunder. They took down the British flag and hoisted the Mussulmans' flag, which was flying till nine in the morning but, meanwhile, the English officers had contrived to send a message to Colonel Gillespie who fortunately came with extraordinary speed to the assistance of those who remained alive, the chief of whom were a company of the 69th, who had taken possession of a place over one of the gateways, and kept possession of it by extraordinary exertions. They were firing their last charges when Colonel Gillespie appeared. They drew him up; the gates were opened, and all the insurgents put to the sword. At least 600 sepoys were instantly killed. Some officers are said to have cut down 20 or 30 with their own hands. It was dreadful slaughter and none were spared; in such a desperate case perhaps nothing else could be done. The British flag was replaced, and a stop put to the proceedings, but a plan had been formed with a design to murder the Europeans both here, and in every station hereabout.[9] Two days afterwards, an attempt of the same kind was made at Hyderabad, a place many days journey distant, and in several places the symptoms of the rebellion appeared at the same time, and indeed it is said that the plan was long ago formed. The affair at Hyderabad was put a stop to by the howling of the women who, when their husbands rose in the night to perpetrate their designs under an idea that the Europeans would finally prevail, raised such hideous yells as alarmed the garrison and prevented them. Some time afterwards they made a second attempt and, upon a signal, a whole company took off their leather stocks and trod them under their feet. The next company were proceeding to do the same when the spirited conduct of Captain Smithies, a young officer, so intimidated them that they took up their stocks again but, upon retiring from the parade, so far recovered their ill-humour as to hoot and hiss. A committee was sent from hence to Vellore to enquire into the particulars of the affair there. You will probably see their reports sooner than we shall for, though we are so near, and though many people are terrified to a great degree by their apprehensions of danger, no particulars are made public. All we hear is the private accounts of people who were present, and have escaped, but all that can be suppressed is, for indeed the rulers may well be ashamed of inciting so horrid a measure by ignorance and idle arrogance and one, too, of so mischievous a nature that years may not do away the consequences of it. Hitherto every officer with a handful of Europeans led an army of sepoys with confidence. The sepoys have now learned to turn their arms upon their commanders and, by so doing, the rest have obtained redress of their grievances, though a few have been sacrificed. The melancholy state of things was such that all sorts of concessions have been made to the sepoys.

9 Colonel Gillespie of the 19th Dragoons was something of a violent desperado. His summary execution of large numbers of sepoys took no account of the probability that some of them were innocent, and not party to the mutiny. After the mutiny was over his reputation took on mythical proportions, and many of his supposed exploits in the raising of the siege were greatly exaggerated.

One of the sons of Tippoo alone appears to have been implicated in this attempt, however they now no longer inhabit the magnificent palace of Vellore. They were all brought down, to the number of thirteen and a few of their chief women, and put on board a ship prepared for the purpose about a week ago, and I suppose are now in Bengal, there to be kept at less expense, and in a stricter state of confinement. Their wives the Begums, the children, a numerous train, are to proceed to Bengal by land and the Palace at Vellore is to be applied to some other purpose, perhaps as a college.

Nothing could exceed the timidity of the Governor during this affair. He is said to have ridden round his garden for exercise, being afraid to venture into the roads, and all concerned are trying to shift the blame from one to another. I cannot guess who will appear to be the culprit when the accounts reach you! The lowest will be likely to bear the burden of blame. The Commander in Chief blames Col Agnew; he blames Captain Pearce. The C. in C. says he did read the orders, though he is contradicted. A censure has been published in orders of the native officers. It is said that they ought to have come forward and to have communicated to Government the dissatisfaction of the troops about the shaving and the caps. Now nothing can be more unjust than this, for how could they think of coming formally forward to communicate a thing so well known. They would have been punished if they had, and the answer would have been; "we know it; we are putting a whole regiment to public scorn by making them do duty without caps, and we have nine men in irons." Mary has got a copy of poor Mrs Fancourt's narrative which she wrote after she had recovered herself, but she was for a fortnight in a state of stupor. She is a very quiet innocent woman. She was for some time concealed with her children under a bed, and afterwards in a stable, as she and some other ladies and children were missing for a while. The first accounts we received stated that they had been killed. The unhappy sepoys, however, furious as they were, killed no woman. They met the wife of an officer in the dark, flying with her child in her arms. They were firing, but the first who saw her distinctly cried out, "it is a woman, don't touch her," and on going near her and perceiving her terror and weakness, he took her to an outhouse in a retired part, and sent his wife to nurse her child for her. Is it not extraordinary to think of such tenderness in the midst of fury? And is it not a pity that a being with such a heart could not, (however he had been misled), have been spared from the general slaughter that followed? One child alone they killed. It was a dreadful murder; a murder intended as a piece of revenge, and unhappily the revenge fell by mistake on the wrong person, if indeed any parents could have deserved such a dreadful calamity. To this affair hangs a story.

A young officer, with the carelessness too common with young men in India, was amusing himself with shooting and, not perceiving everything around him but black men and trees, he did not take great pains to call out, and shot an infant belonging to a wedded pair. He was seized, however, or at least so noticed as to be complained off to the regiment, but as the military men here are extremely averse to all judicial proceedings, instead of sending the officer down to take a public trial, they first held what I'm told they had no right to do, a court martial to ascertain whether or not he ought to be sent before a grand jury. They decided that he ought not as he did not shoot with a design to kill the child. The parents of the child, however, were much dissatisfied with this easy way of dismissing a man whom they considered as the murderer of their child. I do not know the name of this officer but, in the darkness of the night at this fatal time, the parent of this infant met a young man, a Lieutenant Ely and his wife, with her child in her arms and, mistaking him for the young officer who had shot his child, he killed him before his wife's face and then, taking the child from her arms, shot it crying "blood for blood."

Mrs Fancourt is a daughter of a Mr Farrer, an attorney, perhaps you may remember the name of Farrer in large letters at the high house in Lincoln's Inn Fields, at the corner of Queen Street. Poor woman, she picked up a ball that was shot into the room whilst she, with her children and the maids, were concealed under a bed. It came close to her.

I wish I could know who you intend to send us out for Governor *(General)*. We have heard Lord St John, and we have heard the Lord John Townshend; anything would be good for a change. This is dreadful; nothing but intrigue and contrivance. I question, for my part, whether a chicken in the government house ever gets its throat cut by the cook in the ordinary way. I dare say they are all circumvented by some extraordinary contrivance. Lady William

(Bentinck), I have told you before, is a friendly girl to sit and sew with you. You would like her; that is whilst you believed her sincere. She is very simple, very weak I should say, and has had a miserable education. There is not a man in the house; nothing but a set of boys, for the most part very ill taught, and these are employed to go everywhere to enquire all sorts of family anecdotes, and these they retail to Lady William, and she to her husband. What is worse, he acts upon them without considering that the information these spies give is not once in ten times true, not only because they fail in veracity but that these people are too cunning for them. There is not a soul here who does not understand their plan. Those who have anything to conceal are fully careful to do it, and those who wish to mislead easily form a contrivance to fill the enquirers with falsehoods, well knowing the purposes for which they go about it. Lady William herself is not inactive. She sees people all day long, and has not one pursuit but that she makes enquiries about private families. So a set of clacking women go from house to house to collect and convey all sorts of idle stories about men and their wives, or rather I should say in many cases, children and their wives or sweethearts. She is rather pleasant, as a quiet ill-educated simple young woman, but silliness with an attempt to be politic is quite ridiculous and, something worse, very mischievous.
September 22nd.

I have this night been informed that a ship was in sight at sunset and that it was supposed to be the Sarah Christiana, which is that by which I am to send this. I therefore hasten to close it having now the happiness to say that we are all well, after having passed four months of the most severe weather I ever experienced in India.

On the 10th September, which was Biss's and Mary's birthday, we had a grand gala. Twenty seven sat down to dinner. I suppose they will tell you about it, and that you know that their birthdays fall upon the same day. The young men go out upon their surveys in the beginning of December, and heaven knows when we may see them again. They have improved to the satisfaction of their teachers, which I rejoice at for they were a very fine set of young men, and this institution is the very best thing which Lord William has done, as it furnishes employment, of a most goodly kind, for a set of men too often idle or worse.

From Elisabeth Gwillim to her sister Hetty. November 1806

I wrote seven sheets of paper in form of a letter to you. I was about six weeks in writing it, during all that time imagining that the Sarah Christiana would sail. My letter has been on board this fortnight, or these three weeks, yet the vessel is still in the roads and I am not sure that she will sail even with the fleet, for she is the ship destined to convey the accounts of government, and they are not ready. However my letter is in it, and cannot be recalled, and I trust you will have it as soon as the rest. The fleet is not yet come in; God knows when it may.

We saw Mr Graham; he dined with us; I'm glad he brought things safe, but there is no reliance on these young men. He slept here one night and Richard lent him a change of Regiment pantaloons, and he went on board and never sent them back.

We have now been in mourning (the most sorrowful I ever wore) nearly 4 months and I conclude that you have sent us out some mourning *(clothes)*. We must keep it by us for court mournings and compliments. I hope that I shall have nothing more serious to use it for. If it should come soon, it would yet be very useful to us, having such difficulty to get anything. I have been a perfect slave to try to keep myself in something respectable, and fit for the memory of one I loved as much as anything on earth, but it has taken all my time.

I send a bag of seeds which you will please send to Mr Whitley as they contain many seeds which I should be glad to see growing. I send the bag of seeds by a Mr Hoseason, who is going hence with a large fortune. They have so much to carry for themselves that I cannot ask them to take anything else home for me, but he will take the bag to Trincomalee in Ceylon, where ships are waiting for the remainder of the fleet and will then deliver it to them. I have besides added a packet of flower tree seeds, and some others fit for a present to anybody you may chance to give them to, and who wants them whilst they are fresh. You never told me you wanted them, or I would always send them, but indeed they are of little use to any but those in the profession, for private gentlemen's gardeners would either give them away, or never take pains to raise them.

From Mary Symonds to her sister Hetty. November 1806.

The account of the sad event of our mother's death was received on 27 June, and at the same time Sir Thomas Strange arrived in India after his unworthy and unsuccessful journey. He brought out the news of his mother's death, which happened after he left her, and which he heard a few hours before he sailed. When they came to India old Lady Strange was in good health, and quite flushed with spirits in the supposed success and greatness of her sons, the eldest of whom was married to the daughter of a great Minister (Lord Melville); rich and powerful. The second, a chief justice, and the third, whom she had not seen from a boy and consequently knew very little of, was a Colonel in the Army. All this, from so humble beginning as hers, might well be supposed to fill her heart with joy and pride, and how terrible must the great change have been which she just lived to see. A visit, which her son the Colonel paid her, must have convinced a woman of her understanding that he could not be respected by anyone; an idiot and a sot. The eldest son, and great support of all, became a bankrupt and forced to quit his country at 53 years old, and Sir Thomas, having quitted his employment most dishonourably in hopes of regaining the wealth his brother had wasted, became the tool of a weak government whose paltry or wicked vices he intended to forward by Lord Melville's interest. His object was defeated by the disgrace of the Minister, himself on the verge of losing his employment and obliged to return disgracefully, the bearer himself of a public letter from his sovereign, addressed to the courts in India, an expression of high disapprobation of his quitting the appointment his King had honoured him with. What a melancholy parting must this mother and son have had, poor woman! It was too much for her; she sunk under it and died in three days afterwards.

Sir Thomas Strange is the most altered man in the world, since his brother came out to India, and he now seems to be running headlong into all the follies he can think of. He is just going to be married to a girl of features ugly enough, God knows, but he being 52, she has persuaded him that his resistless charms have won her heart, and she had fallen so much in love with him during a month she has been staying at his house, that he is obliged to take compassion on her young heart and marry her.

She is the daughter of Mr William Burroughs, the youngest of two who accompanied him here on his way to Bengal. He left this place a few days ago with his eldest daughter, leaving the love struck lass behind him. She is under the protection of Lady William Bentinck till the happy union takes place. The Misses Burroughs have been dashing about London in a great deal of showy, but I suppose not a very good, company for the father came to India a barrister about 15 years ago. He never practised his profession at all, but he made a large fortune entirely by gaming; it is said above a hundred thousand pounds. This, like other ill-gotten pelf *(money dishonourably obtained)* soon melted, for he went home only seven years ago with all this money, lost every penny of it in the same way he gained it, and is now very much in debt and come out here (to the shame of those who appointed him) a judge on the Bengal establishment here, with these two girls absolutely brought to market to sing and play to any stupid booby that has got a mass of money to lose at hazard, and to marry themselves off as well as they can.

We have had no news from England, either public or private, since April, an unusually long time to be without an overland dispatch, and we are all very anxious to hear what is going on under your new administration, and what new appointments are intended for India. We hope to hear of some man of sense to be sent out to govern this important country and, whomsoever he may be, he will find employment enough for his interest, exertions and abilities in undoing, if that be possible, the mischief the foolish obstinate people have done before him. Your newspapers will of course be filled with accounts of the dreadful disasters in this country, particularly the massacre at Vellore. With this letter I shall send you some papers which will be curious to yourself and your friends. One or two, if I can procure them, as I think I shall, of the ridiculous orders of government which principally occasioned the mutiny. The discontent of the troops has been quite general throughout the country. Inexpression and obstinacy, and extreme weakness, characterise our government and all its measures. The concessions now made to the natives may probably be more mischievous than even the tyrannous orders themselves. The Indian Army is formed partly of Hindus and partly of Musselmans. They have, until this time, shown great attachment to the English. They submitted quietly to every regulation, and fought our battles faithfully and well, and this because a few harmless prejudices of theirs have not before been interfered with. The Hindus think themselves polluted by the touch of leather and the Musselmans, it is well known, abominate the hog and everything belonging to it, yet the wise heads here must needs contrive, either from want of employment or want of brains, to make a new turban in which a piece of pig' s skin was introduced, and a stock of cow' s leather, and with this turban an order was given out to inform the sepoys to wear it. The Musselmans objected to the pig's skin, and the Hindus to the form of the turban, which they said resembled that of a pariah, or outcaste. They remonstrated, but were punished and commanded to comply. Another order was given immediately after this, in which it was directed that uniformity in the looks of the sepoys should be preserved; as much as possible they were to cut their whiskers for that purpose, and the Hindus were to appear without marks on their foreheads. Now to tell a Hindu that he shall not mark his forehead is much the same thing as if you were forbid to use the sign of the cross in baptism, besides the timid fears of these poor people and their superstitions. They were persuaded at one time that the English intended to convert them all to Christianity by force and, at another, that they intended to make them and their families slaves forever. Finding this was not enforced, they have gradually complied. Had these orders for the dress of the army been given to the officers commanding the regiments, to be brought forward at their discretion, possibly in the course of a few years they might have been submitted to, or at least the principal part of them. But no, these weak obstinate people would take no advice, the order was issued and to be enforced at once. The poor natives, persuaded that this strict edict was firm, determined to oppose and resist this thing that they so much dreaded.

There is no doubt but a general massacre of the English was intended throughout the country. To talk of cutting or pulling the Mussulman's whiskers is the greatest insult that can be offered to him, and the folly of requiring uniformity among the faces of a regiment is surely the most ridiculous thing ever heard of. If I was to write volumes, I could not relate half the ridiculous things which have been done here lately, in direct opposition to all the advice of the most experienced persons in the country. Certain it is that the mischief done cannot be undone in many years perhaps, now our mutual confidence has been so completely shaken. Poor Mrs Fancourt's narrative I shall send you a copy of, and also another account given us by a gentleman who was at Vellore. Col and Mrs Fancourt, and indeed many, or almost all, the officers who were killed we knew, some only by sight but others intimately. The Governor has now ordered all the sepoys to wear what marks they please, and when they please. Now this is running into a contrary extreme for, although a general order frightened them, yet they have for many years been in the habit of complying with the request of their officers not to mark their faces till after parade.

If admitting that the sons of Tippoo (or princes as they choose to call them; though no princes at all) have been the sole cause of this shocking affair, then why were these men placed in such a situation as to suffer them to do so much mischief? Why were men left in such a wretched state? These sons had very large allowances which they had no use for. They were guarded by troops which had for the most part been in their father's service, and of course they were easily able to bribe with the gold they were so imprudently supplied with. You will see by a paper I send you how many British lives this business has cost, besides which two battalions of sepoys were utterly cut to pieces and destroyed. All this has been owing to the folly of changing the form of a sepoy's cap.

I hope long before this you have seen our friends Mr Keene and Mr Prosser, and that they have both succeeded in getting the packages ashore which they were so kind as to take charge of. Mr Tappenden, the master of the Airly Castle, took a large case containing an argus pheasant, and many loose feathers of the same kind of bird, and also of some other curious birds, which may be worn as ornaments. Should he have been so fortunate as to convey them safely to you, you will see a curiosity which may be amusing to yourself and your friends. However, should it be lost, do not be uneasy about it for Betsy has another complete bird lately given to her, which she will send whenever any opportunity offers, but at this time we do not know any person going home whom we could ask to carry so large a package.

I shall shortly send to you a portrait of my most excellent friend Richard Clarke, which I have done for his father, but it is his particular wish that it should be first sent to you, and that you will show it to whomsoever you think amongst your friends will feel an interest in his favour. If you have received my letters, which I wrote to you last March, you will not be surprised to hear that you have one friend in whose mind he is particularly desirous of attaining that interest. But lest you should not have received those letters, I shall make use of the same contrivance I did then, and on a separate half sheet repeat as nicely as I can scribble what I then said. You will be so good as to send the picture to Mrs James Clarke, when you have done with it, and she will forward it. I am sorry to say my representation is very far from doing him justice, for he has not much beauty of feature but a peculiar sweetness of expression which is very difficult to represent, at least too difficult for me to catch though I feel its influence, as everyone does who knows him. He is most wonderfully beloved, and is a proof that virtue must be pleasing to people of all descriptions. The picture has a dullness in the eyes, which he has not, and it is altogether greyer and heavier looking, which I believe is owing to his not being able to sit to me regularly, only at scraps and spare bits of time when perhaps he was tired with business. The mouth and lower part of the face is, however, somewhat better, but his eyes have a very slightly arch look when he speaks. He is a well-proportioned young man, and a good height; about 5 foot 10 inches. His disposition is infinitely better than that of any young man I ever knew, for he inherits all his father's generous benevolence yet, having much experience in the world in early life, he is rather more cautious and attentive to worldly concerns. His temper is sweetness itself; he is never ruffled by trifles or soured by misfortunes, but he has occasionally shown that he has no want of proper spirit. This temper is joined to a mind perfectly virtuous, and to habits of industry. He has avoided all the irregularities which young men usually fall into, and that most honourably to himself, for he has had the same opportunity and been exposed to the same temptations but, fortunately for him, not till he had had sufficient experience to see the folly, and great danger, of doing wrong. He has strong feelings; a very warm and tender heart, with extreme delicacy of manners. A great proof of their pleasingness is the high opinion those young men, his acquaintances, have of him. They consult him as a superior in the understanding and knowledge of business, yet with a confidence which his sweetness of temper naturally inspires. I do assure you I have never seen his equal, although I have seen many good and, unless we could visit with beings of a superior order, I am persuaded that in no one can be found less to condemn, or more worthy of admiration. I believe you will have a letter from him. Both he and Mr Biss threaten you with saucy ones too, in return for the rubs you gave them in your last letter to Mr Biss about their not writing regularly, and giving a proper account of the things you send them out.

Poor Richard was rather unlucky in his investment, having to this time never received the cloth for coats which you mentioned, or the cotton stockings and three pairs of the silk. We suppose you must have made a separate package of those articles, and sent them by some other ship. The box of prints also, which you have repeatedly mentioned, we have never received but, as the India ships have been so unlucky lately, we concluded that those things, and doubtless many letters, have been lost. The loss of the Lady Burgess, from the last fleet which arrived here, was a dreadful thing and, as she was the only ship for this place direct, she of course had all the Madras letters in her, except those which came by private hands. We thought ourselves very fortunate in having those you sent us by Mr Graham. They were a great relief to our minds, and it was particularly gratifying to us at that time to see a person who had seen you. We were very anxious for the arrival of our packages, as we had great difficulty in procuring any decent mourning *(clothes)*, having really been forced to wear wretched things. We have had muslin dyed in this country for every purpose, which looks well enough, but they have not thought of fixing the colour, so that our poor skins are every night as black as our gowns. The smell of the dye they use is very odious.

General Trent will no doubt be anxious to see the accounts of the Vellore business, and so I shall refer him to you for them as I cannot get them copied again in time. Richard has sent copies to his father, and I believe to his uncle. We have a very fine young man living with us at present; he has been with us these three months. His name is Gwetkins. He is from a very genteel family in Cornwall, and has been sincerely well educated in every respect. He is in the civil milieu and was introduced to us by a letter from Mr Cove, who is somehow distantly related to his father. His mother is a niece of Sir Joshua Reynolds. We are never without one, two or three young men in the house, nor indeed are any of the families in

Madras, for it is thought both dangerous and disreputable for any young man to live at a hostel. In general they take houses of their own as soon as they have appointments, but Sir Henry and Richard are both so fond of Mr Gwetkin that, although he has had a very good appointment some time, they cannot make their minds to part with him. Poor young Bennington, whom I mentioned to you in my former letters, is lately dead. He came out with Lord William Bentinck, which circumstance his parents thought would secure his fortune being made, but unfortunately they forgot that the poor boy had not abilities to do himself credit, and consequently their having him in the ship was rather a disadvantage, as it gave them an opportunity of knowing his weakness but too well, and they never paid him the slightest attention. Poor creature, he was both weak and faulty for, when he left us and joined his Regiment, he fell into all the follies of the young men he met with, and they are a very profligate set in his Regiment. He gambled, swore horridly and practised other vices; in short he destroyed his health, and came here such an object, so thin and ghostly, that he was a shocking spectacle, and quite a hopeless subject. For, by the account of Biss and Richard, he declared that all his sufferings had not improved his principles. He was so very ill that the surgeon who attended him advised his going to Penang, and there he died.

I have kept this letter open as usual,[10] till I am threatened with the packet closing without it, but I always like you to have the latest information possible. I have copied the paper I sent you last March, and enclose it lest you should wonder what I'm talking about in some parts of this, and I think you will not guess who is the person therein alluded to.

10 See note 14–1801, *page 32*.

Attached document.

On the morning of the 10th of July an insurrection, which had been planned and concerted between the Princes and the native troops of the garrison of Vellore, broke out in that fortress at half past five o'clock. The smallest alarm was not incited, or the least suspicion of what was to take place felt by any of the Europeans within the fort, till the moment of the mutiny taking place. From the result of long and careful enquiries it appears that the resolution to attempt the insurrection and to effect the massacre of all the Europeans on that night, was not taken till the evening of the same day, when the intention was communicated to the Palace, and to Prince Moizuddeen. Preparations were accordingly made, and the principal conspirators took the duty of the main guard, and the different guards. Most of the non-commissioned officers in charge of the different guards were those who were principles in the conspiracy, and bound by oath to attempt the establishment of a Mussulman government, and the destruction of all the Europeans. It appears that the men on the main guard were ordered, after being relieved, to load, by which precautions the greatest proportions of the men on the guard were loaded by 12 o'clock. The 1st Battalion: 1st Regiment had the whole of the guards. The 2nd Battalion; 23rd Regiment had been warned for a field day the following morning, and had been supplied with blunt cartridges. To be ready for the field day, a greater proportion of men than usual slept in the barracks, and it appears to have been from this circumstance that it was resolved by the principal conspirators that the attack should be made that night. The garrison guards consisted of 256, including non-commissioned men, and about 535 of the 23rd were in the barracks. Exclusive of the garrison guards, it may be estimated that the number of men of the 1st Battalion 1st Regiment on regimental duty, and off duty in the barracks, amounted to 103 men. There would therefore be about 900 men within the fort. As soon as the hour of two was struck, and in consequence of messages having passed from the main guards to the barracks, Subidar Sheikh Adam, and Jemidar Sheikh Hussain, of the 23rd awakened the sepoys of that corps, and ordered them to rise, arm, and fall in. Those who were dilatory, or questioned the motive for such orders, the Jemidar struck and abused. The regimental piquets were the first that got ready, and the two light companies of each corps. The two native officers broke open the regimental stores, brought out barrels of ball ammunition, and ordered the sepoys to fill their pouches. As soon as a sufficient number were ready and formed, they were marched down to the European barracks which they surrounded. About 2:30, a single musket was fired as a signal; at this instant the sepoys of the main guard, who had previously loaded, jumped up and fired upon the Europeans at the guard who were sleeping and, at the same instant, the sepoys who had surrounded the barracks commenced firing upon the men who were sleeping. The firing became immediately general and the drum of the main guard, which commenced beating to arms, was instantly silenced and the drummer shot. The three officers on the main guard were also instantly shot; the firing continued and the sepoys, having surrounded the houses of the officers, prevented them getting to the barracks. The Europeans in the barracks had only six rounds of cartridges in their pouches, and the sepoys had possessed themselves of their magazine, as well as the arsenal. A heavy and destructive fire was kept up upon the barracks through the windows. About five o'clock the sepoys had got 3 six pounders to bear upon the barracks, and opened a fire of round and grape shot, which did great execution. The Europeans being unable to get out of their barracks, the sepoys had entire possession of the fort, and were dispersed all over it and along the ramparts, firing in every direction and by word of command.

It might have been hoped that at daylight this horrid mutiny would have ceased, but the fire became much heavier and smarter. It now appears that about 6 o'clock the sepoys went to the Palace, and the native officers had a conference with Prince Moizuddeen, and Mahuddein received from his servants the Mysore flag, which was instantly hoisted, and the sepoys were presented with betel, rice etc etc etc in the palace. A great number of the palace adherents came into the fort, and assisted in the insurrection, and Mahomed Hussain, the son of Syed Ghaffer the celebrated General of Tippoo Sultan, assisted in working the guns and taking aim at the European barracks. The guards posted on the outside of the fort came in, and joined the insurgents. The men who had slept outside the fort the preceding night, about 500 men, as well as the sick from the hospital came in, and also great numbers of the inhabitants.

The sepoys had by this time put to death every European officer that was found, and plunder and liquor soon engaged their attention. Every house was plundered of every article in it, and the different cash chests in the public offices began to occupy their attention, most fortunately at this time. Entirely occupied with drink and plunder they soon became unruly, and inattentive to the instructions of the principal conspirators, and every attempt to make them unite for the purpose of securing the hill fort, and adopting the necessary precaution for maintaining the large fort, proved ineffectual. The sepoys and the inhabitants were promiscuously engaged in plundering the paymasters cash chest, and the different officers houses. The firing was still kept up upon the European barracks. It happened by fortunate accident that Mr Jones, Surgeon, Mr Dean, Assistant Surgeon, Lieut and Adjutant Ewing, Lieut Mitchell, and Captain MacLachlan, driven by the fire of the sepoys out of their own houses, assembled in one house and, by disarming a small guard posted at Lieut and Adjutantt Ewing's, they were enabled to defend themselves from the fire of the sepoys till, greater numbers attacking them, they were driven out of their house and succeeded in getting into the European barracks. After getting in, they headed the men of the 69th, made a dash out and, formed, they got upon the ramparts which they soon cleared, and took down the Mysore flag. In this operation one man who had ascended the flagstaff was shot from the outside of the fort. The 69th soon got possession of the gates, and kept them. About this time the alarm was spread that the cavalry were coming. The sepoys, who were busy plundering, threw down their arms and made their escape through the sally port by hundreds. About 10 o'clock, Colonel Gillespie with the advance squadron of cavalry arrived, but having no guns with it, nothing can be done until the remainder of the regiment came up. The Colonel was drawn up with ropes over the walls into the fort, and took the command of the 69th. The remainder of the 19th Regiment, and all the native cavalry, soon after arrived, blew open the gates, and charged into the fort. Very little opposition was made; a smart fire for a few minutes was kept up, but soon ceased. The fort was of course instantly recovered, and the barbarities committed during the morning by the insurgents exposed. The following unfortunate victims to their brutal rage were cruelly, and inhumanely, murdered. The sick Europeans in hospital were also cruelly massacred. Every officer's house was plundered, and the survivors had nothing left but the clothes on their backs. A few officers lived outside the fort. At the commencement of the mutiny, Captain Stevenson of the 23rd fortunately galloped off to Arcot to communicate the alarm of what was taking place at Vellore. His report happily procured the assistance of the cavalry under Colonel Gillespie, as before stated. Lieutenant Colonel Forbes, and Major Trotter who also lived outside, finding they could not get into the fort, went up to the hill fort with Colonel Forbes's family, and were joined by a few other officers. The guards upon the hill received them, and behaved steady, though it is now ascertained some of them were in the secret. Immediate examples were made of some of the insurgents taken in arms, and many were cut up by the cavalry on the outside.

The number of men of both Corps, computed to be killed on the morning of 10 July, is 500 men.

List of officers killed and wounded on the 10th July.

Colonel Fancourt	Commanding Officer
Mr Smith	Paymaster
Mr Mann	Deputy Commissary

Lieut Popham
Lieut Ely
Captn Miller
Lieut O'Reilly
Lieut Smart
Lieut Tichborne
Major Armstrong
Lieut Col McKerras
Captn Willison
Lieut Hinship
Lieut Jolly

<u>Wounded</u>
Captn Bairow
Capt Maclachlan
Lieut Mitchell
Lieut Cutcliff

Several attempts were made to get a party of sepoys to go and secure possession of the hill fort, but owing to their being engaged in plunder, they could not be collected. It appears there were but few native offices within the fort during the mutiny, most of them having gone up to the hill fort.

The insurrection appears to have been planned and matured for two months previous to its actually breaking out. The attack had been resolved upon to take place twice previously, but the day had been changed.

Letters of 1807 and 1809 and Commentary

Commentary

There is only one letter for this year, dated the 4th March, from Mary to her sister Hetty. In this she refers immediately to the situation in which Sir Henry Gwillim has found himself. There is mention of various detailed letters and descriptions, none of which appear in this collection, and of the political and social problems in which Gwillim has become embroiled. There can be little doubt that this has become a dominant factor in the lives of the whole family. Nevertheless she moves on swiftly to comment on the array of goods and foods sent from England by the remarkable Hetty, whose life must have been ruled by constant shopping, wrapping and packing, or at least the supervision of this. The desire in India for an array of choice goods from England was inexhaustible, and they all assuredly had a sweet tooth judging by the interest in candied almonds, little white caraways; barley sugar; and orange candied chips; peppermint lozenges and so on. It is no surprise, therefore, that even in his forties Sir Henry had no teeth. One wonders about the dental situation in the women.

It then seems that Mary stepped into her elder sisters shoes by becoming involved in botanical drawing. She made an accurate image of the newly acquired Calumba root, which was of general interest to the botanists local to her, but also because of its medicinal qualities. She seems to have been rather pleased with herself about this. Otherwise Mary talks of gifts she is sending home; mostly small pieces of jewellery, and most particularly a small heart for Hetty's daughter.

And so ends 1807, with just this one letter from Mary and none from Elizabeth, whose last letter was to her sister in November 1806. As Elizabeth died a year later at the house in Pammal, in December 1807, it is easy to suppose that she was ill, and unable to write. There is no mention of her indisposition in Mary's 1807 letter, however, and in fact there is a comment referring to how much Betsy was 'delighted to see the almonds', which implies that she was then well. It is more probable that her letters were so full of the troubles besetting her husband that they have been removed from the collection, being a somewhat sensitive subject and not of general concern. Nor would they have been relevant to it, the main interest of the letters being the two sisters' experience of, and affection for, India.

Elizabeth's death seems to have been quite sudden. She had from time to time complained of fever and the ague which she treated with cinchona bark, and it seems probable that she had relapsing malaria and eventually, when in a low state, succumbed to this. It was, after all, the biggest killer of the British in India at that time. On the other hand, in May 1806 she reported abdominal pain radiating to the right shoulder associated with itching, and so perhaps she had gallstones or some other biliary complaint. This was more than a year before her death, however, and may well have been incidental.

Letters

From Mary Symonds to her sister Hetty 4th March 1807

I wrote you last month a pretty long letter by Mr Ball, a worthy and much injured man, who I hope will arrive safe in England and succeed in obtaining redress for the wrongs he has sustained under this most arbitrary and oppressive government. He will be able to tell you some particulars of us, and of the situation Sir Henry stands in. He is the only man who has spirit to oppose the measures he can only but condemn. I have written a long letter to the Thoburns, giving them as circumstantial an account as the limits of a letter would admit of, and I shall send to you all the papers on the subject I can collect copies of and, as your communications will of course be mutual, I shall consider it matter of little consequence to whom they are addressed.

In my last, I had the pleasure of acknowledging all the packages you had so carefully and nicely collected and packed for us. We have dressed three of the hams, which are excellent, and the confectionery is all come very dry and good, being packed in bottles. Betsy was delighted to see the almonds, which are the first we have received dry, and she and Sir Henry are pecking at them every day in so much that there is a great appearance of a 'drying' wind having found its way into the bottle. The only things which have suffered in carriage are some bottles of Capilaric, only two of which arrived whole, but that is quite immaterial as we have very little use for it, and the natives understand making beautiful clear syrup which answers the same purpose. Betsy made presents of some of the pieces of muslin, which were very much admired, and all the gowns are neat and elegant. The white beads are a beautiful imitation of cornelian, and the blue and black ones are a very pretty and pleasing variety. All the head dresses appear very pretty but we have not yet worn many of them. The caps, two or three of which Betsy has tried, are very genteel and becoming. The mobs are much worn here, but I cannot say I am an admirer of them for I have seen but one woman who looked well in them, and she is a very handsome and dashing looking lady, a Lady Ogilvie lately come out. The little worked caps and shirts, both made and unmade, I like much; they are so light and so easily done up. The tiara and bands are very pretty, and what I like very much. One of the grey nets I put on as soon as they were unpacked, and have worn it every day since. I am now writing in it. The shoes fit exactly, and I hope the man will not lose the measures, as a straw shorter would not fit, and I do not like them too big. Richard Clarke is much pleased with his clothes, and the soap you have sent is very acceptable. Pray add a bar or two of common mottled soap to the next packages and, if you can without inconvenience, send a dozen or so of bottled gooseberries and currants. They will be an extraordinary treat. The cranberries all come beautiful, and most acceptable they are. I have only opened one pot of your preserves, which was a strawberry pot, and excellent, but I think stone pots are preferable to the white ones, and the preserves which come in them are higher flavoured, and the risk of breaking is not so great. Your old walnuts, and a pot of brown mushrooms, are all we have opened yet;

both are as good as possible. In future do not trouble yourself to send so many varieties of sugarplums for, although they look very pretty and are very ornamental to the table, yet as those which have fruit in them do not keep very well, such as the barbary sugarplums, and as the coloured ones are not admired in flavour, they are scarcely worth the trouble. The desirable things are Scotch caraway; almonds candied, little white caraways; barley sugar; and orange and cinnamon candied chips; peppermint; tolu, and refined liquorice lozenges; raspberry vinegar; mango, cherry and raspberry brandy, and brandy cherries.

I have lately been favoured by Dr Berry[1] with his permission to make the first drawing of a plant which is quite new; this being the first that was ever possessed by an European. This is the Calumba, the root of which is a very fine medicine. A Mr Fortin, who commanded a trading vessel, was requested by Dr Anderson and Dr Berry to procure for them, from the Mozambique, a piece of the Calumba root in the state in which it grows, for the usual method of preparing it for traders is by cutting the root into small pieces, or thin slices, and drying them. Mr Fortin procured, from the people of Madagascar, a large piece of the root nearly a foot long and, when it arrived here, it had the appearance of a dried yam, and it looked so dry and dead that they had not a hope that it would vegetate. However, being fond of experiments of this nature, they determined to put it into a tub of mould to see if it would be affected by it when, to their great surprise and satisfaction, after some time it put forth a green shoot which grew very rapidly. The leaves resembled cucumber leaves, and from the joint of each leaf there grew a cluster of very small flowers which, unfortunately, the botanists found to be all male flowers so there is no fruit, but I believe they say it is a Bryonia. I shall, however, get it accurately described and will send home, by the next ships, a copy of my drawing of the root, leaf and flowers, which you will have the goodness to show to Mrs Whitby and at leisure take a copy if she wishes it, and then present it to Dr Sims. All in good time, you will say, as I do not intend to send it till the next ships,

1 Dr Berry was superintendent of the Nopalry – Prickly Pear plantation – for cultivating rubber plants and the cochineal insect, in collaboration with Dr James Anderson, his uncle.

but my reason is this; Dr Berry has had a drawing made of the root only by a native, and this he intends to send to England by these ships, but it is so very ill done that it gives no idea of the thing either in form, colour or texture. However, as it will be thought a great curiosity by naturalists, it is possible Dr Sims may already have seen or heard of it.

We have no good opportunity of send anything home by these ships, as I do not know any one family who are to sail by them. I believe that passengers are all people from the interior, with whom we are unacquainted. I therefore think you will receive nothing from us, except two or three little curiosities which are not worth mentioning, but I give them to Mr Lee as he wishes to convey something for us. There is a red heart and a pair of drops for Nancy Green; a cross and a pair of drops for you, and a heart, which was presented to me and is made of petrified tamarind tree, of which curious substance I also send you a specimen in the rough state. Mr Biss has been for some time stationed at the village where it is found, and a great number of trees may be seen there, quite whole and perfect in their form. He sent two pieces of it, and I have an account of it, which was collected and written by a Mr Fallofield who is the Resident at Pondicherry, near which place the village is situated. I will send you this account as it may amuse you, and it is curious. The place is very much infested with tigers and leopards. Mr Biss has seen several and one, the other day, crossed the road on which he was riding within three yards of him. They are very bad neighbours, but there never was known an instance of a tiger venturing into a tent, and in the daytime they keep to the woods entirely, except when compelled by thirst they come down to the edge of a river or tank to drink. Mr Biss is vastly indignant about a lecture his sister sent out to him for not writing. He is a curious fellow, for he expects to have long letters from all his friends, filled with most interesting particulars, and to return short ones. My gentleman is so touchy, so very tender, that it is high treason but to find that anything he does is not what you wish it to be. He is a good soul, but I believe he will be spoiled, for everybody loves him wherever he goes, and I find the Pondicherry ladies are setting their caps at him mightily. I wrote him a long letter the other day, and he returned me a small sheet of paper with four short paragraphs, three of which were messages to be delivered to other people, and the one which was to me was only an acknowledgement of my letter. So I sat down immediately and paraphrased his epistle, and sent it to him as a letter, and now he writes to Richard that I have put a sad quiz upon him, and sent him the shape and form of his own letter word for word. He seems to be a little annoyed by it, but he is not angry, as I know he would have been if I had used any other method of reproving him. He says he is getting on extremely well with his survey, and has done twice as much as is required of him in the time he has been at work, which of course is very creditable to him. I am most happy in hearing of your having such charming companions as his two sisters for, from all I hear of them, I am convinced they must be excellent fine girls. I wish the eldest, who is so healthy and lively, would take it into her head to pay her brother a visit. She would be a great comfort to him and, if she wished to marry, I will answer for her having plenty of opportunities of good young men with fair prospects, which it is ever in the power of a good wife (who begin early to take care for him) to realise. I shall write to Mrs Biss this time to thank her for her kind letter to me, and her excellent hams and pickles. I wrote to Miss Biss by the last ships and, I assure you, glad enough I was of the opportunity, for I have ever wished for a correspondent in Hereford. I know enough of the place and people to make me relish an account of their proceedings, and I shall feel a strong attachment to it as the place in which the happiest days of my life have been spent, and as having more or less real beauty to recommend it, which I never was truly sensible of until the last visit I paid, when I looked at each object (as I then thought) probably for the last time. It will at last be a long, long interval between my last look and any next, should I have the happiness to see that hour, as I hope and trust in God I one day shall.

You make me most happy by the pleasing accounts you send me of your dear little girl *(presumed to be Mary James, Hetty's only daughter)*. I cannot tell you how much I long to see her sweet face, and to be known and loved by her. I find among my treasures a little heart as white and true as her own, and therefore I have put it up with the others for her.

Final letter of the collection

From Sir Henry Gwillim to his sister in law, Hetty James.

15th January 1809 Cape Town, Cape of Good Hope

With much difficulty have we gotten to this place after a tedious passage of 11 weeks and two days, in the course of which we encountered a most tremendous gale which lasted three days and three nights, and for nearly four and twenty hours we had little expectation that we should be able to weather it. We left Madras in company with eight other Indiamen under convoy of the Albion, man-of-war of seventy-four guns, but we have not seen or heard of one of them since the gale.[1] Should we get no intelligence soon, they must either be lost, or have been so damaged as to be obliged to put into some port to repair. We suffered much in ship and cargo to the amount, I am told, of thirty thousand pounds but, happily for us of, our injuries were not such as to be irreparable at sea, so as to dissuade us from prosecuting our voyage. We left Madras roads on the 25th of October; the storm began on the evening of the 19th of November, and we anchored in this bay on Thursday afternoon the 12th instant, and came ashore the next morning. Our ship is the Phoenix. We like our captain and officers much, and I like this place as far as relates to climate and situation, but everything is most extravagantly dear and, should we be detained here long, which I think very probable, I must be ruined. The common passage from Madras to the Cape is eight weeks or thereabouts. Dick Clarke and Pol, who are with me, are both very well. Though exposed to such severities during the storm, we none of us suffered at all in our health. It is now the height of summer at this place, and we have abundance of fruit and vegetables. I pay for each of us sixteen shillings a day for board and lodging, besides other expenses. Would to God I were safe in England, though

1 Three East Indiamen were lost; the Lord Nelson, the Glory and the Experiment.

I have much that is disagreeable to encounter when I get there. What my enemies are doing I know not; I hear from no one. Not a letter have I had, except two or three of no consequence, for above a twelvemonth. I never was more anxious in my life to hear from my friends than I am now, and I never had more reason to be so. I shall hope to find a letter from someone when I get to Saint Helena.

You, I hope are well. I shall be most glad to see you again, for I can never forget the kindnesses I have had from you and James. How is little Hetty? The poor Bishop of Ely I see is dead: it was the first thing I saw upon turning over the English papers upon my arrival at this place. My losses have been very severe of late.

I enclose a bill upon Messr's Coutts and Co for a hundred pounds, drawn by a Lieut. Tilly Kettle in my favour, and endorsed by me to James.[2] This is the first of the set; the second I put in the Preston, one of the ships I left Madras with, and from which we were parted in the gale: the third I have with me. A letter of advice also accompanies it.

I should think that we shall scarcely be able to get to England before the end of May. We must stay here some time in the hope of being joined by the other ships, or some of them. We cannot go without convoy, and the Admiral will not give convoy to a single ship. We have indeed found an Indiaman here; the Wexford; from Bombay. She has been here more than a month, but in the present state of things that circumstance is not likely to be of much use to us. Our own ship must stay some time, as she wants further repairs, and some of her cargo is so much damaged that I imagine it must be sold for the benefit of the insurers. I have thoughts of making an excursion into the country

Pray remember me very kindly at Brompton. I hope they are all well. It will be a great pleasure to me to see them again. I love them dearly; I feel their value every day more and more.

2 This Tilly Kettle, who had paid Sir Henry Gwillim £100, is unknown. By coincidence it is the same name as a well-known portraitist who painted in India, but who had died in 1786.

Assure James of my kindest regards, and deep sense of the many friendly acts he has done me. Pol joins in love with, my dear Hetty, yours affectionately,

To Mrs James.

January 17th. I send this by the Rose, a Botany Bay ship; but as the Camel, which is a store ship and armed, will sail in two or three days, that should seem to be the safer conveyance. I have taken out the bill and letter of advice, and will put them into the Camel's packet.

Put the accompanying letter for my brother into the Post Office.

The Background of Politico-Legal Tension

After the Regulating Act of 1773, Calcutta (Bengal) introduced a Supreme Court of Judicature. Madras, meanwhile, continued with the Mayoral Court system under the control of the East India Company until 1801 when, as a consequence of a growing population, a Crown-appointed Supreme Court was introduced there also, with Sir Thomas Strange as the first Chief Justice. The subsequent experience in Calcutta had been that, far from providing a means of better disciplining the Company's servants, the fact that the judges were Crown-appointed led to a degree of antagonism from Company representatives, such as Governor and Council, as their jurisdiction was at odds with the policies of the Company's own courts which acted for the population of the interior, outside the Presidency towns. Such also became the case in Madras. The Supreme Court was entirely independent of the rural, or 'country', courts, and was distinct from them, and did not act as an appeal court for them. As these rural courts represented the governing authority of the East India Company, this meant that this latter executive body was frequently in conflict with the precepts of the Crown judiciary. This was especially relevant to the Indian population. The supreme court acted for all Europeans everywhere, but only for Indian, and other nationals, in Madras itself. Indians in Madras were subject there to the protection of English law under the terms of the Crown charter of justice, for example with habeas corpus, but out in the country this was much less clear. Within Madras itself any Indian person, or other national, could use the Supreme Court as the venue for the determination of any major civil or criminal action.[1] This geographical conflict of function and jurisdiction could seem discordant to

1 Cocks, Raymond, *Social Roles and Legal Rights: Three Women in Early Nineteenth-Century India*. The Journal of Legal History. 2002 Vol. 23, No. 2. pp.77–106. See also initial references therein.

Company personnel, and the irascible Welshman, Sir Henry Gwillim, another judge to the Court, did nothing to appease this. Matters deteriorated following the appointment of Sir William Bentinck as Governor in 1803. Bentinck, better known much later as Governor General of India (1828–1835), had grave concerns about the value of the Crown-appointed judiciary, although it is quite clear that some of the activity of British residents badly needed reining in, which was less likely to happen under the East India Company's original mayoral court system. They were opposed because they felt their behavioural freedom was unreasonably restrained by the King's court. As Elizabeth Gwillim commented in her letter of 6 March 1805 "Sir Thomas has always exerted himself, with Sir Henry, in the suppression of all the violent measures of a set of people who, till the establishment of the Courts, were unrestrained by law."[2]

Political hostility towards the crown judicial system by the East India Company executive in India was by no means confined to Madras. The same thing was happening to Sir Edmund Stanley in Penang (the Fourth Presidency) at about the same time;[3] had a few years earlier been the experience of the first Chief Justice in Calcutta, Sir Elijah Impey[4] and, within a few years, would happen to Sir Edward West in Bombay, also the first Chief Justice there.[5, 6] The eventual consequence in Madras was that Sir Henry Gwillim was effectively nudged into a backwater, being at odds with both Sir Thomas Strange and Sir William Bentinck.

He had crossed swords early on with council members and senior civil servants when issuing a decree of habeas corpus for an English army officer who had been dismissed from India following a court martial. When this individual forcibly resisted the action of Company officials in trying to

2 Letters: 6 March 1805, Elizabeth Gwillim.

3 Edmund Stanley Papers. India Office Records, British Library, IOR/G/34/198.

4 Sir Elijah Impey. Oxford Dictionary of National Biography. ref:odnb/14371

5 Drewett, Frederick Dawtrey, *Bombay in the Days of George IV: Memoirs of Sir Edward West. Chief Justice of the King's Court during its Conflict with the East India Company* (London, 1907)

6 Edward West Papers. British Library, India Office Records 1822–28 MSS Eur D888.

arrest and deport him, he was indicted, but this action was then rejected by the Supreme Court. A writ of habeas corpus was issued by Sir Henry Gwillim and the matter was eventually closed. William Bentinck accepted that the habeas corpus was justified but remained unhappy about the principle being extended to Indian citizens.[7]

Before long Gwillim fell out with Bentinck when he was invited to be a trustee of a Church charitable fund, on the grounds that there was, in his eyes, a legal problem in its structure and administration. His letter in response was hasty, blunt and a little impolite and Bentinck took great exception stating that "I shall be under the necessity of declining all further communication unless I am addressed in the language of polished intercourse rather than in that of judicial rebuke." This letter was sent via a third party, namely the Advocate-General, Anstruther.[8] The somewhat irritable Welshman obviously had a tendency towards intemperate outbursts. As his letter almost illegibly mentions "young Lords", one is tempted to suspect that he may have been inclined towards patronising this young soldier, spared a university education, and some 15 years his junior.

For some time William Bentinck had wanted to introduce a police force in Madras for the protection of its population,[9] and this need was reinforced by the public fear and anxiety following the Vellore mutiny in July 1806. In early 1807 Henry Gwillim learnt of it whilst presiding, with Sir Thomas Strange in attendance, over the case of a man from out of town who had been charged with subversion. It seems that the wrong person was arrested; a local person whose plight was reported by one of the dubashes of Sir Henry Gwillim's household, and an affidavit had been made on his behalf for a writ of habeas corpus. Sir Henry was vigorous in his criticism of the circumstance, and somewhat tart in his comments about the Governor, the Advocate-General Alexander Anstruther stating that he demonstrated "agitation of manner and voice". A particularly pungent quotation was "It is impossible none of the noble blood of the Cavendish's can flow in the veins

7 Portland (Welbeck) Collection, Lord William Bentinck in Madras, University of Nottingham Libraries, Manuscripts and Special Collection Pw Jb 80/473-7 *Hereafter Portland Pw Jb.*

8 Portland Pw Jb 133.

9 Portland Pw Jb 761 C4 (Minute).

of this man. He must be some spurious changeling that has been palmed upon that noble family and contaminated it."[10] Not the most tactful remark, but clearly inspired by the fact that the police force was headed by an apparently disagreeable army officer (Captain James Grant) whose approach to the native Indian population was abrupt. He was liable to arrest here and there, sometimes incorrectly, while ignoring any protection given by habeas corpus under the King's Supreme Court charter, which the Indian people understandably valued. His appointment had of course been made by Governor Bentinck and, furthermore, Sir Thomas Strange had shortly afterwards given the principle very public support.[11]

Sir Henry Gwillim was not opposed to the concept of such a force, but was frustrated by the fact that he hadn't been told about its structure, and the Supreme Court had been bypassed in its planning. His major concern was that it was militarised, run by a renegade army officer, and contained military personnel. He therefore saw it as a potential instrument of military tyranny. Such a possibility was already a matter of public concern at home in England at that time. He again made his feelings public when delivering a Charge to the Grand Jury in the Supreme Court in July 1807 in which he challenged its legality. This was upheld by the Grand Jury's response which declared "that we hold it to be an inviolable maxim of our most excellent laws, and constitution, that military force cannot legally be employed, excepting in aid of the civil power, and this only."[12] In the same Charge he also strongly supported the overall principles offered to the Indian people contained in the Charter of Justice. In it he stated that "Suppose, gentlemen, that there were some danger in admitting the natives to this regulated freedom, in giving them the benefit of equal law - we are bound to do it, bound by the laws of God and of man - they are our equals by nature, our brethren, and the good policy of the British legislature has fearlessly acknowledged their common rights. But even if there were a somewhat greater danger in it, than I am sure there possibly can be, still I should, speaking for myself, prefer it to continuing them in a state

10 Portland Pw Jb 209.
11 Portland Pw Jb 694.
12 India Office Records, British Library; H431 ff.308.

of depression."[13] Here Gwillim clearly stands by the Charter, and also perhaps reveals a real empathy towards the ordinary Indian. In this one could suppose him to have a similar solicitude and concern as was held by his wife, Elizabeth. Bentinck, however, claims to have been personally insulted by the wording of the charge,[14] but a letter by Benjamin Sullivan contains the claim that he himself had examined the written charge before its delivery, and that there was nothing offensive within it.[15] He concluded that the facts must have been misrepresented to Bentinck, who perhaps was referring in any case to the Supreme Court comments made much earlier that year. Given William Bentinck's views on both the police and Supreme Court issues, it is hardly surprising that he became even more irritated by Sir Henry.

For some time Bentinck had been instinctively opposed to the power of the Supreme Court for the protection it offered to the native population. He felt it would lead to a "lack of respect by the natives to their superiors" and a desire for "independence and resistance" and that it could encourage loss of political control, and thus to insurrection and even the loss of India.[16] He was happy that all Indian people should have civil liberty, but not political, and so he finally planned to destroy the Supreme Court to remove this risk and install provincial courts, each to be headed by a Crown-appointed judge assisted by two others who would be Company appointed.[17, 18] He believed that British rule in India should be despotic, although just, and he did not trust the more powerful Indian, as neither did his senior in Bengal, Richard Wellesley, the Governor-General. During his four years in Madras there is no sign that he ever discussed policy with a single Indian, his view being that "universal corruption prevails among the natives."[19] In his Supreme Court abolition plans he eventually had the support, remarkably, of the Chief Justice, seemingly because Strange saw in

13 Ibid.

14 Portland Pw Jb 85/73.

15 Portland Pw Jb 85/86.

16 Portland Pw Jb 761 C4.

17 Rosselli, John. *Lord William Bentinck: The Making of a Liberal Imperialist, 1774–1839*. Page 267 *Hereafter Rosselli.*

18 Portland Pw Jb 725/260.

19 Rosselli. p. 127–131; p. 141.

it advantage to himself with the assurance made that he would be created President of the Company Courts, on an even greater salary.

And so Sir Henry Gwillim had made an enemy of Governor Bentinck but unfortunately, driven by his principles, he also found himself at odds with his Chief Justice, Sir Thomas Strange. Sir Thomas was initially a supporter of the Supreme Court, as one would expect. He could hardly have been otherwise, but he too was distancing himself from Sir Henry. This at first appears to have been related more to personal ambition, and perhaps a personality difference, than anything legal or political, which is mildly surprising given that they both studied law at Oxford together, and from the same college (Christ Church), with no more than two years between them. Strange left Madras suddenly in early 1805, leaving Henry Gwillim to carry out all the court work alone and, despite requests, gave no clear explanation as to his reasons for doing so, nor any apology. There was little assistance from the third of the judicial trio, Benjamin Sullivan, because of chronic and persistent illness. Strange returned in 1806 after about eighteen months, when it gradually became clear that he had been to London to obtain an extension of office until 1816 largely, as it turned out, by blaming the stress between the Court and the Madras government on the behaviour of Sir Henry.[20]

The tensions developed. The resentment at Sir Thomas Strange's unexpected departure smouldered in the minds of the two sisters, in view of the extra strain it had placed on Henry Gwillim. They thought they had perhaps been a little seduced by his "tender manner".[21] Often, in the not so distant past, they had exchanged visits and gifts, and his attitude to the two women seems always to have been polite. Strange was conscientious in his relationships with the society of Madras. In fact he was a stickler for protocol both in court and outside it. He was said by one contemporary, a number of years later, to be "in love with the flimsiest kind of popularity – the petty applause of dinner tables and coteries; - a dangerous passion in a judge, whom no whisper of the chronicles and gossipings of the society in which he lives should be permitted to reach."[22] This attention to protocol

20 India Office Records, British Library; H431.

21 Letters: 11 Feb 1806. Elizabeth Gwillim.

22 New Monthly Magazine and Literary Journal April 1828 vol XXII. No. LXXXVIII.

led him and Lady Strange to make every effort to be on good terms with Governor Bentinck and his Lady. Nevertheless he had to surmount some difficulties over the arcane procedures of the ranking system in India at that time. As Chief Justice he ranked second to the Governor, and so theoretically did his wife, except that she was outranked in English terms by those with the titles that she herself did not possess, which certainly irked Sir Thomas.[23, 24] The ranking system was rigid, and enshrined in law, and the consequences for his immediate family further reinforced Strange's intent to ally himself to his chief, the Governor. He himself was nevertheless assuredly well-connected. His older brother James was married to the daughter of Henry Dundas, Lord Melville, formerly President of the Board of Control of the East India Company, and father of a later President, Robert Dundas, 2nd Viscount. Furthermore the Advocate-General in Madras was Alexander Anstruther, a schoolfriend of Thomas Strange's and married to his sister, and later knighted and to become a judge in Bombay. Henry Gwillim, by comparison, was something of a social outsider and, although intelligent and learned in the law, his correspondence, and the claims of Sir Thomas Strange, suggest that he could at times be pugnacious and self-opinionated. His manner was too abrupt and argumentative to conciliate and compromise, and he clearly lacked an instinct for diplomacy.

So Henry Gwillim's outspoken beliefs had already set him at odds with Governor Bentinck from a fairly early stage after the latter's arrival in 1803, and in a letter to Sir Thomas Strange, the latter had said, "Sir Henry, God knows, has no claim upon my attention."[25] These private disputes were sufficiently intense that Bentinck eventually concluded that they could not write to one another as gentlemen, and future communications would have to take place through a third party. While steadily falling out of favour with the Governor and Council he continued to alienate Sir Thomas Strange, the Chief Justice, and by 1807 he too was only communicating with Gwillim through a third party, and before too long Sir Henry was no

23 Cocks, Raymond. *Social Roles and Legal Rights: Three Women in Early Nineteenth-Century India*. The Journal of Legal History. 2002 Vol. 23, No. 2. p. 89.

24 Portland Pw Jb 39/45.

25 India Office Records, British Library; H431 ff. 54.

longer attending the court.[26] Initially this schism was because Strange disagreed with his colleague, and supported Bentinck on those issues already described but there is also the strong suggestion, as already alluded to, that Strange was keenly concerned about his own future, and the fulfilment of his personal ambitions. When he returned to London at the beginning of 1805 he had only six months of his term of office remaining, and yet faced a minimum of eight months sailing home and back, and so the reasons for why he did so were a mystery to most people. It seems, however, that Bentinck knew why, later admitting that it was to plan a reconstruction of the judiciary, although when Strange was challenged by Gwillim shortly before departure on his reasons for going, no information was given, and Sir Henry is said by Strange to have been discourteous, even rude. Another black mark – and more asperity against Strange from Elizabeth and Mary in their letters.[27] As already indicated, it turned out that his visit home was to obtain an extension of his contract in Madras, and seemingly to sow the seeds of growing discontent with his Judge colleague, Sir Henry. The latter was obliged to hold the fort in Madras for a good 18 months alone, because of the ill-health of his colleague Sir Benjamin Sullivan, and during this time Sir Henry finally discovered for himself the true reasons behind Strange's return home. So on the latter's return to India, he demonstrated his ire by refusing to see Strange when he called at his house. Elizabeth received him, and sat with him, politely no doubt, but presumably embarrassed that her husband would not show himself out of pique, for which there may have been some justification, although a more diplomatic, and less emotional, person might have remonstrated face to face.[28] From this point on, relations between the Chief Justice and his Puisne Judge, broke down completely. Effectively they did not communicate.

Such was the turmoil amongst the authorities in Madras at that moment, that something had to be done, at least in the eyes of Governor Bentinck and the Chief Justice. At some point in 1807, the President of the Board of Control of the East India Company, in London, received

26 Portland Pw Jb 312.

27 Letters: 6 March 1805, Elizabeth Gwillim.

28 India Office Records, British Library; H431 ff. 89.

a letter from Bentinck[29] in which it was stated that the Governor and Council considered the conduct of Gwillim to "be fraught with danger to the state" and "a hazard to Empire", and that he degraded with "scurrilous contempt" the authority of Council in the minds of the natives.[30] He wished for his suspension, but recognised that he himself did not have the power to order this. This was because Henry Gwillim was not an employee of the East India Company but a Crown appointment. Strange, as Chief Justice, did of course have the authority to make such a request, and in early 1807 he wrote a lengthy submission to H.M. the King requesting Henry Gwillim's recall. The document seems somewhat obsequious, perhaps not surprisingly, as Strange had himself received a letter of reprimand from the King for returning to England without his permission.[31] One is inclined to believe that his charge to the King was couched in terms that demonstrated his efficiency and conscientiousness.

The submission detailed all the complaints against Sir Henry, including those already discussed, namely the matter of the police force and the relevance of the Charter of Justice to the Indian people. The other complaints were numerous. An interesting one related to the practice of appointing Indian legal experts (a Pundit and a Moulavie) on Hindu or Muslim law to assist the court, if matters went beyond English law. This had been usual practice, according to Rosselli, having been used by Sir Elijah Impey in Calcutta, with the encouragement of Warren Hastings when Governor-General. Both Henry Gwillim and Benjamin Sullivan attempted to introduce this while Sir Thomas Strange was away in England, but Strange objected on his return, and blocked the move on the grounds that such people were rarely needed, and were both unreliable and corruptible.[32] He regarded himself as an expert on Hindu law, and it is certainly true that he later wrote books on the subject, and developed some reputation in this regard. Other complaints of Strange's were to do with Court procedure, such as the use of the Court Seal by the Puisne Judges for non-judicial matters, and his expressed desire to countersign court rulings made by the two

29 India Office Records, British Library; H431 ff. 127.

30 Portland Pw Jb 761 C17.

31 India Office Records, British Library; H431 ff. 111 etc.

32 India Office Records, British Library; H431 ff. 57.

of them, to which they both objected. They believed that together they should have the same authority as the Chief Justice, in a spirit of "coordination and co-equality". Strange disagreed, wishing to assert his superiority. Gwillim and Sullivan both felt their authority to be debased by such an imbalance, and resented Government and Council's backing of this view and, more so, the disrespect shown to them by a letter to this effect, which they unsuccessfully requested be withdrawn. These instances of antipathy by Thomas Strange suggest an unusual degree of sensitivity about his status and position of authority in court, perhaps reflecting some insecurity about his standing in the community generally.

In his written statement to the Crown, Thomas Strange further described the personal insults and invective to which he felt he had been subjected by Sir Henry Gwillim. Expanding as he did on all these charges, the document requesting suspension was weighty, and highly censorious. The authorities in England had little else to go by than these lengthy writings by Strange. Henry Gwillim's defence seems hastily, and rather scrappily, written.[33] The impression is of a man under pressure, and in a hurry. He wrote of hearsay, exaggeration and distortion of the facts, and how insulted he felt by the attitude of both Thomas Strange and Governor Bentinck. There are several subsequent letters, but the overall impression somehow doesn't seem so carefully prepared and worded as Strange's original declaration. It is particularly interesting that Benjamin Sullivan frequently fully supported Henry Gwillim's various convictions, including his sympathy towards the Indian people, but Sullivan was not castigated. He was excused by his chronic illness, and his letters are more polite and less fractious. The inescapable conclusion was that the whole maelstrom was not based on incompetence or even, necessarily, erroneous attitudes, but on personality. Sir Henry was intelligent and learned, but a tetchy outsider. His disagreement with Thomas Strange and William Bentinck, was not necessarily because he was wrong, but because he was a loose cannon, with a habit of frequently revealing undisguised indignation, and even outrage. He did not have the conciliatory skills, or the patience, to further his points of view and his ideas. Even his wife, Elizabeth, was moved to comment, "Mr Gwillim is

33 India Office Records, British Library; H431 ff. 139.

sometimes full strong in anger and I think not a little ill-natured."[34] It is reasonable to conclude that Sir Henry Gwillim had his heart in the right place, but perhaps not his tongue.

All this antagonism, estrangement and bitterness went on through 1807, and Elizabeth and Mary can only have been aware of it. Not perhaps all the detail, but certainly the emotional overtones. This must have caused a degree of turbulence at home, and perhaps both women took refuge in their painting. Their social life was much quieter, and they weren't invited to major social events to the same extent. If not exactly ostracized, they preferred detachment and distance, which they achieved by moving out of central Madras to Pammal. It is possibly a pity that they did not more often visit the houses of senior civilians at this time. If they had, they might have learnt from William Petrie, a distinguished member of Council, that according to Cocks, he had misgivings about the way Government was attacking a judge when some of the problem may have lain in the misguided attitudes of the Grand Jury.[35]

Sir Henry learnt from England of his suspension and recall late in 1807, about the time that Elizabeth, his wife of 23 years, died. This cannot have been an easy episode in his life. From a correspondence point of view, Elizabeth had continued silent throughout 1807, and it is possible any letters were abstracted because of depressing personal and family contents. At about this time Bentinck was also recalled following the Vellore Mutiny of 1806. The Commander in Chief, Sir John Cradock, had been recalled as well, having been the chief architect of the extraordinary insensitivity to the customs of the Indian troops that underlay that event. Bentinck, himself, was thought not to have been sufficiently perceptive to Cradock's high-handed alteration of Indian dress regulations, and Sir Henry Gwillim made it quite clear that he agreed with this conclusion. For some time Bentinck had had an uncertain position vis-à-vis the Court of Directors in London. They were unhappy with him for a number of administrative reasons in Madras, as well as for his continued support of Richard Wellesley, and disfavour was automatic anyway as the Foxites were in power, and they

34 Letter: 14 August 1803, Elizabeth Gwillim.

35 See Cocks, R. Ref. 67.

were strongly opposed to the Duke of Portland, former Prime Minister and William Bentinck's father.[36] As Bentinck's return was a little before Gwillim's, the latter must have gained some satisfaction from that sequence of events. It has even been suggested, moreover, that Gwillim's return was partly a counterweight to that of Bentinck's, in order to avoid leaving a rebellious influence in Madras that was unbalanced.

Despite his censure by its Council, and the Board of Directors of the East India Company, Madras was sorry to see Sir Henry leave. He was greatly appreciated by the ordinary man, especially the ordinary Indian, and before his departure 1006 people presented him with a farewell address, as follows: "We the undersigned Europeans, descendants of Europeans and native inhabitants of Madras, reflecting on your accurate knowledge of the law, your ardent love of justice, your disinterestedness, your easiness of access .....[and your desire to] establish the laws of Great Britain in a place where by many they have never been known,..... offer our grateful and warmest thanks for your indefatigable exertions to make the laws known and respected, and to support us in our liberties and rights."[37] This must have been some consolation to the beleaguered Sir Henry Gwillim, but such expressions of support and sympathy were mostly suppressed in Madras. The die was cast; too many powerful individuals had been alienated and, like a renegade politician, he was consigned to history, in India at least. Nevertheless a principle had been aired, namely that Indians, like Europeans, should have access to the writ of Habeas Corpus. Governor Bentinck's plan to dismantle the Supreme court was not pursued any further, despite the several more years that Sir Thomas Strange presided in that Court. In all probability it was realised that such a move would seriously divide the European community and alienate the Indian one. Conceivably also, Sir Thomas no longer needed to ingratiate himself with the Governor to establish his social authority in Madras, because Bentinck's successor was an ordinary Council member, well-known to him, namely William Petrie.

36 Rosselli. p. 49–50.

37 Portland Pw Jb 634, in Cocks, Raymond, *Social Roles and Legal Rights: Three Women in Early Nineteenth-Century India*. The Journal of Legal History. 2002 Vol. 23, No. 2. pp. 77–106.

The last letter in the collection is one by Sir Henry from the Cape, describing the adversities encountered in their passage from India, and the further battles he must face on his return home. His departure, and that of Mary and Richard, was not until October 1808, almost a year after his wife's death and his recall. There were no further saved letters from 1808 either. His return to England was marked by a note to the India Office reporting his arrival at Hetty's house in Bishopsgate on the 25th May 1809. It appears that his difficulties were gradually resolved, and that he was finally awarded a pension, eventually retired and, three years after his return, married again and lived to a good age.

Postscript

Mary settled back into English life quite quickly and married her East Indiaman Captain, John Ramsden. She had one son, John George Ramsden, who was educated at Charterhouse and Cambridge and went into the law as a barrister. He had no children. Hetty had one surviving daughter, Mary, who married Joseph Blunt in 1834 and they had five children. Two of these themselves had children, and those of their daughter Mary can be traced to the present day. Part of Elizabeth's legacy to the world was her letters, which remained unread and un-transcribed for years. The greater contribution was her paintings, which were also unknown for a long time until a chance discovery by the Canadian ophthalmologist and comparative zoologist Casey Wood. After retiring from his medical career in 1920 he developed his interest in ornithology, intending to found a library in this subject, and continue contributing to the Blacker Library in Zoology at McGill University, Montreal. When in London on a buying expedition in 1924, he found himself in an antiquities shop looking at some paintings of fish and flowers, by an artist with the initials E.G. At this point a member of staff remembered seeing a portfolio of paintings of birds in the cellar, before the First World War. Having brought this up, it proved to be a substantial brass-bound, and locked, collection measuring five feet broad and four high, which contained some very fine quality watercolours of Indian birds, numbering 121 in all. Many bore zoological details about the species, which indicated that the artist was very well informed for his or her time. This artist was of course Elizabeth Gwillim, and it was soon recognised that her work was as good quality as that of the well-known American artist John James Audubon, but dating some 20 years earlier. The paintings were returned to what became the Blacker-Wood Library at McGill, where they have remained ever since. For many years they received little attention, except from academics and some other historians, but latterly there has been interest at McGill in bringing awareness of their existence and quality to a greater audience. This would be an admirable tribute to a remarkable and gifted woman, long forgotten, and lying still in that foreign land where her capability had flourished.

Elizabeth Gwillim's bird paintings are available to view on the website below.

<https://archive.org/search.php?query=subject%3A%22Gwillim%2C+Elizabeth%2C+--+1763-1807.%22&page=2> or more easily 'archive.org' and search for Gwillim, Elizabeth

There are also paintings of fish and, elsewhere, some botanical and larger animal paintings.

Many of Mary Symonds paintings are held at the South Asia Collection Museum, Norwich, UK.

Bibliography

Books and Manuscripts

Balfour, Edward, The Cyclopaedia of India and of Eastern and Southern Asia, Commercial, Industrial and Scientific (India, 1885).

Botanical Journal of the Linnaean Society 113/4 (1993), 351–388.

Cameron, Alan, *The Vellore Mutiny*. PhD thesis submitted to the University of Edinburgh 1984.

Cocks, Raymond, 'Social Roles and Legal Rights: Three Women in Early Nineteenth-Century India', *The Journal of Legal History* 23/2 (2002), 77–106.

Dalrymple, William, *White Mughals. Love and Betrayal in Eighteenth Century India* (London, 2002).

Dalrymple, William, *The Anarchy: The Relentless Rise of the East India Company* (London, 2019).

Devine, Tom, *Scotland's Empire. The Origins of the Global Diaspora* (London, 2012).

Drewett, Frederick Dawtrey, *Bombay in the Days of George IV: Memoirs of Sir Edward West. Chief Justice of the King's Court during its Conflict with the East India Company* (London, 1907).

Edmund Stanley Papers. India Office Records, British Library, London. IOR/G/34/198.

Edward West Papers, including the diary of his wife Lucretia West, 1822–28. India Office Records, British Library, London. MSS Eur D888.

Elisabeth Gwillim Letters, and those of Mary Symonds her sister. 1801–08 MSS Eur C240. India Office Records, British Library, London.

Gunnis, Rupert, A Dictionary of British Sculptors, 1660–1851.

Gupta, Maya, *Lord William Bentinck in Madras 1803–1807* (1969 & Capital Publishers, 1986).

Logbook of Honourable East India Company's Ship Hindostan, Asia, Pacific and Africa Collection (APAC), British Library, London.

Madras Ecclesiastical Returns, Asia, Pacific and Africa Collection (APAC), British Library, London.
New Monthly Magazine and Literary Journal April 1828 vol XXII. No. LXXXVIII.
Parkes, Fanny, *Wanderings of a Pilgrim in Search of the Picturesque* (London, 1850).
Parkinson, C. Northcote, *Trade in the Eastern Seas, 1793–1813* (Cambridge, 1937).
Portland (Welbeck) Collection, Lord William Bentinck in Madras, University of Nottingham Libraries, Manuscripts and Special Collection, Pw Jb.
Robb, Peter, *Sex and Sensibility, Richard Blechynden's Calcutta Diaries 1791–1822* (Oxford, 2011).
Roberts, Emma, *Scenes and Characteristics of Hindostan with Sketches of Anglo-Indian Society. Volume 1* (London 1835; 2005).
Rosselli, John, *Lord William Bentinck: The Making of a Liberal Imperialist, 1774–1839*. Sir Henry Gwillim correspondence. India Office Records, British Library, London., IOR H/431
The East India Register and Directory for 1803, and 1804, Asia, Pacific and Africa Collection (APAC), British Library, London.
Wheeler, Patrick, *Ribbons among the Rajahs. A History of British Women in India before the Raj* (Pen and Sword History, 2017).
Yule, Henry, and Hobson Jobson, *A Glossary of Colloquial Anglo-Indian Words and Phrases, Etymological, Historical, Geographical and Discursive* (London 1903; Oxford 2013).

Oxford Dictionary of National Biography

Anderson, James
Bewick, Thomas
Chinnery, George
Clive, Edward. First Earl of Powis
Dundas, Henry. First Lord Melville
Godwin, William
Impey, Sir Elijah
Keene, Henry George
Marsden, William
Rainier, Admiral Peter
Samuel, George
Strange, Sir Thomas

Index

Printed by
CPI books GmbH, Leck